Understanding African American Rhetoric

Understanding African American Rhetoric

Classical Origins to Contemporary Innovations

Edited by
Ronald L. Jackson II
Elaine B. Richardson

Routledge
New York London

Published in 2003 by
Routledge
29 West 35th Street
New York, NY 10001
www.routledge-ny.com

Published in Great Britain by
Routledge
11 New Fetter Lane
London EC4P 4EE
www.routledge.co.uk

Routledge is an imprint of the Taylor & Francis Group.
Printed in the United States of America on acid-free paper.

10 9 8 7 6 5 4 3 2 1

Library of Congress Cataloging-in-Publication Data

Understanding African American rhetoric : classical origins to contemporary innovations / edited by Ronald L. Jackson II and Elaine B. Richardson.
p. cm.
Includes bibliographical references and index.
ISBN 0-415-94386-8 (alk. paper) — ISBN 0-415-94387-6 (pbk. : alk. paper)
1. African Americans—Languages. 2. English language—United States—African influences. 3. English language—United States—Rhetoric. 4. African languages—Influence on English. 5. African Americans—Communication. 6. Black English. I. Jackson, Ronald L., 1970– II. Richardson, Elaine B., 1960–

PE3102.N42 U53 2003
427' .973'08996073—dc21

2002015432

To my son and daughter,
Niles Hasani Jackson and Niyah Simone Jackson.
You are gifts from God that I will cherish forever
and from whom I expect great things!

Ronald L. Jackson II

Dedicated to those who still wonder
if African American rhetoric exists
and to those who are expanding
its teaching and study.

Elaine B. Richardson

Contents

Foreword

ORLANDO L. TAYLOR

The word *access* is often the first word that comes to mind when asked about the impact of the civil rights movement of the 1960s on American life. This is certainly a reasonable designata for capturing the rights achieved by African Americans and others as a result of what might easily be considered as the most important social justice advocacy period of the twentieth century. The movement led directly to access for all Americans and included such important aspects of democratic citizenship as voting rights, fair housing, equal employment opportunity, and accessibility, as well as public accommodations. The civil rights movement hastened the issuance of legislative mandates, judicial rulings and executive orders that advanced the principles of social justice for all that constitute the cornerstone of a democratic society.

As important as access has been in achieving a semblance of inclusion for African Americans and other people of color in American life, empowerment of voice in academia has been at least of equal importance as an outgrowth of the civil rights era. This sort of empowerment means, among other things, both agency and access to the tools for projecting the voices of historically marginalized individuals or groups to mass audiences and, in the academic world, recognition of the significance of a group's voice in the formulation of the core theories and values of a discipline. Both came about in the wake of the civil rights movement for African Americans in the discipline of communication, as well as other fields.

In the academy, empowerment of voice cannot be overstated. With it, scholars from historically marginalized groups acquire access to the vehicles needed to disseminate one's perspectives and paradigms across mass academic venues—journals, books, and programs of professional and disciplinary meetings. It also results in these voices being recognized by the gatekeepers of the disciplines as legitimate contributors to their perceptions of truth. That is to say that the voices of the historically marginalized come to be seen as essential contributors to the discipline's theory and practice with equal status alongside other voices. Truth, after all, in most disciplines, especially in the social sciences and humanities, is typically a *perception* of truth viewed through a prism of culture. Unless the views and voices of diverse groups are heard by a discipline, fair and balanced truth telling can *never* be achieved. At best, we will have acquired only a narrow perception of that truth, indeed a fragmented accoutrement of the truth.

The mainstream communication academic community before the civil rights movement placed little value on the voices of African Americans or of African American scholars. One needs only to peruse the annual indexes of the mainstream communication journals before the civil rights movement to validate this claim. Certainly there was scholarship conducted on African American communication before this period, but it was often articulated with a White voice and often depicted in uncomplimentary terms. Even such eminent scholars as H. L. Mencken, along with countless others, typically portrayed African American communication as being primitive, backward, and childlike. It was often portrayed in the media as a form of mumbo-jumbo and was used frequently to entertain White audiences (e.g., minstrel shows) or to portray White supremacy and Black inferiority (e.g., D. W. Griffith's *Birth of a Nation,* one of the first major talking movies to hit the silver screen).

Most important, African American communication and its philosophical roots rarely, if ever, made it into the mainstream communication literature. African American scholars were rarely heard in public scholarly discourse, and little room was given to African American communication as a major contributor to human communication and its theoretical foundations. In my day as a graduate student in communication, for example, the roots of rhetoric were largely attributed to the Greek philosophers, most notably Aristotle. This was done with no regard for the need to consider other classical rhetorical legacies. With this particular book, *Understanding African American Rhetoric,* comes a greater recognition and understanding of the concept of *orature* from the African rhetorical tradition—which dates back to *before* the rise of Greek civilization.

Even still, it is mystifying that we continue to witness a largely historical and intellectual amnesia within rhetorical studies that may be remedied only by books such as the one you hold in your hands. Volumes such as these interrogate the flawed singularity of truth telling in rhetorical studies not only by exposing the limitations of the European-centered literature's hegemonic intent, but also by centralizing and celebrating the uniqueness of another rhetorical tradition, that of African Americans. More recently, there has been increasing acceptance of such theories as Afrocentricity, as described by Molefi Asante, within the core framework of communication theory. This book contributes to that advancement, with several chapters explicating and critiquing Afrocentricity, in addition to a chapter written by Molefi Asante.

With eighteen chapters and twenty-two contributors, *Understanding African American Rhetoric* is able to deliver a compelling and truly remarkable range of historical and contemporary insights, each of which offers brilliant excursions into the quest for truth. Each essay in *Understanding African American Rhetoric* is well written, lucid, and conceptually heuristic. It is refreshing to participate in this honest, empowering, and engaging array of dialogues concerning the confluence of African American rhetoric and history, ethics, language, gender, spirituality, popular culture, public memory, family, media, politics, and civil rights. This empowerment of voice promises to give rise to a significant body of interdisciplinary literatures, including but not limited to the communication and African American studies fields. I am confident that it will elicit healthy and revolutionary conversations across fields that remain seemingly bereft of culturally diverse intellectual legacies.

Understanding African American Rhetoric also provides us with a glimpse into the future with respect to the intellectual leadership within the fields of communication and African American studies. As increasingingly newer and younger voices continue to explode on the intellectual scene, and as they, in some cases, replace the traditional voices within these disciplines, one cannot help but feel an excitement as we experience firsthand the emergence of new truths, new ideas, and new paradigms. These new voices juxtaposed with older voices—as they are in this book—provide the type of continuity that is required to maintain the vitality of any discipline.

There is a final note. Empowerment of voice leads to empowerment for listeners—or in this case readers. With the assumption that all of us should be seeking the type of fair and balanced truth described above, it is clear that when we learn more from the diverse voices among us, and as we know more about the human experiences and the realities of others who have viewed life through a different lens, each of us becomes more empowered. I salute Ronald L. Jackson II and Elaine B. Richardson as editors for bringing us this sophisticated and pioneering volume of impassioned writers and writings, and most of all, for granting us access and expanding our vision!

Acknowledgments

All glory and honor that accompanies publication of this volume goes to God, through whom all things great are possible.

I am thankful for my co-editor and friend, Elaine B. Richardson, for her persistence, meticulousness, intelligence, and blessed spirit. I also owe a debt of gratitude to the contributors to this volume, many of whom have been or have become good friends. My mentors and influences are countless, but I must say I am grateful for the constant guidance of Sharon Prather, Ronald L. Jackson Sr., Ricci Jackson, and Drs. Melbourne Cummings, Lyndrey Niles, Debbie Atwater, Richard Wright, and Molefi Asante, all of whom started me on my intellectual journey as members of my doctoral committee several years ago and encouraged me to pursue this project. A special thanks goes to my close relatives, including the Prather, Jackson, Singleton, Hughes, Gross, Lee, Bush, Gould, Beauchamp, Shabazz, Morrison, Hogue, and Gabbidon families. Thank you for your undying support and love.

Ronald L. Jackson II

I must thank my co-editor, Ronald L. Jackson II, for his eloquence and integrity and for leading by example. I would like to thank all of the contributors, especially Ella Forbes and Felicia Miyakawa, two scholars I met recently at different conferences who trusted me and believed in the project enough to allow us to publish their scholarship. I must always thank my mentor, Geneva Smitherman, for constant guidance and for giving me the opportunity to earn a Ph.D. Finally, I must thank my beautiful daughters, Evelyn, Ebony, and Kaila, for allowing me to get my work done and sometimes miss their wonderful events.

Elaine B. Richardson

Introduction

RONALD L. JACKSON II AND ELAINE B. RICHARDSON

BACKGROUND: UNDERSTANDING AFRICAN AMERICAN RHETORIC IN THE FIELD OF COMMUNICATION

The study of African American rhetoric as orature has been a significant advance in the field of communication, though relatively few scholars of African American rhetoric in speech communication have integrated African American rhetorical theories and methods to encase discussions of this culturally unique set of rhetorical experiences. Instead, a large number of African American rhetorical studies, textbooks, and monographs tend to offer engaging intellectual treatments of African American rhetoric within the limited purview of public address. Although several of these volumes are exciting to read, they contribute to a narrow understanding of African American rhetorical traditions laced in everyday discourse and leave the less knowledgeable reader with the impression that European and European American culturally generic paradigms are fully sufficient tools for examining culturally specific phenomena and artifacts. There is clearly a place for dramatistic, narrative, neo-Aristotelian, and postmodern rhetorical approaches, among other such paradigms. Alongside these proven methods, there must also be intellectual spaces for culture-centered rhetorical critics and criticism. This book claims one such space for African American rhetoric.

Daniel (1995) explains that in the late 1960s, the National Communication Association (formerly Speech Association of America) convened an "Open Meeting on Social Relevance," out of which emerged a heightened consciousness among some White scholars of the need for African American intellectual and political participation in the discipline. Even after this genesis, there were persistent verbal harassment and death threats from those who would rather espouse the White racial separatism so characteristic of the 1960s than embrace the possibilities of a diversified intellectual front. Despite this, scholars such as Charles Hurst, Molefi Asante, Jack Daniel, Dorthy Pennington, Lucia Hawthorne, and Lyndrey Niles began to conceptualize the Black Rhetoric Institute, an entity that would be dedicated to rhetorical inquiry by, for, and about Black people throughout the diaspora. Although their mission was intentionally exclusionary for political reasons, Daniel (1995) explains, it quickly became apparent that the study of Black rhetoric needed to extend beyond the proposed institute. The scholar-teachers of the institute would need to teach Black rhetoric to Whites who attended their respective universities and also would need to influence how scholars studied Black discourse throughout the profession. Consequently, African-derived concepts such as nommo (the generative power of the spoken word) were introduced to make sense of Black orature. Daniel (1995, 12) asserts, "Instead of analyzing Malcolm X's discourse with modifications of Aristotle's categories, we proposed to teach African American graduate students the role of 'nommo' in Malcolm X's discourse." The Black Rhetoric Institute was underfunded and understaffed; therefore, it never became a reality. Soon after, the Black Caucus became a unit of what was then called the Speech Association of America and is now named the National Communication Association. The National Communication Association Black Caucus still remains today.

Fortunately, almost all of the founders of the Black Caucus are still very active with the unit itself and with the National Communication Association. We are even more fortunate to have essays by several of the founders and subsequent presidents of the Black Caucus in the present volume. This is significant, because this book seeks to facilitate the realization of a vision they set forth in the mid- to late twentieth century. In many ways, this book is a celebration of their early endeavors to institutionalize the study of African American rhetorical and communicative experiences. Although up until November 2001 there was still no journal in communication dedicated exclusively to culture and rhetorical research, there is now one forming that will accent critical studies of rhetoric; it will be the first of its kind in the field of communication. This important historical moment, at which point this culturally focused book emerges alongside the first issues of the nascent critical-cultural communication studies journal, is very important and only reinforces the timeliness of this volume. The writers of the insightful and refreshing essays you will read in *Understanding African American Rhetoric: Classical Origins to Contemporary Innovations,* whether well known already or neophytes in their respective fields, are part of a growing contingent of scholars writing on the major themes of African American rhetoric: ethics, history, spirituality, language, politics, nationality, religion, gender, popular culture, law, and aesthetics.

PURPOSE AND RATIONALE

The title *Understanding African American Rhetoric: Classical Origins to Contemporary Innovations* purports to accent the retentive nature of this volume. African American rhetoric, by nature, is interdisciplinary. We acknowledge that speech communication has no monopoly over the broad range of African American rhetorical studies, and this book does not pretend to survey the full range of African American rhetoric—only as it pertains to how African American rhetoric is conceptualized in communication studies. With this in mind, it must be noted here that there are several scholars outside of communication who are contributors to this volume. Sociolinguists, African American and Africana studies scholars, and English studies scholars provide us with a grounding in African American rhetorical history, ethics, literature, and other interdisciplinary perspectives. Their role is very significant, since African American rhetoric, no matter the disciplinary angle, still inherits conceptual and methodological imports from several disciplines. For us, this is necessary, not problematic, because it defuses the presumption of linearity so common in extant rhetorical studies in communication. It is important to note that, given the limited scope of this volume, we define African American rhetoric as it relates to Black African descendants and their experiences in the United States of America. In other words, this book does not specifically address or offer any scholarly treatment of the rhetorical legacies of African descendants living in Central or South America or Canada, though we recommend that future book-length scholarly manuscripts fill this void with an equally rigorous set of analyses.

By exploring ancestral and rhetorical, discursive and linguistic continuities and traditions present in African American orature, several of the contributing authors here facilitate the reconnaissance of ancient African rhetorical perspectives. Although it is not the intent of this book to present a full discussion of Ebonics or African American language issues, several of these issues are discussed within the realm of rhetorical studies. That is, since rhetorical studies in the communicological tradition refer to the conceptual and analytic dimensions of oratorical character, verbal *and* nonverbal features, and ultimate delivery of the spoken word, it is necessarily distinct from, and yet adjacent to, linguistics. Several authors of essays account for that adjacency in this volume without portending an exhaustive analysis of language studies pertaining to African Americans. Meanwhile, other authors introduce, develop, or expound upon contemporary innovations that shape the study of African American rhetoric.

In many ways, it is unfortunate that a volume of this nature is just now appearing; however, it is also timely, especially since most contemporary scholars seem prepared to agree that rhetoric coincides with the existence and civilization of a people and is a primary vehicle of communicating culture, meaning, and traditions. If that is an agreeable point of entry into our discussion of rhetoric, then as Cheikh Anta Diop (1974) and others remind us, we must examine discursive activity during the origins of humankind in order to gain access to truly classical rhetorical systems. Diop and others (Asante, in this volume; Karenga, in this volume; Williams 1987) have explained that rhetoric must be at least 6,500 years old, since the estimated birth of human civilization has been dated at 4500 B.C. With this in mind, the Greek and Roman classic rhetorical paradigms can no longer occupy a restrictive space of anteriority, since there are clearly civilizations, cultures, and traditions that existed before the Greeks and Romans. As Asante (1999, 84) has persistently argued in an effort to clarify the objectives of Afrocentricity and to assuage the fears of Greek classicists:

> It is not true that Afrocentrists have replaced White Greeks with Black Egyptians; we do not mind everyone standing in his or her own ground. The Greeks can remain firmly in control of whatever cultural legacy they bring to the world. We simply believe that is important to demonstrate that ancient Egyptians must be seen in the correct light. . . . Historical correctness is better than political posturing.

African American rhetoric, along with its ancestral traditions, has been dislodged from our purview of what rhetoric is and how it gets defined. Hence, it is fortunate that there is at least this formal attempt to rescue African American orature from its arrested agency, from its seeming inability to be studied alone as a legitimate line of inquiry independent of classical Greek philosophy.

FURTHER EXPLORATION OF THE "CLASSICS"

According to James (1992), Diop (1974), and Williams (1987), Greek philosophy, which dominates the intellectual landscape in classical rhetorical studies, began around 640 B.C. with the Persian conquests. In fact, there is only one "classical rhetoric" that is ever mentioned, and it refers to Greek and Roman traditions. Naturally, if the genealogy of classical rhetoric begins in 640 B.C.E. and human civilization began in 4500 B.C.E., almost four thousand years of rhetorical innovations have gone largely unexplored by present-day rhetorical scholars. It is impossible for any one book to promise a complete compilation of analytic works that systematically survey and examine all of the rhetorical innovations within that four-thousand-year interval. Within this edited volume, we seek only to introduce and demonstrate definitions, paradigms, and analyses of African American rhetoric. Although many of the contributors in this book use Africological and Afrocentric ideas to frame their arguments, each of the chapters represents a commitment to and is exemplary of historical retentions and/or contemporary innovations in the study of African American rhetoric.

Africology refers to the systematized study of the African continent, with its multiple civilizations, traditions, ideals, and contributions to humanity. Afrocentricity can be defined as a cosmological, axiological, aesthetic, ideological, or generally philosophical orientation toward the world (Asante and Abarry 1996; Jackson, 1995). When rhetorically examining phenomena via Afrocentric lenses, one approaches and apprehends the critical object by encasing one's analysis from the standpoint of African ancestral traditions, mores, and ideals in an effort to ascertain the possibilities of human potential and liberation. Each essay in this volume seeks to demonstrate the presence and utility of epistemes indicative of African-derived African American orature, and to that end many of the contributors can be said to have, if not an Afrocentric orientation, a liberation-centered one. The fact that many of the essays here are Afrocentric is testament to the significance of Afrocentricity as a conceptual and methodological tool; it also indicates a collective thirst for new paradigms to encapsulate a diversified set of rhetorical and discursive experiences too frequently ignored or misunderstood.

Jack Daniel's classic *Changing the Players and the Game* chronicles the development of the National Communication Association's Black Caucus, and in doing so, it also maps the genesis of African American communication scholarship. Although there are those who would like to believe that African American communicology, and more specifically African American rhetoric, began in the 1960s, several studies have proven otherwise (Asante 1996, 1998; Hamlet 1998; Niles 1995). Clearly, the composite body of scholarship often referred to as African American rhetoric is a derivative of ancestral oral traditions, discursive practices, and cultural nuances. Just as it is critical to contextualize the twentieth-century revision of Aristotelian canons by revisiting the original text and context of Greece from 366 B.C. to 322 B.C., it is also necessary to contextualize contemporary paradigmatic revisions of African oratorical traditions found within African American rhetoric by revisiting ancient African sources and concepts such as the Egyptian texts of Ptah Hotep and the Dogon concepts of nommo and magara.

THE LAYOUT

Understanding African American Rhetoric: Classical Origins to Contemporary Innovations is organized, as the subtitle suggests, so that the reader acquires a grasp of the breadth and scope of African American rhetoric. There is a conceptual and coherent logic to this arrangement. It is our belief as co-editors of this volume that any book entitled *Understanding African American Rhetoric* must systematically examine the historical origins, daily manifestations, definitions, intellectual politics, critical analyses, trends, and innovations as well as future directions of African American rhetorical inquiry. Moreover, a volume of this nature must feature some of the most brilliant intellectuals who, in their establishment of heuristic ideas concerning African American rhetoric, succumb neither to tactical relativism nor to uninformed skepticism; instead, they must be courageous and visionary, steadfast and critical, progressive and humanistic. That is the volume you hold in your hands, and the contributing authors have assisted in bringing it to fruition. From the beginning chapters discussing classical origins of Egyptian rhetoric to the final remarks from Molefi Asante and Dorthy Pennington on the future of rhetoric, the scholarship here represents much of the subdisciplinary pulse of African American rhetorical inquiry.

There are six sections in this book: "Classical Egyptian Origins of African American Rhetoric," "Manifestations of African American Rhetoric and Orality," "Politics of Defining African American Rhetoric," "African American Rhetorical Analyses of Struggle and Resistance," "Trends and Innovations in Analyzing Contemporary African American Rhetoric," and "Visions for Research in African American Rhetoric."

Section One offers a historical context for the grounding of rhetorical investigations. This section has two essays, authored by Maulana Karenga and Adisa A. Alkebulan. Karenga returns skillfully to Egyptian texts and autobiographies to introduce classical Egyptian foundations of rhetoric, which accent ethics as the means through which we acquire a fundamental understanding of the power of the spoken word. Alkebulan continues the conversation on ethics as one of seven virtues of Maat, which means truth, balance, justice, and right thinking. He also assembles the ideas concerning nommo and Maat in a cohesive framework that engages the relationship between language, rhetoric, and spirituality.

Section Two combines rhetoric and orality in an attempt to highlight the underlying commonalities and subtle distinctions between the two. Thurmon Garner and Carolyn Calloway Thomas offer a nice segue into this section of the book by tending to the nuances between rhetoric, which is traditionally understood in speech communication as the art of persuasion, and orality, which is immersed in the culturally based oral features of language and tropes of discourse. Melbourne S. Cummings and Judi Moore Latta follow up on this idea and demonstrate how rhetoric and orality are manifested in a church context. Finally, Deborah F. Atwater and Sandra L. Herndon conclude the section with a discussion of how cultural museums are rhetorical artifacts that stimulate public and collective memory.

Section Three is concerned with the politics and definitions of African American rhetoric. This is not to be mistaken for a set of essays that timidly approach the study of African American rhetoric in order to appease some political agency such as the field of communication. Instead, the three authors in this section explore the parameters of African American rhetorical inquiry and note points of caution, for example, where scholars are not sure whether to characterize African American rhetoric as canonical, cosmological, and/or perspectival. Likewise, many scholars are unsure how to avoid being called essentialist as they attempt to discuss African American experiences. In this section, Richard Wright, Mark L. McPhail, and Ronald L. Jackson II offer definitions and direction for the novice reader and scholar of African American rhetoric with these issues in mind. Richard Wright begins this section with a remarkable exploration of the philosophical machinery that transforms, influences, and epistemically undergirds the spoken word. Through revisitation of several noteworthy essays and texts in African American rhetoric, Mark Lawrence McPhail contends that the discipline of rhetoric must prepare itself for the embrace of multiple and ideologically distinct African American rhetorical approaches. Ronald L. Jackson II's essay concludes this section and tends to the disciplinary pulse and paradigmatic tensions in defining African American rhetoric from an Afrocentric orientation while acknowledging that Afrocentricity has challenged the insular nature of rhetorical studies.

Section Four includes essays that analyze the rhetoric of African American struggle and resistance. Jeffrey Lynn Woodyard begins this section and seems to have heeded the call of the Black Rhetoric Institute. His essay is exactly what the institute had in mind, as previously noted—a discussion of nommo as the generative power of the spoken word in the context of Malcolm X's inspirational discourse of liberation. Ella Forbes follows Woodyard's essay with a riveting survey of resistance struggles for justice and equality from the nineteenth century to the present. Felicia M. Miyakawa continues this discussion by examining Black nationalistic messages of Five Percent rappers. Finally, Carlos D. Morrison offers a detailed analysis of the elegies of slain rapper Tupac Shakur in order to reveal a consistent theme of death and dying. His analysis demonstrates how resistance and resilience have become major themes in rap and hip-hop music.

Section Five introduces some of the cutting-edge trends and innovations in African American rhetorical inquiry from popular culture to Black hair to legal rhetoric and then the rhetoric of a mayor who is also a minister. This section transitions nicely from the last section as Celnisha L. Dangerfield discusses womanist themes in Lauryn Hill's award-winning album *Miseducation of Lauryn Hill.* Her essay is followed by Regina E. Spellers' innovative exploration of Black women's hair as a rhetorical artifact. She examines Black women's discourse and attributed meanings concerning hair. Felicia R. Walker offers yet another innovation by conducting an Afrocentric analysis of Johnnie Cochran's closing arguments in the O.J. Simpson trial. Shauntae Brown-White's Afrocentric study also accomplishes something unique, as she critically analyzes the rhetoric of preacher and politician Emanuel Cleaver II. She closely examines his shifts in discourse and rhetorical style from the podium to the pulpit.

Section Six is the final section of the book and features two important essays that address future directions of African American rhetoric. Molefi K. Asante offers an insightful discussion of human and intellectual liberation. By exploring African American women archetypes, Dorthy Pennington thoroughly explains several everyday epistemological facets of African American women's discourse and explores the intersections of that discourse and spirituality. Moreover, Pennington cogently articulates the significance of a richly diverse set of liberating and practical rhetorical experiences among African American women and also a need to access the power to define the range of perspectives, themes, and ideas that constitute the composite we have identified as African American rhetoric.

The ideological fragmentation that plagues the field of communication works to forcefully expunge non-European rhetorical traditions. This book is a recovery initiative; it is a comprehensive effort to reintroduce African American culture and humanity as manifested in African American rhetorical experiences. The challenge, since the 1960s, has been to offer such a volume in speech communication and have all of those who study African American rhetoric embrace it. We are confident that the intellectual legacies, traditions, and innovations we present here will be an important academic and practical resource that will contribute to our collective understanding of African American rhetoric for years to come.

REFERENCES

Asante, M. K. (1999). *The Painful Demise of Eurocentrism: An Afrocentric Response to Critics.* Trenton, NJ: Africa World Press.

Asante, M. K., and A. Abarry (Eds.) (1996). *African Intellectual Heritage.* Philadelphia: Temple.

Daniel, J. (1995). *Changing the Players and the Game: A Personal Account of the Speech Communication Association Black Caucus Origins.* Annandale, VA: Speech Communication Association.

Diop, C. A. (1974). *The African Origin of Civilization: Myth or Reality?* New York: Lawrence Hill.

Hamlet, J. (1998). Understanding African American Oratory: Manifestations of Nommo. In J. Hamlet (Ed.), *Afrocentric Visions: Studies in Culture and Communication* (pp. 89–106). Newbury Park, CA: Sage.

James, G. M. (1992). *Stolen Legacy: Greek Philosophy Is Stolen Egyptian Philosophy.* Trenton, NJ: Africa World Press. Originally published 1952.

Jackson, R. L. (1995). Toward an Afrocentric Methodology for the Critical Assessment of Rhetoric. In L.A. Niles (Ed.), *African American Rhetoric: A Reader* (pp. 148–57). Dubuque, IA: Kendall-Hunt.

Niles, L. A. (Ed.) (1995). *African American Rhetoric: A Reader.* Dubuque, IA: Kendall-Hunt.

Williams, C. (1987). *The Destruction of Black Civilization: Great Issues of a Race from 4500 B.C. to 2000 A.D.* Chicago: Third World Press.

Section 1

CLASSICAL EGYPTIAN ORIGINS OF AFRICAN AMERICAN RHETORIC

CHAPTER 1

Nommo, Kawaida, and Communicative Practice: Bringing Good into the World

MAULANA KARENGA

SCOPE AND FRAMEWORK

The central project of this essay is to make a useful contribution to the ancient and ongoing conversation around the definition, field, and function of African communicative practice, using classical African sources, principally ancient Egyptian (Kemetic) texts, as a fundamental point of departure and framework for understanding and engaging African American rhetoric. It contains an implicit critique and corrective for the dominant consumerist conception of a rhetoric pressed into the service of vulgar persuasion, advertisement, seduction, and sales. It assumes that not only has the dominant European paradigm abandoned the classical Aristotelian understanding of rhetoric as deliberation and action in the interest of the polis, but also that it is not informed by the possibilities inherent in the rich resources of multicultural contributions to this field (Logan 1999; Asante 1998; Hauser 1998). I will begin with a discussion of tradition and themes in African American rhetorical practice and then continue with a critical engagement of the conceptual construct nommo, its evolution in the 1960s as a central category in Black rhetorical studies, and its usefulness in providing conceptual space not only for African-centered grounding in the field of rhetoric but also for exploring alternative ways of understanding and approaching communicative practice (Hamlet 1998; Niles 1995; Walker 1992).

Within this framework, the communal character of communicative practice is reaffirmed and rhetoric is approached as, above all, a rhetoric of communal deliberation, discourse, and action, oriented toward that which is good for the community and world. And it is here that communicative practice is posed as both expressive and constitutive of community, a process and a practice of building community and bringing good into the world. This understanding brings into focus and complements the ethical teaching of the *Odu*

Ifa 78:1, the sacred text of ancient Yorubaland, that "humans are divinely chosen to bring good into the world" and that this is the fundamental mission and meaning in human life (Karenga 1999a, 228).

I will also examine the ancient Egyptian concept of *mdw nfr,* eloquent and effective speech, delineating its socioethical concerns and retrieving and articulating these concerns as an essential component of the conception and pursuit of the central interests of this project. It should be understood that my intention here is not to construct a causal relationship between ancient Egyptian and African American rhetorical practice. Rather, it is to identify shared insights and orientations in a larger African tradition of communicative practice and to recover and employ these classical African understandings to expand the range of useful concepts in defining and explicating communicative practice in general and the African American rhetorical project in particular. This approach parallels the use of classical Greek rhetorical insights by European scholars to develop and explicate theories of rhetoric and its practice by various European cultures without needing to show causal links of rhetorical practice between ancient Greece and, let us say, Vikings or Victorian England. Framing the discussion within Kawaida philosophy, I will then consolidate the multiple ranges of meanings of African communicative practice into four enduring socioethical concerns and use this conceptual construct to demonstrate coherence and continuity in the African communicative practice tradition, from ancient origins to modern ethical engagement with the critical issues of our times. These enduring socioethical concerns are the dignity and rights of the human person, the well-being and flourishing of family and community, the integrity and value of the environment, and the reciprocal solidarity and cooperation for mutual benefit of humanity.

Again, the approach to this project is essentially an Afrocentric cultural approach rooted in Kawaida philosophy, which defines itself as an ongoing synthesis of the best of African thought and practice in constant exchange with the world and is directed toward the enduring historical project of maximum human freedom and human flourishing times (Karenga 1997a, 1997b, 1980). It poses culture as a unique and instructive way of being human in the world and a fundamental framework for self-understanding and self-assertion in it. Kawaida also maintains that as persons in general and intellectuals in particular, we must constantly dialog with African culture, asking it questions and seeking from it answers to the fundamental and enduring concerns of humankind. This dialog with African culture requires that one ask at every critical juncture of research, writing, and discourse the crucial question of what Africa (i.e., African people and African culture) has to offer in efforts toward understanding human thought and practice, improving the human condition, and enhancing the human prospect. Moreover, to dialog with African culture is to constantly engage its texts, continental and diasporan, ancient and modern. This will include engaging its oral, written, and living-practice texts, its paradigms, its worldview and values, and its understanding of itself and the world in an ongoing search for ever better answers to the fundamental, enduring, and current questions and challenges of our lives.

TRADITION AND THEMES

To engage in rhetoric as an African is to enter an ancient and ongoing tradition of communicative practice, a practice that reaffirms not only the creative power of the word but also rootedness in a world historical community and culture, which provides the foundation and framework for self-understanding and self-assertion in the world (Asante 1998; Karenga 1997b; Obenga 1990). It is a tradition that from its inception has been concerned with building community, reaffirming human dignity, and enhancing the life of the people. It has expanded in more recent times to include vital contributions to the struggles for liberation in the political, economic, and cultural senses as a rhetoric of resistance. Thus, whereas Herbert Simons (1978, 50) talks of "distinctive and recurring patterns of rhetorical practice" as defining a genre, I want to identify these defining patterns of African rhetorical practice and locate them into the larger context of a distinct and ongoing *tradition*. By tradition I mean, within the framework of Kawaida philosophy, a cultural core that forms the central locus of our self-understanding and self-assertion in the world and which is mediated by constantly changing historical circumstances and an ongoing internal dialog of reassessment and continuous development (Karenga 2002, 1997a, 1995, 1980).

Here tradition is not simply an obvious source of authority, but also in the Asantean sense the source of *location,* "the constantly presenting and re-presenting context, the evolving presentation context, the perspective—that is history to us" (Asante 1990, 5–6). It is, he says, the source of "codes, paradigms, symbols, motifs, myths and circles of discussion that reinforce the centrality of African ideals as a valid frame of reference for acquiring and examining data." Again, then, this corresponds to the Kawaida concept of tradition as a core source out of which the materials, methods, and methodologies of rhetoric and other communicative practices are made. And as part of the larger cultural context, it becomes an essential source of our self-understanding and self-assertion in the world (Karenga 1997a). It is a tradition that incorporates unity and diversity, consensus and disagreement, affirmation and opposition, criticism and corrective, and a critical integration of the past with the understanding and engagement of the present and the aspirations and strivings for the future.

As an expression and constitutive process of community, African rhetoric is first of all a *rhetoric of community*. In other words, it evolves in ancient

African culture as a rhetoric of communal deliberation, discourse, and action, directed toward bringing good into the community and the world (Karenga 1999, 1994; Asante 1998; Parkinson 1991; Assmann 1990; Gyekye 1987; Perry 1986). In the context of historical and current oppression, African rhetoric is also a *rhetoric of resistance*. Clearly, given a community forcibly transferred to America during the holocaust of enslavement and systematically oppressed since then, a central aspect of the corpus of African American rhetorical practice is rooted in and reflective of constant resistance (Logan 1999; Hamlet 1998; Niles 1995; Walker 1992; Howard-Pitney 1990; Smith 1972; Foner 1972; Bosmajian and Bosmajian 1969; Woodson 1925; Dunbar 1914). Thus, some of African America's greatest addresses and messages are, like the people themselves, conceived and forged in the crucible of struggle (see Glenn 1986 for an extensive bibliography).

In these same texts and others, one finds that African American rhetoric is also a *rhetoric of reaffirmation*. It is self-consciously committed to the reaffirmation of the status of the African person and African people as bearers of dignity and divinity, of their right to a free, full, and meaningful life, and of their right and responsibility to speak their own special cultural truth to the world and make their own unique contribution to the forward flow of human history (Karenga 1980). But in reaffirming their own human rights and social and world-historical responsibilities to bring good into the world, at the same time they frame the discourse in such a way that the claim is on behalf of and in the interest of all people, especially the most vulnerable and marginalized (Karenga 1999, 1984). This is the meaning of Asante's statement concerning the central themes and intentionality of Black speakers: "In a real sense their speeches document the search by all men for the basic and fundamental rights of dignity, respect and equality." And he concludes that "because they record the speaker's response to the living issues of justice and freedom, these addresses are part of America's greatest heritage" (Smith 1971, vii). Finally, African rhetorical practice is a *rhetoric of possibility*. It seeks not simply to persuade, but to share, to inform, to question, and to search for and explore possibilities in the social and human condition. And it is in this regard that it is an active call to counsel and collaboration in the ongoing quest for effective ways to solve human problems, elevate the human spirit, reaffirm the right, create expanding space for maximum human freedom and human flourishing, and constantly bring good into the world.

NOMMO AND THE REAFFIRMATION OF THE '60s: SOCIOHISTORICAL SETTING

As I have noted elsewhere, "the Reaffirmation of the 60's stands, after the classical period and the Holocaust of enslavement, as one of the modal periods of African history" (Karenga 2002, 183–84). By modal periods I mean periods that define the conception and practice of Black life in profound and enduring ways and speak to the best of what it means to be African and human in the fullest sense. The classical period in the Nile Valley reflects the African commitment to knowledge, ethical, and spiritual grounding and cultural excellence, introducing and developing some of the basic disciplines of human knowledge and contributing to the forward flow of human history. It is here that the oldest texts on rhetoric as well as other disciplines are found (Freeman 1997; Diop 1987, 1991; El Nadoury 1990; Harris 1971).

The holocaust of enslavement tested and tempered African people; it called forth and demonstrated their adaptive vitality, human durability, and internal capacity to persevere and prevail. And it also reinforced their commitment to human freedom and human dignity in profound and active ways of struggle, of resistance, and of holding on to their humanity in the most inhuman conditions. The modal period of the '60s was above all a *reaffirmation*—a reaffirmation of *our Africanness* and *social justice tradition,* which had at its core a flowering of creativity and struggle, rhetoric, remembrance and resistance (Woodard 1999; Conyers 1997; Van Deburg 1993; Williams 1987; Pinkney 1976; Brisbane 1974). It is in the 1960s, a decade of storm, steadfastness, and struggle, that African Americans not only reaffirmed their identity and dignity as an African people, but compelled U.S. society and its academies to recognize and respect this most ancient of human cultures and civilizations and to teach them in the universities in newly established departments, programs and centers. And it is in this decade that we struggled to return to our own history, speak our own special cultural truth to the world, and self-consciously make our own unique contribution to how this country is reconceived and reconstructed.

Likewise, African Americans reaffirmed our commitment to our social justice tradition, a social justice tradition that is the oldest in the world, reaching back to the ethical teachings of ancient Egypt (Kemet) and continuing in the teaching of the Odu Ifa of Yorubaland, through the holocaust of enslavement and post-holocaust segregation to the '60s (Karenga 1999, 1994; Wilmore 1998; Fulop and Raboteau 1996; Hayes 1996). As I (1995, 2) noted elsewhere, it is a tradition that requires at a minimum "respect for the dignity and rights of the human person, economic justice, meaningful political participation, shared power, cultural integrity, mutual respect for all peoples, and uncompromising resistance to social forces and structures which deny or limit these." Indeed, the reaffirmation of our Africanness and social justice tradition permeates Black rhetoric of the period and points toward a profound change in the way African Americans understood and asserted themselves in society and the world (Golden and Rieke, 1971; Hill 1964; Smitherman, 1970, 1972, 1977; Boulware 1969; Smith and Robb 1971; Williams and Williams 1970).

NOMMO, THE CREATIVE WORD

The category of nommo evolved in the '60s not only as a conceptual framework for understanding and engaging in African American rhetorical practice, but also for communicative practice in the broadest sense of the word. It reflects the efforts to recover and reconstruct African culture and to use the past as a foundation and framework for present and future projects. The word *nommo* or *nummo* was taken from the creation narrative of the Dogon people of Mali (Griaule 1965; Griaule and Dieterlen 1986). According to the Dogon sage Ogotommêli, the Creator, Amma, sends nommo, the word (in the collective sense of speech), to complete the spiritual and material reorganization of the world and to assist humans in the forward movement in history and society. It is through the word, Ogotommêli tells us, that weaving, forging, cultivating, building family and community, and making the world good are made possible. Inherent in the concept of nommo are the triple aspects and elements of water, wind, and word, symbolizing, respectively, the life force (animation), life essence (spirit), and life creation (creativity). Moreover, nommo is "the completion of the perfect series [of creation], symbol of the total union of male and female, that is to say of unity" (Griaule 1965, 26). It is this sacred, indispensable, and creative character of the word, as an inherent and instrumental power to call into being, to mold, to bear infinite meanings, and to forge a world we all want and deserve to live in, that seizes the hearts and minds of the African American creative community and becomes a fundamental framework for developing, doing, and understanding rhetorical practice—both its oral and literary forms.

THE ASANTEAN INITIATIVE

It is Molefi Kete Asante who introduced the category of nommo into rhetorical discourse and criticism in his joint work with Stephen Robb (Smith and Robb 1971). Although this is a collaborative work in terms of speech selection and editing, a careful reading of Asante's work as well as the similarity of the text in this and his *Afrocentric Idea* (1998) show a distinctive theoretical development and conceptual continuity that is unquestionably Asante's. In this earlier work, then, Asante begins to explore concepts that ultimately lead to his development of Afrocentricity as a methodology, not only for rhetoric but for Africana studies as a whole. He notes in the introduction that "the African brought to America a fertile oral tradition, and the generating and sustaining powers of the spoken word permeated every area of his life" (Smith and Robb 1971, 1). Moreover, prohibited by law from reading and writing, "the African in America early cultivated his natural fascination with *Nommo,* the word, and demonstrated a singular appreciation for the subtleties, pleasures and potentials of the spoken word that has continued to enrich and embolden his history." Moreover, Asante is interested here also in drawing a distinction between African communicative practice and European practice. He argues that "[i]t is a cardinal mistake of our society to operate on the basis that language functions of Whites are everywhere reducible in Black societies in terms of influence and ends" (Smith and Robb 1971, 2).

Asante argues that this distinctive communicative practice of African Americans is rooted in their African heritage—in its oral tradition and in its continuing embrace of the concept and practice of "transforming vocal communication" (Smith and Robb 1971, 2). From this heritage and continuing practice, "the Afro-American developed, consciously or subconsciously, a consummate skill in using language to produce his own alternative communication patterns." Again, the concept that captures this process and practice is nommo. Thus, he contends, "to understand contemporary Black rhetoric in America means one must understand that Nommo continues to permeate Black activities." He cautions that "[t]his is not to say all Black people or most Black people are conscious of Nommo in a technical sense, but rather that most Blacks, given the situation can immediately identify the transforming power of vocal expression."

Finally, Asante calls attention to the fact that it is the practice of everyday life that shapes and reshapes the rhetorical practice as it puts forth and develops its transforming and constantly transformed expressions. For him, the holocaust of enslavement and its continuing effects "stand astride every meaningful rhetorical pathway like a giant colossus." And "while the stated theme of a given speech may be White racism, Black pride, freedom, crime, poverty, desegregation, poor housing conditions and voting rights, the underlying issue is always the slavery experience" (Smith and Robb 1971, 3, 4). This insight raises questions of what this inhuman and brutal physical and cultural genocide means, how we deal with its "residual effects," and how Black people can "regain their pre-slavery indeed pre-American heritage" (see also Asante 1998, part 2). Asante continues to develop these themes in his next book (Smith 1972), but his work takes a definitive turn in terms of his critical understanding of the rich resource of African culture and his development of Afrocentricity in the late '70s as a methodology for understanding and engaging not only the field of rhetoric, but also the discipline of Africana studies, in which it is located (Asante 1988, 1990, 1998).

In *The Afrocentric Idea,* his latest work on communicative practice, Asante states, "[B]y the nature of traditional African philosophy, rhetoric in African society is an architectonic functioning art, continuously fashioning the sounds and symbols of people even as it reenacts history." Moreover, he says that "the word is productive and imperative, calling forth and commanding." And "because the word is imperative, it is the fundament as well as the fashioning instrument of traditional African society" (1998, 81). Here Asante reaffirms the ancient African understanding of speech as a world-creating power and process. For the ancients, this refers to creative activities in the divine, natural, and social worlds. However, my essential interest here is to privilege the creation of the social world in this project without prejudice toward or neglect of the more inclusive ancient concept of world creation. In this context, Asante argues further:

> [T]he African sees the discourse as the creative manifestation of what is called to be. That which is called to be, because of the mores and values of society, becomes the created thing, and the artist or speaker, satisfies the demands of society by calling into being that which is functional. And functional, in this case refers to the object (sculpture, music, poem, dance, speech) that possesses a meaning within the communicator's and audience's worldview, a meaning that is constructed from the social, political and religious moments in the society's history. (1998, 75)

Asante's contribution to the development of the concept of nommo was instrumental in its evolution in the '60s as a central category in Black rhetorical studies. Nommo, as a conceptual construct that sought to recover and engage African modalities in understanding and approaching rhetorical practice, has been particularly useful in providing conceptual space not only for African-centered grounding in the field of rhetoric, but also for exploring and developing alternative ways to conceive, critique, and conduct this defining human activity. Within this framework one perceives that the communal character of communicative practice and rhetoric is engaged, above all, as a *rhetoric of community,* in a word, a rhetoric of communal deliberation, discourse, and action oriented toward that which is good for the community and world. And it is here also that rhetoric is most definitively understood as a communicative practice in the fullest sense, as both an expression of community and a constitutive practice of building community and bringing good into the world. What I want to do now is to explore this concept and process from a Kawaida perspective, using Kawaida philosophy and its understanding of classical African conceptions of rhetorical practice as a foundation and framework.

KAWAIDA AND THE CONCEPT OF *MDW NFR*

The assumptions and contentions about communicative practice made at the beginning of this essay are rooted in and reflective of the Kawaida retrieval and reading of the classical African sources, especially those of ancient Egypt (Kemet) (Karenga 1994, 1984). Fox has noted that although "[r]hetorical theory is traditionally thought to have originated with the Greeks," the ancient Egyptians can claim "their rightful place in the history of rhetoric" (1983, 9). And that, of course, is a place of anteriority. For as the records show, "the rich literature of pharonic Egypt . . . does offer us theories of rhetoric . . . , that is a conceptual rhetoric of good speech . . . expressed both incidentally and explicitly in the context of advice about the efficacy." Fox also rightly states that there is in ancient Egyptian texts an equivalent for the English word *rhetoric* (1983, 11–12). In fact, in the *Book of Ptahhotep,* there are two expressions for rhetoric, rhetoric as eloquent and effective speech itself (*mdt nfrt—medet neferet*) and rhetoric as the rules or principles of eloquent and effective speech (*tp-ḥsb n mdt nfrt—tep-ḥeseb en medet neferet*). Fox uses the latter and argues that the use of the singular form of *tep-ḥeseb,* "principle" or "rule," is significant, for Ptahhotep, in whose work it is used, "sees himself as presenting not just a variety of counsels about good speech, but as offering instructions that *together* form 'the principle of good speech.'"

Fox concludes that given this, for the ancient Egyptians "[e]loquence is a unity." This contention concerning the unity of the principles of eloquent and effective speech is correct and reflects the Kemetic understanding of rhetoric as a craft (*ḥmwt*) not simply to persuade through mastery of technique (*technē*), but to exchange in pursuit of the good for the community and the world. This is why the three modes of appeal identified in Aristotelian rhetoric—*logos,* the rational appeal; *ethos,* the ethical appeal; and *pathos,* the emotional appeal—are in Kemetic rhetoric bound together in an inseparable unity.

Indeed, the ancient Egyptians conceived of speech as essentially an ethical activity, an activity of tremendous power that could be used for good or evil. The very concept and category, *medu nefer,* literally means "good speech," and *nefer* (good) here, like in other African languages (i.e., Swahili *zuri* and Zulu *hle*), means both "morally good" and "aesthetically beautiful." Therefore, *medu nefer,* at its best, was always ethical, and it was truly worthy not because it was technically logical, but because it was appropriate and effective in the context of an ethical value system, Maat, the moral ideal in ancient Egypt. *Maat* is a polysemic word, but in the simplest terms it means "rightness in the world," that is, in the divine, natural, and social realms. It is informed by seven cardinal virtues: truth, justice, propriety, harmony, balance, reciprocity, and order (Karenga 1994). And as Fox (1983, 15) notes in discussing the canons of Kemetic rhetoric, "most important and most characteristically Egyptian, is the canon of *truthfulness.*" Indeed, "[t]ruthful speech is effective speech because it creates your ethos and because it is in and of itself persuasive." It is this ethical core of the project that makes it resistant to the artifice and dissimulation that are so prevalent in much of what passes as rhetoric and rhetorical instruction in a consumerist society committed to seduction and sales.

In addition to Ptahhotep's advice on good speech, the *locus classicus* of eloquent and effective speech in practice is the *Book of Khunanup* (Parkinson 1991; Perry 1986; Karenga 1984, 29–35; Lichtheim 1975–80, 1:169–84). It is important to note that the classic work in Kemetic rhetoric is at the same time the definitive text on Maat, the moral ideal in ancient Egypt (Assmann 1990, chap. 3). The text is a narrative whose central focus is the eloquent and effective petitions for justice by Khunanup, a peasant (whom most Egyptologists call "The Eloquent Peasant") "whose speech is truly beautiful," that is, eloquent and effective and who has been abused by an official and seeks redress from the magistrate of the region (Lichtheim 1975–80, 1:172). The text again stresses that good speech, called here *mdw nfr—medu nefer,* is not the sole possession of the learned or well established. Indeed, peasants, women, servants, and all kinds of everyday people can be eloquent and effective speakers for truth and justice in the world. Given the use of *medu nefer* to describe Khunanup's eloquent and effective speech, I use it as the principal term of Kemetic rhetoric rather than the alternative form *medet neferet* except when quoting Ptahhotep directly.

EXCURSUS: REVISITING ARISTOTLE

It is at this point that one can rightfully argue that the dominant European paradigm of classical rhetoric, which was based on Aristotelian and neo-Aristotelian rhetorical understanding, has been seriously compromised, if not abandoned altogether. Aristotle (1991) understood rhetoric as deliberation and action in the interest of the polis and thus valued the ethical aspect of the practice (Furley and Nehamaus 1994; Garver 1994; Beiner 1983). In fact, Aristotle notes in his *Rhetoric* (1354b) that in principle, arguments based on truth are presumed to be stronger than those that are not. In one case Aristotle, defining rhetoric, says that "rhetoric is a combination of the science of logic and the ethical branch of politics," but if we try to make rhetoric what it is not, a science, we tend to destroy its true nature (1354b). As Calvin Schrag (1986, 181–82) states, rhetoric has to do with both discourse and craft or art (*technē*). But "the Aristotelian notion of technē should not be confused with the modern notion of 'technique' as an affiliate of technology." Thus "[r]hetoric as an art is not a technique for control, an instrument for manipulation, a routine that can be mapped out in advance."

> Such construal of technē leads directly to the technification of discourse, inviting a gimmickry of emotional appeals, twists of language, if not outright deception, designed to win someone over in accepting beliefs and practices without regard either for understanding or for availability of evidence.

Schrag reasons that Aristotle had anticipated this degenerative practice of rhetoric and "installed a distinction between forensics and the deliberative rhetoric of political oratory" (1986, 182–83).

Indeed, Aristotle does call attention to the existing preference for modes of oratory that win points in argument and debate, and notes that he favors deliberative discourse for the common good of the polis. Thus he says that "although the same systematic principles apply to political as to forensic oratory . . . the former is a nobler business and fitter for a citizen than that which concerns relations with private individuals." And "the reason for this," he concludes, "is that in political oratory there is less inducement to talk about non-essentials." Moreover, "[p]olitical oratory is less given to unscrupulous practices than forensic, because it treats wider issues" (1354b). Certainly, no one with a modicum of awareness of U.S. politics and political discourse can claim they do not deal with "non-essentials" much of the time, from the sexual habits of opponents to catering to vulgar tastes of various constituencies. Likewise, Aristotle's statement about political oratory being "less given to unscrupulous practices than forensic, because it treats wider issues" shatters on the same rock of reality, that is, the actual practices of politics in the established order of things in the United States. But one cannot help sensing that inherent in this degenerative tendency of rhetoric is Aristotle's simplest and most often used definition of rhetoric: "the faculty of observing in any given case the available means of persuasion" (1355b). For it is this focus on *persuasion by any and all available means* that has become not only the defining practice of political rhetoric, but also the central focus of instruction for communication classes in the academy and other structures.

RETURN TO THE KEMETIC PARADIGM

As stated above, the Kemetic concept of rhetoric, *medu nefer,* requires a unity of the principles of rhetoric in which all three modalities of appeal form an inseparable unity and the ethical concern serves as hub and hinge on which the entire enterprise turns. This concept is essentially worked out in the genre of ancient Egyptian texts called *sebyt* (sebait), which literally means "instructions," but also is found in other texts such as the autobiographies (Lichtheim 1988; Karenga 1999b). These "books of instructions" are essentially social and political ethical texts designed for and dedicated to instructing members of ancient Egypt's large bureaucracy in the principles of right conduct in governance (Lichtheim 1975–80; Karenga 1984, 37–71). Most of this instruction on *medu nefer* applies to both personal relations and the public conduct of governance. It includes advice on verbal exchange in the family, in public, at court, and in court. This reflects the ancient Egyptian commitment to a unified life—private and public—and the commitment to Maatian thought and practice in both spheres.

In discussing Kemetic rhetoric, Fox (1983, 16) lists five fundamental canons of ancient Egyptian rhetoric: silence, good timing, restraint, fluency, and truthfulness. These are obviously not exhaustive of the canons of ancient Egyptian rhetorical practice, but they are useful in highlighting some of the most important aspects. However, Fox's category of "silence" can be collapsed into "restraint," for the conceptual elasticity of the category *gr* (*ger*), which he uses for "silence," allows for a more expansive meaning of "self-control," which he himself notes (1983, 13). In fact, the paradigmatic Maatian person, the *geru maa,* posited in the *Sebait of Amenomope* (Lichtheim 1975–80, 2:146–63) is not simply the truly silent man, as Fox indicates, but more accurately the *truly self-controlled* person, who, as Fox himself states, "succeeds by virtue of his unflagging inner repose and self-control."

CLASSICAL AFRICAN RHETORIC AS COMMUNAL AND ETHICAL PRACTICE

However, I am interested not so much in canon as technique and rule as I am in rhetoric as a communicative and communal practice to build community and bring good in the community and world. Thus, I want to turn now to four overarching ethical concerns of classical African rhetoric, which, as I stated at the beginning of this essay, find resonance in African American rhetoric since its inception. These are the dignity and rights of the human person, the well-being of family and community, the integrity and value of the environment, and the reciprocal solidarity and cooperation for mutual benefit of humanity. Clearly, these rhetorical and ethical themes vary in emphasis and intensity of appeal, depending on the audience and context or ground of engagement. But they form a unity of moral and public vision and purpose, and thus are interrelated explicitly and implicitly in the classical paradigm.

THE DIGNITY AND RIGHTS OF THE HUMAN PERSON

The *Sebait of Ptahhotep* is not only the oldest complete text in the world, it is also the oldest rhetorical treatise in the world. It is written by the prime minister, Ptahhotep, as a legacy of instruction to his son and by extension to all who perform and aspire to engage in public service (Zába 1956; Lichtheim 1975–80, 1:61–80; Simpson 1973, 159–76). Ptahhotep begins his instructions on the standard of *medu nefer,* good speech, by advising humbleness in learning and respect for fellow human beings whatever their status. And in this he reaffirms the ethical concern for the dignity of the human person as a fundamental aspect of rhetorical practice. He says:

> Be not arrogant because of your knowledge. Rather converse with the unlearned as well as the wise. For the limit of an art has not been reached and no artist [or artisan] has acquired full mastery (of an art). Good speech [*medet neferet*] is more hidden than emeralds and yet it is found among the women who gather at the grindstone. (ll. 52–59, translated in Karenga 1984, 41)

This is the first instruction, thus suggesting its priority as a condition for good speech. It speaks against arrogance in the possession and use of knowledge in rhetorical practice. For the practice is above all a communal and deliberative practice directed toward the good of the community, and this requires respect for all people, regardless of knowledge level, class, or gender. For here they are posed not as an audience, but as fellow participants in the collaborative quest for the common good.

Moreover, Ptahhotep, like Aristotle after him, sees rhetoric as a craft (*hmwt, hemut*), a practice carried out with skill, artistry, and precision. And he demonstrates his respect for it as an art or craft by saying that it is a rare attainment. Furthermore, he says later in the text to "become a craftsman and speak to perfection" (ll. 615–16). Yet he notes that *medu nefer*, eloquent and effective speech, can also be found among the women at the grindstone. Such a position reflects a central pillar of Maatian ethics: the equal dignity and inherent possibilities in all persons, male and female, rich and poor. It is clearly one of Africa's most important contributions to the ethical development of humankind to have introduced the concept of humans as the images of God, *senenu netcher*, and thus as equal bearers of dignity and divinity, as early as 2140 B.C.E. in the *Book of Kheti* (Karenga 1994, 597ff; 1984, 52; Lichtheim 1975–80, 1:106).

This respect for the dignity or inherent worthiness of human beings is also reaffirmed in the narrative of Djedi, in which the sage Djedi tells Pharaoh Khufu, who is about to kill a nameless prisoner, that he must not kill or use any person for an experiment (Blackman 1988). For within the Maatian ethical tradition, "it is not permitted to do such a thing to the noble flock of God," that is, the noble images of God, human beings (Lichtheim 1975–80, 219). This stress on the inherent worthiness and possibilities in each human being emphasizes the ancient Egyptian concept of rhetoric as essentially an ethical practice defined not only by its truth and truthfulness, but also by its respect for the masses of people who are the hearers and participants in the rhetorical and political project of creating and sustaining a just and good society, that is, a Maatian society.

Linked to this recognition of the inherent worthiness of each person and the rhetor's audience or co-agents in collaborative discourse and action is the need for the rhetor to stand worthy her- or himself. Thus, in what Fox calls the literary oratory of ancient Egypt, especially in the autobiographies, there is a rhetorical and moral claim of standing worthy before the people (Lichtheim 1988). Therefore, Nefer-sesham Ra says, "I have spoken truly, I have done justice. I spoke beautifully and repeated what was good so as to stand well with the people" (Karenga 1984, 95). Again, this respect of the audience as worthy respondents and partners in a project of common good is central to Kemetic communicative practice.

In Khunanup, one finds also the concern for the rights as well as dignity of the human person. Indeed, the petitions Khunanup makes for justice for the poor and vulnerable are inherently concerned with the dignity and rights of the human person. Thus, when he seeks justice, it is based on the concept of Maat, which reaffirms and requires equal dignity and basic human rights for all. Khunanup speaks directly to the concepts of rights three times, each time asking the magistrate, Rensi, to allow him to defend his rights. Lichtheim (1975–80, 177, 179, 180) defines these terms, *sp nfr, n-wn-m-̣`, sp n-wn-m-̣`,* and *sp nfr,* as "good cause" and "rightful cause," and Simpson (1973, 42) uses "right cause." But Rodriguez (2000, 364) rightly defines them as meaning "right" or "rights." For in the sense that Khunanup is using them and in the judicial context in which he makes his petition, a right cause or rightful cause is, in fact, a just claim, which is the definition of a right in both the ethical and legal senses. Thus, Khunanup calls on Rensi to recognize and respect his just claim or right, not simply as an Egyptian citizen, but more importantly as a person whose ground is not the state, but that which transcends and grounds the good society, Maat. In this he calls for a cooperative and collaborative practice called "returning Maat to its place," that is, as the framework and foundation of political, judicial, and social practice.

Moreover, the call for collaborative discourse by Ptahhotep speaks to the intentionality of rhetorical practice in the context of what we now call politics and the ancient Egyptians called governance. Although there are various words for governance—*hekat, sekher, seshemet*—I want to use *seshemet* here. For it not only suggests "leadership," "guidance," and "showing the way," but also "working out" and "proving," as in a problem of math (Faulkner 1991, 247). Indeed, the collaborative deliberation of public discourse suggests the need to "work out" the problems and possibilities of society and the world. It is this conceptual framework of collaborative discourse and action that enables us to understand the Kemetic concepts of politics or governance as a collective vocation to create and sustain a just society and good world. And the rhetorician, rhetor or speaker, is charged with eliciting collaborative discourse and action through directedness to the other as interlocutor and coagent in this awesome collective vocation. Thus, given the intentionality of the rhetorical practice and process, the centrality of the ethical becomes obvious and imperative.

THE WELL-BEING AND FLOURISHING OF COMMUNITY

As the reaffirmation of the dignity of the human person is central to the Kemetic rhetorical project, so is the concern for the well-being and flourishing of community. In the autobiographies, this concern is worked out in the moral claims of having done good for family and the people (Lichtheim 1988). Therefore, Count Harkhuf says, "I have come from my city. I have descended from my district. . . . I was one worthy, one beloved of his father, praised by his mother and one whom all his brothers and sisters loved" (Lichtheim 1975–80, 1:24). Having located himself in community and family, he then goes on to declare that he did good for the people, especially the vulnerable, saying, "I gave bread to the hungry, clothing to the naked and brought the boatless to land (Lichtheim 1975–80, 1:24). Iti, the treasurer, says, "I am a worthy citizen who acts with his arm. I am a great pillar of the Theban district, a man of standing in the Southland" (Lichtheim 1988, 31). And finally, Lady Tahabet defines herself not only as a worthy daughter, but also as a worthy citizen. She says,

> I was just and did not show partiality. I gave bread to the hungry, water to the thirsty and clothes to the naked. I was open-handed to everyone. I was honored by my father, praised by my mother, kind to my brothers and sisters and one who was united in heart with the people of her city. (Karenga 1994, 233)

Thus, these persons are concerned with the good of family and community, and their moral self-presentation is not self-congratulatory rhetoric, but rather the presentation of a model of commitment and behavior worthy of a self-conscious member of family and community.

Asante has noted that "African rhetoric is distinguished not only in its concern for coherence and participation, but also its relationship to the stability of the traditional society" (1998, 78). Surely these eloquent autobiographical texts attest strongly to this contention. For what the texts stress is the role of communicative practice in the constitution of the social world, its eliciting and reaffirming a shared investment in creating and sustaining the just and good world we want and deserve to live in. And they also reveal how self is called into being and constituted in community and through the communicative practice it elicits and sustains, that is, a practice of discourse and action within a community. In contrast to the classical European conception of self as a thinking subject, the texts pose the classical African concept of self as a *related and relating subject*. Thus, it is not simply "I think, therefore I am," but rather that *I am related and relate to others, therefore I am*. It is in my *being-with, being-of*, and *being-for* others that I discover and constitute myself. And it is through communicative practice within an ancient and ongoing tradition that I achieve this. As Schrag points out correctly, "the distinctive stamp of rhetorical intentionality is that it reaches out toward, aims at, is directed to the other as hearer, reader, audience" (1986, 198). He continues, "This intentionality illustrates not the theoretical reflection of cognitive detachment but rather the practical engagement of concrete involvement." One must add, however, as Schrag has done elsewhere for his own paradigm, that in the African sense, the listening others are not simply hearers, readers, and audience, but also co-agents, co-participants, in creating and sustaining the just society and good world that point toward and make possible maximum human freedom and human flourishing.

THE INTEGRITY AND VALUE OF THE ENVIRONMENT

The ancient Egyptian autobiographies also yield an ethical concern for the integrity and value of the environment and our obligation to preserve and protect it (Karenga 1999b, 51–53; 2002, 247–49). This principle of communicative practice evolved from the concept of Maat and its central concept of worthiness before nature. As I have noted elsewhere, "Maat requires worthiness before the Creator, nature and the people. The concept of worthiness before nature in the Maatian tradition evolves out of the understanding that moral worthiness, like existence, is interrelated in every area of life" (Karenga 2002, 247). And nature is one of the key areas of moral concern, along with the divine and social realms. As part of this order of rightness, which binds all things together, humans belong to each of these realms. "In their identity as divine images of God, they belong to the Divine; in their identity as social beings, they belong to society and in their identity as living beings, they belong to nature" (Karenga 1994, 723).

The Kemetic concept of *serudj ta* has particular importance here. It refers to the ethical obligation of humans to restore and repair the world with the extended meaning of making it more beautiful than it was when we inherited it. Thus, it speaks to the ancient and ongoing project of renewing and bringing good into the world. This is posed in ancient Egyptian spiritual and ethical texts as a collaborative effort of world maintenance by humans and the divine. Here collaborative communicative discourse and action as Maat-doing restores and repairs the world, which is constantly damaged and undone by things we do wrong and fail to do right. And the damage and the repair occur in the ecological, social, and ontological senses. Therefore, the autobiographies urge us to engage in the collaborative practice of *serudj ta:*

> To raise up and rebuild that which is in ruins; to repair that which is damaged; to rejoin that which is severed; to replenish that which is lacking; to strengthen that which is weakened; to set right that which is wrong; and to make flourish that which is insecure and underdeveloped. (Karenga 1994, 743)

THE RECIPROCAL SOLIDARITY AND COOPERATION OF HUMANITY

Finally, African communicative practice is concerned for and committed to the reciprocal solidarity and cooperation for the mutual benefit of humanity. In its insistence on the ethical criticism of artificial eloquence, deceptive discourse and instrumental reasoning against the greater interest of humanity, it calls for an ethical judgment of rhetoric itself (Hamlet 1998; Garver 1998; Biesecker 1992). Moreover, it raises the issue of the closed and limited public square and calls for its opening in ways that enhance and nurture meaningful and substantive human exchange (Asante 1998; Hauser 1998; De Certeau 1984). And with the prime minister Rekhmira and the peasant Khunanup, it calls for justice for all the people. For as the *Instructions to Rekhmira* say, "He who does *justice for all the people,* he is truly the prime minister," that is, the rightful leader who governs according to Maat. In the *Book of Khunanup,* Khunanup, the eloquent peasant, gives nine rhetorical disquisitions on Maat in his petition for justice in society and the world to the high steward, Rensi (Parkinson 1991; Assmann 1990; Karenga 1984, 29–35). Certainly he stands symbolically for all marginalized and oppressed people who step forward to speak truth and insist on justice based on an ethical system, Maat, that transcends the established order. It is he who gives the classic Kemetic critique of hegemonic discourse and action and calls for truth and justice in the land, saying, "Speak truth. Do justice. For Maat (Rightness) is mighty; it is great, it endures and it leads one to blessedness." In fact, he says, "Maat (truth and justice) is breath to the nose." And again, "[t]he balancing of the earth lies in doing Maat."

The principle of reciprocal solidarity is also stressed by Khunanup. He says that "a good deed is remembered," therefore to "do to the doer that he may also do" (Lichtheim 1975–80, 174). Jan Assmann (1990, 66ff) states that Maat, expressed in the *Book of Khunanup,* yields a concept of solidarity that has two basic aspects—a solidarity of action and a solidarity of understanding. In these forms of solidarity, there is not only the mutual acting for one another (*Füreinander-Handelns*), but also mutual consideration and thoughtfulness with and toward each other (*Aneinander-Denkens*). But the conceptual grounding for both of these is *communicative solidarity,* which is based on the art of hearing (*Kunst Hörens*), a profound and ongoing mutual responsiveness and responsibility to one another. Lady Ta-Aset also speaks to the virtue of reciprocity, saying that "doing good is not difficult; just speaking good is a monument for one who does it. For those who do good for others are actually doing it for themselves" (Karenga 1994, 229). This ethical orientation is reaffirmed later in the teachings of Orunmila in the *Odù Ifá* when he says that "doing good worldwide is the best example of character" (166:2). Indeed, it is a fundamental African understanding that all great good is a shared good, that is, requires being shared with others for its true fulfillment and just enjoyment. Among these goods are life, freedom, justice, family, friendship, and love. It is in this context of the focus on rhetoric as ethical activity in pursuit and benefit of the common good that Carter G. Woodson argues that "true oratory, then, has regard to truth and justice. There must be some lofty purpose in the eloquent appeal which stands the test of time" (1925, 7). And again, this "lofty purpose" must be rooted in and reflective of the enduring ethical concerns of shared human good.

It is important to reiterate the central importance Africans have placed on the creative power of the word, nommo, *medu nefer,* eloquent and effective speech. This is reaffirmed in the Hon. Marcus Garvey's assertion in one of his many speeches that "as soon as we were freed, we made *a rush to get the book*" and to master its materials in the interest of self-determination and human progress (1983, 119, italics mine). For we understood the power of the word, written as well as spoken, and its key role as knowledge in enhancing our capacity to control our destiny and daily lives and live truly free, full and meaningful lives. But again, as argued above, we treasured the spoken word in a special and expansive way, even when we also wrote it down throughout history. Perhaps no one has summed up this expansive concept and profound appreciation of speech—spoken and written—better than Frederick Douglass, a master orator in his own right. He says,

> Great is the miracle of human speech—by it nations are enlightened and reformed; by it the cause of justice and liberty is defended, by it evils are exposed, ignorance dispelled, the path of duty made plain, and by it those that live today, are put into the possession of wisdom of ages gone by. (1979, 476–77)

It is this retrieved and reaffirmed understanding of speech that forms the core and consciousness of African communicative practice, which at its best is directed toward the ongoing historical project to build and sustain community and constantly bring good into the world.

REFERENCES

Allen, J. P. (1988). *Genesis in Egypt: The Philosophy of Ancient Egyptian Creation Accounts.* New Haven: Yale University Press.

Aristotle (1991). *On Rhetoric.* Trans. George Kennedy. New York: Oxford University Press.

Asante, M. K. (1988). *Afrocentricity.* Trenton, NJ: Africa World Press.

Asante, M. K. (1990). *Kemet, Afrocentricity and Knowledge.* Trenton, NJ: Africa World Press.

Asante, M. K. (1998). *The Afrocentric idea.* Philadelphia: Temple University Press.

Assmann, J. (1990). *Ma'at: Gerechtigkeit und Unsterblichkeit im alten Ägypten* [Maat: Justice and eternity in ancient Egypt]. Munich: C. H. Beck.

Beiner, R. (1983). *Political Judgment.* Chicago: University of Chicago Press.

Biesecker, B. (1992). Michael Foucault and the question of rhetoric. *Philosophy and Rhetoric* 25: 351–64.

Blackman, A. (1988). *The Story of King Cheops and the Magicians.* Transcribed from Papyrus Westcar (Berlin Papyrus 3033). Reading, PA: JB Books.

Bosmajian, H., and H. Bosmajian (1969). *The Rhetoric of the Civil Rights Movement.* New York: Random House.

Boulware, M. H. (1969). *The Oratory of Negro Leaders, 1900–1968.* Westport, CT: Negro Universities Press.

Brisbane, R. (1974). *Black Activism.* Valley Forge, PA: Judson Press.

Conyers, J. L. (Ed.) (1997). *Africana Studies: A Disciplinary Quest for Both Theory and Method.* Jefferson, NC: McFarland and Company, Inc.

De Certeau, M. (1984). *The Practice of Everyday Life.* Trans. Steven Rendall. Berkeley: University of California Press.

Diop, C. A. (1987). *The African Origins of Civilization: Myth or Reality.* Westport, CT: Lawrence Hill and Co.

Diop, C. A. (1991). *Civilizations or Barbarism: An Authentic Anthropology.* New York: Lawrence Hill and Co.

Douglass, F. (1979). Great Is the Miracle of Human Speech: An Address Delivered in Washington, D.C. on 31 August 1891. In John W. Blassingame (Ed.), *The Frederick Douglass Papers,* volume 5 (pp. 474–77). New Haven: Yale University Press.

Dunbar, A. (Ed.) (1914). *Masterpieces of Negro Eloquence: The Best Speeches Delivered by the Negro from the Days of Slavery to the Present Time.* New York: The Bookery Publishing Company.
El Nadoury, R. (1990). The Legacy of Pharaonic Egypt. In G. Mokhtar (Ed.), *General History of Africa,* volume 2: *Ancient Civilizations of Africa* (pp. 103–18). Berkeley: University of California Press.
Faulkner, R. O. (1991). *A Concise Dictionary of Middle Egyptian.* Oxford: Griffith Institute.
Foner, P. S. (Ed.) (1972). *The Voice of Black America: Major Speeches by Negroes in the United States 1797–1971.* New York: Simon and Schuster.
Fox, M. V. (1983). Ancient Egyptian Rhetoric. *Rhetorica* 1, 1: 9–22.
Freeman, C. (1997). *The Legacy of Ancient Egypt.* New York: Facts on File.
Fulop, T., and A. J. Raboteau (Eds.) (1996). *African American Religion: Interpretive Essays in History and Culture.* New York: Routledge.
Furley, D., and A. Nehamaus (Eds.) (1994). *Aristotle's Rhetoric: Philosophical Essays.* Princeton: Princeton University Press.
Garver, E. (1994). *Aristotle's Rhetoric: An Art of Character.* Chicago: University of Chicago Press.
Garver, E. (1998). Ethical Criticism of Reasoning. *Philosophy and Rhetoric* 31, 2: 107–30.
Garvey, M. (1983). Address at Newport News, October 25, 1919. In R. Hill (Ed.), *The Marcus Garvey and Universal Negro Improvement Association papers,* volume 2 (pp. 112–20). Los Angeles: University of California Press.
Glenn, R. W. (1986). *Black Rhetoric: A Guide to Afro-American Communication.* Metuchen, NJ: Scarecrow Press.
Golden, J. L., and R. D. Rieke (Eds.) (1971). *The Rhetoric of Black Americans.* Columbus, OH: Charles E. Merrill.
Griaule, M. (1965). *Conversations with Ogotemmêli: An Introduction to Dogon Religious Ideas.* London: Oxford University Press.
Griaule, M., and G. Dieterlen (1986). *The Pale Fox.* Chino Valley, AZ: Continuum Foundation.
Gyekye, K. (1987). *An Essay on African Philosophical Thought: The Akan Conceptual Scheme.* New York: Cambridge University Press.
Hamlet, J. (Ed.) (1998). *Afrocentric Visions: Studies in Culture and Communications.* Newbury Park, CA: Sage Publications.
Harris, J. R. (Ed.) (1971). *The Legacy of Egypt.* Oxford: Oxford University Press.
Hauser, G. (1998). Civil Society and the Principle of the Public Square. *Philosophy and Rhetoric* 31, 1: 19–40.
Hayes, D. (1996). *And Still We Rise: An Introduction to Black Liberation Theology.* New York: Paulist Press.
Hill, R. L. (Ed.) (1964). *Rhetoric of Racial Revolt.* Denver: Golden Bell Press.
Howard-Pitney, D. (1990). *The Afro American Jeremiad: Appeals for Racial Justice in America.* Philadelphia: Temple University Press.
Karenga, M. (1980). *Kawaida Theory: An Introductory Outline.* Inglewood, CA: Kawaida Publications.
Karenga, M. (1984). *Selections from the Husia: Sacred Wisdom of Ancient Egypt.* Los Angeles: University of Sankore Press.
Karenga, M. (1994). Maat, the Moral Ideal in Ancient Egypt: A Study in Classical African Ethics. Ph.D. dissertation, University of Southern California, Los Angeles.
Karenga, M. (1995). *The Million Man March/Day of Absence Mission Statement.* Los Angeles: University of Sankore Press.
Karenga, M. (1997a). African Culture and the Ongoing Quest for Excellence: Dialog, Principles, Practice. *Black Collegian* (February), 160–63.
Karenga, M. (1997b). *Kawaida: A Communitarian African Philosophy.* Los Angeles: University of Sankore Press.
Karenga, M. (1999a). *Odu Ifa: The Ethical Teachings.* Los Angeles: University of Sankore Press.
Karenga, M. (1999b). Sources of Self in Ancient Egyptian Autobiographies: A Kawaida Articulation. In James Conyers Jr. (Ed.), *Black American Intellectualism and Culture: A Social Study of African American Social and Political Thought* (pp. 37–56). Stamford, CT: JAI Press, Inc.
Karenga, M. (2002). *Introduction to Black Studies,* 3rd edition. Los Angeles: University of Sankore Press.
Lichtheim, M. (1975–80). *Ancient Egyptian Literature: A Book of Readings,* 3 volumes. Berkeley: University of California Press.

Lichtheim, M. (1988). *Ancient Egyptian Autobiographies Chiefly in the middle kingdom.* Fribourg, Switzerland: Biblical Institute, University of Fribourg.

Logan, S. W. (1999). *"We Are Coming": The Persuasive Discourse of Nineteenth Century Black Women.* Carbondale: Southern Illinois University Press.

Niles, L. A. (1995). *African American Rhetoric: A Reader.* Dubuque, IA: Kendall-Hunt Publishing Co.

Obenga, T. (1990). *La philosophie africaine de la péroide pharonique, 2780–330 avant notre ère* [African philosophy in the pharonic period 2780–330 B.C.E.]. Paris: Editions L'Harmattan.

Parkinson, R. (1991). The Tale of the Eloquent Peasant, volume 2. Ph.D. dissertation, Oxford University, Oxford.

Perry, E. (1986). A Critical Study of the Eloquent Peasant. Ph.D. dissertation. Johns Hopkins University, Baltimore.

Pinkney, A. (1976). *Red, Black and Green: Black Nationalism in the United States.* Cambridge: Cambridge University Press.

Rodríguez, Á. S. (2000). *Diccionario jeroglíficos egipcios* [Egyptian hieroglyphic dictionary]. Madrid: Alderabán Ediciones.

Schrag, C. O. (1986). *Communicative Praxis and the Space of Subjectivity.* Bloomington: Indiana University Press.

Simons, H. W. (1978). "Genre-alizing" About Rhetoric: A Scientific Approach. In Karlyn Kohrs Campbell and Kathleen Hall Jamison (Eds.), *Form and Genre: Shaping Rhetorical Action* (pp. 33–50). Falls Church, VA: Communications Association.

Simpson, W. K. (Ed.) (1973). *The Literature of Ancient Egypt: An Anthology of Stories, Instruction and Poetry.* New Haven: Yale University Press.

Smith, A. L. [Molefi Kete Asante] (1969). *Rhetoric of Black Revolution.* Boston: Allyn and Bacon.

Smith, A. L. [Molefi Kete Asante] (1970). Socio-Historical Perspectives of Black Oratory. *Quarterly Journal of Speech* 56: 264–69.

Smith, A. L. [Molefi Kete Asante] (1972). *Language Communication and Rhetoric in Black America.* New York: Harper and Row.

Smith, A. L. [Molefi Kete Asante] and S. Robb (Eds.) (1971). *The Voice of Black Rhetoric.* Boston: Allyn and Bacon.

Smitherman, G. (1977). *Talkin and Testifyin: The Language of Black America.* Boston: Houghton, Mifflin.

Van Deburg, W. (1993). *New Day in Babylon: The Black Power Movement and African Culture, 1965–1975.* Chicago: University of Chicago Press.

Walker, R. J. (Ed.) (1992). *The Rhetoric of Struggle: Public Addresses by African American Women.* New York: Garland, Inc.

Williams, J. (1987). *Eyes on the Prize.* New York: Viking Penguin.

Williams, J. C., and M. Williams. (Eds.) (1970). *The Negro Speaks: The Rhetoric of Contemporary Black Leaders.* New York: Noble and Noble.

Wilmore, G. (1998). *Black Religion and Black Radicalism,* 3rd edition. Maryknoll, NY: Orbis Books.

Woodard, K. (1999). *A Nation Within a Nation: Amiri Baraka (LeRoi Jones) and Black Power Politics.* Chapel Hill: University of North Carolina Press.

Woodson, C. G. (Ed.) (1925). *Negro Orators and Their Orations.* Washington, DC: The Associated Publishers, Inc.

Žába, Z. (1956). *Papyrus prisse. Les maximes de Ptahhotep* [Papyrus Prisse. The maxims of Ptahhotep]. Prague: Académie Tchécoslovaque de Sciences.

CHAPTER 2

The Spiritual Essence of African American Rhetoric

ADISA A. ALKEBULAN

The purpose of this essay is to examine spirituality as a significant component of African American rhetoric. A historical foundation will be established by demonstrating the cultural continuity of language and rhetoric that Africans have with one another all over the world. The aim of this undertaking is also to identify how aspects of African culture associated with spirituality are manifested in African American rhetoric. Crucial to our understanding of the spiritual essence of African American rhetoric are the Kemetic (ancient Egyptian) concept of Maat and the Dogon concept of nommo. These concepts will be explored in detail.

Furthermore, the study of African American rhetoric is also a study of African languages (continental and diasporic, ancient and modern). It is difficult to speak of African American rhetoric absent a discussion of language, given the paramount nature of the oral culture. I argue that African American rhetoric is best understood within the field of linguistics associated with culture, called cultural linguistics. Sermonizing, signifyin', playin' the dozens, stylin' out, soundin', lyricism, improvisation, indirection, repetition, poetry, spirituals, history, style, culture, rhythm, and the very creation of the language of Africans in the United States (commonly called Ebonics) are all significant aspects of language and African American rhetoric that are firmly rooted in the African oral tradition. A true discussion of rhetoric, in an African context, cannot be separated from a discussion of language.

THE AFROCENTRIC PARADIGM

Afrocentricity is placing African ideals at the center of any analysis that involves African culture and behavior (Asante 1998, 6). In other words, any study that is concerned with the study of African phenomena should be examined from the perspective of the African person. Crucial to our understanding of Afrocentricity is the idea that Africans should be viewed as subjects in their own right and as acting as agents in their own historical and cultural reality rather than as objects on fringes of Western scholarship and civilization. According to Mazama, "methods and methodologies are derived from and informed by a particular paradigm." Further, "a people's worldview determines what constitutes a problem for them and how they solve problems" (2001, 398–99). For Asante, all analysis orbits around culture and evolves from ideology. Linda James Myers agrees with both assertions and holds that worldview is yielded by a particular set of philosophical assumptions that are represented in the conceptual systems those assumptions structure (1998, 74). She also maintains that "a cohesive set of philosophical assumptions create a conceptual system, a pattern of beliefs and values that define a way of life and world in which people act, judge, decide and solve problems." She asserts that it is this conceptual system that structures the worldview at the level of deep structure, to be reflected in surface structure across time and space. Furthermore,

> in the analysis of the sacred and secular dynamics of the African American communication system, Daniel and Smitherman . . . identify the traditional African worldview as significant for understanding patterns of Black communication in the United States, and the call response pattern as exemplary of a "deep structure" cultural difference. (Myers 1987, 75)

Similarly, Terry Kershaw maintains that Afrocentricity, as a paradigm, requires its practitioners to have a knowledge base that comes from the life experiences of people of African descent (1992, 163). This collective experience, worldview, or deep-structural cultural phenomenon informs the paradigm. Our understanding of the unique ways in which African people in the United States communicate can be established in part by our understanding of African rhetorical culture.

MAAT AS THE BASIS FOR AFRICAN SPIRITUALITY

In this essay, spirituality will not be defined or conceptualized in religious terms, for we know that the African religious community worldwide is quite diverse. Africans practice African religions, Christianity, Islam, and others. So to define spirituality in religious terms would prove fruitless, and it would prevent us from understanding the nature of spirituality at the core of the African person both in Africa and in the Diaspora regardless of religious affiliation. Rather, spirituality will be defined in cultural terms to show the cultural connection between Africans all over the world.

The lifelong quest for balance and harmony within oneself and within society is the essence of the spiritual being. Therefore, spirituality is defined as the search for personal balance and harmony as well as that of society. Asante writes:

> It is the quest for harmony that is the source of all literary, rhetorical, and behavioral actions; the sudic ideal, which emphasizes the primacy of the person, can only function if the person seeks individual and collective harmony. . . . One must understand that to become human. . . . The person is defined as human by performing actions that lead to harmony; our attitude toward this person creates the dynamism necessary to produce a harmonized personality. (1998, 200)

For Africans, life is predicated on the belief that the attainment of spiritual harmony is possible. In fact, one's humanity hinges on one's pursuit and fulfillment of harmony.

The concept that best embodies the African conceptualization of spirituality is the ancient African principle of Maat. According to Asante (2000), Maat is the "Kemetic (ancient Egyptian) quality of order, justice, righteousness and balance" and without Maat, he further maintains, "there is no understanding, no harmony and no possible restoration of balance . . . [We] are without power or direction" (p. 89–95). However, he points out, none of these terms individually encompasses the total nature of Maat. He surmises that "Maat is like a vast ocean with many waves" and maintains that it is correct to recognize Maat as the ruling force between good and evil. Moreover, he writes, "when you speak of it as the organizing principle of human society, the creative spirit of phenomena, and the eternal order of the universe, you come close to understanding what the ancient Kemetic civilization understood" (p. 89). He further explains that Maat's special character was the righteousness and rightness in the individual. Further, justice, truth, and righteousness referred to Maat; one cannot *be* righteous, but rather "it is a continuous process by which we align ourselves with the harmony we find in nature" (pp. 83–84). For the ancient Egyptians, Maat imposed order and direction and provided adequate meaning to their lives while serving as a major force against chaos. In other words, as we have been discussing, it was "the cosmic principle of harmony " (p. 95).

Key to our understanding of Maat is the relationship between humanity and the universe. This principle guided the ancients and provided them with an understanding of their role and interdependence with the universe. Obenga asserts that Maat connected the ancient Egyptians with all things in the universe. For the Egyptians, Maat provided an understanding of the universe, giving them a sense of divine order, balance, symmetry, geometry, truth, and immortality. Maat wove all aspects of life and reality "into a well-matched globality" (1995, 109–10). To understand the ancient Egyptians' ethical thought, we must understand the concept of Maat. There was no aspect of this ancient society in which Maat was not present. It guided the ancients in all of their daily rituals.

For the ancient Egyptians, Maat seemed to have been the guiding ethical principle at the core of their society. In fact, according to Monges, even "the role of the ruler was to balance the activities of the state so that Maat would be achieved. . . . It became an ethical system which guided the activities of the king" (1997, 106). In other words, if the pharaoh wanted eternal life, he or she had to abide by the guiding ethical principles set forth by Maat. The pharaohs of ancient Egypt were not simply kings, but also the "epitome of Maat" (Asante 2000, 90).

The concept of Maat did not confine itself to the borders of ancient Egypt. Nor did this spiritual and ethical principle die with the demise of Kemetic civilization. According to Obenga, "the word/concept Maat, 'truth,' can be found everywhere in Black Africa. It is a key concept throughout the entirety of African culture" (1995, 103). Asante also reveals a connection between the ancient Egyptians and other Africans. His argument is that all African societies owe Kemet as the common source for intellectual and philosophical ideas:

> These manifestations are shown, for example, in: the conversations of the Dogon's blind philosopher Ogotommeli; Zulu oral poetry, as brought to us by Masizi Kunene; Yoruba Ifa divination rights; Nsibidi texts, and in the practices and words of the Shona spirit mediums. . . . This is the position I take with respect to the dissemination of the Maatic concept throughout the African world. (1990, 92)

Further, the principles of Maat, according to Asante, extend to Africans in the Diaspora as well. He also maintains that "the Brazilian, Jamaican, Cuban, Haitian, or United States African all share the same experience or forms of the experience: Samba, Sango, Candomble, Santeria, Voodoo, Macumba, Umbanda, and Mial. At the center of all of these forms of human expression is the same source of energy" (1998, 198).

AFRICAN AMERICAN RHETORIC AND SPIRITUALITY

Adetokunbo Knowles-Borishade conceptualizes the relationship between language, rhetoric, and spirituality, affirming that African orature takes place within a certain ritualistic format, one that is created "based upon certain understandings and beliefs that Africans hold in common; understandings about the universe and human beings' place in it, and beliefs about humans' relation to God and to each other" (1991, 492). "Africans inject spiritual elements into their oratorical events, and thus seek and expect to reach a higher consciousness during such events. The speaker, or caller as she refers to it, initiates this process by invoking spiritual entities at the very beginning of the event to establish the ritualistic format" (p. 492). She further writes:

> There is no line of demarcation between the spiritual and the secular in African oratorical events, which is a prime consideration in classical African orature. Robert Faris Thompson discusses the traditional African belief that an improved character improves the art form. This means that in African orature, the Word (Nommo) gains in power and effectiveness in direct proportion with the moral character, strength of commitment, and vision of the caller, as well as the skill s/he exhibits . . . the caller must become a poet-performer and direct her/his creative powers toward a higher level of consciousness by activating spiritual and psychic powers. (pp. 490–91)

Knowles-Borishade maintains that traditionally, Africans view humanity as a spiritual force, and the speaker is viewed as having the power to access "cosmic forces for a higher truth by merging her/his vibratory forces with the rhythmic vibrations of the universal cosmic energy." She further surmises that the African rhetor is "preoccupied with human welfare, and this accounts for her/his profound sense of humanism" (p. 494). In other words, the orator's concern is with the spiritual harmony of the audience or community, again abiding by the guiding principles of Maat. The word set forth by the rhetor demonstrates "what is morally good is what benefits a human being; it is what is decent for man—what brings dignity, respect, contentment, prosperity, joy to man and to his community." "What is morally bad is what brings misery, misfortune, and disgrace" (p. 494).

Finally, Knowles-Borishade asserts that "spiritual entities" act as judges, witnesses, and enablers in rhetorical events. These include the creator God, lesser deities, angels, the Holy Spirit, ancestors, the recently deceased and the unborn. Furthermore, nommo (which we will discuss in greater detail later) invokes these spiritual entities. She writes: "The ritualistic format is the initial stage for classical African rhetoric. It is established by the caller's opening remarks acknowledging and often giving obeisance to Spiritual Entities: 'I give honor to Almighty God and the Holy spirit'; 'All praise is due to Allah, the God of the universe.'" She provides these examples to demonstrate the African belief in spiritual entities (1991, 495).

THE AFRICAN PHILOSOPHICAL BACKGROUND OF RHETORIC

Let us consider how Africans view language and rhetoric. The ancient Egyptians or Kemites called their language, *mdw ntr.* The translation of *mdw* is "speech," and for the people of the Nile Valley, speech was divine—a gift of the Creator. In fact, the literal translation of *mdw ntr* is "divine speech." *Medew nefer,* however, literally means "good speech" and was reserved for the realm of humanity. Carruthers writes, "Only Medew Nefer was in accord with Medew Netcher. In fact, it was through the consistent practice of Medew Nefer that human beings finally attained Medew Netcher, Divine Speech" (1995, 40). It is also important to point out that the concept in this ancient language of divine speech also refers to an authoritative utterance. Rhetoric, the theory of authoritative utterance, and oratory are intertwined with Egyptian life. The spoken word, in fact, was the primary method of cultural and spiritual transmittal of values (Asante, 2000, 81). Asante points out that good speech must have an ethical base: "There are no speeches by hatemongers that have gone down in the history as great speeches. There will never be such speeches because the overwhelming judgment of history is a moral one and the speaker who imperils the forward march of human dignity will not live in the minds of the future. It is the champion of righteousness that is the true victor in rhetorical traditions" (Asante, this volume). Speech was not merely a series of codes that fostered communication. Rhetoric was spiritual, a human quest for what was good and divine.

Nommo, the "generative and productive power of the spoken Word" (Asante, 1998, 17), is an African concept of communication rooted deeply in traditional African philosophies. The power of the word, or of speech in general, has always been rooted in Africans' oral tradition. According to Smitherman, the word "is believed to be the force of life itself" (1998, 208).

NOMMO

The Dogon of Mali believe the concept of nommo carries the vital "life force, which produces all life, which influences 'things' in the shape of the spoken word" (Jahn 1990, 124). According to Ogotemmêli, a Dogon elder who through years of study acquired a vast knowledge of the Dogon spiritual belief system, states, "The voice of man can arouse God and extend divine action" (Griaule 1970, 138). In other words, by human utterance or through the spoken word, human beings can invoke a kind of spiritual power. But of course, the word began with Amma or God, who created the world by uttering three successive words. According to Ogotemmeli, "The life-force, which is the bearer of the Word, which is the Word, leaves the mouth in the form of breath, or water vapour, which is water and is Word . . . the Word came from the deepest and most secret part of the being" (Griaule 1970, 140).

In *Muntu,* Jahn deeply explores this African concept of Nommo, revealing the paramount nature of the power of the word for African peoples:

> Nommo, the life force, is . . . a unity of spiritual-physical fluidity, giving life to everything, penetrating everything, causing everything. . . . And since man has

> power over the word, it is he who directs the life force. Through the word he receives it, shares it with other beings, and so fulfills the meaning of life. (1990, 124)

As such, all of human creation and natural phenomena emanate from the productive power of the word, nommo, which is itself a life force. For the Dogon, all magic is ultimately word magic, whether the Word is manifested in incantations, blessings, or curses. In fact, "if there were no Word, all forces would be frozen, there would be no procreation, no change, no life" (Jahn 1990, 133). Furthermore, the word or the power of nommo rests not solely with the Creator but also with human beings. It does not "stand above and beyond the earthly world." After all, he notes, it is humans who have mastery over the Word. Jahn further writes: "In the gospels the Word remains with God, and man has to testify to it and proclaim it. Nommo, on the other hand, was also, admittedly, with Amma, or God, in the beginning, but beyond that everything comes into being only through the Word, and as there is muntu (human beings), the word is with the muntu" (p. 132). For the ancient Egyptians, the power of the word was linked to the ethical principle of Maat. According to Asante, the ancient Egyptians believed that the nature of Maat was to be alive. "[T]o live in Maat is to live the living Word, the ankh mdw. It becomes the only path to ankh nehen, that is, life eternal. . . . [Maat] is active, dynamic, and alive in the everyday lives of humans at work, at play and at worship" (Asante 2000, 113). The Dogon's conception of the word and its life-sustaining power is no different from the ancient Egyptians'.

Jahn notes the hierarchical nature of nommo. The power of the word is different from one individual to the next. Furthermore, the word power of the Creator is more powerful than that of any other being. Jahn also asserts that in African philosophy, individuals have, by the power of their words, dominion over things, which they can change and make work for their purposes and command them. "But to command things with Words is to practice magic" (1990, 135). Asante is in concert with Jahn's assertion when he writes, "[T]he more powerful the speaker, the more fascinated the audience will be. And power is derived from the experience of the 'orality' and spirituality of the presentations" (1998, 91).

Knowles-Borishade takes a more spiritual approach in her discussion of nommo. She contends that morality is the prime consideration for African orature. "Nommo gains in power and effectiveness in direct proportion with the moral character, strength of commitment and vision of the [individual], as well as the skill he or she exhibits." The speaker "must direct his or her creative powers toward a higher level of consciousness by activating spiritual and psychic powers" (1991, 490). Knowles-Borishade also maintains that "Africans traditionally view humanity as a spiritual force and the speaker is seen as having the ability to tap cosmic forces for a higher truth by merging his or her vibratory forces with the rhythmic vibrations of the universal cosmic energy" (pp. 490–91). Nommo, she proclaims, is the embodiment of "Afri-Symbols." In other words, the word is "pregnant with value-meanings drawn from the African experience which, when uttered, give birth to unifying images that bind people together in an atmosphere of harmony and power" (p. 490).

> The potency of Nommo is drawn from mental and physical faculties. Once the process of mental conception formulates an idea, the attending action is the declamation, the Nommo, the Word that speaks creation into being. Although Nommo is vibrantly potent, that potency evanesces if utterance does not emerge from and apply to the African experience. Classical African rhetoric must address . . . the social, political and religious moments in the history of a society, if it is to be relevant. (p. 495)

Ultimately, according to Knowles-Borishade, spiritual harmony is the objective of the speech act. The attainment of harmony from the beginning of the event is the aim of all participants when the community is called together for a common cause. When there is harmony, the rhythms and vibrations imparted by spirit consumes the participants. A new creation comes into being, and there is a mystical kind of joy and sharing in spirit. "A synergistic relationship locks in, with the rhythms of spirit, the [speaker], Nommo, and the [participants] all throbbing together in the experience of the shared moment" (p. 498). In the African oratorical tradition, Knowles-Borishade maintains, harmony is viewed as the "supraordinate objective of African speech events, because it serves as empowerment for moving or acting on solutions that are presented by the caller, validated by the chorus, and sanctioned by the responders." However, solutions are secondary considerations; harmony is the paramount prerequisite to solutions.

Asante surmises that the contemporary African preacher in the African American church is probably the best example to illustrate the power of nommo. He asserts that in order to understand the nature of African communication, one must understand that nommo continues to permeate African existence in America. He acknowledges that not all or even most Africans, given the nature of American history of slavery and subsequent racism and oppression, can immediately recognize the transforming power of vocal expression. However, he maintains, "it is apparent when a person says, 'Man, that cat can rap.' Or one can identify it through the words of the sister leaving a Baptist church, 'I didn't understand all those words the preacher was using, but they sure sounded good.' Inasmuch as the Nommo experience can be found in many aspects of African American life, one can almost think of it as a way of life" (1998, 97–98).

The effective African preacher or lecturer understands the transformative power of the word. We know that words, speeches, or sermons have power when we walk away from them invigorated, ready for revolution or "praisin the lawd." We will explore this concept of call and response in a later section. Smitherman also contends that the African church in the United States is the most significant force that nurtures African linguistic and cultural traditions. Thus, the sermon or sermonizing has become a significant component of African American rhetoric.

African culture is an oral culture, and as such, rhetoric is paramount. Language, after all, produces and structures thought (Haskins and Butts 1973, 39). To better understand the concept of nommo and why it is crucial in understanding African American rhetoric, we will now turn our attention to the African oral tradition.

ORAL TRADITION

The African oral tradition provides a framework with which to study language and rhetoric for African people. Within the African oral tradition, language is not simply a regularized code that includes syntax, lexicon, and phonology. Rather, the nuances of African culture assists in defining language. And rhetoric, after all, is the articulation of language. The term "oral tradition" means "that tradition whose origins stretch back to pre-colonial Africa and the beliefs associated with it" (Conteh-Morgan 1991, 126). The oral tradition, also termed "oral literature" or "orature," refers to a "comprehensive body of oral discourse on every subject and in every genre of expression produced by a people" (Asante 1998, 96). Knowles-Borishade maintains that African orature should be characterized as classical, based upon certain factors drawn from the African world experience. The first factor, she asserts, is historical. The African oratorical format, style, and dynamics can be traced back to ancient Kemet (Egypt). Second, African orature "conforms to particular African cultural expectations, so that it is standard and authoritative." In other words, it is traditional. And third, orature is an art form that can be analyzed in accordance with an approved and recognized set of traditional standards. She also points out that African orature does not conform to a Western style of speechmaking. The nature of the African oral tradition is drawn from African belief systems and traditions (1991, 498–99).

The corpus of African oral literature goes hand in hand with its performance. You cannot have one without the other. Bodunde further explains that the oral tradition is the complex corpus of verbal or spoken art created for the purpose of remembering the past based on a people's ideas, beliefs, symbols, assumptions, attitudes, and sentiments. He further states that there are two main categories of orature, literary and historical. The literary includes poetic genres, divination poems, and songs. It also includes proverbs, parables, and incantations. The historical includes narratives based on myths, legends, and historical plays or epics (1992, 24).

The poet serves many functions in traditional African society. Okpewho notes that the griot or court poet for the Mandinka of West Africa was charged with not only singing the ruler's praises, but also documenting through songs historical events surrounding the royal or ruling family. He is also the linguist or spokesman for the king. The umusizi in Rwanda in Central Africa, the imbongi of the Zulu in southern Africa, and poets in other ethnic groups all served the same purpose. Moreover, Okpewho explains, "poets are trained to handle some of the rather delicate tasks peculiar to their profession" (1985, 4–5). Certainly the contemporary African preacher, lecturer, or activist in the United States, it can be argued, serves the same purpose as did the traditional poet.

Ever present in African orature is the productive power of nommo, the word. The African poet "is not an artist using magic, but a magician, a sorcerer in the African sense" (Jahn 1990, 135). In other words, the poet commands things by using words according to traditional African philosophy—not to be confused with the evil sorcery of witches and warlocks in European mythology. Not only are these "magical" poets used at the discretion of royalty, but others consult them as well. For example, goldsmiths often call upon poets to work their "word magic" for the creation of their art. Within this tradition, writes Marimba Ani, "the praise singer (griot) is hired by the customer to recount the glories of the goldsmith's ancestors and thereby energize him" (1981, 229). Jahn asserts that goldsmiths transform "the gold into an ornament with the help of Nommo" (1990, 137). In African poetry the word precedes the image. It is nommo that creates the image. The poet speaks and transforms things into "forces of meaning, symbols, images" (p. 151).

The African poet is a *muntu,* a person, which means sorcerer, prophet, and teacher. Jahn goes on to write: "[The poet] expresses what must be. His 'I' is not therefore 'collective' in the European sense; it is not non-individual. He speaks to the community and for them" (Jahn 1990, 149). Okpewho puts it this way:

> [T]he essence of true poetry . . . lies in its power to appeal strongly to our appreciation and in a sense, lift us up. There are basically two ways in which a piece of poetry can appeal to us. One is by touching us emotionally, so that we feel either pleasure or pain; the other is by stirring our minds deeply so that we reflect on some aspect of life or some significant idea. (1985, 7).

While at the same time appreciating the oral skill of the poet, Africans recognize their orature and its performance (again, you cannot have one without the other) as a functional part of society. The purpose of orature is not merely to entertain or appeal to some romantic sensation, but to enlighten and stir the audience into some productive action, or initiate or facilitate spiritual action.

Ojaide underscores Okpewho's position and also asserts that Africans traditionally value oratory in verbal communication. He elaborates on the nature of the African poet as well as discusses the importance of oral skill:

> The place of otota/spokesperson is highly coveted among Urhobo and other African peoples. Who presents and responds to issues on behalf of a group is an orator who weaves words artistically to open up avenues and soften difficult issues. The frequent use of proverbs, anecdotes, axioms, and other wise sayings by African poets confirms the broad poetic repertory of the tradition. (1996, 23–24)

African orature, according to Okpewho, does not departmentalize literature into poetry, prose, and drama. Examples of the use of language rooted in the indigenous African culture are numerous. This is important because it demonstrates that there is no line drawn between a speech act and a performance in African communities. They are one and the same. To speak is to perform. Traditional African literature, or, as we have been calling it, African orature, exists alongside or within African languages. It is not compartmentalized into separate and distinct categories. Thus, the whole notion of public speaking or rhetoric is not separated from performance, as in the Western tradition. When we discuss traditional African orature, we are speaking of artistic verbal expressions and its performance in the form of poems, songs, proverbs, myths, legends, incantations, sermonizing, lecturing, testifyin', signifyin', and other modes based on a complex worldview designed to elevate and transform society.

In Africa and the Diaspora, Asante notes, past and present, the spoken word dominates communication culture. This, he maintains, is part of the continuity with the ancient African past. He suggests the importance to Africans in the United States is that they "maintained an expressive sense that manifested itself as a life force in dance, music, and speech" (1998, 71–72). He further holds that the word is not the captive of the written word; to the contrary, it is the word revealed in life.

AESTHETICS

When discussing the spiritual essence of African American rhetoric, it should be noted that it is also a discussion of aesthetics. African aesthetics must be employed to get the full spectrum of what African American rhetoric is. Culture-inspired perceptions of beauty are articulated in the language. For Africans, language and rhetoric are beauty. Language is not merely for fostering communication. Rather, language in a cultural and theoretical sense defines who we are. Furthermore, the rhythm in African languages reflects the rhythm of African lives—our cultural lives.

Aesthetics is a function of culture. Its principles are cultural principles. In this vein, aesthetics and culture are inextricably linked. Africans' perceptions of beauty or what is good give their cultures their essence and organizing principles. African worldview, then, is a reflection of African culture. Welsh-Asante (1994) points out that in many African languages, the words for "good" and "beautiful" are the same (1994, xiii). A person who has beauty is a good person. Inversely, someone who is good is beautiful. By "African worldview" I mean the guiding principles and values that determine how Africans see and respond to life and interact with the universe. Worldview is the means by which culture determines what is beautiful and what is not. In other words, aesthetics is the part of African worldview that is associated with beauty.

It should also be noted that when *aesthetics* is used here, it refers to what Welsh-Asante calls pan-African aesthetics, which "transcends geographic or ethnic boundaries and functions on certain commonalties" (1993, 2). Only geography separates Africans in the Americas from Africans at home. At no point in Africans' history in the Americas did Africans stop being Africans (whether we know it or not).

African aesthetics are found wherever you find African people. In regards to rhetoric, the same holds true. Lorenzo Turner's landmark work *Africanisms in the Gullah Dialect* (1949) and Salikko Mufwene's *Africanisms in Afro-American Language Varieties* (1993) are important texts. Their works and others have been monumental in our understanding of African communication systems created in the Western Hemisphere. But the question that arises is as follows: Are there Africanisms among African people and within African languages? Naturally, the answer is yes. This is like asking if there are religious overtones in a church sermon—of course there are. Joseph Holloway briefly defines Africanisms as "those elements of culture found in the New World that are traceable to an African origin" (Holloway 1991, ix). African people create what is African regardless of their geographic location. To refer to "African elements" in what are essentially African creations in the Western Hemisphere subconsciously, or perhaps not so subconsciously, denies their African essence or their legitimacy. Moreover, it denies that African people in the West are in fact African people. These may be considered "X-isms." Carrington suggests that the term *isms* implies "peripheralness and peculiarity" (1993, 36). He further asserts that the African in the United States "is the product of contact between Europe and Africa. The African legacy cannot therefore be described as either peripheral or peculiar" (p. 38). This "contact" has not stripped the African of his and her Africanity. Rather, what we find among Africans in the West is simply African continuity with other features that can be attributed to European sources. What had been lost or weakened as a result of Africans' enslavement has only been re-formed along the same cultural-aesthetic principles.

Welsh-Asante (1994) teaches that spirit, rhythm, and creativity are the key criteria in discussing any aesthetics for African people. Furthermore, she maintains, they derive from epic memory or a sense of ancestorism (1993, 4). Indeed, these are all crucial for our understanding of African American rhetoric. We must grasp the concept of epic memory to understand the nature of rhetoric for Africans in the United States. The poetry and power of African American rhetoric speak to the spirit, rhythm, and creativity of African people. Since I consider African rhetoric in general and the rhetoric of Africans in the United States in particular an art form, I am bound to place aesthetic value on them like other art forms. And traditionally for African people, art for art's sake simply did not exist. This is also crucial in understanding the nature of African American rhetoric. Language is an important instrument in conveying complex ideas and transmitting the values of society. Language is the expression of African culture and values. Furthermore, Africans, being the product of an oral tradition, attach music, poetry; and other verbal art forms to language because they are all means of creating, recreating, and maintaining African culture.

RHETORIC AND AESTHETICS

Crucial to our understanding of African American rhetoric is the relationship between language and art for African people. As we have referenced in other sections, Africans place a high value on spoken art forms. The individual charged with imparting information to the community through speech is expected to deliver words in a way that not only gets the point across, but also is aesthetically pleasing. As Asante puts it, "To stimulate one's fellow to cooperative action through the use of rhetoric is no lean task; it requires skill, knowledge of human nature, and the necessary physical organs to utter sounds" (1998, 74). By failing at this task, the rhetor risks having his or her message lost. This is not to say that Africans only need to be entertained or to have their sensibilities struck to be moved to some action. The message and the messenger's motivation, in terms of their intent, must reflect the values and best interest of the community as well. If the community feels otherwise, the message most certainly would be lost. Asante notes that in ancient Egypt,

> [i]n order for an orator to perform at the highest levels he had to know the special duties of the speaker, which related to Maat. No orator could effectively speak with the eloquence of Thoth unless he understood the special character of Maat. "Know thyself," the admonition written on the temple at Karnak, reverberated deep in the heart of the ancient Egyptian orator. (1990, 81)

In ancient Egypt, the orator knew that to be skillful, he or she had to embody the principles of Maat: harmony, justice, righteousness, balance, and reciprocity (Asante 2000, 113).

Let us take art a step further. Traditionally, art in African society is not art for the sake of mere artistic expression and creativity. Rather, it is always functional. For the artist, everything is functional. There can be no art without a functional objective. The piece of art must "do something, perform something, or say something" (Asante 1998, 75). In an African context, public discourse as an art form can take place only when the objective is productive and functional. Asante further maintains that Africans highlight the creative process of the artist. To be an observer, he notes, is to be primarily interested in the product, or what is given through speech. But for the artist or speaker, the creation and its function in society are paramount. Therefore, the African sees discourse as the creative manifestation of what is called to be. And what is called to be, which is determined by the mores and values of the society, "becomes the created thing; and the artist, or speaker, satisfies the demands of the society by calling into being that which is functional." Further, he writes: "Functional, in this case, refers to the object that possesses a meaning within the communicator's and audience's worldview, a meaning that is constructed from the social, political and religious moments in the society's history" (1998, 75).

If we accept this scheme, we see that the artist's, or for our purposes here the speaker's, objective is to help transform and elevate society through his or her artistic expression. The role of art, traditionally for Africans, is to serve as a vehicle for improving society, balancing it harmoniously. While the creativity of the rhetor is essential, the artist as a transforming agent is paramount. Asante writes that, "the intelligent speaker knows that speaking is an emotional as well as an intellectual process, and that how one alters a phoneme or a word in vocal expression is significant. To know how to say 'cat' or 'man' is to know the secrets of word magic" (1987, 60). The mores and values of society serve as the artist's canvas, on which to paint the nature of the African dilemma or situation and at times present a narrative for addressing the condition. The oral artist's work must be rooted in the social reality of the community and he or she is expected to be the "conscience of the nation" (Ogede 1992, p. 73).

In this volume, Jeffery Woodyard, in some detail, explores aspects of African American rhetoric crucially linked to aesthetics. For example, he discusses stylin' out, soundin', lyricism, improvisation, indirection, repetition, and others to point to how nommo is manifested artistically in African American rhetoric. So there is no need to elaborate here, but the topic is certainly important and relevant in the discussion of African American rhetoric.

Verbal responses are also a part of this cultural-linguistic phenomenon. Call and response is deeply rooted in the African oral tradition. The listener or audience is as much a part of the orature as is the orator.

CALL AND RESPONSE

Finally, one of the defining characteristics of rhetorical situations for Africans or the oral tradition is the involvement of the community in the speech event, commonly referred to as call and response. For example, "in a creative performance, members of the audience neither listen silently nor wait for the chief performer's invitation to join in. Instead, the audience breaks into the performance with their additions, questions and criticism" (Bodunde 1992, 24–25). Traditionally, the rhetor "usually performs before an audience which is a living presence before the artist, with whom the performer establishes a rapport by engaging the audience as both observers and participants in the events enacted" (Ogede 1992, 74). In fact, as Okpewho points out, the rhetorical event "achieves its forcefulness not only at the hands of the performer himself. Part of this forcefulness comes from the participation of various persons (present at the scene of performance) in the creative act that is taking place" (1985, 8). Through Maat, Asante maintains, the speaker creates a connection with his or her audience and realizes the life force embedded in the principle. "Maat, ultimately a spiritual concept, is the central notion in the quest of life. Yet an orator can only become truly Maat oriented in the company of a thousand gods. . . . A speaker needs an audience" (1990, 82).

Throughout the African Diaspora, audience participation is an integral part of the performance. And for our purposes here, the performance is the speech act involving enlivened spontaneity within a speech community (Saakana 1995). The rhetor is not a singular voice in sending out the word. Rather, the audience confronts the speaker-poet or rhetor with the expectation that the truth will be rendered. Knowles-Borishade also holds that the rhetorical event is never a lone voice that produces the word; "utterance is accompanied by the echoes of the chorus, with cries of 'teach,' 'that's right,' 'preach,' 'Amen,' and 'Go ahead on'!" (1991, 321–23). It is the communal or collective voice that represents the use of the pronoun *we.* "In African culture," she explains, "the concept symbolizes and perpetuates the ultimacy of the collective, whereby decisions are made and actions are taken by consensus rather than by solitary decree" (p. 494). Therefore, a rhetorical event is a communal one. The absence of audience participation invalidates the event. The rhetor or caller during call and response fails to invoke the power of nommo or deliver Spirit if there is no audience participation or call and response. She elaborates further on the call-and-response phenomenon:

> Responders (audience) are the community who come to participate in the speech event. They are secondary creators in the event, containing among them a vital part of the message. It is they who either sanction or reject the message—the Word—based upon the perceived morality and vision of the Caller (rhetor) and the relevance of the message. This notion of community or group sanction is the basis of the African call-and-response tradition. (pp. 497–98)

The audience, then, is a direct expression of public sanction and opinion. Consequently, call and response is fundamental in determining the rightness of popular response to the action of the rightness in the speaker; hence, response in juxtaposed to ethicism.

The audience is an active participant. In fact, it is the audience who allows the speaker to know whether or not his or her words have power. "Teach," "preach on," "dats right," or "amen" are popular responses to a speaker in predominately African American churches. Smitherman further explores this when she explains that constant exchange is necessary for meaningful communication between African people. We witness this in the African American church, with the exchange between the preacher and the congregation during the sermon (1998, 208). Even outside of the church, Smitherman holds, whenever Africans in the United States communicate, call and response abounds. She further chides: "The only wrong thing you can do in a Black conversation is not respond at all because it suggests that one 'ain't wit the conversation' i.e., disengaged, distant, emotionally disconnected with the speaker or speakers" (p. 208).

Call and response, therefore, is a necessary component of the African oral tradition. It is a reciprocal process. The speaker-poet, who according to African philosophy is a magician, calls on the power of the spoken word, invokes the spirit and elicit a response from the audience and they, in turn, empower the rhetor based on their reaction. He or she is not a magician in the sense that his or her role is to be an illusionist, but instead his or her role is to facilitate transference of the word's inherent power to the audience in an effort to convey the full strength of an articulation. In that conveyance, there is a communing with the spirits of the interactants. Once that communion is achieved, it is highly unlikely that the audience will be motivated to strip him or her of that power by rejecting the speaker-poet's message. After all, it is the community, based on its values, belief system, and morals, that can sanction the message. An orator, Asante holds, is most effective when he or she "creates a union" with the audience (1990, 87)—in other words, obtains a spiritual and harmonious balance.

CONCLUSION

Crucial to our understanding of African American rhetoric is the recognition of spirituality within rhetorical events. It has been demonstrated that for Africans, public discourse is about far more than communicating thoughts or ideas. Rather, the objective is the elevation of the community or society and the attainment of spiritual harmony and balance. Public discourse in the African community in the United States is intended to move the audience to positive action, either collective or individual. The response to the spoken word by Africans in general and Africans in the United States in particular speaks to the legacy of African oral traditions and the energizing power of the word. At the core of African American rhetoric is the spiritual force that places its speakers on a humanistic mission for justice, freedom, balance, and harmony.

REFERENCES

Akbar, Na'im. (1984). Africentric Social Sciences for Human Liberation. *The Journal of Black Studies* (June), 395–414.

Alleyne, Mervyn (1988). *Roots of Jamaican Culture*. London: Pluto Press.

Ani, Marimba (1981). The Nyana of the Blacksmith: Metaphysical Significance of Metallurgy in Africa. *Journal of Black Studies*, 12(2), 218–238.

Asante, Molefi K. (1995). *The Book of African Names*: Trenton, NJ: Africa World Press.

Asante, Molefi K. (1998). *The Afrocentric Idea*, revised and expanded edition. Philadelphia, PA: Temple University Press.

Asante, Molefi K. (2000). *The Egyptian Philosophers: Ancient African Voices from Imhotep to Akhenaten*. Chicago, IL: African American Images.

Asante, M. K. (1990). *Kemet, Afrocentricity and Knowledge*. Trenton, NJ: Africa World Press.

Bodunde, C. A. (1992). Oral tradition and modern poetry: Okot p 'Bitek's Song of Lawino and Okigbo's Labyrinths. In E. D. Jones (Ed.), *Orature in African Literature Today* (pp. 24–34). Trenton, NJ: Africa World Press.

Carrington, Lawrence (1993). On the Notion of "Africanism" in Afro-American. In Salikoko Mufwene (Ed.), *Africanisms in Afro-American Language Varieties* (pp. 35–46). Athens: University of Georgia Press.

Carruthers, Jacob H. (1995). *Mdw Ntr: Divine Speech*. London: Karnak House.

Conteh-Morgan, J. (1992). French language African drama and the oral tradition: Trends and Issues. In E. B. Jones (Ed.), *Orature in African Literature Today* (pp. 115–132). Trenton, NJ: Africa World Press.

Gilyard, Keith (1997). *Let's Flip the Script: An African American Discourse on Language, Literature and Learning*. Detroit: Wayne State University Press.

Griaule, M. (1970). *Conversations with Ogotemmeli*. London: Oxford University Press.

Haskins, James, and Hugh F. Butts (1973). *Psychology of Black Language*. New York: Hippocrene Books, Inc.

Holloway, Joseph E. (1991). *Africanisms in American Culture*. Bloomington: Indiana University Press.

Jahn, Janheinz (1990). *Muntu: African Culture and the Western World*. New York: Grove.

Kershaw, Terry (1992). Afrocentrism and the Afrocentric Method. *The Western Journal of Black Studies* 16, 3: 160–68.

Knowles-Borishade, Adetokunbo F. (1991). Paradigm for Classical African Orature: Instrument for Scientific Revolution? *The Journal of Black Studies* (June), 488–500.

Mazama, Ama (2001). The Afrocentric Paradigm: Contours and Definitions. *The Journal of Black Studies* (March), 387–405.

Monges, Miriam (1997). *Kush: Jewel of the Nubia*. Trenton, NJ: Africa World Press.

MuFwene, Salikoko (1993). (Ed.). *Africanisms in Afro-American Language Varieties*. Athens: University of Georgia Press.

Myers, Linda James (1987). The Deep Structure of Culture: Relevance of Traditional African Culture in Contemporary Life. *The Journal of Black Studies* (September), 72–85.

Obenga, Theophile (1995). *African Philosophy in World History*. Princeton, NJ: Sungai Book Sun-Scholars Series.

Ogede, O. S. (1992). Oral echoes in Armahis Short Stories. In E.D. Jones (Ed.), Orature in African Literature Today (pp. 73–83). Trenton, NJ: African World Press.

Ojaide, Tanure (1996). Poetic Imagination in Black Africa: Essays on African Poetry. Durham, NC: Carolina Academic Press.

Okpewho, Isidore (1985). The Heritage of African Poetry. London: Longman Group, Ltd.

Smitherman, Geneva (1998). Word from the Hood: The Lexicon of African American Vernacular English. In Salikoko S. Mufwene, John R. Rickford, Guy Bailey, and John Baugh (Eds.), *African American English: Structure, History, and Use* (pp. 203–25). New York: Routledge.

Turner, Lorenzo (1949). *Africanisms in the Gullah Dialect.* Chicago: University of Chicago Press.

Welsh-Asante, Kariamu (1994). The Aesthetic Conceptualization of Nzuri. In Kariamu Welsh-Asante (Ed.), *The African Aesthetic: Keeper of the Traditions* (pp. 1–20). Westport, CT: Praeger Press.

Section 2

MANIFESTATIONS OF AFRICAN AMERICAN RHETORIC AND ORALITY

CHAPTER 3

African American Orality: Expanding Rhetoric

THURMON GARNER
CAROLYN CALLOWAY-THOMAS

African American approaches to rhetoric have not strayed far from the codified view set by the Aristotelian tradition. We still rely on the language developed two thousand years ago to talk about rhetoric. The categories of disposition, elocution, invention, memory, and pronunciation continue to control our investigation of African American discourse. The discourse of known and not-so-known African American public figures remains an important voice that contributes to our understanding of the social condition of the mass of Black folks. Since the early 1970s African American rhetorical approaches have consisted of little more than anthologies or critical examinations of African American orators and oratory based on formalistic categories. We are reminded of the saying "The more things change, the more they remain the same." What we continue to do in African American rhetoric is what we have always done, explored great orators and great texts.

A new orientation is needed. Where do we start when we talk about African American rhetoric? What do we include? Certainly we should not abandon the traditional approaches to rhetoric. Great African American orators and great texts by or about African Americans yield useful and important insights. Yet it makes sense to speak of an everyday rhetoric within African American culture. Indeed, as McPhail (in this volume) asserts, "[t]he building of Black communication as a discipline involved an important movement from the descriptive studies that had dominated critical analyses of African American rhetoric to a theoretical examination of its unique and culturally influenced dimensions." The widely held notion that African American discourse is primarily based on an oral culture is an appropriate starting place from which to rethink African American rhetoric. A new beginning must take into account the idea that rhetorical print or writing as a means of acquiring knowledge, developing consciousness, and defining literacy continues to dominate Western thought, exclusive of any other rhetorical posture. At the same time we should understand that the rejection of orality, especially that of African Americans, as a source of rhetorical expansion is firmly entrenched in the sociocultural consciousness. With orality as a base, we can rediscover rhetoric as a social art grounded in the uses of everyday language.

This essay is an attempt to chart the space between the rhetorical practices of African Americans and the landscape of African American orality. African American communication scholars have often overlooked the theoretical but overpowering influence of an oral tradition in understanding the rhetorical qualities of Black sense and sensibilities. Our concern is with the search for broader rhetorical forces that focus or explain African American oral rhetorical communication. Toward that end we concentrate on articulating the contours of an African American rhetorical perspective represented in the oral nature or everyday use of language and supportive of an African American rhetorical presence. What, then, constitutes a Black oral presence in the discourse on or about African Americans? Our discussion centers around the notion of orality as generating rhetorical means of investigating private or personal discourse habits made public by varied media. We are concerned with the rhetorical features of an African American oral tradition and how such features can serve as means for understanding not only traditional forms of rhetorical discourse, but the new electronic forms of delivery. Finally, we discuss signifying as part of an oral rhetorical tradition and as a system of exploration for the rhetorical critic.

BLACK RHETORICAL PRESENCE

Any innovative approach to understanding an African American rhetoric would have to determine what makes rhetoric African American. Another way of presenting this concern is to ask whether there is anything Black about rhetoric or discourse except that it is written or spoken by African Americans. Does a Black presence exist in African American rhetoric? Certainly at the present time such a quality exists, and that existence is a defining moment in any consideration of an African American rhetoric. The idea of a Black rhetorical style is not new, and African American communication scholars have accepted such a notion but have too often publicly avoided articulating a point of view. While we are not attempting to make the case for a Black aesthetic, which has already been done, nor refocus Afrocentic approaches, African American rhetorical critics must take into account the notion of an African American presence as they interpret and explain the text of Black discourse.

What, then, makes for a Black presence in a rhetorical work? A simple but not simplistic answer would be, especially for the rhetorical scholar, a culturally bound way of practicing and framing language, discourse, and patterns of behavior. The most obvious point is that in African American rhetoric a Black presence is generated when we find in the text cultural combinations of African American rhetorical patterns of sufficient frequency and intensity. In other words, African Americans are foregrounded or represented in terms of principled cultural experiences. An innovative rhetorical posture develops when African Americans are elevated as subject (foreground) or represented as main characters in the dramas of cultural life rather than relegated to the status of other (background) or supporting actor. Such a presence should position African American rhetors at a point where they no longer concern themselves with how they write or talk about Black people or human beings in general because they automatically foreground Black perspectives. Like Black literary figures, communication scholars must see Blacks as the norm when examining works on African Americans. Therefore, the grounding for a Black presence would include exploring how much and in what ways the collective consciousness and/or cultural habits of African Americans are developed and used within the text under study.

A Black presence is signaled when the cultural intensity or emotional energy of African Americans is demonstrated. Rhetorical scholars should be admonished against accepting the visual insertion of a Black character or the delivery of a speech by an African American as a Black presence. One might ask if African American political commentator Ward Connally of California, who speaks for a color-blind merit system for matriculation into California schools, is Black enough. Connally speaks within the tradition of African American political thought; color should not matter. What may anger people is that Connally forgets or ignores another part of the collective consciousness of African Americans, which is that color still matters in the real world, especially in the education of African Americans, and cannot be separated from tests of merit. Even when characters are recognizably African American, that does not necessarily constitute a Black presence in a text. Let us take movies, for example. In the film *Switchback* African American actor Danny Glover's character is devoid of a Black presence except for his visual image as an African American. There is nothing else in the film to suggest that Glover's character is grounded in African American culture. Morgan Freeman in *The Shawshank Redemption* is another good example of a Black actor stripped of an African American presence when playing a role. In a color- and race-blind society we appreciate these presentations. But we are not there yet. Interestingly enough, the bodily texts of Connally, Glover, and Freeman can be explored rhetorically from an African American perspective if a critic articulates the social impact of including or excluding traits that suggest a Black presence. A Black presence, in the examples above, would turn upon the articulation of other social and political themes, patterns of behavior, and modes of discourse that reflect a Black sensitivity.

We are not without examples of what might characterize a Black presence based upon the frequency of identifiable cultural sensibilities. Literary figures and scholars have provided the public with a better understanding of the common orientations that are found in African American music, including rap or hip-hop, dance, athletics, religion (especially preaching), rituals, literature, oral tradition, and so on. Grayl Jones remarks, "During the Harlem Renaissance, then, folklore or oral tradition was no longer considered quaint and restrictive, but as the core for complex literary influence" (1991, 9). It was Zora Neale Hurston, Jean Toomer, and Langston Hughes, among others, who "provided the base for contemporary African American writers, who make use of folklore cognizant of its multiple and complex linguistic, social, historical, intellectual, and political functions" (Jones 1991, 9). Importantly, these literary figures have demonstrated a link between their particular concern, whether music or literature, and what some researchers consider "vernacular" or oral tradition. A single phone call, while an ordinary event, can contain multiple indicators of a Black presence: tone, rhythm, enunciation, and metaphorical use (Rickford and Rickford 2000; Hecht, Jackson, and Ribeau 2003).

Having already suggested that it is connected to folklore, we continue to struggle to give voice to those features that constitute an African American oral tradition. Did the improvisation we find in jazz call into being a similar improvisation in African American discourse? Or did the improvisation exist in the discourse of the oral tradition and was then applied to jazz? Our search takes us beyond examining the context of cultural storytelling, literature, or music for oral qualities to a study of orality itself. Rhetorical scholars are in a unique place to rethink the oral tradition and its impact on African American culture and what would constitute through language an African American presence. The innovative posture for the rhetorical critic is to cast the complexity of African American oral culture into rhetorical discourse worthy of the culture. Orality is, without doubt, rhetoric in its practical daily use.

ORAL-BASED RHETORIC

The oral discourse tradition continues to be central to African American culture because of the composite yet shared heritage within the Black community and "because the structural underpinnings of the oral tradition remain basically intact even as each new generation makes verbal adaptations within the tradition. Indeed, the core strength of this tradition lies in its capacity to accommodate new situations and changing realities" (Smitherman 1977, 73). Black cultural communication has been influenced by a rich oral tradition with ties to American slavery and African culture. The impact of both influences are explored in other writings (Abrahams 1970; Kochman 1981; Levine 1972; Gee 1985; Smitherman 1977; Asante 1988, 1990). We see that "Nommo, the magic power of the Word," is as strongly felt in African culture (Smitherman 1977) as respect and value for the "man of words" is in African

American communities throughout the United States (Abrahams 1976; Hannerz 1969; Kochman 1981). Therefore, research on Black communication has revolved around identifying and exploring expressive uses of language. Although we are provided with a better understanding of uses and functions of expressive Black speech acts such as boastin', braggin', playin' the dozens or soundin', signifyin', and rappin', which call attention to the speaker, we do not fully understand these speech acts as rhetorical discourse. What is needed now is an understanding of how these and other speech acts contribute to an African American rhetorical presence.

Any attempt to construct an African American rhetorical presence based on written texts without critical and extended investigation of the orality out of which they came limits our knowledge of the African American rhetorical process. African American rhetorical scholars have no need to reinvent the wheel, but they have to work hard at refining and refitting it. A good place to start would be with rethinking what it means to note that African Americans have an oral culture. Is it an oral-based culture, an oral-conscious culture, or a secondary oral culture? Do we include in our definition aural and visual aspects of culture? What distinguishes African American orality from the orality of others? Why is there a Black presence to African American oral-based culture? Perhaps specific definitions do not matter, but what matters is explaining how Black culture is made distinctive by the oral rhetorical quality of its discourse.

In oral cultures, communication is direct and immediate. It is free of a medium. One has to act and react spontaneously, because there is instantaneous feedback. The oral person is personally involved in the acts of communication and "makes decisions, acts upon them, and communicates the results through an intuitive approach to a phenomenon" (Sidran 1971, 4). An oral approach may seem intuitive since there is an urgency for a response, but what seems intuitive is culturally bound and learned from experiences, allowing community members to act respectfully toward each other. In oral cultures no distinction is made between the speaker and the audience. The communication that transpires between them is the creation and sharing of one's personhood, so that one retains a personal humanism. There are rhetorical positions, patterns, and modes of discourse that allow members of the African American community to act out their daily personal interactions. And there are cultural logics that lead participants to interact effortlessly and competently with each other as different communicative situations arise. There are also hidden assumptions underlying communication interaction in African American culture. Innovations in African American rhetoric demand a new way of explaining the connection between formal aspects of a rhetorical tradition and the everyday intuitive approach to an oral-rhetorical tradition. In other words, a Black presence is signaled when we recognize the African American rhetorical traits of an oral-based discourse.

Repositioning African American rhetorical presence means explaining how orality is a rhetoric of everyday use. Traditional or classical Greek explorations of rhetoric position rationality and logic at its center. African American oral rhetoric positions ethics, critical thinking, and personal logic as its core (Karenga, in this volume). Traditional Greek rhetoric emphasizes persuasion and influence, while an oral-based perspective would emphasize judgment in decision making for the daily acts of living. An African American oral presence seems not to divide rhetoric into private and public, nor does it privilege the public logic/rhetoric over the private; it merges the two and anything in between that helps people make sense of the world. Oral-based rhetorical discourse is the way that human beings confront unpredictable issues in daily life. African American orality is the basis for performance or the ability to develop and apply sound judgment to issues that cannot be predicted with certainty. Oral-based discourse is active, not passive. In any society, critical thinking is needed in daily interactions, and the study of how to articulate an oral discourse is essential in understanding the rhetorical thinking and judgment making that characterize an African American presence.

A new perspective on African American orality can be developed from exploring the rhetorical implications suggested in the writing of others. Scholars such as Walter J. Ong, J. Goody, J. P. Gee, E. A. Havelock, and Deborah Tannen can yield insights about African American orality. Which, if any, of the "psychodynamics" of "oral cultures untouched by writing," as identified by Walter Ong, apply to the African American mode of communication? Of the nine dominant oral traits—additive rather than subordinate, aggregative rather than analytic, redundant or "copious," conservative or traditionalist, close to the human lifeworld, agonistically toned, empathetic and participatory rather than objectively distanced, homeostatic, and situational rather than abstract—which ones apply to Black culture, and how or why are they rhetorical? Likewise, how does Tannen's feature of relative focus on interpersonal involvement add to our knowledge or guide us in our understanding of an African American oral-based rhetoric?

There is, we assume, an oral-based rhetorical posture and connection to the oral traits of Ong and the relative focus of Tannen. African American scholarship would need to determine not only which features apply to an African American oral discourse mode, but how and why these traits are rhetorical. Importantly, one would have to demonstrate how these traits contribute to the ability of African Americans to make judgments in a spontaneous and unpredictable daily world. What does it mean for the rhetorical scholar to say that African American oral discourse is "agonistically toned" or that it is "situational rather than abstract"? For the rhetorical critic, articulating what makes Black orality Black and rhetorical is a step toward understanding the ways in which an African American presence is signaled in a text.

African American literary scholars also serve as sources from which to explore a Black oral presence. They have provided voice to language that presents African American oral discourse linguistically, thematically, socially, and rhetorically. Important writers of the Harlem Renaissance and those who followed used the oral tradition in their works; therefore, we can assume that they understood the folk and oral traditions to make their renderings as authentic as possible. Their understanding of rhetoric was probably closer to "figurative rhetoric," "figurative uses of language," or "figurative speech" than to rhetoric as argument, persuasion, identification, influence, a search for meaning, or the understanding of misunderstanding.

Rhetorical features, not just the figurative kind, exist in oral traditions. Rhetoric is a figure of speech when it is stylized or considered an embellishment, but when a point is being made or an attempt to change one's perspective is initiated, the form of expression is rhetorical in the sense of shifting meaning or adding emphasis to an idea. Since Aristotle, rhetoric has been considered the art of speaking on a subject that is constructed and appropriately stylized for audience, purpose, and occasion. The aim of rhetoric in the Aristotelian sense has been moral suasion and is concerned with questions of justice and injustice, good and bad, equity and inequity, desirability and undesirability, praise and blame, and right and wrong. Oral features are especially rhetorical when they address questions that have a moral tone, such as justice and injustice or right and wrong. They are particularly rhetorical when infused in the more formal rhetorical process of public speaking. An important innovation to African American rhetoric would involve exploring formal rhetorical texts for oral-based rhetorical traits that represent a Black presence (Bacon 1999).

An exploration of a Black presence is a search for understanding of the rhetorical features of the oral tradition that represent African American cultural habits. Rhetoric has always been more than persuasion and influence, and in particular rhetoric has been concerned with language (Welch 1999). Individual scholars are working toward explaining African American cultural patterns. We have in various texts assumptions about the African American oral tradition that signal particular cultural views. Indirection is essential to understanding African American oral communication. It is one of the assumptions found in African American orality. African Americans have retained, it appears, an essential circular quality of African discourse. Sidran notes, "In language the African tradition aims at circumlocution rather than at exact definition. The direct statement is considered crude and unimaginative; the veiling of all content in ever-changing paraphrases is considered the criterion of intelligence and personality" (1971, 6). Researchers have noted the same phenomenon in African American culture. According to Kochman, "Blacks regard direct questions as confrontational, intrusive, and presumptuous" (1981, 99).

Rhetorically, for the African American community, the strategy behind indirection suggests that direct confrontation in everyday discourse is to be avoided when possible. Indirect message preparation has a latent advantage. Mitchell-Kernan observes, "Such messages because of their form—they contain explicit and implicit content—structure interpretation in such a way that the parties have the option of avoiding a real confrontation" (1973, 318). Consequently, indirection is not just a speech event in African American communities, but a rhetorical strategy or tactic employed during the daily ritual of communicating. As a strategy, it is a rhetorical method and philosophy for attacking and handling communication behaviors. Therefore, as a concept, indirection implies something about how African Americans understand what is appropriate cultural discourse conduct (Hecht, Jackson, and Ribeau forthcoming). Normally, indirection has been treated as a function of the speech acts and not as a rhetorical strategy in oral discourse. Boasting, bragging, loud talking, rapping, signifying, and, to a degree, playing the dozens have elements of indirection.

It goes without saying that spontaneous daily communication interactions are unrehearsed. Orality and rhetorical preparedness require that speaker and audience devise, originate, compose, or invent without preparation when engaged in dialogue. The spontaneous nonanalytic nature of an oral tradition demands such action. African Americans place a high value on spontaneity, inventiveness, and improvisation in language behavior. Although writing about music, Sidran makes an important point about oral improvisation when he states, "The complexity of this rhythmic approach is in large part due to the value placed on spontaneity and the inherently communal nature of oral improvisation" (1971, 7). Each moment is a unique experience, and "the celebration of the feeling of any given moment as a unique experience, rather than as a part of some elaborate syntactical structure, has made the Black man flexible and helped him to improvise" (p. 18). "Improvisation is based on the ability to 'hear' with internal ears the sound of an internal voice. This reliance on 'internal hearing' is part of the more general approach of the oral orientation" (p. 62).

Rhetorically, Black use of improvisation maintains the integrity of the individual's personal voice in the context of group activity. Black metaphoric language is a vehicle for individual expression, perfectly suited to improvisation and spontaneous composition. It stimulates and increases the importance of innovation or, at least, of individuation within a normally group-oriented society. This integration of the individual into the society at such a basic level of experience is the root of Black group actionality. One effect of the oral mode of perception is that individuality, rather than being stifled by group activity or equated with specialization, actually flourishes in a group context. Thus, members of the oral culture are differentiated not by their specialist skills but by their unique emotional mixes. African American communication, then, is "an act to be performed on a stage of life; the creation and sharing of one's person hood with others of similar acculturation" (Holt 1975, 90).

Ong notes that oral cultures are "antagonistic in their verbal performance and indeed in their lifestyle" (1982, 44). He also observes that orality situates knowledge in a context of struggle. Riddles, proverbs, and stories are used to store knowledge as well as "to engage others in verbal and intellectual combat" (p. 44). At the same time, he claims that "violence in oral art forms is also connected with the structure of orality itself" (p. 44). Verbal communication by nature, direct word of mouth, dynamic give-and-take, and a high degree of interpersonal relation add to the antagonisms of daily life.

VERBAL PLAY IN AFRICAN AMERICAN DISCOURSE

If Ong is correct, the antagonistic nature of orality is found in any culture that uses verbal behavior as its primary means of communicating in interpersonal relationships. It seems clear that African Americans tend to engage in these daily verbal struggles, influenced by orality, in a more noticeable manner than White Americans. A distinctive difference between cultures might be in how each handles, practices, and controls the antagonistic nature of verbal communication. Abrahams appears correct when he concluded that "perhaps the clearest indication of the distinctiveness of the Black speech community lies in the use of speech in the pursuit of public playing" (1976, 37). Play (or playing the dozens), in African American communities, is a nonserious, sometimes nonthreatening, verbal exchange. It is a symbolic exchange of selves, an entertainment of each by the other (Hannerz 1969).

Abrahams' discussion of play provides some insights about the way antagonistic practices might be understood in African American culture. Beginning with the idea that play is difficult to describe in any culture, he considers that play as practiced in African American cultures relies on distinguishing between it and the "real" or the "serious." For play as entertainment to operate successfully, he finds that "there must be a sense of threat arising from the 'real' and 'serious' world of behavior" (Abrahams 1976, 40). That threat must be constant, and the constant message must be ambivalent. The message is carried out by the use of curses, boasts, and devices of vilification used in real arguments. These explanations provide critical commentary concerning the inability of other participants to determine if one is cursing in a playful or serious tone.

Verbal play in the African American community is both performance and entertainment, oriented like sandlot football or card playing at picnics. But it can, on occasion, be as serious a kind of play as competitive football or bid whist tournaments. Still, play is an entertainment of each by the other and a symbolic exchange of selves. The question for the audience or listener is to decide when the play is or is not a serious exchange of selves.

African American culture has found through verbal play a mechanism to reduce and restrict daily hostilities brought on by the antagonism and struggle inherent in oral communication. It is not enough to know that play exists as an important phenomenon in African American culture. Cultural understanding demands that you know when to use it. Understanding the importance of play as a strategy in public discourse allows a speaker to interact. Play in the African American community appears to be a normal aspect of daily life on street corners, in barber shops, pool halls, garages, churches, and homes, where people congregate to enjoy themselves. Play in African American communities functions in a recreational and performance sense. Verbal play is found in much of the good-natured banter of African Americans. But when the unexpected happens and confrontation takes place, the use of playfulness can often quell emotionally charged conflicts that may bring the contestants to fisticuffs (Folb 1980, 92).

The notion of verbal play or entertainment suggests that in African American culture the same speech acts or language behaviors function both expressively and instrumentally. An expressive or stylistic function is one in which communication is used to influence an audience by drawing attention to the character of the speaker. An instrumental or rhetorical function is one in which communication is used in the traditional sense of influencing or manipulating others. The decision as to which function to use is often a matter of the speaker's personal assessment of the relationship between play and seriousness. If a situation is considered serious or the potential for hostility is great, the speaker uses the instrumental function. In contrast, if the shared cultural knowledge is that participants are in play, then the expressive function is used. We will return to the importance of shared knowledge at the end of the following section.

SIGNIFYING: A RHETORICAL ACT

In the previous section we noted that African American rhetorical theory and criticism must take into account an examination of the everyday oral-based discourse of an African American presence. Therefore, our concern in this section is to explain the rhetorical qualities of signifying as a speech event in the African American oral tradition. We claim that traditional speech events and discourse must be examined as rhetorical events in African American oral communication. While our exploration is brief, we hope to provide an understanding of the speech event of signifying as an example of what we find when African American voices are foregrounded for a Black presence.

Signifying as an African American speech event has been explained by scholars according to its functions (Abrahams 1970; Kochman 1972), as a rhetorical stance, an attitude toward language, a means of cultural self-definition (Gates 1988; Smitherman 1977), and as a critical means of exploring the

African American literary tradition (Gates 1988; Lee 1996). But it is Claudia Mitchell-Kernan's insightful observations that provide the basic structure for a rhetorical understanding of signifying in the oral tradition. Signifying, she explains, is an alternative message form and embedded in a variety of discourses. Importantly, she notes that a speech act could not be considered signifying without the element of indirection. By indirection she means that for the correct interpretation of an utterance one cannot rely upon dictionary meanings or syntactic rules. Consequently, "[t]he apparent significance of the message differs from its real significance. The apparent meaning of the sentence signifies its actual meaning" (1973, 325). In signifying, shared knowledge is important in helping a listener interpret the indirection. The notion of signifying is made more difficult because of the obscurity of where interpretation lies: the meaning or message, the audience addressed, or the intent of the speaker.

Carol Lee's contribution to the notion of signifying, especially as a response to the process of literary interpretation, is based on a metaphoric or figurative understanding, which she equates to characteristics assigned to manifest meaning and ironic or latent meaning. African Americans, through signifying, read between the lines using their own cultural codes and system of analysis as means of interpretation. Lee comes to the conclusion that signifying is a rhetorical stance—an attitude toward language—that is empowering and culturally self-defining.

Signifying as a traditional form of African American discourse is familiar to the African American community across class, gender, generations, and urban and suburban environments (Lee 1996; Gates 1988; Kochman 1972; Abrahams, 1970, 1976). Signifying is important because it can be employed as a rhetorical device to using written and oral forms of communication, especially African American rhetorical discourse. The ability to think critically about a literary text is based on one's prior social knowledge and cultural codes. While signifying is a way of encoding a message, one's shared cultural knowledge is the basis on which any reinterpretation of the message is made. Theoretically, signifying (Black) as a concept can be used to give meaning to rhetorical acts of African Americans and indicate a Black presence. Rhetorically, one can also explore texts for the manner in which the themes or worldviews of other texts are repeated and revised with a signal difference, but based on shared knowledge.

Gates (1988) and others note that the audience of a double-voiced word is therefore meant to hear both a version of the original utterance as the embodiment of its speaker's point of view (or semantic position) and the second speaker's evaluation of that utterance from a different point of view. The silent second text corresponds to the shared knowledge, which must be brought to bear upon the manifest content of the speech act and employed in the reinterpretation of the utterance. The point here is that the second speaker's evaluation of an utterance and shared knowledge suggests that the listener draw upon all of his or her rhetorical background to interpret the message and that multiple interpretations can exist or coexist depending on the shared social knowledge of the rhetorical tradition with which an audience identifies. Shared knowledge is cultural knowledge. Therefore, shared knowledge must exist as part of the logics of everyday life. Shared knowledge, in African American culture, consists of those cultural patterns of communication, behaviors, worldviews, and philosophy understood by members of that community. The shared knowledge relied upon in speech events, rhetorical and otherwise, to decode meaning is what is important to understanding a Black presence.

Any speculation about signifying leads to other interesting theoretical questions about the nature of orality. For example, are meanings in people? Some evidence points to the conclusion that in oral cultures meanings are more public rather than private. Therefore, the notion that meanings are in people is misleading when applied to oral cultures because in oral culture it appears that the truth, intent, or accuracy of a statement has to be analyzed in terms of what is common knowledge to the culture. In the African American act of signifying, the apparent meaning of a sentence differs from its real meaning, and a listener is required to interpret meaning by attending to shared knowledge of the group before real meaning can be discerned. Consequently, meanings ultimately are in people, but in the oral tradition meanings are tempered by the text, the context, and the pretext (i.e., the shared social knowledge that people have to draw upon to interpret the message).

CONCLUSION

Rhetorical understanding in any culture may mean that one understands some of the basic assumptions people have about the culture. In the case of African Americans, the use of cultural understanding in orality signals a Black presence. Oral discourse is the mechanism by which interactants work out their daily routines. At the same time, cultural preparation implies a recognition of the rhetorical tactics in daily use and the names of speech acts that signal a particular rhetorical strategy. In African American culture, learning to act rhetorically is a lifelong process. How such practice develops—that is, how a culture goes about instructing members in rhetorical assumptions and rhetorical acts that lead to rhetorical understanding—will require continued exploration. Importantly, a Black presence for rhetorical scholars will rely upon explaining how shared cultural knowledge of African Americans is recreated and constructed in everyday texts.

REFERENCES

Abrahams, R. D. (1970). *Deep Down in the Jungle: Negro Narrative Folklore from the Streets of Philadelphia.* New York: Columbia University Press.

Abrahams, R. D. (1976). *Talking Black*. Rowely, MA: Newbury House.
Asante, M. K. (1988). *Afrocentricity*. Trenton, NJ: Africa World Press.
Asante, M. K. (1990). *Kemet, Afrocentricity, and Knowledge*. Trenton, NJ: Africa World Press.
Bacon, J. (1999). Taking Liberty, Taking Literacy: Signifying in the Rhetoric of African American Abolitionists. *Southern Communication Journal* 64: 271–87.
Caponi, G. D. (1999). *Signifyin(g), Sanctifyin', and Slam Dunking*. Amhurst: University of Massachusetts Press.
Folb, E. A. (1980). *Runnin' Down Some Lines: The Language and Culture of Black Teenagers*. Cambridge, MA: Harvard University Press.
Garner, T. (1985). Instrumental interactions: Speech acts in daily life. *Central States Speech Journal, 36*, 227–238.
Garner, T. (1998). Understanding Oral Rhetorical Practices in African American Cultural Relationships. In V.J. Duncan (Ed.), *Towards Achieving Maat* (pp. 29–44). Dubuque, IA: Kendall/Hunt Publishing.
Gates, H. L., Jr. (1988). *The Signifying Monkey*. New York: Oxford University Press.
Gee, J. P. (1985). The Narrativization of Experience in the Oral Style. *Journal of Education* 167: 9–35.
Hannerz, U. (1969). *Soul Side: Inquires into Ghetto Culture and Community*. New York: Columbia University Press.
Hecht, M., R. Jackson, and S. Ribeau (2003). *African American Communication and Identity*. Mahwah, NJ: Erlbaum.
Holt, G. (1975). Metaphor, Black discourse style, and cultural reality. In R. L. Williams (Ed.), *Ebonics: The True Language of Black Folk* (p. 89). St. Louis, MO: Robert L. Williams and Associates. Inc.
Jones, G. (1991). *Liberating Voice: Oral Tradition in African American Literature*. Cambridge, MA: Harvard University Press.
Kochman, T. (1972). Toward an Ethnography of Black American Speech Behavior. In T. Kochman (Ed.), *Rappin' and Stylin' Out: Communication in Urban Black America* (pp. 243–64). Urbana: University of Illinois Press.
Kochman, T. (1981). *Black and White Styles in Conflict*. Chicago: University of Chicago Press.
Lee, C. D. (1996). *Signifying as a Scaffold for Literary Interpretation: The Pedagogical Implications for an African American Discourse*. Urbana: University of Illinois Press.
Mitchell-Kernan, C. (1973). Signifying as a Form of Verbal Art. In A. Dundes (Ed.), *Mother Wit from the Laughing Barrel: Readings in the Interpretation of Afro-American Folklore* (pp. 310–28). Englewood Cliffs, NJ: Prentice-Hall.
Ong, W. J. (1982). *Orality and Literacy: The Technologizing of the Word*. London: Methuen.
Rickford, J., and R. Rickford (2000). *Spoken Soul: The Story of Black English*. New York: John Wiley and Sons.
Sidran, B. (1971). *Black Talk*. New York: Holt, Rinehart and Winston.
Smitherman, G. (1977). *Talkin and Testifyin: The Language of Black America*. Boston: Houghton Mifflin.
Welch, K. E. (1999). *Classical Rhetoric, Oralism, and a New Literacy*. Cambridge, MA: MIT Press.

CHAPTER 4

"Jesus Is a Rock": Spirituals as Lived Experience

MELBOURNE S. CUMMINGS
JUDI MOORE LATTA

INTRODUCTION

In African American folk communities, where new sacred songs are created by each emerging generation, a certain dynamic redundancy exists. Lyrics are repeated, musical phrases are borrowed, and whole songs—once retired—reemerge. Folklorist Mellonee Burnim explains the phenomenon as resulting from the fact that "texts have such significance that they cannot be discarded . . . [and are consequently] revived and revitalized by being fused with a more contemporary sound" (Burnim 1980, 166). The lyrics come from situations that seem to reinvent themselves. The importance of examining what Walter F. Pitts called "the ritual and structure . . . [of] 'little communities'" (Pitts 1993, xiii) involved in such revitalizing activity cannot be underestimated.

This study of an aspect of African American communication and culture connected to the group that produces it makes several assumptions:

- that religion plays an important role in shaping and reflecting a worldview
- that the indigenous sacred music of African Americans is tightly woven in text and performance with the lived experiences of individuals
- that linguistic meanings and insights into cultural communities are produced through such music
- that the "pervasiveness of nommo, the generating and sustaining power of the spoken word, permeates all aspects of Black life" (Smith 1972, 296).

Further, this study uses a methodological approach that involves a serious contemplation of lives in action, as it draws from ethnography, with its liberal use of personal interviews and field observations ultimately translated into "thick description" and analysis. In the tradition of Walter Pitts, who in his dual role as anthropologist and church pianist observed the parallels between the sanctity of his "little community" and the vast expanse of the African Diaspora that formed its backbone, this study examines the symbol of "spiritual transformation in ritual" (Pitts 1993, 175) as it occurs in the context of an African American reality.

A WORSHIP SCENE

The 8:00 A.M. service was well under way. The prayer and praise portion that precedes the regular worship had been rich with testimonies and songs as people witnessed about "how good the Lord had been" in their lives—saving the Boy Scouts from a terror-filled night in the middle of a flood, rescuing a teenage son from drugs, delivering one woman's "baby girl" from cancer, opening one window on a job opportunity when another had closed.

This was a typical Sunday at the People's Community Baptist Church, the largest Black congregation in the richest county in Maryland. Now, two prayers and a hymn later, the service had turned to song once again. On this second Sunday of the month, the forty-five member Chancel Choir, directed by thirty-year-old Jonathan Davis, was singing what might be considered a gospelized spiritual, and the tenor of the worship in the sanctuary was quite exciting.

Jesus is a Rock in a weary land,
A weary land, a weary land.
Jesus is a Rock in a weary land,
A shelter in a time of storm.

The words rang out, percussive, forceful. The voices were sharp and clear, sometimes supported by the synthesizer and drum, sometime standing alone in a cappella isolation. The choir swayed and stepped on beats one and three. Some members of the congregation began to stand, waving their hands in silent agreement. Others moved in their seats and clapped. Half the choir sang, "I know He is a Rock," and the other half responded, "In a weary land." Tenors and basses joined forces to sing, "He's a Rock." Altos and sopranos finished the line, "In a weary land"—repeating an antiphonal call-and-response relationship that was centuries old.

The spiritual's musical arrangement, by Glenn Burleigh, was new, but the function of the song as a rhetorical text—a narrative embedded in history, memory, and faith—was not. This was a nineteenth-century religious song—a spiritual, a dynamic redundancy—speaking to and for twenty-first-century worshipers. In many ways it was more than just one of Du Bois' "sorrow songs." It bore out James Cone's projection of the spiritual as a way of dealing with trouble, a means of persevering, "a joyful expression . . . and a vibrant affirmation of life" (Cone 1972, 33).

SPIRITUALS: A LOOK BACK

> African American spirituals are songs born in the souls of enslaved men and women as they toiled long and hard in the fields, sawmills, seaports, and "big houses" of the South; as they endured lashes across their backs; and as they gathered together in the still of the night for prayer, worship, and peace. They are songs that have, at various times, been called "slave songs," "jubilees," and "sorrow songs," but they are, fundamentally, religious folk songs composed from Black folk-English. They are songs that cry out about the slaves' daily encounters with brutal oppression and their struggles to be free. (Reagon et al. 1994, 11)

Spirituals have always been a powerful source of strength in African American communities—even before they were named. African Americans came to understand the importance and the centrality of religion in their lives as embodied in sacred music that reflected their troubles, as well as everything they were and what they aspired to do or be. It was their life force; it was the virtual essence of their worldview.

During slavery religion offered solace and refuge from lives filled with trials and tribulations. Because of the promise of a better life, at least in the hereafter, if not on earth, African Americans embraced Christianity. As a religion focused on reversing the adverse conditions in which slaves found themselves, Christianity promised its converts a life free of woes.

Clearly there were sacred songs that attended this new acceptance of Christianity. However, it was not until African Americans began to rework the songs so that they reflected their belief system that this new religion was completely embraced. Christianity became a reality to slaves, its first New World converts, as they began to voice songs of patience, forbearance, love, faith, and hope. Slaves took complete refuge in Christianity, and though they were forged of sorrow, the songs, later called Negro spirituals, took on a fervor, often of joy, peace, and relief (Levine 1977, 20).

It is generally believed that slaves would not have survived the inhuman treatment of slavery in the way they did had it not been for their faith in the promise that Christianity offered and through communication with the Holy Spirit in the spirituals that they sang. Those songs were spirituals like "Jesus Is a Rock in a Weary Land" or "Nobody Knows the Trouble I See." The singing of spirituals not only represented ways in which slaves were able to comfort themselves or find peace in a "weary land," but they served as a way of coping with life and as ways in which important messages were conveyed from one slave to another or one plantation to another (Southall 1973, 47).

Some of the most provocative, reverent, and imaginative songs were spirituals that passed messages about upcoming rebellions or events that were being planned (Southall 1973, 46). On occasions such as these, spirituals such as "Didn't My Lord Deliver Daniel" became useful. Or when an escape was to take place, a spiritual such as "Steal Away" might be sung at a night gathering or a camp meeting to alert people to the impending activity or let them know when to be ready. One of the enduring qualities of spirituals was their ability to be misinterpreted (Douglass 1855, 87). It is believed that had it not been for the dual nature of the lyrics, many a conspiracy that led to the freedom through escape of numerous slaves would have been foiled (Du Bois, 1903, 200). The spiritual referred to above proclaimed that if God saved Daniel from the lion's den, He would certainly deliver slaves from the brutality of their existence; if God saved the Hebrew children from the fiery furnace, He would save them from the sting of the lash; if God delivered Israel from bondage, then God would deliver the slaves to freedom.

Spirituals were never static. The lyrics had no final version; they were communal. Always the community felt free to alter and re-create. These songs, like the church, had a significant impact on the congregation (Taylor 1975, 1). The fact that these songs continue to survive in the same or altered forms is testament not only to the perpetuation of significant elements of an older worldview among the slaves, but also to the continuation of a strong sense of community. They allowed individual as well as communal expression (McKim 1967, 58).

The structure of the spirituals (the traditional call-and-response pattern or lining out hymns) kept individuals in touch or in a kind of dialog with the community. A point that is often made is that slave music (spirituals) is testimonial to the fact that despite the inhumanity of the slavery system that did everything to destroy African American communality, it was unable to destroy it totally or to leave the slaves without defenses before their White masters. As a matter of fact, the spirituals presented the slaves with a potential outlet for individual feelings, even while they drew the slaves back into the communal presence and permitted the shared feelings, experiences, and assumptions of other like-minded individuals (Levine 1977, 23).

In examining spirituals, we see that some of these shared assumptions surface in lines that identified the slaves as "children of God" or "the chosen people." Such is the case in songs such as "Go Down Moses," "Swing Low Sweet Chariot," or "Looks Like My Lord's Coming in the Sky." Some of the songs show the personal identification with God that the slaves shared, like in the song "Who'll Be a Witness for My Lord" or "My Lord's a-Writing All the Time."

There is hardly a spiritual that shows God as remote; He is always shown as a personal friend, as in "I'm Going to Talk with King Jesus by Myself" or "Massa Jesus is My Bosom Friend." Additionally, there are always the shared experiences of the conversion. People profess being "born again," which entails reaching out beyond the world to the heavens and seeing Jesus, as in the song "Father, I Stretch My Hands to Thee." Most of these lyrics continue to be sung today (Lomax 1977, 1).

Spirituals were psychologically uplifting to the slaves, for the lyrics that they sang were completely devoid of the feeling of unworthiness. Instead, the lyrics were filled with a sense of self-worth, of belonging, and of the probability of justice and a sense of the earthly life and surrounding conditions being temporary. Life after death was depicted as being permanent. In other words, the spirituals were to the slaves, as they are to Black people presently, about hope (Taylor 1975, 389).

Even when the spirituals were "sorrow songs," as they are often called, such as "Sometimes I Feel Like a Motherless Child" or "This World Is Not My Home," they were not pervasive or permanent. They were almost always overshadowed by a triumphant note of affirmation, as in the case of "Dust, dust and ashes, fly over my grave, But the Lord shall bear my spirit home" (Du Bois 1903, 199). There is a version that states, "Sometimes I feel like a eagle in de air, spread my wings an fly, fly, fly." In the lyrics of the mournful "Nobody Knows the Trouble I See," one version has its mood changed to:

One morning I was a-walkin' down
Saw some berries hanging down,
I pick de berry and I suck de juice
Just as sweet as the honey in de comb.

For all the sadness inherent in slave songs, they were characterized more by a feeling of confidence than despair. There was confidence that the conditions under which they lived were not unchangeable, as in the lyrics

Did not ol' Pharaoh get lost in the Red Sea?

or

Jesus make de dumb to speak
Jesus make de cripple walk
Jesus give de blind sight
Jesus do most anything.

The lyrics showed confidence in the rewards of persistence:

Keep a-inchin' along like a
Po' inch worm
Jesus will come by and by.

Spirituals also showed confidence in the prospects of the future, the faith that someday slavery would be no more:

We'll walk de golden streets
Of de New Jerusalem

or

No more rain for wet you, hallelujah
No more sunshine for burn you

Dere's no hard trials
Dere's no more whips a-crackin'
No evildoers in de Kingdom
All is gladness in de Kingdom

Spirituals reflected slaves' way of life. They were based on biblical passages or stories from the Bible, even on Protestant hymns (Southern 1972, 9), but for the slaves who reshaped them, they were songs, as Frederick Douglass wrote, that spoke "to the sorrows of their hearts" (Douglass 1855, 83). Over the years these spirituals have been given additional words and rhythms to suit the times. But they still remain true to the original intent: They encourage the heart, they give hope for the future, and they speak to "the soul of the thoughtful" (Douglass 1855, 83).

AN AFRICAN AMERICAN COSMOLOGY AT WORK IN SPIRITUALS: THEORETICAL FRAME

In traditional anthropological research, cosmology is a reference to a cultural group's system of meaning that helps shape its view of the world or universe. Historically among African Americans, this cosmology has involved a relationship between the self and God and has been reflected in the expressive culture originating in the church—particularly the music.

While a comprehensive exploration of a cosmology is beyond the scope of this essay, C. Eric Lincoln and Lawrence Mamiya offer an overview of just such a construct. They call cosmology "the best prism to cultural understanding" because it addresses sacred values held by people and it describes the nature of their encounter with the divine (Lincoln and Mamiya 1990, xi). In so doing, it prescribes the nature of the encounters with the worldly. According to their study *The Black Church in the African American Experience,* 78 percent of all African Americans are "churched," and most of the estimated thirty million to thirty-five million Blacks who acknowledge having had a Christian religious experience have participated/worshiped in what is called the Black church.[1] Using the idea that the Black church is a sociological/theological construct encompassing the pluralism of Black Christians in the United States, Lincoln and Mamiya explore the Black sacred cosmos and assert that there are six common principles that form its tent poles. They include the centrality of Jesus; the symbolic importance of the word *freedom* as a communal and shared concept; intense enthusiasm; belief in the personal conversion of the individual worshiper; recognition of the African heritage; and commitment to racial parity, justice, and equality.

Putting human narrative experience (the spiritual in particular) at the center of the study of culture and in dialogue with the elements of an African American cosmology provides an opportunity to examine the connectedness of cultural systems. It reinforces the point made by folklorist popular culture scholar Jay Mechling, who suggests that "texts have no objective 'real meaning' but have meaning through the act of interpretation" (Mechling 1989, 3).

How does the spiritual "Jesus Is a Rock in a Weary Land," sung as part of worship in a Sunday morning service by a full gospel choir participating with a congregation, embody an African American cosmology? How does a song whose lyrics were first sung by people who were property and who were faced with the realities of the auction block, the lash, and family separation have meaning for middle-class church members in an air-conditioned sanctuary with cushioned seats? An explanation is available by examining the words of the text (both the historical originals and the contemporary additions), the actions and nonverbal behaviors of the worshipers, and the context of the experience. The choir intones the verse:

Jesus is a Rock in a weary land,
A weary land, a weary land.
Jesus is a Rock in a weary land,
A shelter in a time of storm.

The lyrics of this song present a worldview that privileges a direct human relationship with Jesus and puts people comfortably on a first-name basis with Him. This is African American cosmology at work. While all Christians profess a belief in Jesus as the Son of God, this primarily Black American congregation gives voice to a connection between oppressive conditions and the humiliation/death/promise of divine rescue offered by Jesus. To position Jesus in the central metaphor of the song ("Jesus is a Rock") is to place Him as the solid foundation on which all else is built.

The song advances, each verse moving the congregation higher and higher toward a more intense worship experience. Convicted by the oratory and the relationship it has to their lives, more people stand when the choir sings the chorus, "I know He is a Rock." The shift from third person ("Jesus is a Rock") to first person ("I know He is a Rock") is a step toward personal affirmation and allows a public confession of the personal conversion of the individual.

While the "weary land," repeated as a recurring line in both the refrain and the verse during the contemporary singing of this spiritual, is *not* the space referenced by a people in bondage two centuries ago, it is the space of modern-day psychological, economic, and physical oppression. For those worshipers participating in the singing, Montgomery County, Maryland—a part of metropolitan Washington, D.C.—is the territory in question. It is indeed a "weary land"—a place where drive-by shootings claim lives each year; a community where parents routinely drill their teenage boys on how to cope with police brutality; a community that sees excessive racial profiling, resulting in false arrests and mistaken identity; a community where workers are routinely downsized from middle-management positions; a community where the unemployment rate among young African Americans is higher than any other group; a community where the rate of HIV infection is at its highest among young Black women and where the rate of rape victims exceeds the rate of new readers; a community where domestic violence is at an all-time high regardless of class and shelters for battered wives and their children have no vacant beds.

Little wonder, then, that such passion resonates throughout the congregation when the choir reaches the third section of the song, with its set of contemporary interrogatories:

> Has He ever made a way when you didn't have a dime?
> Has He ever stepped in just right on time?
> Has He ever picked you up when you were down?
> Has he ever placed your feet on solid ground?
> Then you know He is a Rock.

One of the choir members, Andrea Hines, talks about her response to the lyrics:

> For me, a weary land is my particular job. I'm thankful for my job, but it's quite a challenge every day. I pray every day for God to guide me because the tasks are so overwhelming and sometimes I don't know what I'm doing. . . . So just making it from day to day on that job with the people I have to deal with, that's a weary land for me.

SPIRITUALS ALIVE IN THE CHURCH

Music is an important part of the Sunday service at the People's Community Baptist Church and offers a window on worship for the parishioners. Not all songs sung are spirituals. Many are what some worshipers call "the hymns of the Church"; others are the gospel songs that embody the energy, intense enthusiasm, and upbeat Christian fervor embraced by Thomas Dorsey (called "the Father of Gospel Music") in the 1920s and '30s and taken to new heights by artists such as the Winans and Donnie McClurkin in contemporary times. The singing in the 8:00 and 11:00 A.M. services is generally led by one of the four choirs that rotate Sundays at People's. In addition to the Chancel Choir, there are the Men's Choir and the Youth Choir, which, like the Chancel, draw from a repertoire traditionally known as gospel, while the People's Angelic Voices, or PAVs, usually sing traditional anthems. All of them at one point or another, in one service or another, sing spirituals.

Jonathan Davis, the director of the Chancel Choir and a third-generation choir director, remembers first hearing spirituals when his mother taught them to her choir in the 1980s. He "didn't know what to call them" at the time, but he was aware that they were "something special." Now, the lyrics "have a message" for him:

> When you mention the word *spirituals* I think most musicians might think of traditional, very easy chord progressions, those types of things our grandmothers and great-grandmothers and grandfathers did and they say, "That's nice." But we really do . . . connect with them in a different way.

Jonathan's choir-directing mother, Reba Davis, "connects" with spirituals because their historical role is intertwined with a personal identification and a religious conviction. "Deep River," for example, has earned its place as her personal favorite because she remembers hearing it sung as a bass solo in her home church in Philadelphia. Associated with it are all of the memories of the public performance, the private worship, and the passionate longing for relief from "trouble." The value of spirituals as both the record of Black people's striving for earthly freedom and the story of her ancestors is not lost on Reba Davis. She says, "The people who first sang those songs look just like me."

> When I hear spirituals, I think about the suffering of our people, even the joy of "Nobody Knows the Trouble I've Seen" and "My Lord, What a Morning" and those kinds of things . . . "In that Great Getting Up Morning". . . I sort of relate to and I can picture hundreds of years ago what people were going through even though I wasn't there. I'm still thinking, we're singing these today and there's a relationship. There's a binding.

Spirituals create a "binding" and connection for others like Gloria Baker, a real estate broker in her everyday life and a deaconess/soprano who sings on the first Sunday of every month with the PAVs. Just as the songs provided a way to hold together the personhood of the eighteenth- and nineteenth-century creators of the music, they provide a sense of pride and dignity for Gloria.

> I think of our forefathers and mothers and all the suffering that went on that they actually put some of that in the music. . . . It gives me a kind of feeling of responsibility when I listen to those songs. . . . It makes me feel a certain responsibility to do well, to pass on, to help improve whatever I can.

Gloria Baker loves spirituals. Connecting "in a different way" for her means remembering her growing-up years in southern Georgia, when she lived next door to a sanctified church where spirituals and gospel music were sung. Gloria recalls seeing Mahalia Jackson bring the songs to life on television:

> She was one of the first Black persons I heard on television singing spirituals. And I remember the story circulated in our little town that they offered her all this money just to sing a non-spiritual song, a rhythm and blues . . . and she turned it down because her music was her faith.

Gloria's introduction to singing spirituals was in a concert setting where she, as a member of her high school choir, sang with the Harmonizing 75 in Abbeyville, Georgia. Today she is moved whenever any choir sings spirituals:

> I think of the goodness of God when I hear spirituals. It's like it's similar to when one prays to God. You're praying to God to bring him closer to you. So singing the music and understanding the words is really a prayer in music.

Tanya Brown, the youth choir director, is not as passionate about traditional spirituals as Gloria Baker and Reba Davis are, possibly due to a difference in age. Tonya, however, remembers being taught spirituals in Sunday school as young as five years of age.

> I grew up in the church and I remember learning spirituals through scriptures . . . and I remembered we learned about where we came from as a people. Most of the experience we talked about was based on the troubles we went through as a people. Our history told us that. I believe that spirituals are the foundation of our faith.

CONCLUSION

The roles that African American congregations such as the People's Community Baptist Church have played in perpetuating and preserving spirituals have been vital. Spirituals have always been significant to African Americans as a means of discourse, shrouded with sometimes hidden meanings and enveloped at other times in blatant narratives. When it comes to traditional Black rhetoric, what Blacks say in the form of stories, dance, and songs is the way they communicate their feelings, beliefs, desires, values, and way of life. If it is too strong to say that this sacred music has helped Black people survive, then the spirituals—capturing the essence of an embattled existence—certainly have made living more bearable.

At once, spirituals have been a source of consolation, a means of expression, and a reflection of a perspective that is both collective and individual. In fact, it is through spirituals that we can look to comprehend Black people's worldview because these songs embody in many ways the cosmology Blacks brought from Africa. It is a cosmology that afforded them the possibility of adapting to and transcending their situation.

In both their historical incarnation and their contemporary form, spirituals have maintained rhetorical elements that place them clearly in the African oral tradition. Call and response is at the center of the songs' performance; communal composition is at the heart of the songs' source; inventiveness is the crux of the songs' creative formulation.

Spirituals, like certain other forms of rhetoric in Black discourse, deal with the distressed and abused conditions that attend the people. They are functional and practical, yet one hundred years after Du Bois characterized spirituals, many people would argue that they remain "the most beautiful expression of human experience born this side of the seas."

NOTE

1. Their use of the term "Black church" refers to Black Christians in the United States who are part of "independent, historic, and totally Black controlled denominations" (Lincoln and Mamiya 1990, 1)

REFERENCES

Bryan, A. (1974). *Walk Together Children: Black American Spirituals*. Hartford: Atheneum.

Burnim, M. (1980). The Black Gospel Music Tradition: Symbol of Ethnicity. Ph.D. dissertation, Indiana University, Bloomington.

Cone, J. H. (1972). *The Spirituals and the Blues: An Interpretation*. New York: Seabury Press.

Du Bois, W. E. B. (1903). *The Souls of Black Folk*. Chicago: McClurg.

Douglass, F. (1855). *My Bondage and My Freedom*. Boston: Dover.

Johnson, J. W., and J. R. Johnson (1926). *The Book of American Negro Spirituals*. New York: Viking.

Levine, L. (1977). *Black Culture and Black Consciousness*. New York: Oxford University Press.

Lincoln, C. E., and L. H. Mamiya (1990). *The Black Church in the African American Experience*. Durham, NC: Duke University Press.

Lomax, A. (1977). *Georgia Sea Island Songs* [liner notes]. New World Records.

Lovell, J., Jr. (1972). *Black Song*. New York: Macmillan Company.

McKim, J. M. (1977). Negro Songs. In B. Jackson (Ed.), *The Negro and His Folklore in Nineteenth Century Periodicals*. (pp. 148–149). Austin: University of Texas Press.

Mechling, J. (1989). An American Culture Grid with Texts. *American Studies International*, 37, 1.

Pitts,W. F. (1993). *Old Ship of Zion: The Afro-Baptist Ritual in the African Diaspora*. New York: Oxford University Press.

Reagon, B. J., T. Bolden, J. Moore Latta, and L. Pertillar-Brevard (1994). *"Wade in the Water: African American Sacred Music Traditions" Educator's Guide*. Washington, D.C.: National Public Radio.

Smith, A. L. (1972). *Language, Communication, and Rhetoric in Black America*. New York: Harper and Row.

Southall, G. (1973). *Black Composers and Religious Music: The Black Perspective in Music*. Minneapolis: University of Minnesota Press.

Southern, E. (1972). An Origin for the Negro Spiritual. *Black Scholar* (summer): 8–13.

Taylor, J. E. (1975). Somethin' on My Mind: A Cultural and Historical Interpretation of Spiritual Texts. *Ethnomusicology* (September): 387–99.

CHAPTER 5

The Use of Public Space as Cultural Communicator: How Museums Reconstruct and Reconnect Cultural Memory

DEBORAH F. ATWATER
SANDRA L. HERNDON

It is a peculiar sensation, this double-consciousness, this sense of always looking at one's self through the eyes of others, of measuring one's self through the eyes of others of measuring one's soul by the tape of a world that looks on in amused contempt and pity. One ever feels this two-ness, an American, a Negro; two souls, two thoughts, two unreconciled strivings; two warring ideals in one dark body, whose dogged strength alone keeps it from being torn apart. (Du Bois 1903, 15)

The use of public space and what that space signals to all who encounter and interact in it is fertile ground for study for communication scholars. In this paper, we are concerned specifically with how museums, as public spaces, can display and reveal the intersection of race and culture in the recovery of a society's historical and cultural memory. We briefly discuss the intersection of race and culture in an examination of two museums, the National Civil Rights Museum in Memphis, Tennessee, and MuseumAfrica in Johannesburg, South Africa, and we discuss the formation and connection of cultural memory between Africans and African Americans. Lastly, we examine how museums can be a constructive way to engage an African past and the sense of double consciousness for African Americans. What are the similarities and differences that bind us together as a people? The genesis of this project began with a fifteen-day National Communication Association Study Tour of South Africa in August 1999, during which we visited MuseumAfrica in Johannesburg. We also visited the National Civil Rights Museum in Memphis. Both of these museums commemorate the struggle of a group of people seeking to liberate themselves from an oppressive and racist social system.

Writers across many disciplines are asking difficult questions about the role of public memory. In particular, just what is public memory, and who creates and owns it? According to Browne (1995), recent works collectively emphasize text as a site of symbolic action, a place of cultural performance, the meaning of which is defined by its public and persuasive functions.

The origins and uses of public memory can be divided into two cultures—official and vernacular. Official culture, according to Bodnar, Browne (1995) notes, is communicated by and on behalf of the nation-state and seeks through its sponsorship to retain loyalty, to keep itself perpetual, and to stress the virtue of unity. Its language of commemoration emphasizes the idealistic and the abstract as well as promotes patriotism as the highest realization of duty. Its realm is sacred and timeless. Vernacular culture is situated locally; it is given material and symbolic expression by the individual and community. Vernacular culture seeks its end in change and is much more ambivalent about the meaning of its past. Vernacular culture speaks of rights, the secular, the here and now. At the intersection of these two cultures lie the symbolic aspects of public memory and the fundamental issues concerning the very existence of a society—the meaning of past, present organization, and the structure of power. For example, Blair, Jeppeson, and Pucci (1991) in their analysis of the Vietnam Veterans Memorial demonstrate the multiple stories and multiple layers of meaning evoked by a public commemorative monument.

In a real sense, public memory refers to having a potential for a shared sense of the past, fashioned from symbolic resources of community, and subject to its particular history, hierarchies, and aspirations. We emphasize the potential of sharing the past, because in the United States, just as in South Africa, different groups have different perspectives and recollections of the historical past. Remembering the past for African Americans becomes important if we as a nation are to reconcile and reconnect with our collective American public memory. One of the most poignant reasons we should remember and honor the past is made evident by the former president of South Africa, Nelson Mandela. In a foreword to *Reconciliation Through Truth,* Mandela says,

> Today it is our hope that, in facing up to our past, we can ensure that never again will South Africa's children have to remain content with accounts of our country that are known to be false. Instead we must insist with quiet resolve on a firm policy of undoing the continuing effects of the past. It is another personal delight for us today to watch how the divisions of the past are giving way to the beginnings of a new South African sense of belonging, shared by all. (Asmal, Asmal, and Roberts 1996, vii–viii)

Asmal, Asmal, and Roberts shed further light on why it is important to remember the past in South Africa and, in explaining the truth and reconciliation process, also provide an important context for the role of the museum in South Africa: "As South Africa faces its past, we must faithfully record the pain of the past so that a unified nation can call upon that past as a galvanizing force in the large tasks of reconstruction" (1996, 6).

According to Asmal, Asmal, and Roberts, memory is significant:

> This talk of shared memory must not be misunderstood or mystified. It is not the creation of a post-apartheid era, or a stifling homogeneous nationhood, nor a new Fatherland. The process of forging a collective memory is a flaring up of debate; it is the creation of a public atmosphere in which the seemingly unimportant memories and annals of the past achieve a new public importance. Private reminiscence achieves public currency and manifest worth. (Asmal, Asmal, and Roberts, 1996, 10)

Given the past of both South Africa and the United States, those who encounter it in a public space, such as a museum, are left with the possibilities of multiple messages and effects, some more enduring than others. In any culture, museums are both significant arbiters of public memory and the spaces in which that memory is interpreted. In the best-case scenario, museum experiences may even be liberating.

Thus, we come to the purposes of this essay. In it, we discuss the role of museums in communicating culture, with their potential to reach a broad cross-section of each society and thereby wield significant influence on the meanings generated on the subject of race. The formation of cultural memory and its impact on the history of two countries. Race and its role in the public forum of the two museums mentioned at the outset is examined precisely because the relationship between public space and race in the history of the two nations involved is both implicit and profound. And finally, in the process, we hope to build on previous research and scholarship in the area of public space and public memory. We also offer our own perspective on how we encountered and reacted to the two museums.

THE FORMATION OF CULTURAL MEMORY

As Marita Sturken discusses in *Tangled Memories: The Vietnam War, The AIDS Epidemic, and the Politics of Remembering* (1997), memory establishes life and the very core of identity. It gives meaning to the present. What is cultural memory? What does it mean for Africans and African Americans to remember? What does it mean for a culture to remember? Can the collective memory be similar to the individual political stakes and meanings? Are there dangers associated with political and cultural amnesia?

In his book *The Recovery of Race in America,* Gresson argues why recovery is vital to everyone in this country. Specifically, he says, "Recovery is a human necessity: whenever and wherever there are losses, we must respond . . . it is an attempt to gain back something of the balance—whether good, bad or indifferent—that we once knew" (1995, x).

For Gresson, there are two major American losses: White Americans' loss of moral hegemony and Black Americans' loss of the myth of racial homogeneity (p. ix). If we look at the phenomenon of recovery,

> [w]e can see recovery as the reconnection to, or regaining of, a prior and privileged position or relationship. The Black apocalypse is 1. Recovery of a collectively shared set of ideals by which to conduct civil relations; and 2. Recovery of a mutually binding interracial code of morality. (p. 4)

Two aspects of Gresson's "rhetoric of recovery" are (1) the use of narrative to describe a discovery with inferred relevance for both one's own and the other's ability to deal better with duplicity and uncertainty, and (2) an implicit invitation to identify with and accept the "liberative powers of that discovery" (p. 5).

We argue that one way to recover the past, no matter how painful, is through the use of museums that are constructed to engage the public even though there may be multiple messages or narratives conveyed, for within all cultures various versions of the past can and do exist simultaneously. Cultural memory in the United States relies on various forms such as memorials, public art, pop culture, literature, commodities, and activism. One definition of cultural memory is memory that is shared outside the avenues of formal, historical discourse, yet is entangled with cultural products and imbued with cultural meaning (Sturken, 1997, 3). Different stories vie for a place in history, just as personal memories of public events are shared. There is no single narrative for history, although for many years in the United States that was indeed the norm for lessons of American history.

MUSEUMS AS PUBLIC SPACE

In his 1990 presidential address to the Museums Association's annual conference, Patrick Boylan cited the definition of a museum, provided by the International Council of Museums, as a "non-profit-making institution *in the service of society* and its *development,* and open to the public, which acquires, conserves, researches, communicates and exhibits, for the purposes of study, education and enjoyment, material evidence of people and their environment" (1990, 32). Given this frame, he argued that museums have a responsibility "to take seriously the needs of the disadvantaged sectors of their population, whether that disadvantage is the result of poverty, ethnicity, disability, age or social disaffection" (p. 32). According to Katriel, museums "have, indeed, become major participants in contemporary efforts to construct culturally shared, historically anchored representations of 'self' and 'other'" (1993, 70). However, Black museums are important, for according to Fath Davis Ruffins, "Black museums founded in the last thirty years are places where alternative versions of the African American and African past can be debated and disseminated to a wider public" (1992, 567). But more importantly, she argues that "Black museums have served as the principal repositories of the memory of the individuals, families, and communities. Black museums continue to be an outlet for the mythopoetic narratives of the special destiny of African Americans" (p. 570). Inevitably, these collections are the resources upon which we build our own interpretations of the past.

Describing museums as "truly unique institutions whose functions include collecting, preserving, documenting, and interpreting material culture," Fleming asks, "How do museum professionals determine what lessons from history the museum visitor should learn?" (1994, 1020). Foote, in examining the origins of the National Civil Rights Museum in terms that may also be applicable to MuseumAfrica, posits that some "sanctified sites" begin by "marking minority causes" that provide "meaning immediately for the minority group," but also that acceptance by the larger society usually requires the passage of time (1997, 18). Foote describes the source of the conflict over the establishment of the National Civil Rights Museum as a "fight over place [that] had much to do with the fight over history—who will be remembered, how, and why" (p. 74).

Put simply, "archives, libraries and museums are political" in that the choices curators make are inherently value-laden, explicitly or implicitly (Brown and Davis-Brown 1998, 22). Adams encourages museums to create settings that encourage and stimulate dialog in order to create "forums, not temples" (1999, 976). The two museums examined in this essay were designed explicitly to focus attention on the experiences of historically marginalized people whose lives have been inadequately represented in such spaces. The next section of this paper provides a brief overview of each of the two museums.

THE NATIONAL CIVIL RIGHTS MUSEUM, MEMPHIS, TENNESSEE

The National Civil Rights Museum at the Lorraine Motel in Memphis, Tennessee, was the first of its kind in the United States. Opened in the fall of 1991, the twenty-thousand-square-foot space memorializes the site of the assassination of Dr. Martin Luther King Jr. in April 1968. The museum has as its primary goal educating visitors about the civil rights movement in the United States and its impact on worldwide movements for social and human rights. The museum exhibits re-create the brutality of segregation so graphically that visitors cannot help but experience some kind of emotional impact. Even those unfamiliar with the events of the 1960s sense the drama and significance of the civil rights era and the Black freedom movement that propelled it forward (see Eisterhold 1992; National Civil Rights Museum 2000).

The arrangement of photos, audio recordings, and documentary footage, along with life-size statues and artifacts, helps to create the look and feel of the era and help the viewer visually grasp the emotional and sometimes violent conditions facing civil rights activists of the time (Eisterhold 1992; National Civil Rights Museum 2000).

Coretta Scott King, widow of the slain leader, noted, "They have taken the site of tragedy and made it a place where the dream is redeemed" (cited in Eisterhold 1992, 53). The place of a national tragedy was successfully transformed into a space of cultural and educational significance as well as part of the formation of American cultural memory.

MUSEUMAFRICA, JOHANNESBURG, SOUTH AFRICA

MuseumAfrica is located at 121 Bree Street, Newton, Johannesburg, South Africa. It professes in an official brochure to be "All South Africa Is and All South Africa Was." This is the only museum that attempts to tell the story of life in southern Africa from the stone age to the nuclear age and beyond. It is the first major museum to give credit to Blacks' contributions to the development of the city.

Constructed in 1913, the building that now houses MuseumAfrica was Johannesburg's fruit and vegetable market until 1974. The converted building opened as MuseumAfrica in August 1994. Part of the Newton Cultural Precinct, the museum is next door to the world-renowned Market Theatre and a close neighbor to a host of other cultural and entertainment venues (MuseumAfrica n.d.).

The exhibition "Johannnesburg Transformations" examines some of the ways in which change has swept through the lives of the city and its people. "Johannesburg's Earth Roots and Early History" explores the origins of the region. "Gold" traces the impact of the substance on the lives of the Black population, including the miners forced to live in male-only hostels, as well as looking at the monetary, symbolic, and decorative importance of the precious metal that spawned the city itself. "What About the Workers?" focuses on the hard work of the masses of people, unseen and unknown, whose work undergirds the city. "The Sounds of the City" examines the music of the city, from the township jazz of Sophiatown's shebeens (bars) in the 1950s to the rhythms of resistance against apartheid in the 1960s and later. "Birds in a Cornfield" portrays homelessness in South Africa's biggest city and guides the visitor through the shantytown shacks of "informal settlements" to show how human creativity can make something from almost nothing. It re-creates the burgeoning townships with their squatter camps and shebeens. "The Road to Democracy" explores the politics of the anti apartheid struggle, including the role of women, the significance of gaining the vote, and the changes that are occurring postapartheid (MuseumAfrica n.d.). This museum successfully focuses attention on the experiences of the majority populations of South Africa, who had previously been oppressed under the system of apartheid.

COMMUNICATION, PUBLIC SPACE, AND RACE

In analyzing the changes that have been taking place in museums, Hooper-Greenhill presents two theoretical perspectives on the communication and educational functions that lead to differing notions of the role of the museum. The traditional role of the museum, she argues, assumed an "information transmission" (2000, 12) model of communication based on a "behaviourist view of teaching" (p. 13). In contrast, Hooper-Greenhill presents a cultural approach to communication based on constructivist learning theory to reconceptualize the role of the "museum as a communicator" (p. 12). This redefinition of the museum focuses on fundamental components of communication: "what is said and who says it, issues of narrative and voice" as well as "who is listening . . . an issue of interpretation, understanding, and the construction of meaning" (p. 18).

It is a truism in the study of communication that space is communicative, that is, it evokes meaning. According to Weisman, "There is a striking parallel between space and language. . . . Space, like language, is socially constructed; and like the syntax of language, the spatial arrangements of our buildings and communities reflect and reinforce the nature of gender, race, and class relations in society" (1992, 2). The emergence of the National Civil Rights Museum in the United States in 1991 and MuseumAfrica in South Africa in 1994, commemorating the experiences of oppressed people in these two societies that had, each in its own way, disenfranchised, marginalized, and brutalized them for decades, even centuries, calls attention to the changes that have occurred. One can argue that the very existence of these two museums heralds a new attempt at the recovery of race and public memory.

At the same time, it may be that things are not exactly as they seem. That is, perceived change in racial arrangements may give rise to an illusion of influence or power, as yet insufficiently realized, that does not comport well with the aspirations and goals of those previously oppressed. Few would argue that Black people have achieved full equality with White people in all aspects of society in either of these two societies. Indeed, Foote notes that some of the opposition to the museum in Memphis derived from the argument that "if money was to be spent in King's honor . . . it would be better invested in programs to aid Memphis' African American population," precisely because the disparities remained so great (1997, 78).

One can conclude not merely that space is communicative, but also that space and social interaction are interdependent. As Ardener suggests, "Space reflects social organisation . . . behavior and space are mutually dependent" (1993, 2). Inside the museums re-created spaces illustrate the interdependence of space and social interaction as well. For example, in the National

Civil Rights Museum, the "Montgomery Bus Boycott" exhibition directs the visitor to the back of the city bus in a manner reminiscent of the experience of Rosa Parks, complete with the threatening voice of the bus driver. In MuseumAfrica, the visitor is guided through a re-creation of a shantytown with cramped, crowded, miserable shacks for living quarters. Even though we never forget the fact that we are in a re-created space in a museum, in each case the effect is powerful. Weisman observes, "Space provides an essential framework for thinking about the world and the people in it," (1992, 9) and there is "an ongoing dialectical relationship between social space and physical space. Both are manufactured by society" (p. 10). In these museum spaces, almost inevitably, we viscerally experience the psychological, even physical shrinkage as our attention turns to the role that race has played in creating and determining these societal conditions.

There is a reciprocity of influence regarding space. As space defines the individual, so too does the individual define the space. The two are mutually interactive (Ardener 1993). Blair suggests that memorial sites, and by analogy museums such as the ones we are writing about, "by their very existence, *create communal spaces*" (1999, 48, emphasis in original). Young notes that such places "provide the sites where groups of people gather to create a common past for themselves, places where they tell the constitutive narratives, their 'shared' stories of the past; they become communities precisely by having shared (if only vicariously) the experiences of their neighbors" (1993, 6–7). As an inevitable consequence, the museum itself, as a space and a culture that is a language, is influenced by the experiences and responses of those individuals who populate its spaces.

The location of the National Civil Rights Museum remains controversial because it displaced inhabitants and buildings in the area. This engendered an extended protest by Jacqueline Smith, whose countermemorial is located directly across the street. She has made a commitment to protest the site of the museum because it destroyed the homes of those previously living there, and she has taken the position that the site could have been put to better use. Her presence constitutes a site of conflict in which visitors must engage even before entering the museum and the King memorial. Jacqueline Smith would likely argue that the more things change, the more they stay the same.

The presence of these museums "speaks" about what is valued. They are attempts to fill in missing pieces, to give voice in shaping the cultural and social environment, to help define "real" history and achieve cultural memory, albeit not without controversy even about the physical space itself.

RACE IN THE UNITED STATES AND SOUTH AFRICA

As a nation, we continue to struggle with how to deal with race and diversity. The 1998 report *One America in the 21st Century: Forging a New Future* states:

> America's greatest promise in the 21st century lies in our ability to harness the strength of our racial diversity. The greatest challenge facing Americans is to accept and take pride in defining ourselves as a multiracial democracy. At the end of the 20th century, America has emerged as the worldwide symbol of opportunity and freedom through leadership that constantly strives to give meaning to democracy's fundamental principles. These principles—justice, opportunity, equality, and racial inclusion—must continue to guide the planning for our future. (Franklin 1998, 1)

Ellis Cose, author of *Color Blind: Seeing Beyond Race in a Race Obsessed World* and Columbia University political science professor Anthony Marx, author of *Race Making and the Nation,* discuss some of the differences and similarities between South Africa and the United States with regards to race.

Both countries had legally encoded racial domination or segregation in the form of Jim Crow laws and apartheid. Both authors point out that top officials from both countries would say that neither country practices racism anymore; however, the enemy in both countries now has to do with the more subtle ramifications of racism and the legacy of racism. The important issue of inequality continues here and in South Africa. There is, according to Cose, "magical thinking" when it comes to race, where people act in ways that are clearly discriminatory, institutions clearly discriminate among people, outcomes are clearly unequal, but people in both countries say, "There's no bias, no racism, here."

The current discourse on race is one of inclusion, as stated by former president Clinton's initiative on race (One America in the 21st Century). We would argue that there is in the case of Africans and African Americans a shared or tangled memory of oppression and exploitation that intertwines, reinforces, and invites a shared identity and a shared historical narrative. The cultural and historical memory for Africans and African Americans is entangled rather than oppositional. The move from second-class citizenship to equality is a struggle shared by both groups, and we are not sure that we are ahead of the South Africans on this issue. Harvard law professor Lani Guinier delineates the merits of a proportional form of government. Guinier says that in South Africa, each party gets seats in the legislature in proportion to the number of votes it receives. Instead of a winner-take-all situation, in which the loser feels completely unrepresented when its candidate doesn't get the top number of votes, each vote counts to enhance the political power of the party of the voters' choice. Under South Africa's proportional representation and party-list system, if a party gets 10 percent of the votes, it gets 10 percent of the seats in the legislature. This represents a shift from counting specific populations to empowering the people and organizations that most effectively mobilize and motivate the voters to go to the polls (Guinier 2000, 226). Proportional representation would favor African Americans and other minorities in this country.

Another difference between both countries is how race is defined and legally established. Informally, the "one-drop rule" has come to denote in the United States that if you have any degree of African heritage or one drop of African blood in you, then you are Black (Davis 1996). In South Africa, the classification system is more flexible, with the designations as Black, Colored, and White. Each year people get the documentation necessary to reclassify themselves. In some cases, siblings from the same family have different racial classifications, which can contribute to conflict and turmoil within the same family. Due to this conflict and those found in both societies, it is no wonder that Marx and Cose agree that in both countries, if you are Black, chances are you are going to have significantly lower assets or wealth, and lower educational opportunities and attainments.

Both countries are dealing with an equality that is being newly acknowledged and or challenged. In the end, South Africa may emerge as a racial democracy, provided redress for past grievances are realized. Those vast inequalities are housing, level of Black education, health issues, and economic issues, none of which is going to change quickly in South Africa. A major difference for Black South Africans is that they have the confidence that at some point, if race is ignored, it would still leave them with considerable power, simply by virtue of being the majority in a democracy. Unfortunately, African Americans do not have that privilege or luxury. And there are many who would argue that the knowledge of being in control is a powerful psychological difference. You can give up political power but maintain economic power, and here lies a difficult problem for South Africans to resolve in this time of transition. True, both countries have much that should be forgotten if real progress is to be made, but we argue that it is important for both countries to remember and to remember the complete narrative, despite the pain.

We agree with Milan Kundera when he proffers that forgetting is a form of death ever present within life (1980, 235). Organized forgetting or cultural amnesia occurs when a big power wants to deprive a small country of its national consciousness. A nation that loses awareness of its past gradually loses itself. Just think of the implications that this has for Africans and African Americans. Both continue to and must recapture and reclaim our cultural identity. One historical past without the other would be incomplete and not authentic. What memories tell us more than anything else is the stakes held by individuals and institutions in attributing meaning to the past. The institutions of Jim Crow and apartheid have shaped and impacted our collective identity and in some instances continue to do so.

If we consider the technologies of memory, then cultural memory is produced through objects, images, and representations. Like the United States, there are numerous sites of memory in South Africa, including Museum-Africa and Robben Island (near Cape Town). These sites allow us to experience and re-create in different ways events in the past that are both painful as well as inspiring, and they lend themselves to the revelation of the spirit of humankind. How we engage with our pasts speaks much about how we live in the present and how we hope to live in the future.

The sharing of memory gives meaning to the past. Reading about our history and experiencing the origin of that cultural identity is a far more difficult communicative endeavor or encounter than anything else, because it goes to the very core of identity and self-esteem. Lauren Berlant describes a process by which a national symbol transform individuals into subjects of a collectively held history (Berlant 1991). What is the collectively held history of South Africa and the United States? Is it unthinkable to expect to live in a world without racism? A world before and after Jim Crow and apartheid? Nietzsche reminds us that only that which never ceases to hurt stays in the memory. In both countries, despite the inhumane treatment of some by others, there continues an effort to find the good. Both countries are dealing with a disruption of master narratives that deal with White supremacy and imperialism, and both countries are dealing with the destruction of previously held sacred truths. Cultural memory is produced and resides in cultural reenactment (Sturken 1997). Cultural memory serves the need for catharsis and healing. Specifically, memory for both Africans and African Americans provides a means to confront loss and transform that loss into healing and reaffirmation.

Both countries are experiencing the complicated issues of how one speaks about a cultural history and, even more importantly, who will listen. In this quest for cultural memory and history, each country must continue to contend with images shaped by the media, both positive and negative, and each country must deal with an inaccurate and sometimes hidden history. And so we reiterate that museums and the messages that can be conveyed within them can cause meaningful interactions with the public. The next section deals with our reaction to the National Civil Rights Museum and MuseumAfrica and how both museums reconnected our cultural heritage and past.

IMPACT OF TWO MUSEUMS

Young's questions help in articulating how museums evoke different meanings: "[W]hat meanings are generated when the temporal realm is converted to material form, when time collapses into space[?] . . . What is the relationship of time to space, place to memory, memory to time? . . . How does a particular place shape our memory of a particular time? And how does this memory of a past time shape our understanding of the present moment?" (1993, 15). When one stands as a descendant of those enslaved, the recreations of time and space inevitably evoke different meanings than they do for the descendants of those who were responsible for enslaving a race of people. Below is a description of the first author's situated response to these public spaces and the meanings experienced by the first author.

In June 1999, we were attending a national conference on race and ethnicity in higher education, and several of our colleagues (three males, one White and two Black) decided to visit the National Civil Rights Museum. The first time we found it, we immediately noticed that it was located in a deteriorating part of town. What type of statement is the city of Memphis making by placing the museum in this area? By the time we arrived, it had closed for the day, but we were able to see the balcony where Dr. King was assassinated. A flood of emotions caused all of us to be silent and introspective. We were in a place that demanded silence. We also knew that we had to return the next day to experience the entire museum.

When we later gained entry, we were moved by several exhibits in particular—the Rosa Parks bus experience, around which we lingered longer than we had anticipated, and Dr. King's two rooms, frozen in time. His last meal was on display, the one he had before he stepped on the balcony and into a sacred space in history.

For us, the museum was not only an intersection of race and space, but a disturbing intersection of past, present, and future. We were able to see and feel the past while being in the present, but we also had a discomforting vision of the future. We asked ourselves over and over again, "What has really changed?"

There has been progress in this country as far as race relations are concerned, but we concluded that it is not nearly enough progress. The experience was both inspirational and depressing at the same time in the same space. Although we teach courses dealing with civil rights and race relations, we still wondered how one race could hate another so. We also wondered if the issue of race would ever be resolved in this country in our lifetime.

The fact that this museum was able to speak to us in such a profound manner convinced us that the goal of the museum can be and must be realized by all people who live in this country. This history, this museum, must exist in a public way for all audiences to experience in varied and unique ways. The interactive exhibits do engage all of the viewer's senses, and for us this is one of the most effective ways to deal with the issue of race.

A few months later, along with our National Communication Association colleagues, we visited MuseumAfrica, located in Johannesburg, South Africa. We spent time in the Gandhi exhibit on the first floor of the museum, and for us it brought up Dr. King's connection to Gandhi's philosophy of nonviolence and the American civil rights movement. The most vivid memory and experience I (the first author of this essay) had was the exhibit "Birds in a Cornfield," which depicts the shantytowns of Black South Africans. Walking through the display of a township settlement brought a surge of dreadful emotions so strong that I had to withdraw from the rest of the group. I was literally overwhelmed to the point that I had to find a place to sit down. This space brought about a connection with the African American experience that was hard not to feel. Although I knew it was for display purposes, it was difficult for me to separate from this experience and merely be an observer. I suddenly realized that this was the same intense feeling that I had had at the National Civil Rights Museum in Memphis several months before. But what had this space communicated to me? It had communicated a feeling of oppression, hopelessness, and dismay.

We had read about the townships, and we had seen numerous images in the media, but none of that prepared us for what we experienced. It was much too real for us to comprehend. Later, after visiting some of the shantytowns in Soweto, we were amazed at how the museum accurately captured the feel and look of a township.

As in the case of the National Civil Rights Museum, we discussed with one of colleagues why we chose not to buy souvenirs. We felt that doing so would somehow trivialize our visit. Although we understand why people purchase T-shirts and other items from the National Civil Rights Museum, we sought in each case more information about the museum, and when possible, we purchased postcards depicting those exhibits that moved us. Ultimately, we used the information for educational purposes.

Both museums continue to have an impact on us, primarily because in a public space, each museum was able to provide exhibits necessary for us to encounter history, race, and culture on our own terms and in our own time. It was also a way to feel a stronger connection and bond with our African heritage and thus decrease the sometime frustrating experience two-ness in America. There was something calming about feeling that connection with one's ancestors.

CONCLUSION

This essay has focused on the role of race and its relationship to public space as demonstrated in the case of two museums—the National Civil Rights Museum in the United States and MuseumAfrica in South Africa. We have discussed the formation and role of cultural memory and in particular the historical and cultural connection between Africans and African Americans. We have also attempted to articulate the ways these museums as public spaces communicate meaning about history, values, race, and memory in these two countries, and we have also attempted to show why it is important for the past, however painful, to be remembered.

Our goal was to highlight the significance of two museums, and others like them, as well as their communicative function in society. We were concerned with the formation of cultural memory and the connection between African and African Americans. We hope to stimulate further research in the area of connections between Africans and African Americans by exploring the ways and forms in which public space can communicate cultural memory and identity.

REFERENCES

Adams, R. M. (1999). Forums, Not Temples. *American Behavioral Scientist* 42, 6: 968–76.
Ardener, S. (1993). Ground Rules and Social Maps for Women: An Introduction. In S. Ardener (Ed.), *Women and Space: Ground Rules and Social Maps,* rev. ed. (pp. 1–30). Providence, RI: Berg.
Asmal, K., L. Asmal, and R. S. Roberts (1996). *Reconciliation Through Truth.* Claremont, South Africa: David Philip.
Berlant, L. (1991). *The Anatomy of National Fantasy.* Chicago: University of Chicago Press.
Blair, C. (1999). Contemporary U.S. Memorial Sites as Exemplars of Rhetoric's Materiality. In J. Selzer and S. Crowley (Eds.), *Rhetorical Bodies* (pp. 16–57). Madison: University of Wisconsin Press.
Blair, C., M. S. Jeppeson, and E. Pucci (1991). Public Memorializing in Postmodernity: The Vietnam Veterans Memorial as Prototype. *Quarterly Journal of Speech* 77: 263–88.
Boylan, P. J. (1990). Museums and Cultural Identity. *Museums Journal* 90, 10: 29–33.
Brown, R. H., and B. Davis-Brown (1998). The Making of Memory: The Politics of Archives, Libraries and Museums in the Construction of National Consciousness. *History of the Human Sciences 11,* 4: 17–32.
Browne, S. H. (1995). Reading, Rhetoric, and the Texture of Public Memory. *Quarterly Journal of Speech, 81,* 237–50.
Davis, F. J. (1996). *Who Is Black? One Nation's Definition.* University Park, PA: Penn State University Press.
Du Bois, W. E. B. (1903). *The Souls of Black Folk.* Chicago: McClurg.
Eisterhold, G. L. (1992). National Civil Rights Museum. *Museum News 71*: 52–53.
Fleming, J. E. (1994). African American Museums, History, and the American Ideal. *The Journal of American History* (December): 1020–26.
Foote, K. E. (1997). *Shadowed Ground.* Austin: University of Texas Press.
Franklin, J. H. (1998). *One America in the 21st* Century: Forging a New Future. The President's Initiative on Race, The Advisory Board's Report to the President. Washington, D.C.: U.S. Government.
Gresson, A. D., III (1995). *The recovery of race in America.* Minneapolis: University of Minnesota Press.
Guinier, L. (2000). Back Talk: Voter Empowerment. *Essence.* (November): 226.
Hooper-Greenhill, E. (2000). Changing Values in the Art Museum: Rethinking Communication and Learning. *International Journal of Heritage Studies 6,* 1: 9–31.
Katriel, T. (1993). "Our Future Is Where Our Past Is": Studying Heritage Museums as Ideological and Performative Arenas. *Communication Monographs 60*: 69–75.
Kundera, M. (1980), Afterword: "A Talk with the Author Philip Roth." In *The Book of Laughter and Forgetting.* Trans. M. H. Heim. New York: Penguin.
MuseumAfrica (n.d.). Johannesburg, South Africa: MuseumAfrica.
National Civil Rights Museum (2000). Available at: http://www.midsouth.rr.com/civilrights/museum.html.
Ruffins, F. D. (1992). "Mythos, Memory, and History: African American Preservation Efforts, 1820–1990," in J. Karp, C. M. Kreamer, and S. D. Lavine (Eds.), *Museums and Communities* (pp. 506–611). Washington, D.C.: Smithsonian Institution Press.
Sturken, M. (1997). *Tangled Memories: The Viet Nam War, the AIDS Epidemic and the Politics of Remembering.* Berkeley: University of California Press.
Weisman, L. K. (1992). *Discrimination by Design: A Feminist Critique of the Man-made Environment.* Urbana: University of Illinois Press.
Young, J. E. (1993). *The Texture of Memory: Holocaust Memorials and Meaning.* New Haven, CT: Yale University Press.

Section 3

POLITICS OF DEFINING AFRICAN AMERICAN RHETORIC

CHAPTER 6

The Word at Work: Ideological and Epistemological Dynamics in African American Rhetoric

RICHARD L. WRIGHT

The dominant insight that surfaces throughout the history of African American rhetoric is captured by Langston Hughes in his poem "Freedom's Plow." That is, like the plow, which parts the earth in preparation for the planting of the seed, the word does work in the world. In the same way that the hand must hold fast to the plow and guide its action, the mind must grasp the word and hold on to a special relationship with it. The character of that relationship is best expressed through the often-cited African concept of nommo, which in essence is the word at work. Contrary to the Western lexicographical approach to the word, which defines it as "a sound or a combination of sounds, or its representation in speech or writing, that symbolizes or communicates a meaning" or alternatively as "something said: an utterance, a remark, or a comment" (both definitions are quoted from *The American Heritage Dictionary,* third edition, 1997), the nommo principle propels itself outward into and onto the world of being and doing. The spoken word (released through human agency) is not merely an utterance skillfully manipulated, but rather an active force and companion to human activity, which gives life and efficacy to what it names or verbally affirms. In effect, the African principle of nommo acknowledges that the word is both generative substance and mystical force, which are activated within a rhetorical event. As such, with nommo under one's command, the speaker is empowered to act in and on the world as Langston Hughes' plow acts in and on the earth. Both the plow and the word act to prepare the way for what follows from their necessary and prior activity.

For African Americans, given their history of struggle against the individual and institutional forces/structures of exploitation, marginalization, isolation, degradation, and annihilation, one might conclude that the primary work of the rhetoric produced by African Americans has been essentially in protest against such conditions, thereby utilizing all of the verbal skills at their command to mount a verbal assault upon such conditions in the hope of challenging, persuading, cajoling, frustrating, exhausting, and so on in order to prepare the ground for the seeds of Black liberation. Dominant and necessary as this rhetorical approach has been in the struggle of a people, where the word has been their primary defensive and offensive weapon, a closer look into aspects of African American rhetoric reveals the active presence of strong ideological and epistemic foundations regarding what it means to be in the world and to engage the world. In effect, to be different is to experience the world differently, which leads one to know the world differently, which leads one to think and feel differently and, ultimately, to talk differently. Much of African American rhetoric can be understood as a journey from being in the world to discourse about being and doing in the world, where the word is the primary means of forming, informing, and transforming consciousness.

Much of contemporary rhetorical theory has benefited from the work of language-oriented philosophers such as Mikhail Bakhtin (1973), Michael Foucault (1961), and Jacques Derrida (1976), who have produced important studies on questions of language and its relation to thinking, knowledge, power, discipline (social control), and the reproduction of structures of domination. It is insightful to apply concepts such as these to an analysis of aspects of African American rhetoric, especially since the African American community is a discourse community, and its discourse, like all discourse, is imbued with ideology (ways of thinking and believing) and epistemology (ways of knowing and relating to the world). Language is constructed socially, and its group-defining forms and functions emerge out of the contexts, contingencies, and communities that constitute it and which, in turn, are constituted by it. This constructive approach to African American rhetoric opens up valid and valuable perspectives on the role that language as discourse has played in the struggles of African Americans in an unfriendly land.

LANGUAGE AS IDEOLOGY AND EPISTEMOLOGY

We live, act, and have our being within the age of science, which means that the ideology of science is generally accepted as the dominant paradigm for validating what counts as knowledge of the world. In formal terms, this amounts to affirming that the modern world has embraced a "realist epistemology" that assumes there is an objective, material world external to and independent of our perceptual and cognitive processes, a world that possesses properties and qualities accessible to human experience and human understanding. It assumes further that it is possible to establish a mode of inquiry or rules of discourse that determine how to make claims, propositions, or hypotheses about this world, and how to present evidence and argument so that others can independently assess the issue of truth or falsity. Lastly, realist epistemology assumes that humans share a core of common characteristics as processors of information that allow them to agree about the accuracy or inaccuracy of statements made about this objective, external world. In this regard, the American pragmatic philosopher Charles S. Pierce stated, "The opinion which is fated to be ultimately believed by all who investigate, is what we mean by the truth, and the object represented in the opinion is the real" (1956, 306). In even stronger realist epistemological terms, Pierce affirmed:

> There are real things, whose characters are entirely independent of our opinions about them; whose realities affect our senses according to regular laws, and, through our sensations are as different as our relations to the objects; yet, by taking advantage of the laws of perception, we can ascertain by reasoning how things really are, and any man, if he have sufficient experience and reason enough about it, will be led to the one true condition. (p. 26)

What this epistemological perspective fails to acknowledge is its own perspectival character. That is, the realist consensus theory of truth is itself a perspective on truth.

Ironically, the scientific paradigm of the eighteenth-century Enlightenment was initiated as a challenge to and break with the perceived oppressive theocracy of Christianity, which privileged its theodicy in order to explain and legitimize an established social structure and hierarchy of power. In their assault upon the authority of the Christian church, the Enlightenment men of science argued that if the structures and arrangements of social life and the associated distribution of material surpluses and political power are the work of humans rather than ordained by God, then these man-made conditions could be remade by other humans, who could be empowered through the paradigm of science to search for new truths in a totally new way. In effect, the shift was away from a theocratic or theocentric worldview to an anthropocentric worldview. In the new challenge to the nature of truth, it was argued that nothing should be taken as true unless it could survive the tests of truth. This attitude or perspective elevated the uniqueness and worth of individuals, and contributed to the validation of human personality and individual human conscience. This attitude of science—that is, that humans had access to truth in ways that privilege human thinking—was intimately linked to the struggle for human liberation and human dignity that began during fifteenth-century Renaissance humanism, the manifesto of which was written by Pico della Mirandola:

> I have given you, O Adam, no fixed abode, and no visage of your own, nor any special gift, in order that whatever place or aspect or talents that you yourself will have desired, you may have and possess them wholly in accord with your desire and your decision. Other species are confined to a prescribed nature, under laws of my making. No limits have been imposed upon you, however; you determine your nature by your own free will, in the hands of which I have

> placed you. I have placed you at the world's center, that you may behold from this point whatever is in the world. And I have made you neither celestial nor terrestrial, neither mortal nor immortal, so that, like a free and able sculptor and painter of yourself, you may mold yourself wholly in the form of your choice. (Davies 1996, 479)

In effect, the challenge to theodicy placed the science of free inquiry into the domain of ideological critique and, therefore, at the center of the push for human liberation. The Enlightenment philosophers, in their attempt to weaken the power of the Church, argued that humans were enslaved in three ways: by physical coercion, by material deprivation, and by the tyranny of false ideas and institutionally imposed systems of belief. By breaking with the ideology and epistemology of the church, the new practitioners of science sought to place responsibility for the human condition and human action in human hands, preferring to seek answers to fundamental questions about the world within the concept and practice of human reason. As a liberation dynamic, the new science elevated and empowered human reason as an active agent in the process of understanding and changing the world.

Supportive of this notion of human action on the world was the Kantian view that all humans share the same set of fundamental moral interests, analogous to the shared realist epistemological assumptions about the material world. Therefore, as Kant argued, humans are able to exercise unconstrained reason and can arrive at common agreement on a desirable moral order. Kant, however, believed that this moral order, much like the physical laws of the universe, was already given and needed only to be "discovered," rather than produced through scholarly debate and resulting consensus. Although science as realist epistemology was linked to the struggle for human dignity and human liberation, it assumed that all humans share a common core of interests and reasons for their actions, such that it is possible for them to arrive at a common knowledge base about the external world as well as a common set of judgments as to the rightness or wrongness of any action in the light of these common interests.

It must be noted that the thinking that projected formal science as a dominant epistemological system failed to recognize the pivotal role of language in the process of cognizing and structuring reality. The energy of the new science was committed to the concept of reason or human rationality, and to a philosophical realism that affirmed the existence of a world exterior to human beings, with given or intrinsic properties that could be revealed via the new scientific mode of inquiry through which empowered minds were beginning to explore and describe the world. Proponents argued that it was through science that humans came to what was projected as a "true understanding" of the world, and were able to share this understanding through the vehicle of their respective languages.

THE CLASSICAL/OBJECTIVIST THEORY OF CATEGORIES

The worldview implicit in this approach together with the theory of categorization that supports it are predicated on a set of fundamental assumptions about the nature of reality, which can be explicitly stated as follows:

1. *Objectivist ontology.* Reality consists of objects or entities with fixed properties and relations, which are amenable to observation and description.
2. *Essentialism.* Among the properties of all entities, there are those essential properties that make the thing what it is, and without which it would not be the thing that it is. Other properties are purely accidental—that is, they may be present but are nonessential to the nature of the thing.
3. *Objectivist categorization.* All those entities that share a given property (or given properties) form a necessary category. The set of essential properties constitute the conditions that define the category.
4. *Objectivist knowledge.* Knowledge consists in correctly conceptualizing, categorizing, and articulating the identified objects and relations that constitute the real world.
5. *Language isomorphism.* Language is an adequate instrument for the formulation and communication of knowledge. Properly used, language is isomorphic in expression with the world that exists external to language. In effect, language reflects reality.

The realist epistemology is founded on these premises, which advance important claims regarding the perceptual, cognitive, and ideological nature of human beings. One such claim is that humans are capable of experiencing and conceptualizing "reality" as it is, in itself (i.e., the Kantian *an sich*). A second major claim is that human language functions adequately to state real-world dynamics in a straightforward and revealing manner. Both of these pivotal claims must be challenged in the light of (1) culture-specific differences in conceptualizing and categorizing "the world" and (2) the fact that in learning a language, the child must discover which domains of experience are relevant to categorization, together with the language-specific ways by which these categories are to be constructed. Finally, it is generally acknowledged that language never encodes all the features or dynamics of any situation or experience, no matter how much the language user seeks to accomplish that end. In effect, language is never a simple matter of choosing the right words that are isomorphic with or that reproduce in words what exists "out there" in the world. In this regard, Emile Durkheim stated the following:

> It is not at all true that concepts, even when constructed according to the rules of science, get their authority uniquely from their objective value. . . . In the last resort, the value which we attribute to science depends upon the idea which we collectively form of its nature and role in life; that is as much as to say that it expresses a state of public opinion. In all social life, in fact, science rests upon

> opinion. . . . Science continues to be dependent upon opinion at the very moment when it seems to be making its laws; for it is from opinion that it holds the force to act upon opinion. (1965, 486)

DISCOURSE, IDEOLOGY, AND EPISTEMICS

For much of the history of rhetoric, rhetoricians tended to agree with positivistic claims that only formal science yields *episteme* (knowledge and truth), whereas all else is *doxa* (mere opinion). Contemporary approaches have emphasized the essentially political nature of all discourse, together with the realization that all reality is constructed through symbolic/linguistic interaction. As a result, all theories of knowledge, including Kuhnian paradigm shifts, pragmatism, hermeneutics, existential phenomenology, ordinary-language philosophy, structuralism, poststructuralism, and postmodernism are all conceptions of knowledge embedded within a sociohistorical world. Within this conception, all explicit theories, like fictional narratives, sermons, or political speeches, require a discourse of formulation and articulation, which reflects particular perspectives and practices related to the intersubjective construction of reality. In effect, all knowledge and truth are embedded within the pragmatic, political, and linguistic/discourse processes that motivate their construction. In all forms of constructed knowledge, we are engaged in the creation and advocacy of some perspective on reality through the invention, manipulation, elaboration, and imposition of discourse. In this sense, there can be no such thing as a natural, neutral, or rhetoric-free language/discourse that merely reports the world as it is. Weigert claimed that analysts engage in "a naïve rhetoric of possible identity deceptions" whenever they "adopt the epistemological position that insists that a group of concepts and propositions is unbiased and value-free because it is labeled a 'theory'" (1970, 112). As such, words, expressions, and propositions have no determinate meaning value except within a determinate discursive formation. As noted, all discourse participates in the political. It was Marx who, in his thesis regarding the nature of domination, outlined the political role of a set of ideas or propositions, as well as the functional role of individual and class consciousness within the social formation and reproduction of domination. It is in this sense that discourse is, by nature, ideological in that it necessarily involves both social signification as well as the exercise of social power. Although Marx advanced a view of ideology as false consciousness (i.e., specific domination in thought of one class over another), he also viewed ideology as a necessary feature of the institutional structure of social formation: In this regard, Marx stated:

> The distinction should always be made between the material transformation of the economic conditions of production . . . and the legal, political, religious,

> aesthetic, or philosophic—in short, ideological—forms in which men become conscious of this conflict and fight it out. (1970, 79)

Informed by Marx's contribution, it was Althusser who framed the relevance of ideology to communications in a way that made it useful to analysts of rhetoric and discourse. His approach created a synthesis and allowed for an epistemological or epistemic theory of ideology:

> Ideology is indeed a system of representations, but in the majority of cases these representations have nothing to do with "consciousness" . . . it is above all as *structures* that they impose on the vast majority of men, not via their "consciousness" . . . it is within this ideological unconsciousness that men succeed in altering the "lived" relations between them and the world. (1969, 233)

Discourse as ideology works to create a certain subject formation (resulting from a particular social formation), projecting the individual (or group) into a particular structure of consciousness, which becomes the basis for acting to alter the character of the perceived conditions that sustain the formation of subjects. Within this conceptualization, individuals and groups as social formations exist and function, indeed live and have their being within discourse, itself the product of power relations and associated forms of domination. Whereas many rhetorical approaches limit their perspective on power and discourse dynamics to the power of discourse to accomplish certain intended effects or to the personal power of particular rhetors in given situations, the present argument supports the much broader approach that views all discourse as a constructive dynamic inseparable from the ideological and the epistemic. Indeed, one might ask what all of this means for individuals and qroups who seek to empower themselves though the use of new or alternative ideological/discursive formations, thereby claiming to alter the conditions for the generation and functioning of knowledge.

LANGUAGE, VOICE, INNOVATION, AND LIBERATION

The present discussion is sensitive to the complex dynamics involving language, ideology, knowledge, forms of domination, and liberation. In a liberating sense, it is an empowering act to problematize the nature and function of language and discourse as mediating forces in the construction of reality. That is, liberation begins with intellect in the form of critical consciousness, with a "knowing that," which essentially means that discourse, as an inherently ideological and epistemic system, serves to locate people into prescribed (and out of proscribed) places in the world. To problematize the world, given our fleeting, fluctuating understanding of it, is to be engaged in the business of making and remaking "what is" and, more importantly, "what is not." As the nineteenth-century German philosopher Wilhelm Humboldt creatively expressed it:

> Man lives with his objects chiefly—in fact, since his feeling and acting depend on his perceptions, one may say exclusively—as language presents them to him. By the same process whereby he spins language out of his own being, he ensnares himself in it; and each language draws a magic circle around the people to whom it belongs, a circle from which there is no escape save by stepping out of it into another. (Quoted in Cassirer 1946, 9)

Although Humboldt had in mind the linguistic (in the sense of a unitary system) and its cross-linguistic transfer, the present discussion argues that the "magic circle" can also operate within a language, through the activity of alternative discourses and their associated ideological and epistemic leanings. It is indeed sobering to know that language does not reflect reality in any direct and unmediated manner, but rather that language simultaneously has the power to reveal and the power to conceal, the power to clarify and the power to distort, the power to create and the power to destroy. By the simple act of constructing language in the naming and framing of reality, the individual commits the ultimate irony: Rather than naming and, thereby, exposing reality to him/herself, the individual reveals him/herself to him/herself as well as to others. In effect, what gets known through the use of language is not the nature of things, but the nature of the mind that attends to things. As such, humans live within the world (or is it the "whirl"?) of language as much as they live within the world outside of language. As Stein noted in this regard:

> One speaks of finding, losing, appreciating, recognizing, rejecting, searching for meaning, as though the referent of meaning were experienced to lie outside the self, occupying an objective reality distinct from the self. (1983, 393)

The knowledge that language/discourse reveals more about the knower than about the known and participates fully in the process of invention must be viewed as a positive, empowering, and liberating dynamic. It has been said that in the ultimate analysis, we are governed by force or by language. This being the case, scholarly study of discourse, as it relates to liberation, must concern itself with the following specific issues: (1) who constructs the language or discourse, (2) in what way(s), (3) for whose consumption, (4) for what purpose(s), and (5) with what effects or consequences for things cognitive and sociopolitical. Even a cursory glance at publications throughout the social sciences since 1960 reveals that a wide variety of *voices* are actively engaged in the business of describing, analyzing, critiquing, revising, constructing, and deconstructing the "essentialist" categories of knowledge as mere "inventions" of the general sociocultural constructedness of the world (e.g., Sollers 1989; Anderson 1991; Bernard-Donals and Glejzer 1998).

Within the academic community, it is now generally understood that all knowledge is the product of textual strategies found in language and rhetoric, which are best seen as productive forces that frame the ideological terms for the creation of new knowledge and new sources of power. New voices appropriate the word and through politicized use become actively engaged in the formulation of new or alternative perspectives. They function, in effect, as primary agents of liberation from the status quo of knowledge and its oxymoronic "invented essentialisms." Conceptualized in this way, the vaunted and lofty pursuit of truth as an absolute is not a productive scholarly activity. Rather, since truth is itself a constructed phenomenon, originating within and emerging from a particular discourse, what must be pursued are the "social, historical, and political conditions under which statements count as true or false" (McHoul and Grace 1998, 29).

By accepting the appropriated word in action, it is productive to conceive of discourse or rhetoric from the perspective of the varied contexts within which realities are constructed and lives lived. Within such an approach, we come face-to-face with the realization (1) that there are alternative truths, (2) that there are alternative ways of truth telling, (3) that the tellers of truth must be responsible for the ways in which they tell their truths, and (4) that all constructed truth presupposes a community of truth consumers whose individual and collective consciousnesses emerge from their rhetoric or discourse practices. Clearly, language as both a sociocultural institution and a politico-ideological practice is the agentive synergy that mediates between consciousness and the objects of consciousness.

From a liberation perspective, the critical question that must be pursued, then, is not so much what is true, but what is privileged! Bakhtin expressed this insight into the empowering and liberating potential of language in claiming that

> [l]anguage, for individual consciousness, lies on the borderline between oneself and the other. The word in language is half someone else's. It becomes "one's own" only when the speaker populates it with his own intentions, his own accent, when he appropriates the word, adapting it to his own semantic and expressive intention. Prior to this moment of appropriation, the word does not exist in a neutral and impersonal language (it is not, after all, out of a dictionary that the speaker gets his words!), but rather it exists in other people's mouths, in other people's context, serving other people's intentions: it is from there that one must take the word, and make it one's own. (Quoted in Gates 1988, 1)

REFLECTIONS AND CONNECTIONS TO AFRICAN AMERICAN RHETORIC

By "doing language" within the context of unrelenting existential oppression, African Americans have been compelled to create and to continually recreate themselves and their world(s). The word as weapon in the liberation dynamic is brought into relief by Zora Neale Hurston, who reminds us in her novel *Mules and Men* (1935) that "language is the last weapon left to the powerless (135)." Through the constructive act of doing language, by taking the word and making it their own, African American users of rhetoric have demonstrated that they live as much "in the word" as they live "in the world." An early reference to this alertness that African Americans have had to develop comes from Frederick Douglass in an article that he published in his newspaper *The Liberator* (May 26, 1865):

> It has been called by a great many names, and it will call itself by yet another name; and you and I and all of us had better wait and see what new form this monster will assume, in what new skin this old snake will come forth. (Quoted in Mullane 1993, 311)

An excellent example of how African Americans have dealt with "the old snake" from a rhetorical perspective is found within Ebonics or African American vernacular English. Throughout the decade of the 1960s, there was pervasive social, political, and academic attention focused on "lower-class" African American speech patterns in terms of their presumed linguistic and cognitive inadequacy. The self-serving arsenal of condemnatory establishment characterizations of African American speech patterns included such social science notions as "culturally and linguistically deprived," "language-deficient," "language of poverty," "language disadvantage," and "cognitive retardation." Through the use of such dismissive naming practices, the dominant group through the presumed neutrality of social science research, affirm their right to judge the Other and to impose its ideology as legitimate. However, consider the following exchange between a White middle-class social reformer and an African American gang member:

> *Student:* I know you have been deprived and are impatient with the power structure . . .
> *Gang Member:* Let me tell you something. I have never been denied 'cause I go out and steal what I want, man, take what I want, man, and I get it, boy! Anything I want in life, I'm going to get. And I'm not going to let no fool tell me, well, look here, Jack. You can't do this here because it's against the law, and that kind of bullshit. (Quoted in Brown 1987, 5)

In this language exchange, it is clear that the student as social reformer claims a right to alter some societal reality on behalf of the gang member, and in so doing presupposes knowledge and competencies superior to those of the gang member. Clearly, those who benefit from the status quo of power and domination tend to be more willing to align themselves with the normative rules and structures that ensure continuity and control in their daily lives. This is symbolized through the use of standard English, with its formal and distancing vocabulary and grammar.

However, consider the attitude and orientation of the gang member together with the language through which these are asserted. From the social reformer's perspective, the gang member's language is clear evidence of the roughness and crudity of a lower-class African American lifestyle. From an alternative rhetorical perspective, the gang member has taken the word and made it his own. His directness and resistance to powerlessness capture a dynamic often missed in most discussions and analyses of the African American vernacular. From a power perspective, Brown claims that there is "an inverse relationship between the degree of control over one's conditions of existence and the degree of control over one's existential actions" (1987, 19). This being the case, the use of standard English represents conformity to sanctioned norms of behavior, which buys one the security that conformity usually affords. Since the gang member has so little control over the actions of those who create the conditions of his existence, his aggressive and self-authorizing vernacular functions as a powerful and highly rational coping strategy for persons of his existential condition, who choose to confront uncertainty and lack of control with the language of self-empowerment, spontaneity, daring, self-assertion, resistance to illegitimate authority, and even hostility.

From a rhetorical perspective, this is hardly the language of "deprivation" or "disadvantage," but rather the language of self-assertion and defiance to imposed restrictions. In effect, the gang member is "doing language" in a way that serves as an authentic measure of his life and his rational approach to coping with what has been unfairly meted out to him. (Recognition of the gang member's aggressive "languageing" of his situation is not an endorsement of his actions, but rather an acknowledgment of the rationality embedded in his refusal to succumb to the conditions of his existence. The moral issue, of course, is the societal responsibility to hold accountable the forces that have created and sustained such conditions out of which such rationality emerges.) It is critical that the diagnostic power of rhetoric, language in action, and discourse studies continue to advance the frontiers of thinking about how humans have constructed their world and their relationship to the world. Those groups that have suffered the most from the conditions of marginalization and disempowerment have the most to teach about the role of language as ideology, as synergy, as catalyst, as force, as weapon in the ongoing and unrelenting struggle for liberation. More than any other, African American rhetoric is rich in traditional forms of expression as well as in its variable transformations over time, in response to the changing character of domination and the conditions of existence that it seeks to impose. As seen rhetorically, African Americans have been and continue to be actively engaged in the complex processes of reality construction through dynamic linguistic action through which they author, and are authorized by, their words.

This spirit of resistance and self-affirmation is no modern thing. Indeed, it has been the invisible hand that has accompanied African Americans throughout their experiences on American soil, and which was so well expressed by Zora Neale Hurston in an essay written in 1928 entitled "How It Feels to Be Colored Me," where she states:

> I am not tragically colored. There is no great sorrow damned up in my soul, nor lurking behind my eyes. . . . I do not belong to the sobbing school of Negrohood who hold that nature somehow has given them a lowdown dirty deal and whose feelings are hurt about it. . . . No, I do not weep at the world—I am too busy sharpening my oyster knife. (Quoted in Mullane 1993, 523)

Consider also Hurston's poignant phrase "tragically colored," which brings African Americans face-to-face with the thorny issue of race. As a sociopolitical construct, race was used throughout American history as an extension of Western eighteenth- and nineteenth-century academics who sought to study, describe, and rank the various peoples of the world, with the European always at the apex of any ranking. With the support of science and its essentialist epistemology, the word *race* was used to refer to a biological community with essentially innate characteristics, dispositions, and abilities. The presumed "scientific" underpinnings regarding the different "races" functioned not so much to advance knowledge about human diversity, but as a needed rationale for the imperialist politics of categorization, isolation, subjugation, exploitation, humiliation, and decimation. However, recognition of the origin and application of a phenomenon (however brutal) does not resolve the issue. That is, it is not enough to know, for example, that the founding fathers were members of the landed aristocracy and, therefore, guilty of blatant hypocrisy when they wrote and adopted the Declaration of Independence in 1776. Like the issue of race, the critical question is not what has it made of us, but what will we make of it. The fact that the founding fathers were hypocrites is insufficient in itself for this and future generations to dismiss their document as merely the tainted legacy of the noble dead. The rhetoric of the Declaration of Independence can be appropriated anew and made to be what it must be. It was Langston Hughes who said it best when he defined democracy as "what we do not have, but cannot cease to want."

As African Americans struggle with the thorny issue of race, they would do well to heed the argument being advanced in this essay: the sociocultural construction of reality together with the pivotal role of rhetoric and discourse in that process. As noted, the construct of race is of sociopolitical origin, and finds its foundation in the need to rank in order to rule. Indeed, the sinister invention of ethnic purity as an extension of the construct of race was exposed for what it was as early as 1905 by Charles Chestnut, the African American writer and political activist, who said, "We are told that we must glory in our color and zealously guard it as a priceless heritage." Recognizing the need to be responsibly skeptical about anything that the oppressor might desire for the oppressed, Chestnut resisted this plunge into the joys of ethnicity with a statement that deserves to be quoted at length:

> Frankly, I take no stock in this doctrine. It seems to me a modern invention of the White people to perpetuate the color line. It is they who preach it, and it is their racial integrity which they wish to preserve; they have never been unduly careful of the purity of the Black race. . . . Why should a man be proud any more than he should be ashamed of a thing for which he is not at all responsible? . . . Are we to help the White people to build up walls between themselves and us to fence in a gloomy back yard for our descendants to play in? (Sollers 1987, xvii)

Rhetoric is the dynamic constructive force that frames and structures social reality. For African Americans, the word has a special place and does its work in sacred space (our lives). Therefore, we should take to heart the words of Toni Morrison, who has reminded us that as African Americans, "we do language," and, dialectically, as we do language so do we do ourselves.

REFERENCES

Althusser, L. (1969). *For Marx.* Trans. Ben Brewster. London: Allen Lane.

American Heritage College Dictionary, third edition (1997). New York: Houghton Mifflin.

Anderson, B. (1991). *Imagined Communities.* London: Verso.

Bakhtin, M. (1973). *Marxism and the Philosophy of Language.* Trans. L. Matejka and I. R. Titunik. New York: Seminar Press.

Bernard-Donals, M., and R. Glejzer (1998). *Rhetoric in an Antifoundational World.* New Haven: Yale University Press.

Brown, H. B. (1987). *Society as Text: Essays on Rhetoric, Reason, and Reality.* Chicago: University of Chicago Press.

Cassirer, E. (1946). *Language and Myth.* Trans. S. Langer. New York: Harper and Row.

Davies, N. (1996). *Europe: A History.* London: Oxford University Press.

Derrida, J. (1976). *Of Grammatology.* Trans. G. Spivak. Baltimore: Johns Hopkins University Press.

Durkheim, E. (1965). *The Elementary Forms of Religious Life.* Trans. Joseph W. Swain. New York: Free Press.

Foucault, M. (1961). *Madness and Civilization: A History of Insanity in the Age of Reason.* Trans. R. Howard. London: Tavistock.

Gates, H. L. (1988). *The Signifying Monkey: A Theory of Afro-American Literacy Criticism.* New York: Oxford University Press.

Hurston, Z. N. (1935). *Mules and Men.* New York: Harper and Row.

Marx, K. (1970). *Contribution to a Critique of Political Economy.* Moscow: Progress Publishers.

McHoul, A., and W. Grace (1998). *A Foucault Primer: Discourse, Power, and the Subject.* New York: New York University Press.

Mullane, D. (Ed.) (1993). *Crossing the Danger Water: Three Hundred Years of African American Writing.* New York: Doubleday.

Peirce, C. S. (1956). *Chance, Love, and Logic.* New York: George Brazziler, Inc.

Sollers, W. (Ed.) (1989). *The Invention of Ethnicity.* New York: Oxford University Press.

Stein, H. (1983). Psychoanalytic Anthropology and the Meaning of Meaning. In B. Bain (Ed.), *The Sociogenesis of Language and Human Conduct.* New York: Plenum Press.

Weigert, W. (1970). The Immoral Rhetoric of Scientific Sociology. *The American Sociologist 5,* 2: 111–19.

CHAPTER 7

The Politics of (In)visibility in African American Rhetorical Scholarship: A (Re)quest for an African Worldview

MARK LAWRENCE McPHAIL

> *America is woven of many strands; I would recognize them and let it so remain. It's "winner take nothing" that is the great truth of our country or of any country. Life is to be lived, not controlled; and humanity is won by continuing to play in the face of certain defeat. Our fate is to become one, and yet many—This is not prophecy, but description. Thus one of the greatest jokes in the world is the spectacle of the Whites busy escaping Blackness and becoming Blacker every day, and the Blacks striving toward Whiteness, becoming quite dull and gray. None of us seems to know who he is or where he's going. (Ellison 1947, 435–36)*

It has been more than half a century since Ralph Ellison articulated his definitive discussion of one of the fundamental preoccupations of the African American experience: the need to assert one's existence—one's visibility—in a culture suffering from a certain kind of blindness, an inability to see the humanity of others and ultimately of self. Ellison believed that African Americans offered the nation a potentially transformative consciousness, one in which difference and diversity could be celebrated instead of subordinated. His insights augured an intellectual trajectory that would manifest itself in critical projects that revealed an underlying coherence despite their different disciplinary perspectives. In philosophy, psychology, political science, literary studies, and communication, African American scholars challenged the prevailing intellectual paradigms of Western thought, making visible the rhetorical, historical, political, and spiritual contributions and influences of peoples of African descent, and unveiling the moral and epistemological incoherence of American culture in particular, and Western "civilization" in general.

In the field of communication the most important challenge to the discipline's European biases and influences emerged in the work of Molefi Kete Asante. Asante's Afrocentric ideas have clearly been the most important and pervasive influence on African American rhetorical theorizing. Although not fully appreciated by scholars in the discipline of communication (Jackson 2000), Afrocentricity has profoundly shaped contemporary Black thought in communication and has significantly influenced the theoretical and methodological directions of research in our field. Although Afrocentricity is often understood to reflect the underlying epistemological and ontological assumptions of an African worldview, many of its critics have suggested that its centrist emphasis has served to obscure that worldview instead of clarifying it. Indeed, at the same time that Asante was beginning to conceptualize Afrocentricity, another scholar of African descent was articulating an alternative conceptualization of the character and consciousness of African-inspired theories of language and communication.

In "The Quest of an African World View" Chief Fela Sowande presented such an approach to communicative inquiry. Unlike Afrocentric theory, which is explicitly premised upon "the belief in the centrality of Africans in post-modern history" (Asante 1989, 6), Sowande's understanding of an African-inspired communication theory assumes that "the world view that is enshrined in African traditions, folklore, and mythology . . . is not the preserve of the African or of peoples of African descent" (Sowande 1974, 111). In this essay I wish to juxtapose the visibility of Afrocentricity and the invisibility of Sowande's perspective in contemporary African American rhetorical theory by comparing and contrasting Sowande's "Quest" with Molefi Asante's essay "Theoretical and Research Issues in Black Communication" (1974a).

Initially, I'll explore the political implications of the visibility of Afrocentricity and the invisibility of Sowande's quest for an African worldview through an examination of how the latter informs two of the less visible trajectories in African American rhetorical scholarship. Next, I will argue that the lack of attention to the issues raised by Sowande almost thirty years ago continues to limit the intellectual and political scope of African American rhetorical thought in ways that call for a (re)quest for an African worldview that would be just as inclusive in practice as it is in theory. Finally, I will suggest that African American rhetorical scholarship, as a field of inquiry that was itself a response to a lack of visibility in "mainstream" publications, can scarcely afford to ignore any perspective on the contributions of people of African descent that enriches our understanding of language and communication in America. While the field of African American rhetorical scholarship has become more inclusive over time, the contributions of many scholars writing in this area remain unseen, and their voices, unfortunately, remain unheard. I offer this essay as an attempt to begin to remedy this lack of attention to the contributions of these writers, and initiate a more critical conversation about the politics of invisibility in African American rhetorical scholarship.

THE MARKINGS OF AN AFROCENTRIC RHETORIC: THE QUEST FOR COMMUNICATIVE VISIBILITY

Although people of African descent have had a significant impact on the quality and character of language and communication in America, the theoretical and critical study of African American rhetoric is a relatively recent phenomenon.[1] In the early 1970s, a number of studies authored by African American scholars surfaced in the literature and established a clear directions for the theoretical and critical development of the study of African American communication. "There are some who are still unwilling to admit the role of institutional and individual racism in stifling scholarship in the area of Black Rhetoric/Language/Communication," (p. 1) explained Jack Daniel in an issue of *Today's Speech* that focused on African American discourse. "However, we have reached a point where further discussion of the causes may serve only to bring further delay and neglect of the study of Black Communication. It is time to build" (1971, 1). The building of Black communication as a discipline involved an important movement from the descriptive studies that had dominated critical analyses of African American rhetoric to a theoretical examination of its unique and culturally influenced dimensions. At the forefront of this movement was a young professor of rhetoric from the University of California at Los Angeles: Molefi Kete Asante (formerly known as Arthur Smith).

Smith's 1974 essay, "Markings of an African Concept of Rhetoric" established the foundations for a reconceptualization of rhetoric that would significantly impact African American studies of language and communication.[2] The essay begins by challenging the hegemonic assumptions of Western rhetorical studies and arguing for the legitimacy and cultural significance of African approaches to, and perspectives on, discourse. "Any interpretation of African rhetoric must begin at once to dispense with the notion that in all things Europe is teacher and Africa is pupil," he explains. "To raise the question of an imperialism of the rhetorical tradition is to ask a most meaningful question, because Western theorists have too often tended to generalize from an ethnocentric base" (1974a, 13). Implicit in Asante's analysis is a critique of the epistemological foundationism of Western rhetorical thought, a foundationism that placed emphasis on rational, "objective," and abstract communicative principles and practice. Asante emphasized the expressive and embodied dimensions of language largely neglected or subordinated by traditional Western rhetorical theory and criticism, and argued that discursive practices were deeply embedded in both cultural consciousness and historical action.

Asante juxtaposed the foundationist emphases of Western rhetorical theory with the integrative impulses of African thought and culture. Drawing upon scholarship that pointed to the communal and collective character of African societies, and the principle of "art for life's sake" that distinguished African and other traditional aesthetic systems from Western formalism,

Asante suggested that while one could not speak specifically of "an African Mind," one could draw generalizations about the role of language and communication in traditional African societies. "African society is essentially a society of harmonies inasmuch as the coherence or compatibility of persons, things and modalities are at the root of traditional African philosophy," he explained (p. 15). In addition to an emphasis on coherence, Asante notes that an African-centered approach to discourse emphasizes relationality in contrast to the Western preoccupation with reductionism, and views discourse in terms of its role in the creation of social stability and transformation.

Indeed, Asante establishes in this essay the strong emphasis on contrasting Western and African cultures that would characterize this theoretical orientation, which would later evolve into an Afrocentric approach to communication. He writes:

> Thus, unlike the Euro-American, the African seeks the totality of an experience, concept or system. Traditional African society looks for unity of the whole rather than the specifics of the whole; such a concentration, which also emphasizes synthesis more than analysis, contributes to community stability because considerations in the whole are more productive than considerations in detail. This concept has a very real bearing upon the making of a public discourse. (p. 17)

The distinctions that Asante drew in this early essay would become much more pronounced in a second essay that appeared three years later. In "Theoretical and Research Issues in Black Communication," Asante drew clear boundaries between the assumptions at work in the discourses of peoples of African descent and those at work in Western accounts of rhetoric.

The three assumptions outlined in the section of the essay subtitled "Metarhetorical Theory" would become foundational preoccupations of much of the rhetorical theory and criticism produced by African American scholars that would emerge over the next thirty years. Asante argued, first, that "[*r*]*hetoric as a concept is foreign to the African ethos*"; second, that "*Africans in America place considerable reliance on rhythm in expression*"; and finally, that "[*s*]*poken discourse by Afro-Americans suggests specific criteria for evaluation*" (p. 139, italics in original). Asante and his colleagues addressed several other key issues that would influence theoretical and critical inquiry in African American public address for several decades, yet none reflected more definitively the theoretical and critical concerns that would emerge in Afrocentric scholarship. The emphasis on metatheoretical and epistemological concerns and the focus on the centrality of African ideals and values as the normative framework for the discussion and analysis of Black communication would become hallmarks of Afrocentric scholarship in the discipline of communication.

Jackson (in this volume) echoes Asante's emphasis on metatheoretical and cultural concerns in his essay "Afrocentricity as Metatheory: A Dialogic Exploration of Its Principles." He notes that Afrocentricity represents a powerful response to the "epistemological and cosmological myopia" of traditional Western scholarship, and offers Afrocentric metatheory as an inclusive and socially responsible method for cultural criticism and intellectual inquiry. He notes that Afrocentricity places a primary emphasis on epistemology, and emphasizes the generative and transformative potential of consciousness and discourse. For Jackson, Afrocentricity offers an alternative to the essentializing tendencies of Western foundationism, and advances an inclusive epistemic stance that values difference and affirms cultural diversity.

Like Asante, he views Afrocentricity as "a direct counternarrative to a most obvious and hegemonic grand narrative presupposing that all that is not of Europe is not of worth." An emphasis on community, collectivity, spirituality, and morality is at the heart of the Afrocentric counternarrative, and unlike Western rhetorical theory, which has traditionally emphasized the representative dimensions of discourse, Afrocentric theory stresses the generative possibilities of language and its potential to shape and transform reality. Jackson's essay provides a clear indication of the continuities that have been sustained in Afrocentric approaches to the study of communication, as well as the evolutionary shifts that have occurred over the past three decades.

Richard Wright's essay (in this volume) also offers insights into how both continuity and change have marked the development of Afrocentric communication scholarship, and illustrates the ways in which Asante's three assumptions have evolved over time. Wright takes into account the transformations that have occurred in traditional Western rhetoric, in particular the shift from representational to generative conceptualizations of language and the corresponding recognition that discourse is always grounded in context. For Wright, rhetoric is no longer reducible to persuasion and thus, like nommo, offers an understanding of discourse as generative, as constitutive of reality.

Indeed, it is not rhetoric per se that is foreign to the African ethos, but the conceptual framework that limits rhetoric to a representational view of language. Wright juxtaposes this traditional emphasis with an understanding of rhetoric "that views all discourse as a constructive dynamic inseparable from the ideological and the epistemic (knowledge)." Rhetoric understood in these terms offers a powerful heuristic for explicating the culturally significant dimensions of African American language and communication that are too often obscured or ignored by the normative constraints of traditional rhetorical inquiry. Historically, Western rhetorical theories have embraced Aristotelian assumptions that define language as representational and amoral. Traditional or classical African thought, in contrast, embraces the creative and constitutive power of the word, and aligns language with morality, spirituality, and social responsibility. While Wright focuses on Ebonics as a specific example of African American discourse that reveals the theoretical complexities entailed by the shift from representational to generative rhetorics, his concluding observation that "the word has a special place and does its work in sacred space" has implications for the critical consideration of Black communication as well.

The visibility of Afrocentricity in African American rhetorical scholarship illustrates its importance for the theoretical and critical understanding of discourse produced by and for persons of African descent. While the uses and applications of Afrocentric methods and theories have developed and evolved over time, Asante's foundational concerns have remained central to the efforts of communication scholars who have embraced this perspective, and in returning to those concerns it is possible to engage in the type of self-critical analysis that Jackson correctly notes must be part of the continued evolution of Afrocentric theory. His concluding statements suggest the need for coherence between Afrocentric principles and practices: "Any theory whose theorists contradict its primary epistemological, axiological, ontological, and cosmological tenets will be ephemeral. Afrocentrists must be clear about what this term [Afrocentricity] means. And, eventually, it will be imperative that its theorists offer candid critiques of its utility as it matures." I wish to pursue this search for coherence by examining Asante's early work in relation to that of one of his contemporaries, Chief Fela Sowande. While I do not believe that my work would be considered part of the Afrocentric tradition, I do believe that my scholarship reflects the underlying assumptions of what Sowande calls "an African worldview." The distinction between the two, I believe, addresses the issues raised by Jackson, and offers important directions for scholars of African American rhetoric.

At the same time that Asante was establishing the foundational principles and assumptions about the African roots and influences of African American rhetoric, one of his contemporaries was engaged in a similar exploration of the significance of African culture and society for our understanding of discourse. Chief Fela Sowande, a Nigerian-born concert organist, composer, conductor, and scholar, contributed an essay titled "The Quest of an African World View: The Utilization of African Discourse" to the collection in which Asante's "Theoretical and Research Essays in Black Communication" appeared. Both men focused on the epistemological, moral, and spiritual contributions of traditional African cultures, and both emphasized the participatory and integrative aspects of African thought and consciousness. Both men also saw in traditional African cultures the possibility of an identity and consciousness grounded in *coherence*—in Asante's words, the "compatibility of persons, things and modalities" (1974a, TK), and in Sowande's an "*inseparable organic unity in an organic relationship to that organic whole* which is life itself" (p. 111, italics in original). The perspectives advanced by the two men, however, were distinguished by the ways in which they conceptualized coherence and its relationship to African culture.

Asante viewed culture as a primary determinant of consciousness, while Sowande believed that both culture and consciousness were subordinate to a more fundamental unity, one that transcended all forms of difference and identity. The centrality of African culture is at the heart of Asante's theory, and it is this cultural orientation that reveals the most fundamental aspects of Afrocentric consciousness and communication. For Sowande, however, African culture reflects an undifferentiated reality, an "indivisible whole, in which the world of the invisible spirits, the world of nature, and the world of humankind are but three 'distinguishable but inseparable' aspects, interdependent, interacting, in an organic relationship" (p. 89). Sowande suggests that this whole is greater than either culture or consciousness, and any attempt to place either of these at the center of existence or inquiry can be problematic. He explains that

> in the concept "African world view" it is the *world view* that is crucial, not *African*. For no consideration whatever can we afford to lose sight of this most vital point; otherwise, any intended quest for an African world view will surely and rapidly degenerate into a feverish hunt for a new ideological gimmick which can be used for questionable ends as political counters with the inevitable results of further intensifying race-consciousness as an ally to race hate. (p. 111)

Unlike Asante's theory of Afrocentricity, which "pursues a voice distinctly African-centered in relationship to external phenomenon" (quoted in Jackson, this volume), Sowande's African worldview eschews attempts to establish as distinct any manifestation of culture or identity. "Once you intend in your mind to compartmentalize the one humanity into this and that unrelated groups, you have ensured that with every step you seem to take toward your objective you are ten times further away" (p. 111). Afrocentricity, as defined and developed by Asante, would in Sowande's terms be "a view of the world," which he suggests is significantly different from a worldview.[3]

For Sowande, the very act of drawing a distinction between Afrocentric and Eurocentric viewpoints undermines the value of an African worldview, which "offers, to Blacks and non Blacks alike, a chance to recover equipoise and stability," and "to shadow forth in our daily lives the beauty of the art of living" (p. 113). Instead of contrasting Afrocentric and Eurocentric thought, Sowande searches for their points of implicature, suggesting that the cosmological principles of the African worldview are affirmed in the works of Western European esoteric thinkers such as Carl Jung, whose theories depart from the dialectical assumptions dominating Western psychology and gravitate toward a recognition of interrelationship and coherence as the foundation for social and symbolic activity. The Afrocentric and Eurocentric are, for Sowande, inseparable and deeply implicated in each other. The belief that they can be separated from each other, even for the sake of analysis, leads to a reification of the very social and symbolic wounds that an African worldview might heal.

Sowande's analysis confronts two seemingly contradictory impulses that have marked the evolution of Afrocentric thought in the discipline of communication. First, his observations anticipate some of the criticisms that have been leveled against Afrocentric scholarship. Second, his articulation of the quest for an African worldview augurs the movement toward inclusivity and self-reflexive critique revealed in the writings of African American rhetorical scholars. Ultimately, he draws the same conclusions as Asante about the ends that the quest for an African worldview achieves: "The utilization of African discourse has but one goal, which is that the individual should gain and learn to use effectively a practical understanding of life, and the processes of life," he concludes, "and with this a clear, accurate, tested, tried, and proven picture of how, where, when, and why man fits into the picture" (p. 114). The quest for an African world view is, for Sowande, a journey toward visibility, wholeness, and a recognition of the inseparability of self and other in the world.

Ironically, however, Sowande's work is largely invisible in the discipline of communication and African American rhetorical studies. This may be attributable to the fact that his contributions to the discipline were limited largely to this essay, and that his major works were in the areas of aesthetics and ethnomusicology. Also, prior to his death in 1987, he "refused to put before the uninitiated public" his opinions and philosophy.[4] His work has, nonetheless, been labeled "Afrocentric," and he is considered by those he influenced at Howard University, the University of Pittsburgh, and Kent State University as an important thinker in this tradition. Apart from my own (1994) research on rhetoric and race, however, I am unaware of any other scholars in either Afrocentric or rhetorical studies who have drawn upon his work. The lack of attention to his work offers scholars in both of these areas an opportunity to pursue the type of self-reflexive inquiry that Jackson calls for, and also provides important insights into the politics of invisibility in African American rhetorical theory.

Those politics result too often not in the inclusive and diverse study of the rhetoric of Black Americans, but in the study of Black rhetoric that is inclusive of some voices and exclusive of others. A very similar situation gave rise to the discipline of Black communication, since up until the 1970s, rhetorical studies of African American discourses were largely authored by European Americans and based upon Western theoretical and methodological approaches. Although that tradition of inquiry has continued up until the present day, there are clear separations between the intellectual trajectories of African and European American scholars writing in this area.[5] From an Afrocentric perspective, African American rhetorical research has largely become defined as studies of Black language and discourse written by African Americans, instead of the more inclusive notion of the study of African American discourse written by rhetorical scholars. The distinction, though subtle, is important: The first perspective implicitly suggests that African Americans, by virtue of race or culture, are more capable of rendering authentic analyses of Black communication. This suggestion is, I believe, at odds with the fundamental assumptions of an African worldview, and reflects a somewhat problematic view of the world.

Scholars in the areas of literary studies have offered compelling critiques of this view of the world, critiques from which researchers in Afrocentric and Black communication studies could learn much. Michael Awkward's excellent essay "Race, Gender, and the Politics of Reading" (1988) advances this argument in relation to the arguments presented by African American and feminist critics who privilege race and gender in terms of "the authority of experience." This position, he believes, merely reifies the assumptions at work in canonical discourses of Whiteness and maleness that subordinate the voices of "others" to the realm of the invisible. Within the context of African American rhetorical studies, reliance upon the politics of experience is even more problematic when the voices of scholars of color are suppressed or ignored because they are not viewed as "authentic" or valid. Perhaps this is why Sowande's important contribution to Afrocentric and rhetorical studies has achieved such limited visibility. The limited visibility of my own work and that of my colleague Aaron David Gresson III in the discipline of communication in general, and Black communication studies in particular, lead me to believe that the politics of invisibility continue to undermine the potential for an inclusive and integrative vision of African American scholarship.

Ron Jackson (2000) has noted the lack of attention to Gresson's work and my own, as well as Asante's, in mainstream communication research. In African American rhetorical scholarship, however, while Asante's contribution has been clearly acknowledged, neither my research nor Gresson's has been recognized or addressed in any systematic manner, despite the fact that between the two of us we have contributed several dozen essays on the subject. I've written elsewhere (McPhail and Dace 2000) how my work on Afrocentricity, in particular, was dismissed by scholars of color and culture, and do not feel the need to revisit these issues here except to note that apart from Jackson's acknowledgment, my work has been largely invisible in research on African American rhetoric and race. I do, however, wish to discuss at length the lack of visibility of Gresson's work, since his contribution to the field of rhetorical studies is extensive and provocative. His early work on minority epistemology (1977) has been ignored by most African American rhetorical scholars, and his important book *The Recovery of Race in America* (1995) has yet to receive the recognition that it deserves from researchers writing in this area, despite being the recipient of an Eastern Communication Association book award.

Gresson's other writings include *The Dialectics of Betrayal: Sacrifice, Violation and the Oppressed* (1982), and a critique of *The Bell Curve,* co-edited with

Kincheloe and Steinberg, *Measured Lies:* The Bell Curve *Examined* (1996). Although his contributions to African American rhetorical theory and criticism have spanned over two decades, Gresson's work has been largely invisible and continues to be so. And yet Gresson's work in theory and practice reflects, I believe, the fundamental assumptions of an African worldview. His concluding comments about the need for a "rhetoric of enlargement" in *The Recovery of Race in America* sound remarkably like Sowande's comments concerning the utilization of African discourse. Enlargement, he writes,

> must be dialectically derived in the context of an existential, day to day struggle. More precisely, it must be part of a global, species-specific maturation. But it requires, as well, that we acknowledge the persistence of racism and that we collectively begin the systematic rebuilding of a healthier, more inclusive set of formative images. We must delimit these images enough to inspire identification and involvement, yet make them expansive enough to embrace the integrity of the world community. (p. 214)

For Gresson, the quest for an African worldview involves the process of recovery, which "is ultimately concerned with the reintegration with, or reconnection to, the group. This may be a clue to the rhetorical format of larger, broader based encounters and dialogues toward relational justice and reconnection. In this sense, we all need to keep talking" (p. 214). Although his work is clearly aligned with Sowande's notion of an African worldview, Gresson's scholarship is not considered Afrocentric. Instead, it advances a critique of Afrocentricity that echoes the concerns advanced by Sowande.

Gresson views Afrocentricity as a recovery narrative that, though problematic on some levels, makes an important contribution to the quest for an African worldview. "Rhetorically, the Afrocentric position is an exigency: it constitutes a part of that great external pressure an individual apprehends as oppression is to be resisted" (p. 55). Afrocentricity refuses to accept invisibility imposed from without by speaking "in the language of the voice within" (Burke, quoted in Gresson 1995, 55). Asante's Afrocentricity, according to Gresson, "implies a mindfulness of the racial past and present: he is all too aware of the immense need for racial loyalty and collective action in American society" (p. 55). It is this immense need, I believe, that at one and the same time creates and undermines the transformative possibilities of language, life, and method envisioned by the architects of Afrocentricity and embodied in the quest for an African worldview.

Thus, for contemporary African American rhetorical scholars, our greatest challenge may be to be as inclusive in our deeds as we have been in our words. We cannot afford to ignore that both Afrocentricity and African American rhetoric are rooted in a double consciousness, neither distinctly African nor European, but something of both. It is this double consciousness that Ellison, like Du Bois (1903) before him, saw as the key to our fate and potential. Our future as Americans was, Ellison believed, "to become one yet many" (1947, 435). This may indeed be the great truth of our time, and whether we choose to pursue Afrocentricity, complicity, recovery, or traditional rhetoric, it is ultimately the path that we must travel in the quest of an African worldview and its coherent understanding of our interrelatedness and implicature. As a definitive statement of the assumptions and values of that worldview, Sowande's observations about the Black experience of religion could just as easily be applied to our experience of rhetoric: "Therefore, Black Experience of Religion must be examined in terms of Human Experience of Religion, and not as something existing outside human experience, that of the Human Race within which, whether we like it or not, the Black Race is totally contained."[6] Like Du Bois and Ellison, Sowande suggests that people of African descent possess an integrative and coherent consciousness that has the power to transform and reconstruct the world and view of the world that historically have been defined and undermined by the color line. In short, Sowande believed that an African worldview offers the possibility of moving beyond the complicity of negative difference and division, and toward a more coherent and cooperative approach to social and symbolic interaction.

FROM COMPLICITY TO COHERENCE: A (RE)QUEST FOR AN AFRICAN WORLDVIEW

Perhaps no area of inquiry in the discipline of communication more clearly reflects the prophetic reading of race that Ellison offers in the quotation that begins this essay than the Afrocentric study of Black rhetoric. Here we witness in the attacks of those who would defend Eurocentricity and the privileges of Whiteness the joke of those who are "busy escaping Blackness and becoming Blacker every day." Yet we also witness, in the words and deeds of those who would merely invert the binaries of difference and identity, "the Blacks striving toward Whiteness, becoming quite dull and gray" (1947, 435). And yet in African American rhetorical studies, despite the politics of invisibility, my sense is that we are coming to a much better understanding of who we are and where we are going. Our greatest challenge now, perhaps, is to decide just who gets included in that "we." Like America, the study of African American rhetoric is made up of many strands, and I believe that it is possible for us to celebrate them all. While we cannot ignore the realities of race, culture, difference, and identity, it is imperative that we take seriously Jackson's call for coherence between our theories of knowledge, existence, and metaphysics and how they reveal themselves in our social and symbolic action.

This is, I believe, the essential end of the quest for an African worldview: not the erasure of race, but a recognition of how easily its logics inflect and infect our view of the world. Asante's commentary on Ellison's *Invisible Man* reveals some of the difficulties we may face in attempting to pursue this quest in the terms outlined by Sowande: "In the United States, Ralph Ellison, even after the metaphorical brilliance of *The Invisible Man*, could identify more closely with James Joyce than with Richard Wright. And Frank Yerby has simply sought the faraway fringes of consciousness to take him away from his African self" (1993, 144). Here we see the privileging of "African" over worldview that so concerned Sowande, and the implicit claim that the racial self must have priority over the human self. Asante goes on to make this claim explicit.

> Too many of our artists and intellectuals have tried to divest themselves of their heritage in order to become "just human beings," by which they almost always mean just Europeans. It is impossible for anyone to be just a human being; we are always, within some context, some culture. I do not say that this is the way things ought to be or will forever be. I am just recognizing the facts of the last five centuries. No conscious person of African descent can allow himself or herself the luxury of talk of being just a human being. (1993, 144)

The contradictions and ironies here are numerous and troubling. Many of the sources from which Asante's theories were derived were based upon European interpretations of African culture, interpretations that African philosophers have dismissed as "ethnophilosophy";[7] scholars of European descent continue to contribute to and be identified with Afrocentric theories and methods;[8] and Sowande, an African by birth as well as descent, if one takes Asante's judgment literally, is attempting to escape from his "true" African self.

Ellison's words again come to mind: "It's winner take nothing." Or at least nothing other than the power to determine who is invisible and who is not. This is the sad truth of our time, and just as it troubled Sowande, so should it trouble us all. Sowande's quest of an African worldview is an affirmation of the very humanity, the very wholeness that Asante would call a luxury, on one hand, yet define as essential to the Afrocentric vision on the other.[9] This seems to me, to use Jackson's terms, to "contradict [the] primary epistemological, axiological, ontological, and cosmological tenets" of an African worldview. It lays the foundation for a context within which some voices will be heard and others will not, where some critical perspectives will be privileged and others dismissed, where the works of some scholars will be celebrated and those of others overlooked. I do not believe that this is how things need to be or are destined to remain. I am just recognizing the facts of my experience as an African American rhetorical scholar whose contributions to the field have remained largely invisible, as have the contributions of scholars such as Sowande and Gresson.

I do not believe that this is simply because our scholarship advances critiques of Afrocentricity, nor because our research is not considered "Afrocentric enough." But I am certain that we are not the only voices in the field of African American rhetorical studies that remain unheard, nor that ours are the only scholarly contributions that remain unseen. Nonetheless, I am hopeful that the continued maturation of Afrocentric and African American rhetorical studies will result in an inclusivity that cuts across race and culture, that defines African American rhetoric in terms of what I have described in my work as "dialogic coherence" (1995): a capacity to integrate diverse conceptions of reality, culture, and identity. In honor of the late Chief Fela Sowande, this is my (re)quest for an African worldview, and I conclude, as did Ellison, with the question that perhaps most clearly reveals the sentiments that accompany that quest: "Who knows but that, on the lower frequencies, I speak for you?" (Ellison 1947, 439).

NOTES

1. Prior to the 1960s, the major journal in the field of communication, *The Quarterly Journal of Speech*, contained few studies in communication that addressed issues of race either directly or indirectly. Prior to the 1950s the few essays that appeared in *QJS* considered the normative and performative implications of "Negro Dialect" "slave speech" minstrelsy (Moody 1944), preaching (Pipes 1945), and speech training in historically Black colleges (Boulware 1947). Little of this research prior to the 1950s was conducted by persons of African descent, and none of it incorporated or valued as unique the perspectives that African Americans brought to the understanding of rhetoric in the American context.

   During the 1950s and 1960s, however, this began to change. Essays appeared that examined the rhetorics of political protest (Kerr 1959), the *Brown v. Board of Education* Decision (Strother 1963), and African American protest and opposition (Haiman 1967; Scott and Smith 1969; Gregg, McCormack, and Pedersen 1969). The 1970s also saw a significant increase in the number of journal articles and book-length studies that addressed issues of African American rhetoric and social protest, as well as writings by African Americans. In the 1960s, studies by Roy Hill (1964), Molefi Kete Asante (née Smith; 1969, 1971), and Robert Scott and Wayne Brockreide (1969) chronicled the politics of racial revolt and Black revolution, while in the 1970s, African American scholars called for an expansion of the communication discipline's boundaries to address and accommodate approaches to rhetoric that departed from traditional notions of persuasion and argument.
2. Asante's contributions to the field of African American rhetorical theory and criticism are extensive. His numerous books include *Transracial Communication* (1973); *The Rhetoric of Black Revolution* (1969); *Language, Communication, and Rhetoric in Black America* (1972); *Afrocentricity* (1989); *The Afrocentric Idea* (1987); and *Malcolm X as Cultural Hero and Other Afrocentric Essays* (1993). His co-authored works include *The Voices of Black rhetoric* (1971); Intercultural Communication (1976); and *Contemporary Black Thought: Alternative Analyses in Social and Behavioral Science* (1980). The "Markings of an African Concept of Rhetoric" essay (1974b) also appeared in *Language, Communication and Rhetoric in Black America.*
3. Sowande describes the difference in this manner: "A world view, in the proper sense of the term—in which sense it is to be understood here—is the essence extracted from certain specific 'substances' or 'elements' which then become the attributes of the worldview. . . . A view of the world, on the other hand, is a stance, the result of an instinctual reaction based on the individual's intellectual, political, religious, economic, scientific, or any other kind of 'convictions,' so called because these are often in themselves complexes born of irrational prejudices and adhered to with mulish obstinacy which the individual regards and demands should be recognized as 'indomitable Will'—from which, of course, it could not be furthest" (p. 68). While I do not believe that Sowande would apply this to all forms of Afrocentric analysis, it would certainly apply to those perspectives that purport to be inclusive and particular but are in practice "exclusive and universalistic."
4. Information about Chief Sowande's life and work can be found at http://hierographics.org/felasowandephilosophyandopinions.htm, and http://hierographics.org/FelaSowande—The LearningProcess.html.

5. There have been numerous innovative studies of African American rhetoric by scholars of European descent written during the past three decades (see, for example, Campbell 1986; Goldzwig 1989; Condit and Lucaites 1990, 1991a, 1991b; Browne 1998; Stewart 1997; J. Pauley 1998; G. Pauley 1998; and Terrill 2000). It is, in my mind, unfortunate that none of the more prolific of these writers has been included in this volume.
6. See http://hierographics.org/felasowandephilosophyandopinions.htm.
7. See my essay "From Complicity to Coherence: Rereading the Rhetoric of Afrocentricity" (1998) for a discussion of the Eurocentric roots of Afrocentric thought.
8. The most well known is, of course, Martin Bernal (see Bernal 1987). Another writer of European descent whose work is described as Afrocentric is Richard Poe, whose book *Black Spark, White Fire* (1997) offers a thoughtful analysis of the role of race in ancient history advanced from an Afrocentric perspective.
9. One sees this tension in Asante's essay "An Afrocentric Communication Theory," included in his book *Malcolm X and Other Cultural Heroes:* "I am concerned with nothing less than human maturity. It is my intention to address in a systematic way the pragmatics of communication, particularly with respect to the way we are affected by our environment. Such a task undertakes a reorientation of the enterprise of social science, a reformulation of assumptions, and a more thorough response to the diversity of human experiences in communication. Some writers have begun to see a crisis in the field of social sciences. I see no such crisis, because those who profess belief in the system are inclined to continue their faith. Perhaps what we see is a need for a new world voice" (1993, 171).

REFERENCES

Asante, M. (1987). *The Afrocentric Idea.* Philadelphia: Temple University Press.

Asante, M. (1989). *Afrocentricity.* Trenton, NJ: Africa World Press.

Asante, M. (1993). *Malcolm X as Cultural Hero and Other Afrocentric Essays.* Trenton, NJ: African World Press.

Asante, M., and E. K. Newmark (1976). *Intercultural Communication.* Falls Church, VA: Speech Communication Association.

Asante, M., and A. Vandi (Eds). (1980). *Contemporary Black Thought: Alternative Analyses in Social and Behavioral Science.* Beverly Hills, CA: Sage Publications.

Awkward, M. (1988). Race, Gender, and the Politics of Reading. *Black American Literary Forum* 22: 5–27.

Bernal, M. (1987). *Black Athena: The Afroasiatic Roots of Classical Civilization.* London: Free Association Books.

Brown, T. (1998). Remembering Crispus Attucks: Race, Rhetoric, and the Politics of Commemoration. *The Quarterly Journal of Speech* 85: 169–87.

Boulware, M. (1947). Speech Training in Negro Colleges. *The Quarterly Journal of Speech* 33: 509–14.

Campbell, K. (1986). Style and Content in the Rhetoric of Early Afro-American Feminists. *The Quarterly Journal of Speech* 72: 434–45.

Condit, C. M., and J. L. Lucaites (1990). Reconstructing <Equality>: Cultural and Counter-cultural Rhetorics in the Black Martyred Vision. *Communication Monographs* 57, 1: 5–24.

Condit, C. M., and J. L. Lucaites (1991a). The Rhetoric of Equality and the Expatriation of African Americans, 1776–1826. *Communication Studies* 42, 1: 1–22.

Condit, C. M., and J. L. Lucaites (1991b). *Crafting Equality: America's Anglo-African Word.* Chicago: University of Chicago Press.

Daniel, J. L. (1971). Column One. *Today's Speech*, 19(2), 1–2.

Daniel, J. L. (1974). *Black Communication: Dimensions of Research and Instruction.* New York: Speech Communication Association.

Du Bois, W. E. B. (1969). *The Souls of Black Folk.* New York: Signet.

Ellison, R. (1947). *The Invisible Man.* New York: Vintage.

Goldzwig, S. (1989). A Social Movement Perspective on Demagoguery: Achieving Symbolic Realignment. *Communication Studies* 40: 202–28.

Gregg, R., A. J. McCormack, and D. Pedersen (1969). The Rhetoric of Black Power: A Street Level interpretation. *The Quarterly Journal of Speech* 55: 151–60.

Gresson, A. (1977). Minority Epistemology and the Rhetoric of Creation. *Philosophy and Rhetoric* 10: 244–62.

Gresson, A. (1982). *The Dialectics of Betrayal: Sacrifice, Violation and the Oppressed. Norwood, NJ: Ablex.*

Gresson, A. (1995). *The Recovery of Race in America.* Minneapolis: University of Minnesota Press.

Haiman, F. (1967). The Rhetoric of the Streets: Some Legal and Ethical Considerations. *The Quarterly Journal of Speech* 53: 99–114.

Hill, R. L. (1964). *The Rhetoric of Racial Revolt.* Denver: Golden Bell Press.

Jackson, R. (2000). So Real Illusions of Black Intellectualism: Exploring Race, Roles, and Gender in the Academy. *Communication Theory* 10: 48–63.

Kerr, H. (1959). The Rhetoric of Political Protest. *The Quarterly Journal of Speech* 45: 146–52.

Kincheloe, J., S. Steinberg, and A. Gresson. (1996). *Measured Lies:* The Bell Curve *Examined.* New York: St. Martin's Press.

McPhail, M. (1994). *The Rhetoric of Racism.* Lanham, MD: University Press of America.

McPhail, M. (1995). *Zen in the Art of Rhetoric: An Inquiry into Coherence.* Albany: State University of New York Press.

McPhail, M. (1998). From Complicity to Coherence: Rereading the Rhetoric of Afrocentricity. *Western Journal of Communication* 62: 114–40.

McPhail, M., and K. Dace (2000). Black as We Wanna Be: From Identity Politics to Intercultural Competence. In R. Lustig and J. Koester (Eds.), *Among Us: Essays on Intercultural Communication* (pp. 148–60). New York: Longman.

Moody, R. (1944). Negro Minstrelsy. *The Quarterly Journal of Speech* 30: 321–28.

Pauley, G. (1998). John Lewis's "Serious Revolution": Rhetoric, Resistance, and Revision at the March on Washington. *The Quarterly Journal of Speech* 84: 320–40.

Pauley, J. (1998). Reshaping Public Persona and the Prophetic Ethos: Louis Farrakhan at the Million Man March. *Western Journal of Communication* 62: 512–36.

Pipes, W. H. (1945). Old-Time Negro Preaching: An Interpretive Study. *The Quarterly Journal of Speech* 31: 22–28.

Poe, R. (1997). *Black Spark, White Fire: Did African Explorers Civilize Ancient Europe?* Rocklin, CA: Prima Publishing.

Scott, R., and D. Smith (1969). The Rhetoric of Confrontation. *The Quarterly Journal of Speech* 55: 1–8.

Scott, R. L., & W. Brockriede (1969). *The Rhetoric of Black Power.* New York: Harper and Row.

Smith, A. (1969). *The Rhetoric of Black Revolution.* Boston: Allyn and Bacon.

Smith, A. (1972). *Language, Communication and Rhetoric in Black America.* New York: Harper and Row.

Smith, A. (1973). *Transracial Communication.* Englewood Cliffs, NJ: Prentice Hall.

Smith, A. (1974a). Theoretical and Research Issues in Black Communication. In J. Daniel (Ed.), *Black Communication: Dimensions of Research and Instruction* (pp. 136–44). New York: Speech Communication Association.

Smith, A. (1974). Markings of an African Concept of Rhetoric. *Today's Speech* 19: 13–18.

Smith, A., and S. Robb (1971). *The Voices of Black Rhetoric.* Boston: Allyn and Bacon.

Sowande, F. (1974). The Quest of an African World View: The Utilization of African Discourse. In J. Daniel (Ed.), *Black Communication: Dimensions of research and instruction* (pp. 67–117). New York: Speech Communication Association.

Stewart, C. (1997). The Evolution of a Revolution: Stokely Carmichael and the Rhetoric of Black Power. *The Quarterly Journal of Speech* 83: 429–46.

Strother, D. (1963). Polemics and the Reversal of the "Separate but Equal" Doctrine. *The Quarterly Journal of Speech* 49: 50–56.

Terrill, R. (2000). Colonizing the Borderlands: Shifting Circumference in the Rhetoric of Malcolm X. *The Quarterly Journal of Speech* 86: 67–85.

CHAPTER 8

Afrocentricity as Metatheory: A Dialogic Exploration of Its Principles

RONALD L. JACKSON II

> *The afrocentric enterprise is framed by cosmological, epistemological, axiological, and aesthetic issues. In this regard the afrocentric method pursues a world voice distinctly African-centered in relationship to external phenomenon. How do we gather meaning out of African or other existence?... What role does the African culture play in the African's interface with the cosmos?... The fundamental assumptions of Africological inquiry are based on the African orientation to the cosmos. By "African" I mean clearly a "composite African" not a specific discrete African orientation which would rather mean ethnic identification, i.e. Yoruba, Zulu, Nubia, etc. (Asante 1996, 256)*

> *For all its pretensions to expanding our vision, the afrocentric movement is not propelled by a desire to bring about any significant enrichment of our American culture. What Afrocentrists almost always want is power—the power to define, no matter how flimsy their cases might be.... [W]hen an afrocentrist is charged with shoddy scholarship, the retort is that his or her revolutionary work arrives through means of research and assessment outside "European methodology." (Crouch 1995/96, 78)*

As expressed in the two quotes above, Afrocentricity, which was born in the discipline of communication (particularly in rhetoric), has both strong proponents and opponents. There is no doubt that Afrocentric inquiry diverges from mainstream rhetorical methodological approaches. That is what cosmologically distinguishes and heuristically privileges this paradigm in its utility and function. But both sets of rhetorical theory, traditional and nontraditional, European and African-influenced, do seek to define certain parameters with which scholars choose to investigate human behavior, whether communicative or otherwise. Naturally, this is characteristic of all cultural rhetorics, including but not limited to ancient Chinese, Japanese, Korean,

Brazilian, and Caribbean rhetorical approaches. Certainly, the disciplinary perspectives of the theorists facilitate increasingly controversial discussions of Afrocentricity as method. As the humanistic scholar Edward Said suggests, intellectuals have a tendency to localize their analyses to the academy while commenting on the declining consciousness of the general populace. We, as American scholars, have frequently insulated ourselves from cultural difference to the extent that it has manifested in our consciousness and our progress as academicians (Jackson 1997).

Afrocentricity, though born and developed in academia, has become a household name. Anything from fabric with an African motif to necklaces and most everything in *Essence* magazine's clothing and accessories catalog can be considered Afrocentric. This widespread usage of the term has led to misconstrual concerning its definition. Before considering the strengths and limitations of the Afrocentric paradigm, it is critical that the volatile climate and incendiary responses to the Africological method be acknowledged. The epistemological and cosmological myopia we are presently experiencing in academe is much more than a stigma that thwarts our vision. It obstructs our collective sight and therefore deserves corrective lenses. One of this essay's objectives is to offer one set of corrective lenses with respect to African American rhetoric. The other objectives are to critique Afrocentricity as metatheory, as culturalized epistemology, and take a brief glance at the emergent literature that has embraced and contested Afrocentrism. Although spirituality is briefly implied, it is not treated here as a central theme. Other scholars in this volume (Cummings and Moore Latta, Alkebulan, and Karenga) attend to this most important continuity; instead, this essay concentrates on deconstructing the dilemmas in extant Afrocentric rhetorical epistemologies with the understanding that African American discourse is epistemic. That is, the apparatus used to apprehend the critical object in African American rhetoric is in fact the epistemes (or discursive formations), which are culturally derived and understood as foundational to the rhetor's everyday life. This is what is meant by Garner and Calloway-Thomas's (in this volume) reference to African American orality as "the rhetorical qualities of Black sense and sensibilities." I will discuss the epistemic implications of African American rhetoric by first discussing the politics of the intellectual discourse concerning Afrocentricity and later by briefly delving into the nature of orality and divine utterance as manifested in African American rhetoric.

The epistemic foundation of Afrocentric movements in the United States is the affinity for peace, harmony, self-knowledge, agency, and liberation among its proponents. Afrocentricity is a conceptual system that structures the way in which human beings engage the world. At the 2000 convention of the National Association of African American Studies, I participated in a formal debate on Africological theory building. During the question-and-answer period, one professor indicated that she was unsure of how this theory would affect Black adolescents' behaviors and lives. My response was that it will do so only to the extent that consciousness shapes behavior and being. I agree with Harris that "an afrocentric orientation is one which asserts that consciousness determines being" (1998, 18). It is a set of ideas about human transformation and a celebration of cultural placement and achievements. However, it does not claim to instantly reform behaviors. I am not sure how any paradigm can do that.

Assumably, if one moves to a developmentally high level of consciousness, then one becomes engaged in the struggle for human liberation, which begins with self-improvement and overall well-being. Afrocentric scholars have constantly reiterated that a "warrior" in the struggle for human liberation is powerless without the armor of cultural consciousness and self-consciousness (Person-Lynn 1996). Additionally, by recognizing that they come from a long lineage of extraordinary leaders and brilliant thinkers, rhetorical scholars may be enticed to learn more about who they are culturally and to understand that no one is solely an individual. Rather, we are individuals within a community that survives only because it is legitimized by a loyal and committed set of persons whose collective strength sustains the whole despite negative external and internal forces.

Naturally, when an "I"/"Other" dialectic is socially devised to evaluate worth and value, such as is in the case of the White/Black dichotomy, it is critical to self-assess the mental and spiritual condition of those who are being affected (see Asante, in this volume)—hence the impetus for the advent of the Black liberation psychology and sociology movements in the 1970s. These movements were not created to align with Afrocentricity, because the construct had not been coined yet, but the fundamental axis upon which the academic liberation movements and Afrocentricity lie is clear—liberation.

Afrocentricity is a direct counternarrative to a most obvious and hegemonic grand narrative presupposing that all that is not of Europe is not of worth. For example, the implication that *classical* is a term reserved for Greek or Roman scholarship is one that mimics the colonialistic instinct undergirding many North American paradigms (Jackson 1995). Although Afrocentricity as metatheory was created about twenty years ago, there is still much confusion, particularly by non-Afrocentric scholars, about the concrete objectives of Afrocentricity. A common misconception is that Afrocentrists are anti-White (Lefkowitz 1995). That is not true; they are anti-oppression (Asante 1999). In some respects, Afrocentricity has been resentfully received by the academy as a hostile takeover rather than a movement to construct space for the study and criticism of Black particularity throughout the diaspora. It is this intellectual xenophobia that has inhibited the progress of cultural models and critical practice within academic institutions.

Although the backlash from both Black (Crouch 1995/96; Gates 1993) and White (Lefkowitz 1995) scholars concerning Afrocentric studies utilizes "essentialism" as an apparatus to justify the critique, essentialist politics and highbrow appropriations of African heritage (in the form of a fictitious and anachronistic "Middle East" Egyptian studies) have been the catalysts for the present Afrocentric movement. How do we, as rhetoricians, make sense of the ambiguous European canon formations grounded in Egyptian ethics (Maat) without references to the indigenous cosmology or philosophers that inspired the axiological system (see Karenga in this volume)? Africanist and Afrocentric scholars such as Cheikh Anta Diop, John Henrick Clarke, and Chancellor Williams have been chastised for introducing their cultural orientations and correcting the chronological schedule and historical context in which those orientations are rooted. They have encountered this hostile climate because it is believed that they have somehow illegitimized European history by countering claims about Greek and Roman primacy in oratorical philosophy.

The fact is that every culture has its own unique perspective on rhetoric, and the Western intellectual tradition must be interrogated and decentralized in order for other cultures to locate where their cultural legacies and sensibilities fit in the epistemological structure of the world in general and rhetorical studies in particular. So, to some degree, Afrocentricity is just one step in the demythologization of "classical" rhetoric, though an important one (Hamlet 1998). McPhail (in this volume) agrees and contends, "In the field of communication the most important challenge to the discipline's European biases and influences emerged in the work of Molefi Kete Asante. Asante's Afrocentric ideas have clearly been the most important and pervasive influence on African American rhetorical theorizing." This means not that we should avoid celebration of Greek and Roman intellectual traditions and their relevance as conceptual and methodological tools for rhetorical criticism, but that those traditions should not be utilized to overshadow other cultural and intellectual legacies. The Chinese (Lu and Frank 1993), Native American (Basso 1970) and African (Nwosu and Taylor 2001) cultures each have their own classical rhetorics. The absence of these cultural rhetorics in major rhetorical theory and criticism texts leaves a void in the study of the rhetorical tradition (Jackson 2000). This fragmentation intensifies the need for the present volume.

The kaleidoscopic nature of metatheory is a bit misleading when discussing Afrocentricity. While a metatheory is defined as a formulated paradigm that outlines how a given set of theories should be structured, oftentimes much more is expected of the Afrocentric method. Paradoxically, Afrocentricity is both complicated and parsimonious, young and antiquated, culturally particular and yet useful for examining other cultures. It is liberatory, yet still held hostage by its opponents for its unwelcomed critique of Whiteness as a colonialistic construct; it is accused of being limited for what it does not say, with little to no regard for what it was developed to say. I must admit, however, that while I feel I am adequately prepared to defend the Afrocentric method, it does have its voids and inconsistencies. Within this essay, I will define Afrocentricity, explore its scope and nature, and distinguish it from Black nationalistic approaches. Henceforth in this chapter, as with most of the book, the terms *Black* and *African American* are used interchangeably. This chapter will conclude with a discussion of its strengths and limitations as a metatheory.

DEFINING AFROCENTRICITY

Certainly, since the 1980 debut of Afrocentricity in Molefi Kete Asante's *Afrocentricity: Theory of Social Change,* there have been varied perspectives on and versions of the Afrocentric approach. Some have heralded it for not being as universalistic as many European-centered models; conversely, others have claimed it to be antagonistic and a mere conceptual replacement of Europe with Africa. These persons claim that Afrocentricity is simply a paradigm shift that attempts to erect Africa as the center of the universe, from which all good things come.

As a social and political construct, Afrocentricity has been attached as a label to describe everything from one's cosmological orientation and theoretical posture to the clothes and hairstyle one wears. The term has become a marketplace commodity used to sell almost any item targeted to the African American community. KFC in several urban centers has employees wearing kente cloth designs on uniforms, and new hair care products appeal to the political side of consumers by using the term to signify a true connectedness to an African heritage (some with product labels reading "African Pride").

Academically, Afrocentricity has been adopted across several disciplines—African American studies, social work, psychology, sociology, communication, English, political science, history, and anthropology, to name a few. Afrocentricity combines "elements of philosophy, science, history, and mythology" to explain the human condition (Asante 1988). This combination is founded upon principles of Afrology, a genuine acceptance of the African past, and the endorsement of a contextual analysis. Afrology is the African-centered study of concepts, issues, and behaviors. As Molefi Asante posits in *Afrocentricity* that an Afrologist has three qualities: competence, clarity of perspective, and understanding of the object.

Competence comprises the relevant skills and abilities utilized to critically assess a given subject matter. Clarity of perspective is the focused engagement of Afrocentric analysis. It is maintaining an analytic interpretation while considering all contingent factors and political ramifications of behaviors and actions. Understanding the subject lends itself to a contextual analysis. The subject and its environmental influences are important, since they implicitly indicate phenomena occurring in and around the subject (Asante 1988).

According to Norman Harris (1998), there are three philosophical assumptions that form the basis upon which Afrocentric orientations rest: an

Afrocentric orientation is one that asserts that consciousness determines being; an Afrocentric ontology is communal; and Afrocentric epistemology validates reality by combining historical knowledge with intuitions.

As mentioned previously, there is a need for a clear, authoritative methodological direction for analyzing discourse Afrocentrically. Asante maintains in *Kemet, Afrocentricity, and Knowledge* that Afrocentricity does not seek to interrogate the Eurocentric tradition within its rightful context; It does, however, question Eurocentric studies that "seek ungrounded aggrandizement by claiming universal hegemony." The European tradition is meant to create, celebrate, sustain, develop, and introduce the totality of the European's existence to the world. The Afrocentric tradition is meant to accomplish these same objectives for African descendants. Afrocentricity intends to expand the repertoire of human perspectives on knowledge (Asante 1990). As an analytic tool, it is grounded in a philosophy of struggle and resistance, the condition that undergirds the African throughout the Diaspora. It seeks to reveal the dialectic present in every sociopolitical instance, and endorses the idiom "Everything is political" (Jackson 1995). Furthermore, it is the contention of this essay that all Afrocentric discourse implicitly and/or explicitly addresses the issue of liberation.

An Afrocentric method cannot and does not ignore the significance of other cultural ideologies, such as those promoted by the I Ching, Kahlil Gibran, Omar Khayyam, Siddhartha, and the Bhagavad Gita. These culturally significant leaders and texts address meaning-centered cosmologies that speak to the values and sensibilities of distinct cultural heritages.

It is characteristic of the Afrocentric epistemology to explore, uncover, and use codes, paradigms, symbols, motifs, and circles of discussion that reinforce the centrality of African ideals and values as a valid frame of reference for acquiring and examining data (Asante 1990). No Afrocentric methodology can afford to ignore this function of Afrocentric discourse. Turner (1991) identifies eight principles of an Afrocentric worldview, six of which were selected here because of their consistency with Asante's explanation of African cosmology:

1. Interconnectedness of all things
2. Collective identity
3. Oneness of mind, body, and spirit
4. Consequential morality
5. Time
6. Spirituality

The Afrocentric method, because of its interdisciplinary nature and scope, must maintain its conceptual foundation. That foundation includes a recognition of the connectedness in the universe.

It is precisely this *interconnectedness,* this observance of circularity, harmony, and dialectic, that was taught to Plato by Socrates. This is why Plato was inclined to use dialogues, for dialogues hinted at circularity. The basic argument has more than one side or one dimension, so by offering a juxtaposed set of contentions, one was able to systematically examine more than a single side of the issue. The term *dialectic,* from an Afrocentric standpoint, suggests not opposites, but rather juxtaposed dimensions. Traditional rhetorical critics conform to a strict, rigid dichotomy. Marcuse's theory of negative reason and Foucault's concept of reversal are very similar. Herbert Marcuse offered the idea that something is because of what it is not. In other words, if you are not one thing, then you are another. This statement implies opposition and a rigid categorization of human understanding. It presumes that the "I" can affirm herself only by first defining the "other." Moreover, the value of the "other" must be discovered via the "I." This never takes into account the possibility that the "I" is the "other"—only that they are different individuals.

When functioning within a *collective identity* or lifeworld, the "I" and "other," just like the mind, body, and spirit, are only figuratively different, since they are directly responsible to the same community. Clearly, when the "I' and the "other" are understood as a paired community that travel together, this idea changes how we conceptualize the nature of Plato's dialogue. We can no longer theorize dialogics as a superior versus an inferior, such as Socrates pitted against the Sophists. Instead, they are universal complements, much like the authentic interpretation of yin and yang, which resists polarity and accents holism.

Consequential morality is of crucial importance. The Afrocentric paradigm clearly envelops the notion that the universe is the true cosmos. All that is in the universe is sacred in origin. Even the word has life within it. The spoken word is not seen as an utterance that is the consequence of skillful manipulation. It is seen as nommo, the life-giving mystical force offered through verbal and vocal discourse (Asante 1987). Although the word possesses its own vivacity and suppleness, its power must positively affect the audience. There is a moral imperative. Just as the Roman orator Quintillian is quoted as saying, "A good speaker speaks well," so is Tehuti, the Egyptian god of truth, wisdom, and the word. Tehuti does not simply *speak* truth, but *is* the spiritual and mythological embodiment of truth, justice, equanimity, peace, and harmony. So to invoke the ancestral power of Tehuti via discourse, one must tap into the peaceful and moral spirit of the word and request that it move through you (the speaker) to the audience. Said another way, within the African diasporic communities throughout the world, the word is affective. It is effective only when the audience emotes as a result of having been influenced by it. The manner in which the range of emotions proceeds becomes an indicator of the effect. The speaker is judged by how much the word "touched" the audience. The orator or writer is directly responsible for the moral character inculcated in the affect and effect.

Spirituality is inherent in discussions of the word, whether in oratorical or literary form (Cummings and Moore-Latta in this volume). Within both, spirituality intercedes within folk songs and Negro spirituals, proverbs, "bosom biscuits" (Daniel and Effinger 1996), sermons, and mythopoeia (such as folktales) and is evoked via signification (Garner and Calloway-Thomas in this volume), metonymy, epanaphora, and other rhetorical means. Essentially, spirituality is contained in the movement of nommo as sustained by magara, which is the driving force behind the word. It is the affective component that when properly placed can influence an audience to perform an act or commit to a stance without revocation. Pouring libations—the pouring of liquid (usually alcohol) upon the ground in homage to the ancestors—is a ceremonial activity that is also representative of a spiritual inclination. It is a part of the African-influenced holiday Kwanzaa, established by Maulana Karenga (Karenga 1998). Libations are preceded by the literal "calling of the ancestors" by speaking their names. This most powerful act is significant because it is a tribute to particular persons whose names are identified and spoken to embrace their spiritual being.

Time, place, and perspective are three essential contextual ingredients of Afrocentric discourse. The temporal arrangement is vital in that it alludes to the past, present, and future. The status quo is linked not only to the time of day, but also to the situation. The mood, tone, and intensity of a presentation may be heightened during wartime compared to peacetime. A speech given at the same location may have been more intense in how it is presented and received during the 1960s as opposed to the 1990s. The place or setting refers to the location of the speech. A speech given at a KKK rally by a Black separatist will be much different from a speech given at an inauguration ceremony. Finally, the perspective refers to the feelings, thoughts, and ideas of the multitude. It is also the ideology the speaker promotes. The perspective is the approach or viewpoint understood by the audience and explained by the rhetor. Time, place, and perspective envelop the whole Afrocentric analysis. Harmony as a response to liberation becomes key. Good is the restoration of harmony, balance, truth, justice, and equality. This concept in Afrocentric discourse is known as Maat. According to Karenga (1994), Maat evolves from and through the seven cardinal virtues of truth, justice, propriety, harmony, balance, and reciprocity. In the African nation of Akan, this is called *dja.* These two ideas address the significance of order, right, and integrity. It is the proper alignment of man and nature, man and animal, and man and man. It is the relationship dually situated between subject and object. Moreover, the appreciation of balance in the universe lends credibility to an Afro-circular, as opposed to a Euro-linear, perspective.

As mentioned, Asante suggests that an Afrologist is one who has competence, clarity of perspective, and understanding of the object. The Afrocentric method must display a sense of interconnectdeness, harmony, time, place, and perspective. Finally, the concept of Afrocentricity as it relates to authentically African discourse must promote balance, order, justice, and equality. The principles of the method are outstanding. The specious interpretations, however, dilute the significance of this paradigm.

AFROCENTRICITY AND THE BLACK NATIONALISTIC APPROACH

James Baldwin asserts that the Black intellectual is a "bastard of the West"—an illegitimate offspring developed and sustained by standards that are foreign yet still treated as familiar. When scholars such as Stanley Crouch criticize the Afrocentric project, they are essentially criticizing the ability to act as an agent in the creation of new knowledge about themselves. They would rather be left incapacitated by a stubborn adherence to culture-general approaches for culture-specific inquiry. There are two major mistakes made by spectators of the Afrocentric movement. First, many people presume that Molefi Asante represents the totality of the Africological venture. Second, it is assumed that Afrocentricity is a unidimensional approach that claims to have made the only worthy contribution to the human experience. The former statement is not meant to discredit or disrespect the groundbreaking works of Molefi Asante. As a first-rate scholar, Asante is more than worthy of praise and respect. However, even he often notes that he is a Diopian, meaning that he is a student of the late anthropologist, historian, linguist, and Egyptological scholar Cheikh Anta Diop. The objective of Africological thought is to reintroduce the African cultural personality to mainstream scholarly discourse. This massive undertaking precedes the Afrocentric movement. The latter statement is a misinterpretation that is inspired by what Martin Bernal calls the "afrocentric scholarly continuum." As Bernal points out,

> the label of "afrocentrist" has been attached to a number of intellectual positions ranging from "all good things come from Africa" . . . to my own shared position that maintains that Africans or peoples of African descent have made many significant contributions to world progress and that, for the past two centuries, these have been systematically played down by European and North American historians. (1996, 86)

Clearly, since its rise in the 1960s, Africological research has been met with intense resistance by the most unlikely critics—White women, Black women, and Black men. Some of the individuals who have led the national conversation in opposition to Afrocentricity are Mary Lefkowitz, Cornel West, Michelle Wallace, Walter Williams, K. Anthony Appiah, Stanley Crouch, and Henry Louis Gates. Among the popular proponents defending Afrocentricity are Molefi Asante, Martin Bernal, Basil Davidson, G. G. M. James, Maulana Karenga, John Henrick Clarke, Marimba Ani, Haki Madhubuti, Yosef Ben-Jochannan, Wade Nobles, E. A. Wallis Budge, Na'im Akbar, and the entire Temple School of Africologists. The arguments have become so inflammatory that Lefkowitz refused to include Bernal's response to her latest polemic in her book *Black Athena Revisited.* Nonetheless, the debate on Afrocentricity between Bernal and Lefkowitz was moved to the Internet in May of 1997 and sponsored by Lefkowitz's publisher, HarperCollins. The tone and content of these discussions are highly technical, and they are written in language that practically excludes the nonscholar. Bernal (1996) mentions several times that Lefkowitz attempts to intimidate Afrocentric proponents who do not have extensive training in classical languages or access to Egyptological documents.

Some of the less technical but still critical commentary has come from Cornel West and Henry Louis Gates. West charges in *Keeping Faith* (1993) that Afrocentrism is misguided since it denounces cultural hybridization, remains silent on issues of class, and proposes retrograde views of women and homosexuals. He suggests a prophetic framework, which he labels a "Black cultural democracy," as a viable replacement for afrocentricity. In *Loose Canons,* Gates notes that "[it is important to have] a tradition not defined by a pseudoscience of racial biology or a mystical essence called Blackness" (1993, 39). Other scholars such as bell hooks and Michelle Wallace have thoroughly contested Afrocentric scholarship, which they contend promotes hegemony and/or essentialism. Postmodern and postcolonial theoreticians have effectively argued against the establishment of an "essentialist" way of knowing, and rightfully so (Dyson 1993, 1996; hooks 1989, 1995; Hall 1997; West 1993). Essentialism is an epistemology characterized by an unchallengeable and unchanging approach to African American cultural particularity. Paul Gilroy (1995) and bell hooks (1993) launch a surprisingly broad-based indictment against Black nationalist thinkers as proponents and self-proclaimed gatekeepers of Black authenticity. While I cannot agree that all Afrocentrists and/or Black nationalist thinkers believe they are spokespersons for "true Blackness," it is important to remind ourselves that culturally specific theories cannot rightfully reduce Blackness (or any other cultural existence for that matter) to a singular perspective.

There is a distinction between Black nationalism and afrocentricity. Black nationalism is both ideological and activistic (Miyakawa in this volume). There are many brands of Black nationalism, such as revolutionary (e.g., pan-Africanism), integrationist (e.g., the NAACP), and separatist (e.g., the Nation of Islam), each concerned with some form of Black self-determination and success as a collective Black community. Nationalism is fundamentally a movement to establish a Black nation-state that is wholly self-sufficient and capable of independent functioning. Maulana Karenga's Kawaida theory is a Black nationalistic theory, not a metatheory, nor is it a conceptual rubric of the Afrocentric paradigm (Karenga 1980). Cheikh Anta Diop's cosmological triad of language, history, and psychology is an identity matrix that predates

Afrocentricity. It is Black nationalistic. As a prime exemplar of Black nationalistic efforts, in 1962 Diop proposed the creation of six institutes (Spady 1986):

1. An institute of nuclear physics and chemistry
2. An electronics institute
3. An aeronautics and astronautics institute
4. An institute of applied chemistry for industry and agriculture (organic synthesis, metallurgy, mineral chemical industry, etc.)
5. An institute of tropical agronomy and biochemistry (soil study, fertilizers, extraction of vegetable products with a view to finding industrial or pharmaceutical applications for certain flora)
6. An institute of health specializing in the study of tropical diseases

Diop's systematic planning, organizing, and institute building is much like Amos Wilson's mammoth 890-page proposal for Black liberation entitled *Blueprint for Black Power* (1998). In it, Wilson structures an insightful and detailed strategy including everything from how to participate in the stock market and invest to the transformation of consciousness into the power to define progress. Afrocentricity, like Black nationalism, is an ideological venture, not an epistemological moment, though it must be understood that Black nationalism is more than ideology or perspective; it is a movement for policy formation and cultural-political activism. Black nationalism and Afrocentricity are not synonymous, and efforts to equate the two are faulty.

Every critical theorist and intellectual understands that one cannot separate the text from the context, nor the theory from the theorist. There is a conjugal relationship between the two. As a result, if I publicly claim to be an Afrocentrist, yet my interpretation of human activity is inconsistent with the postulates of Afrocentricity, then who is at fault, the theory or the interpreter of the theory, me? Against all of what it means to be critical, many people have chosen to dismiss the theory rather than dismiss the interpreter of the theory. I concur with Bernal's "continuum" of Afrocentric scholarship. At the same time, I am convinced that there are so-called Afrocentric persons who have misread the metatheory. A criticism of Afrocentricity is that it does not embrace difference. There is no way that Afrocentricity can maintain its stature as a liberatory method and simultaneously disengage such individuals as women and homosexual intellectuals from the collective venture. Regardless of the fact that Black nationhood can be cosmologically understood with respect to a shared gender community, Black nationalism *can* afford to disengage women and homosexuals, because at the core it is much more restrictive and exclusionary. This is perhaps the most tragic facet of Black nationalism, because there are still those who believe a community must be defined by its potential to exclude and select members it deems worthy, when no strong

Black nation can exist without men and women invested in its potential and continuity (hooks 1995).

It logically follows that if there are variegated social and political preferences and ideologies that contribute to the foundations of diverse communicated Black existences, there must also be concomitant ideologies and biographical narratives that punctuate these experiences. It is imperative that Afrocentric theorists do some self-analysis to uncover these personal and situated commentaries within the discourse and be clear about whose agenda they are promoting—Afrocentrism or Black nationalism.

STRENGTHS AND LIMITATIONS AS METATHEORY

There are three major strengths and limitations of the Afrocentric method. They are as follows:

Strengths	*Limitations*
1. It is historically grounded, conditional.	1. As a liberation metatheory, it does not critically discuss economics.
2. It is culturally particular, contextual.	2. It is not a theory.
3. It demarginalizes and recenters Blacks as agents in human interaction.	3. Often misunderstood as being essentialist and hegemonic, due to enthusiastic researchers who call themselves Afrocentrists.

Afrocentrists have been accused of everything from prostituting Black cultural studies for monetary gain to constructing a fantastical universe that parasitically feeds off Western civilization's entropic tendencies to claim all human activity as universal and hegemonic property. These scholars have been branded as hustlers distributing the placebo of false pride to a weakened populace of marginalized hopefuls like a "street pharmacist" would to his/her clientele. The receiving constituency is not credited with being critical and progressive, but deemed addicts anticipating their next dosage of feel-good stimulants that will facilitate their escape to an imaginary plateau where all that is valuable is Black. The intellectual contortions furnished by the opponents of the Afrocentric enterprise are somewhat brilliant, and yet so vacuous (Asante 1999). Afrocentric proponents are supposed to second-guess their commitment to becoming agent, subject, center, and author in their own humanistic understanding of their cultural self-definitions. Somehow they should be guilt-ridden for having been courageous enough to reject the systematized and insidious structure of psychological, political, and social entrapment known as modernism. The history is compelling enough evidence to sway any victim of this maledictory oppression, but the Afrocentric paradigm is not just based on history. It is based on conditions and contexts. The metatheory simply claims that scholars can best understand Black experiences by using instruments designed to uncover those symbols, codes, and motifs that are culturally particular. These instruments, for African American rhetoric, tend to be Africological in principle.

Africology differs from Afrocentricity in that Africology refers to the systematic study of Africa and African philosophy (including cosmology, epistemology, axiology, ontology, and aesthetics). Afrocentrism is an ideological orientation that places Africa at the center of the analysis of human evolvement. The complexity arises when the interpretations are misleading and/or falsely representative of the Afrocentric paradigm. This metatheory is broad enough to be utilized in any discipline, including forestry or agriculture. It just so happens that it has not expanded into those areas of study yet. It is unrealistic to expect one theorist, trained in the discipline of communication, to be well versed in every area of human inquiry. Asante has proven his ability to be a well-read scholar, but can we expect him to be an economist, agriculturalist, physician, biologist, anthropologist, classical artist, mathematician, and so on? Let's examine whether Afrocentricity has met the criteria for a metatheory. According to Mary John Smith (1988),

> The term metatheory refers to beliefs about the nature of theory. Thus, metatheoretical assumptions address the types of theoretical explanations that are appropriate to human communication. Consistent with the hierarchically interrelated nature of paradigms, a researcher's ontological and epistemological views will largely determine the sorts of theoretical explanations he or she deems suitable. (1988, 311)

Metatheories are developed to express the nature and scope of theory. The historical and cultural qualities of Afrocentricity qualify as nature and scope. Is the metatheory sufficient, adequate, and heuristic? That is the real question. If its scholarly constituency continues to promote it as being exclusive and universalistic, then contributory academic explorations of Afrocentricity will expire quickly. Any theory whose theorists contradict its primary epistemological, axiological, ontological, and cosmological tenets will be ephemeral. Afrocentrists must be clear about what this term means. And, eventually, it will be imperative that its theorists offer candid critiques of its utility as it matures. Just as any viable institution must conduct periodic self-studies, so must the circle of Africologists who are truly Afrocentrists.

Future African American rhetorical studies must not abandon criticism of public address; however, public address must not be our only invocation. The discourse as object must also be fluid, with the discourse as a momentary snapshot of everyday lived cultural experience. It is impossible to disengage completely from our own culturalized humanity while functioning as critic. It seems fitting as we experience this postmillenial cultural revival in rhetorical studies that we revisit what it means to be a rhetorician and what it means to have a classical rhetorical orientation defined by culturalized orature and manifested in spiritual, religious, gendered, nationalistic, political, ethical, and popular discourse.

Just as there are Greek classics, Roman classics, and French classics, there also must be discussion of Egyptian classics and other culturally specific classics in rhetoric. By attending to these cultural traditions and oratorical legacies, the study of rhetoric will be enriched, enlivened and expanded beyond its present intellectually imperialistic condition. As McPhail insightfully suggests, "I am certain that we are not the only voices in the field of African American rhetorical studies that remain unheard, nor that ours are the only scholarly contributions that remain unseen. Nonetheless, I am hopeful that the continued maturation of Afrocentric and African American rhetorical studies will result in an inclusivity that cuts across race and culture." This essay, as with this entire book, is a testament to conceptual yearning for something that is deeply entrenched in our everyday being, something innovative, and something reflective of our diversified humanity. Afrocentricity is a precocious beginning to a disciplinary transformation we will all witness in the coming years with respect to the way we systematically examine the culturalized rhetorics of being.

REFERENCES

Asante, M. K. (1987). *The Afrocentric Idea.* Philadelphia: Temple University Press.

Asante, M. K. (1988). *Afrocentricity.* Trenton, NJ: Africa World Press.

Asante, M. K. (1990). *Kemet, Afrocentricity, and Knowledge.* Trenton, NJ: Africa World Press.

Asante, M. K. (1996). The Principal Issues in Afrocentric Inquiry. In M. K. Asante and Abu Abarry (Eds.), *African Intellectual Heritage.* Philadelphia: Temple University Press.

Asante, M. K. (1999). *The Painful Demise of Eurocentrism.* Trenton, NJ: Africa World Press.

Basso, K. (1970). To Give Up on Words: Silence in Western Apache Culture. *Southwestern Journal of Anthropology,* 26: 213–320.

Bernal, M. (1996). The Afrocentric Interpretation of History: Bernal Replies to Lefkowitz. *The Journal of Blacks in Higher Education* (Spring): 86–94.

Crouch, S. (1995/6). The Afrocentric Hustle. *The Journal of Blacks in Higher Education* (Winter): 77–82.

Daniel, J. and Effinger, M. (1996). Bosom Biscuits: A Study of African American Intergenerational Communication. *Journal of Black Studies,* 27, 183–200.

Dyson, M. (1993). *Reflecting Black: African American Cultural Criticism.* Minneapolis: University of Minnesota Press.

Dyson, M. (1996). *Race Rules: Navigating the Color Line.* Reading, MA: Addison-Wesley.

Gates, H. L. (1993). *Loose Canons: Notes on the Culture Wars.* Oxford: Oxford University Press.

Gilroy, P. (1995). *The Black Atlantic: Modernity and Double Consciousness.* Cambridge, MA: Harvard.

Hall, S. (1997). *Representation: Cultural Representations and Signifying Practices (Culture, Media and Identities).* Thousand Oaks, CA: Sage.

Hamlet, J. (Ed.) (1998). *Afrocentric Visions: Studies in Culture and Communication.* Newbury Park, CA: Sage.

Harris, N. (1998). A Philosophical Basis for an Afrocentric Orientation. In J. Hamlet (Ed.), *Afrocentric Visions: Studies in Culture and Communication* (pp. 15–26). Newbury Park, CA: Sage.

hooks, b. (1989). *Talking Back: Thinking Feminist, Thinking Black.* Boston: South End Press.

hooks, b. (1993). *Sisters of the Yam: Black Women and Self-recovery.* Cambridge, MA: South End Press.

hooks, b. (1995). *Killing Rage: Ending Racism.* New York: Henry Holt and Co.

Jackson, R. L. (1995). Toward an Afrocentric Methodology for the Critical Assessment of Rhetoric. In L. A. Niles (Ed.), *African American Rhetoric: A Reader.* Dubuque, IA: Kendall-Hunt Publishing Co.
Jackson, R. L. (1997). For Those of Us Who Must Move Forward: Diversity Scholarship, Moving into the New Millennium. *NCA Summer Diversity Conference Proceedings* (pp. 67–81). Annandale, VA: National Communication Association.
Jackson, R. L. (2000). So Real Illusions of Black Intellectualism: Exploring Race, Roles, and Gender in the Academy. *Communication Theory* 10, 1: 48–63.
Karenga, M. (1980) *Kawaida Theory: An Introductory Outline.* Inglewood, CA: Kawaida Publications.
Karenga, M. (1994) Maat, The Moral Ideal in Ancient Egypt: A Study in Classical African Ethics. Ph.D. dissertation, University of Southern California, Los Angeles.
Karenga, M. (1998). *Kwanzaa: A Celebration of Family, Community and Culture.* Los Angeles: University of Sankore Press.
Lefkowitz, M. (1995). *Not Out of Africa.* New York: HarperCollins.
Lu, X., and Frank, D. (1993). On the study of ancient Chinese rhetoric/Bian. *Western Journal of Communication*, 57, 445–463.
Nwosu, P., and D. Taylor (2001). Afrocentric Empiricism. In V. Milhouse, M. Asante, and P. Nwosu (Eds.), *Transcultural Realities: A Handbook of Multiple Communication Perspectives.* Newbury Park, CA: Sage.
Person-Lynn, K. (1996). *First Word: Black Scholars, Thinkers, Warriors.* New York: Harlem River Press.
Smith, M. J. (1988). *Contemporary Communication Research Methods.* Belmont, CA: Wadsworth.
Spady, J. (1986). The Changing Perception of C. A. Diop and His Work: The Preeminence of a Scientific Spirit. In I. Van Sertima (Ed.), *Great African Thinkers.* New Brunswick, NJ: Transaction Books.
Turner, R. (1991). Afrocentrism: Affirming Consciousness. In J. C. Everett (Ed.), *Child Welfare: An Africentric Perspective* (pp. 32–49). New Brunswick, NJ: Rutgers University Press.
West, C. (1993). *Keeping Faith.* New York: Routledge.
Wilson, A. (1998). *Blueprint for Black Power: A Moral, Political, and Economic Imperative for the Twenty-First Century.* Trenton, NJ: Afrikan World Infosystems.

Section 4

AFRICAN AMERICAN RHETORICAL ANALYSES OF STRUGGLE AND RESISTANCE

CHAPTER 9

Africological Theory and Criticism: Reconceptualizing Communication Constructs

JEFFREY LYNN WOODYARD

Inventing new designs for interpreting communication behavior and texts is a duty particular to African American scholars concerned with language traditions. Discrete uses of words and their powers by African Americans give access to a more complete idea of what it means to be human in inhumane social contexts. Not only can we rediscover the power of rhetoric for the disenfranchised in pro-democratic societies, but we also can complement the textures of human understanding. By that, I suggest it would be impossible to explain what it means to be human in the Western experience if we do not understand the rhetorical forces influencing historical shifts in the material conditions of African peoples in the United States and elsewhere.

This volume affords a rare opportunity to treat the merits of grounding communication theory and criticism in the life and cultural experiences of African peoples. A conversation toward a diasporic take on how people create shared meanings and understandings and achieve social coordination might open by raising several critical issues.

Among these include: (1) the nature of things Africological, (2) the nature of Africological communication and rhetorical theory building, (3) some of the salient variables resulting from Africological reconstructs, (4) how rhetorical communities express themselves, and (5) how rhetorical activity functions as a symbolic script for spiritual dynamics in human affairs. I will attempt here a consideration of these issues and a demonstration of how Africological theory and criticism is taking shape.

PROACTIVE AFRICOLOGY

First, this notion of being "Africological" deserves our attention. It is not safe to assume the term has any *real* meaning at all. Yet, my orientation to the word begins with Afrocentric tendencies in the exploration of human texts.

As Ronald Jackson (in this volume) demonstrates, the term *Afrocentric* is growing in use and takes on different meanings representing differing bodies of thought. To some, it is a cultural nationalist expressive moment among African Americans, Africans, and Africans in other parts of the worldwide Diaspora. Several close definitions have been attempted in the social sciences. For instance, in Black psychology, it is often related to theories of African personality. In Africa-centered studies of cultural history it requires the embrace of romanticized ideals about host cultures and societies in loosely constructed images of an African past. There are tendencies to conflate "Africa" into a concept before understanding African peoples.

Increasingly the label *Afrocentric* has a growing market value. It is used in the exchange of goods and services from corporate producers to middle-class African Americans and other urban dwellers. African Americans and others at the bottom of Derrick Bell's "well" also have come to understand the term to have some consumable significance. Public education theorists, practitioners, and politicians buy into this market hoping the children under their care will have enhanced self-esteem and higher test scores. They probably will. This is a good thing.

The Temple School of Africologists, where the terms *Afrocentric* and *Africology* seem to have fluid definitions, primarily influences me. There is a strong tendency in my thinking to rely upon Molefi Kete Asante's early definitions. Particularly, in communication studies, his *Afrocentric Idea* (1987) stands as the most serious treatment of rhetorical processes from an Afrocentric perspective. As McPhail (in this volume) notes, "Implicit in Asante's analysis is a critique of the epistemological foundationism of Western rhetorical thought, a foundationism that placed emphasis on rational, 'objective,' and abstract communicative principles and practice." In essence, Asante showed that we could talk sensibly about "placing African values and ideals at the center of analysis" while exploring African American rhetorical activity and texts. By the way, that is Afrocentricity. It is an intellectual orientation to human experiences and their resultant texts. As Richard Wright suggests in the third chapter, Afrocentricity allows me to explore texts from the perspectives of African peoples. Such exploration is politics.

I have attempted, in my contribution to Dyhana Zeigler's edited volume *Molefi Kete Asante and Afrocentricity: In Praise and in Criticism* (1995), to provide a critique of Professor Asante's *Afrocentric Idea* and suggest how the book might be useful for studying human communication. I will resist repetition here, except to say that Asante's metatheoretical attempts gave the promise of expanding the critical conversation about epistemological assumptions involved in communication theory. Because Asante's work responds to and extends critical theory, he provides both an opportunity and a mainstay for Afrocentrists—intellectuals—hoping to build upon the traditions of African American communication scholars of the late '60s and '70s. I am only in a position of gratitude.

Now, the term *Africologist* suggests a particular kind of scholar who assumes Africa, as concept or continent, as a point of departure for raising or attempting inquiry and exploring texts. An Africologist demonstrates that viewing human activity from some constructed African vantage is a sensible, reliable option for reading human experiences.

I suppose that "proactive Africalogy" requires less focus on the limitations of Eurocentric worldviews and paradigms. That said, I should spend no time deconstructing Western chauvinisms, patriarchy, racialization, rationalism, homophobia, enviro-genocidal racism, classism, and the whole host of social maladies plaguing us during American late capitalism. Allow me this, however: Africology, constituted by the collective human sciences of Afrocentric scholarship, in order to make valid contributions to African peoples and to social policy, must provide, at presuppositional levels, the kinds of deconstructive critiques of the West that make room for more humanizing possibilities and manipulations of our current social order. Proactive Africology resists essentializing tendencies at all costs.

The nature of Africological communication studies/rhetorical theory, then, includes a conversation about humanizing tendencies. Asante's call for a new perspective on communication that offers the promise of "making life better for human beings" (1993, 183) pertains in that Africological rhetorical theory and criticism providing "a more humanistic voice which is based on harmony" (p. 184) is the desired end.

CONSTRUCTING AFRICOLOGICAL THEORY

In Africological terms, this amounts to a call to engage a holistic view of the human person (Asante 1993, 181–84). One appropriate response is to privilege the dialogue about metaphysical contexts of human communication. This is a major area of theory building and corresponds to the suggestion that the "acquisition of knowledge occurs in a cultural context" (Asante 1990, 118).

Similarly, the derivation of meaning embraces the cultural arenas in which that process occurs. Culture becomes *the* operative value in understanding communication. Interculturalists have staked their field on this claim (Dodd 1987; Gonzalez, Houston, and Chen 1994; Klopf 1991; Lustig and Koester 1993; Samovar and Porter 1994). Rhetoric and culture are inextricable. The interpretation or critique of rhetoric, as a means of generating knowledge (about people and culture), is coupled with culture as well.

As such, Africological tenets claiming cultural and historical continuities between Africa and the lived experiences of African Americans provide contours for our theory building. Theories that are neither aggressive nor violative of those lived experiences will develop. More humanistic analytical methods are our objectives. The urgencies of our theory building grow out of that which is consistent with diasporic knowledge and phenomena.

Essentially, African and African American phenomena frame reconstructions about human communication and rhetoric. These reconstructions allow us to place both scholar and scholarship on appropriate "psycho-socio/cultural grounds" (Asante 1990, 188).

By exploring Kemetic and other African philosophical orientations, as well as African American and other diasporic orientations, we derive ideas about the creation of meaning that adequately locates our theory building within Africological parameters.

For instance, through an embrace of rationalizations about West African conceptions of spiritual sensibilities, we are permitted an examination of the metaphysical or *spiritual dynamics* that inhere in human communication. Yet spirituality is omitted as a category of analysis in communication models grounded outside Africological frames.

Specifically, one approach I use is to engage magara as a central motive in human communication. The magara principle (reflecting Bantu culture and language) invokes our ability to "strengthen" and/or "weaken" another toward a particular interpretation or understanding. Magara, applied to communication, suggests a system of operations wherein spiritual and material dynamics unite in the production of shared meaning (Jahn 1990, 111).

Issues of harmony, balance, and social coordination can be addressed by arguing that African American rhetoric, as a case in point—occurring within macrostructural dominations that help to determine our rhetorical conditions—can be understood within an ecological framework of material and metaphysical (spiritual) forces operating in accord with ntu. Ntu is assumed as the rhythmic point of derivation of all of life's harmony and balance (Jahn 1990, 101).

To theorize about rhetoric in this way is a departure from tradition. First, such theory seeks cultural contiguity because it will be instrumental as a base for reinterpreting African American rhetoric. It is divergent, too, for its utility in systematic efforts to note manifestations of nommo in African American communication. Third, it connects the discussion about African and African American spiritual ethos with empirical knowledge about communication. That is, we will be able to speak of material—even behavioral—phenomena while attending to the nonmaterial forces at work in generating those material expressions. Once a cogent theoretical base is established around the magara principle of human communication, I proceed toward defining Africological rhetorical critical approaches.

AFRICOLOGICAL RECONSTRUCTIONS: THE MAGARA PRINCIPLE

By now a familiar concept, nommo refers to an African sensibility of word or word force. That is, language use is about the use of power. Nommo in rhetoric represents the spiritual modality through which muntu (human-being-ness) is activated. It is muntu who alone exercises intellect. Muntu, a human person, maintains agency over nommo. Life, meaning, communal understanding: all are created and recreated through nommo in communication. If our hermeneutic interests include spiritual dynamics of human communication, we might ask: To what degree does a rhetor, group, or corporate identity facilitate nommo (power of the word) to influence people and effect social coordination?

This ability to have rhetorical effect—to influence—is understood as the Magara principle. Magara suggests a system of operations wherein spirit force and material force are united in the production of life and meaning. Magara represents the process of "life-strengthening" and/or "life-weakening" (Jahn 1990, 111). Magara signifies a strengthening and/or weakening influence brought to bear alongside rhetorical behavior within and across rhetorical communities. This principle is a spiritual thoroughfare toward understanding persuasion among African populations in the West. It is one Afrocentric approach to *being* rhetorical.

Magara operates in the context of ntu, or universal life force. All forces relate to one another within an ecology of ntu. Ntu, also understood as the universal rhythm of life, is manifest within various African cultural categories, of which muntu, "human being," is the first. Ntu, or rhythm, is constructed as a fundament to living. Ordered human life is centered in accordance with the rhythms experienced upon encounter with the cosmos, or life environment. As an ecological context for living, ntu is the rhythmic space in which rhetorical communities derive available means for negotiating meaning and achieving social understandings.

We can view African American rhetoric within a framework of forces operating in accord with ntu. Ntu is assumed as the rhythmic point of derivation for all of life's harmony and balance that are pivotal to traditional African cosmology. For Jahn, ntu expresses not the effect of these forces, but their being. But the forces act continually and are constantly having effect—influence. Only if one could call a halt to the whole universe, that is, if life suddenly stood still, would ntu be revealed. All human rhetorical activity can be said to occur within the rhythm of ntu. Asante is correct to contend for the centrality of nommo in human communication as "the generative and productive power of the spoken word" (1987, 17).

Clearly, the most significant contribution made by such a theoretical approach is the inclusion of spiritual sensibility in discussions about rhetorical behavior and processes. For example, Griaule (1948) explains nommo is *kintu* or "thing" and functions as "the vital force that carries the word" (165). Another explanation of the confluence between spirituality and logos is Jahn's (1961) assertion that "man has the power over the word, it is he (or she) who directs the life force" (124). Spirit (immaterial force) is elevated.

From this brief treatment, four propositions about rhetoric emerge:

1. Nommo operates in the context of ntu to engender magara within and across varying rhetorical communities.
2. Nommodic rhetorical behaviors (manifestations of nommo) are evident in strategies and behaviors of particular communicators and other participants in rhetorical communities.
3. Magara (effects) are observable in a rhetorical community's responsiveness to discrete rhetorical strategies and behaviors over time. People are, to varying degrees, "strengthened" or "weakened" toward or away from particular ideas, illusions, visions, and prescribed or predicted communal (social) behaviors advocated by rhetors, groups, or corporate identities.
4. Rhetoric, as proscribed by ntu, is the evidence of rhythmic patterns urging shared meanings within and across rhetorical communities.

RHETORICAL COMMUNITIES AS AFRICOLOGICAL CONSTRUCT

The term *rhetorical community* has been implicated. The notion of rhetorical community was explored by Peter Ehrenhaus as a conceptual model that "addresses the sociodramatic processes through which social order evolves, is maintained, can change, and is threatened" (Ehrenhaus 1981a, 4). He later proposed a more precise definition under systems theory rubric. As a point of departure for the study of community, Ehrenhaus posited a rhetorical community as "group of people who identify themselves with a common rhetorical vision (symbolic reality) that gives them a common goal and sense of purpose by which they organize their actions" (1981b, 3).

For my purposes, the concept of a rhetorical community takes on a different meaning. To begin with, any consideration of texts assumes a rhetorical community or intersection of any number of such communities. We understand a rhetorical community as people whose faith options facilitate a reliance upon communal uses of rhetoric as a humanizing force or power, asserting agency in response to overarching power relations that constrain daily life. Clearly, the focus has to do with historical and cultural variables impacting available means of generating shared meanings.

Another distinction with this use of the term is the manner in which overarching patterns of power relations bring themselves to bear on all communication behaviors within and among rhetorical communities. Central to the model is an assumption based on the social construction of agency in response to multifarious oppressions. These ideas do not inhere in Ehrenhaus's use of the term.

One way of understanding my idea of rhetorical communities is to view trends and tropes manipulated in African American nationalist discourse, as Felicia Miyakawa does in this volume. Nationalist rhetorics demonstrate almost sole reliance upon culturally *discrete* language use to empower human agency during varying periods of American political history. Miyakawa's treatment of the nationalist rhetorical ends demonstrates that among the several political options—including armed struggle for liberation—African American rhetorical communities place their faith(s) in the efficacy of oppositional discourse and nommo, the force inherent to the discourse.

A rhetor (any communicator) establishes identity within rhetorical communities being addressed in a text. This is more than a mere discussion of audience, however. For example, Malcolm X's entire premise for having anything of value to express is determined by the manner in which he honors the traditions of his rhetorical communities. Too, this has to do with more than matters of credibility, for the traditions of any rhetorical community are brought to bear not merely to signal authority and believability. It is more complex. Communal traditions for creating understanding and sharing meanings are invoked consistently if anything is to "make sense" within given rhetorical communities.

Rhetoric achieves power in its timeless presence and use throughout the history of such communities. Epic, exigent material conditions resulting from various oppressions move people to believe, or have faith, in the efficacy of rhetorical forces (and sometimes rhetorical forces alone). Rhetorical strategies are arrived at historically, as options. The choices evolve, in part, because they deliver on people's faith. Certainly, in the rhetorical experiences of formerly enslaved African American women, these are humanizing options. Other options presented themselves, but rhetorical ones were preferred. This is most often the case with rhetorical communities.

RHETORICAL TEXT AS SYMBOLIC SCRIPT

This discussion places our concerns appropriately in the realm of the symbolic. As Richard Wright asserts elsewhere in this book, there is so much more, however, in the lives of rhetorical communities than mere manipulation of signs and symbols. Wright's urgencies direct us to the work of language, its power, its force. African thought, ancient and contemporary, as well as African American traditionalisms are characterized by a type of symbolism quite distinct from our common understandings. Rather than a symbolism that "stands for" objects, one that "stands as" is in effect. A symbol may likely be taken to be the thing! Symbols are powerful. In like manner, there is much less subject/object duality in any rationalization or conception. This assists our approach to Africological rhetorical theory and criticism in that we are far more inclined to be open to an awareness of how language, for example, is responsible for calling into being that which may not readily be seen from other cultural venues.

The centrality and function of spirit in African rhetorical activity is better understood, too, through an appreciation for the ways in which material, natural aspects are understood as a form of a "symbolic script" or text (Nobles

1986, 101). The spiritual laws that govern the cosmological order are accessible only through material realities and alignments. They are understood as unified, as whole. As we have seen above, the spiritual finds its manifestation in the material. The material has its meaning in the spiritual.

It is clear that nommo has as its symbolic script, or material text, particular manifestations that are attributable to rhetors and other participants in rhetorical communities. The final turn toward constructing theory is to delineate how such manifestations might take form. This is necessary in that we must be able to connect discussions about spiritual ethos to empirical knowledge about rhetorical behavior.

Building on the metatheoretical approach to discourse use presented by Asante (1987), several traditions of African American rhetorical communities become benchmark indicators or markers of the presence and facility of nommo. That is, various rhetorical behaviors are attributable to an awareness of the presence of nommo by rhetors and other rhetorical participants. More than this, members of rhetorical communities become variously adept in the facility of nommo to engender magara. By facility, I refer to a sensibility permitting verbal and extraverbal manipulations during communication instances that enhances awareness of extant spiritual dimensions.

NOMMODIC RHETORICAL BEHAVIORS (MANIFESTATIONS OF NOMMO)

1. *Rhythm as a frame of mentality.* Communicators reflect an orientation to expression and reception of ideas and feelings that attends to patterns or rhythms, which determine the use of language and the flow of speech. The use of pauses, frequency of modulation of pitch, rate, loudness, and other paralinguistic attributes reflects this attention to rhythms. A speaker's effectiveness is largely determined by her ability to demonstrate a facility of rhythmical communication patterns.

2. *Stylin' out as a quality of oration.* Conscious or unconscious manipulation of mannerisms is employed to influence favorably the hearers of a message. These mannerisms pertain to unique or classical styles of delivery and include gestures, posture, bodily movement, facial expressiveness, and other extraverbal behaviors. They are intended to communicate visual messages. Individual speakers can develop a repertoire for stylin' out that becomes unique, conventional, and expected by others.

3. *Soundin' as verbal artifact.* Vocal mannerisms that function similarly to extraverbal stylin' out; attached to and determined by speaker's facility of rhythm in vocal expression. These vocal cues can also be used as conventional devices with African American listeners or can develop as unique to a particular speaker.

4. *Lyrical approach to language.* The claim here is that in particular rhetorical communities African Americans' public communication is funda-

mentally lyrical: suited for poetry and song. Existential responses are primarily narrative and poetic. These responses are historical and cultural in derivation and transmitted tacitly as part of culture.

5. *Preference for improvisational delivery.* An aesthetic quality of discourse use is the reliance upon an improvisational mode of delivery. This is akin to the function of improvisation in dance and jazz. It involves composition of a call (portion of a message) before delivery and a willingness to finish the composition during delivery. Improvisation anticipates responses from listeners and allows for their participation in creating the message. It permits communicators to create and share meaning in the spaces between call and response.

6. *Call and response of participation.* A speaker knows and anticipates the cultural expectations of listeners in a particular rhetorical community. Listeners will deem a speech, sermon, dance, song, or other form most effective when they have been given space to participate in the creation of the message. The speaker is primarily responsible for sending a call, which is her portion of the created message. Speakers make room for the responses of listeners throughout the speech, for example. The speaker's call is modified depending upon the responses of the listeners. A message or text is not complete until the call is given and the response comes forth.

7. *Reliance upon mythoforms.* Mythoforms determine how we understand our living relationships with one another, our ancestors, and our progeny (see Asante 1987, 96). It operates as a cultural force that rationalizes and structures the illusions constructing our reality (past, present, and future). Mythoforms are generative of myths regarding our explanations of the human condition of multifarious, intersecting oppressions and liberation. Mythoforms are adaptive to the circumstances of history. Myths arise from them to structure our experiences and provide direction. Speakers relying upon storytelling and myths are said to rely upon mythoforms.

8. *Use of indirection.* This involves a circuitous approach to an issue, idea, or image. Rather than a direct approach, a communicator might embellish with imagination, flair, and artistry as the issue, idea, or image is approached from a circular direction—stopping here and there to view the thing from various angles before (if ever) landing on the point to be made. This "stalking" of the issue arouses listener interest and participation.

9. *Repetition for intensification.* Communicators conventionally use repetition of a single idea or image to move from one level of intensity to another until saturation is experienced. The clarity of a point is enhanced each time an idea or image is presented or restated.

EMERGENT CRITICAL APPROACHES

Since Africological formulations reopen questions concerning the available means of creating shared meaning, communal understandings, and social coordination—in other words, *persuasion*—it is incumbent upon us to demonstrate that spiritual dynamics form the substance behind human manipulations. To do this, we explore the rhetoric of Malcolm X. In particular, his text, *Message to the Grass Roots*, because of its prototypical qualities, leaves it suitable for exploration. The question asked here is: To what degree did Malcolm X facilitate nommo in the production of magara through the culturally discrete use of nommodic manifestations in *Message to the Grass Roots*?

Before an audience of mostly non-Islamic responders, Malcolm X, then a minister in the Nation of Islam, was a featured speaker at the Northern Negro Grass Roots Leadership Conference, held concurrently with, and in opposition to, the Northern Negro Leadership Conference in Detroit, Michigan, on November 10, 1963, at the King Solomon Baptist Church. Reverend Albert B. Cleage Jr., a pro-nationalist Christian minister, was instrumental in establishing the grassroots conference after the more traditional Detroit Council for Human Rights refused to allow African American nationalists to participate in its Leadership Conference.

Both conferences convened for two days, beginning on November 9. There was already a heavy pro-grassroots sentiment upon which Malcolm X would play throughout the length of his speech. Available transcripts of his address include nearly half of the entire speech.

For Malcolm X, this was an opportunity to broaden the Nation of Islam's notions about nationalism. Since there had already developed a distancing from the honorable Elijah Muhammad, founding leader of the Nation of Islam, this speech gave Malcolm X an inducement to place his indelible stamp on nationalist ideals.

As well, the moment suggested prime opportunities to target the ideas of those who openly led African Americans away from nationalist ideologies. Much of the text of *Message to the Grass Roots* presents itself as a rebuttal to the more traditional and moderate civil rights ideologues with which Malcolm X disagreed sharply and publicly. His characterization of them and their philosophies was anything but cordial.

This text, perhaps more than any other, reflects Malcolm X's understanding of the civil rights movement of the late 1950s and early 1960s. His was an effort to affirm local African American female and male leadership in their grassroots liberation struggles. It became his burden to demonstrate that most civil rights activists were not capable of responding to the urgencies of commonplace, working-class African Americans, who constituted the legions in the struggle.

Rev. Cleage, two years after the assassination of Malcolm X, reflected on *Message to the Grass Roots* as perhaps Malcolm's "best speech, his most typical statement, and [one] which I personally think is his last will and testament" (Clarke 1990, 14). The speech reflects Malcolm X's own assessment of content. By 1963, he spoke less and less of religion. "I taught social doctrine to Muslims, and current events, and politics" (X 1965, 322). The speech evidences Malcolm X's sharp disappointment with 1963 March on Washington, which had begun as the brainchild of A. Philip Randolph of the Brotherhood of Sleeping Car Porters some twenty years before.

A CASE FOR AFRICOLOGICAL CRITICISM

Critical approaches, as we have seen, emanate from critics' ideological assumptions about significant markers of effective or excellent uses of discursive and nondiscursive communicative forms. Our attention has been turned in this essay to the manners in which nondiscursive forms act as symbolic scripts for discourse. That is, we are concerning ourselves with those dynamics of human communication that are not symbols belonging to some verbal or nonverbal system or language. The dynamics we seek to explore are spiritual.

While such dynamics are immaterial, they re-present themselves in material terms. There are manifestations with which we can associate these dynamics. Magara is generated by a communicator's facility of nommo. The term *facility* suggests that one can offer manipulations of communication variables that will indeed produce "strengthening" or "weakening" responses among respondents in communication. For example, the presence of nommo and one's skill at its facility result in certain manifestations or behaviors constituting a communicator's call. Skilled communicators construct a call that elicits a desired response from listeners, audience members, or (better) responders.

Already, this description of human communication evidences Afrocentric ideological assumptions. The prevailing ideology, or body of givens, is centering on a configuration of African ideals and values. To continue the description, let us assume that an individual articulates an idea, wants to change people's attitudes or actions, or is being expressive in an artistic manner. Our model maintains that nommo is the force that will do the work of engendering meanings in responders that adequately correspond with the idea, desired attitude or action, or artistic value now resident in the individual. The individual assumes the stance of a communicator who, desiring to achieve coordination of meanings, offers a call, which of course is a text of some sort.

We are assured that nommo will be present, for no communication occurs in its absence. What is variable, however, is the communicator's ability or skill at facilitating the presence of nommo so as to produce the desired strengthening of others' ideas, attitudes, actions, or artistic values toward the communicator's. It is for the communicator, then, to offer certain manipulations of the call that will, in fact, induce or enhance the workings of nommo in the production of this magara. This does not suggest that a person has a controlling effect on nommo. To the contrary, a communicator manipulates communicative behaviors, not nommo. It is more accurate to understand human agency as a conduit for the workings of nommo.

Thus, when critics search for rhetorical effectiveness, one fertile area includes a communicator's activity so far as they relate to what I have called "manifestations of nommo." I understand these behaviors to have been learned tacitly as a function of regular encounters within certain rhetorical communities. As it is, African American rhetorical communities tend to rely upon these manifestations to foster shared meaning and understanding to achieve social coordination.

It must be stated that the behaviors are learned, observed, shared, and taught as a part of the life (culture) of African American rhetorical communities. Critical reflection concerns itself with communicators' particular manipulations of the manifestations as a symbolic script for the spiritual dynamics, which are believed to engender the desired coordination. The critical focus is on observable phenomena as expressive evidence of the workings of immaterial forces.

The critical approach useful in tracing manifestations of nommo in the production of magara involves descriptions of communicators' sensibility permitting verbal and extraverbal manipulations during instances of communication that enhance people's awareness of extant spiritual dimensions.

An examination of *Message to the Grass Roots* under this rubric would engage any or all of the nine manifestations. This portion of the essay is confined to an exploration of Malcolm X's use of three of those manifestations: indirection, repetition, and a lyrical approach to discourse use. One result will be the demonstration of how various manifestations operate together to aid in the construction of a text.

USE OF INDIRECTION

One of Malcolm X's trademarks was his penchant for indirection and innuendo. Asante posits indirection as one of the constituent elements for structuring language by approaching "the central issue of talk in a circuitous fashion, in the manner of the cultural temperament" (1987, 51). The effort suggests the veiling of one's true emotions through "duality, irony, and elegancy" (Paznik 1975, 5). Malcolm's veiling tends to be momentary in this text, for though he dances around a matter, it is not long until he circles in with a direct statement. Even so, this eventual directness tends to exhibit a type of caution.

Early in *Message to the Grass Roots,* Malcolm stalks the issue of African American displacement and undesirability within the American social mainstream. Before overtly proposing the idea, he wanders through an indictment of America's social problem:

> We all agree tonight, all of the speakers have agreed, that America has a very serious problem. Not only does America have a very serious problem, but our people have a very serious problem. America's problem is us. We're her problem. The only reason she has a problem is she doesn't want us here. And every time you look at yourself, be you Black, brown, red or yellow, a so-called Negro, you represent a person who poses such a serious problem for America because you're not wanted. Once you face this as a fact, then you can start plotting a course that will make you appear intelligent, instead of unintelligent. (X 1965, 4)

Clearly, it was Malcolm's wish for his listeners to believe that they needed to begin to adopt strategies that would effectively address one central reality: African Americans were among America's undesirables. Yet this notion is cloaked until after he has involved the listeners in a tour around it. Through masterly call-and-response techniques, Malcolm X is able to elicit agreement, all the while dancing around the issue. Moreover, this pre-issue speaking time permitted listeners opportunities to indicate that they not only agreed with the foregoing, but also enjoyed following Malcolm X in the anticipation that he was leading to some agreeable space.

Indirection, in this case, assures both communicator and responders that they are traveling together, as it were, to some safe and mutual point of understanding. Much of the common understanding to be reached when Malcolm lands on his point has already occurred in the journey of indirection. It was more significantly meaningful to agree on the notion that African Americans were not wanted within the American social mainstream after the dance than it would have been if Malcolm X had made the assertion absent these stylistics.

In another early passage in the text of the speech Malcolm X's indirect style allows him to speak to the matter of why African Americans experienced what to him amounted to racial oppression. Rather than moving into accusative territory, he reminds people of the reasons they experience particular hardships as citizens through a series of negations. Similar to definition by negation, this technique required that Malcolm X reflect an understanding of his listeners' life circumstances. He, for example, had to be aware that there were differences among them and that these differences at times prevented them from coming together to address common difficulties. He placed himself in a position to remind them of who they were and were not:

> You don't catch hell because you're a Methodist or Baptist, you don't catch hell because you're a Democrat or a Republican, you don't catch hell because you're a Mason or an Elk, and you sure don't catch hell because you're an American; because if you were an American, you wouldn't catch hell. You catch hell because you're a Black man. You catch hell, all of us catch hell, for the same reason. (X 1965, 4)

There was, by the end of the passage, a no-nonsense directness that appeared to contain unavoidable truth in light of Malcolm X's skillful disqualification of alternative explanations. Asante called attention to the deductive nature of many stylistic uses of indirection (1987, 51). This passage exemplifies this tendency.

Further indirection allowed Malcolm X to place all the responsibility for African American oppression on one target. He was careful to pace himself regarding the degree to which he would exercise precision in naming this target:

> We have a common enemy. We have this in common. We have a common oppressor, a common exploiter, and a common discriminator. But once we all realize that we have a common enemy, then we unite—on the basis of what we have in common. And what we have foremost in common is that enemy—the White man. He's an enemy to all of us. I know some of you all think that some of them aren't enemies. Time will tell. (X 1965, 5)

Certainly, it would be a simple matter for any African American to understand racist oppression as an offense from institutional elements of European American society of the period. It would hardly have been an earth-shattering revelation for a public speaker of Malcolm's ilk to remind an audience of the source of American exploitation. Mindful, however, of the need to permit respondents to share in the creation of the message, Malcolm X approached naming the enemy with customary reserve. Until, through suggestion and inference, it was essentially clear who the enemy was, Malcolm allowed respondents to name the enemy for themselves. Again, by the time the matter had been stalked, it is merely for the purpose of clarifying shared understandings that Malcolm X made the direct reference.

One of the most challenging passages for any communicator to broach involved Malcolm X's response to Dr. Martin Luther King Jr.'s reference to the "Negro revolution" that had been sweeping the nation. In rebuttal form, Malcolm X sought dialog on the appropriate use of the term to signal the nonviolent efforts of the Southern Christian Leadership Council, the Student Nonviolent Coordinating Committee, and other mainstream civil rights organizations.

This is an instance where Malcolm X was called upon to promote a generally negative impression without becoming overtly derogatory. His ideas about nonviolent resistance as a philosophy of social change were clear. Later in the text, he called proponents of such strategies "traitors." In the upcoming passage, he was able to deftly draw distinctions between historical political revolutions and the philosophy of nonviolent resistance:

> Look at the American Revolution in 1776. That revolution was for what? For land. What did they want? Land. Independence. How was it carried out? Bloodshed. Number one, it was based on land, the basis of independence. And

> the only way they could get it was bloodshed. The French Revolution—what was it based on? The landless against the landlord. What was it for? Land. How did they get it? Bloodshed. Was no love lost, was no compromise, was no negotiation. I'm telling you—*you don't know what a revolution is!* Because when you find out what it is, you'll get back in the alley, you'll get out of the way. The Russian Revolution—what was it based on? Land: the landless against the landlord. How did they bring it about? Bloodshed. You haven't got a revolution that doesn't involve bloodshed. *And you're afraid to bleed. I said, you're afraid to bleed.* (X, 1965, 7)

There are two ideas that Malcolm approached. First was the idea that people using this nomenclature to describe the civil rights movement did not command an understanding of the term. Second was the notion that devotees of the civil rights movement simply were unable to bring what is required in a revolution, namely, a willingness to give blood and life for the cause of liberation and independence. For Malcolm X, anyone not willing to ask for land and independence and lay down his or her life to attain them was not worthy of the term "revolution."

It is easy to note that Malcolm X may have been accused of advocating violent revolution and overthrow by such a series of ideas. This analysis assists by demonstrating his stylistic indirection as a way of *not saying* what he meant. It is more important to discover what was not spoken than it is to seek literal interpretations of his words in this instance.

After still more indirection, Malcolm X returned to the theme of a so-called Negro revolution. This time, however, we are permitted a glimpse at his effort to unmask his indirection by being more precise with his distinctions. After a discussion of various global, contemporaneous revolutions, Malcolm X believed his respondents were "ready" to hear his targeted idea:

> So I cite these various revolutions, brothers and sisters, to show you that you don't have a peaceful revolution. You don't have a turn-the-other-cheek revolution. There's no such thing as a nonviolent revolution. The only kind of revolution that is nonviolent is the Negro revolution. The only revolution in which the goal is loving your enemy is the Negro revolution. It's the only revolution in which the goal is a desegregated lunch counter, a desegregated theater, a desegregated park, and a desegregated public toilet; you can sit down next to White folks—on the toilet. *That's no revolution!* Revolution is based on land. Land is the basis of all independence. *Land is the basis of freedom, justice, and equality.* (X, 1965, 7–8)

The passage served two purposes. Not only was indirection useful for dispelling the notion of a nonviolent revolution, it concluded Malcolm X's use of the earlier series of historical and contemporaneous liberatory battles.

In an effort to weaken respondents away from adherence to the strategies of the nonviolent civil rights leaders, Malcolm X spent considerable energy repeating the "house Negro" and "field Negro" myth. To be sure, his intent was to leave the general impression that nonviolent civil rights leaders functioned as "house Negroes." His reliance upon indirection, however, permitted the illusion, so he could finally say:

> Just as the slavemaster of that day used Tom, the house Negro, to keep the field Negroes in check, the same old slavemaster today has Negroes who are nothing but modern Uncle Toms, twentieth-century Uncle Toms, to keep you and me in check, to keep us under control, keep us passive and peaceful and nonviolent. That's Tom making you nonviolent. (X 1965, 12)

While that statement revealed Malcolm's willingness to focus on the sources and character of African American nonviolent resistance, it also marked a skillful reduction of risk. To have named and identified, not by intimation, leaders of the nonviolent struggle as twentieth-century Uncle Toms would have risked the desired "strengthening" of his respondents to his own nationalist, and not necessarily nonviolent, philosophies.

REPETITION FOR INTENSIFICATION

A second critical mark of *Message to the Grass Roots* was Malcolm X's use of repetition for intensification. At issue here are the manners in which he would reiterate single ideas and images until they grew in the minds of responders to represent larger, more intense notions. When leading responders toward agreement on America's "problem," Malcolm X used the term seven times in five sentences. Responders became familiarized with the word *problem,* which aided in their acceptance of Malcolm X's peculiar use of it.

In the "catching hell" passage, Malcolm used the expression, in varying forms, nine times in only four sentences. One of these contains the phrase four times. Clearly, after mentioning "catching hell," at first through negation, so many times in so short a passage, Malcolm X was forging agreement through identification and association, or mutuality. Not much later, Malcolm X reinforced mutuality through repetition of *common.* This demonstrates responder familiarity needed to ensure a kind of weakening away from reliance upon notions that would ally African Americans with European Americans in the liberation struggle.

Another potent passage relies upon repetition of "revolution":

> I would like to make a few comments concerning the difference between the Black revolution and the Negro revolution. Are they both the same? And if they're not, what is the difference? What is the difference between a Black revolution and a Negro revolution? First, what is a revolution? Sometimes I'm inclined to believe that many of our people are using this word "revolution"

> loosely, without taking careful consideration of what this word actually means, and what its historic characteristics are. When you study the historic nature of revolutions, the motive of a revolution, the objective of a revolution, the result of a revolution, and the methods used in a revolution, you may change words. You may devise another program, you may change your goal and you may change your mind. (X 1965, 6–7)

One of the pillars upon which *Message to the Grass Roots* stood was Malcolm X's movement to strengthen responders toward an embrace of the global "Black revolution" that would have placed African Americans of the early 1960s within a pan-Africanist moment. Clearly, the meaning of *revolution* becomes an increasingly important notion for responders after hearing it so frequently within so short a space of time. The intensification of the revolutionary ideas desired by Malcolm X was realized not through a treatise of why revolution suited their case, but by the manipulation of this nommodic manifestation.

A desired intensification of the idea that America was a kind of "prison" for African Americans was economically achieved in the passage:

> When I was in prison, I read an article—don't be shocked when I say that I was in prison. You're still in prison. That's what America means: prison. When I was in prison, I read an article in *Life* magazine showing a little Chinese girl, nine years old . . . (X 1965, 8)

Here again, efficient intensification was achieved by artistic repetition of a single term, as was the case with thirty-eight repeated words or phrases from the available documented portion of the text. Some of these phrases when surveyed help to delineate the thematic imperatives under which Malcolm X operated during *Message to the Grass Roots*. A listing of most repeated words and phrases follows.

	Word/Phrase	*Repetitions*
1.	problem	7
2.	catch hell	9
3.	ex-slave	3
4.	brought here	4
5.	common	8
6.	some of them (were)	8
7.	they didn't have	3
8.	revolution *[three passages]*	43
9.	land, bloodshed	15
10.	you bleed/bled	9
11.	if violence is wrong/right	8
12.	prison	5

13. desegregated	4
14. nation/nationalism	16
15. house Negro/field Negro	31
16. Uncle Tom	4
17. suffer peacefully	5
18. they control you	2
19. started attacking	4
20. march on (Washington)	4
21. that was revolution	3
22. scared to death	3
26. they called in	3
27. I'll welcome/join it	8
28. knows it happened	5
29. it used to be	3
30. it ceased to be	3

LYRICAL APPROACH TO LANGUAGE

A third marker useful for tracing manifestations of nommo in the rhetoric of Malcolm X has to do with his use of lyrical code structuring. The claim here is that significant portions of *Message to the Grass Roots* reflect language styles suitable for poetry. One way to access the poetic approach of Malcolm X's code structuring is to treat thematic sections of the text as though they were, in fact, presented as lyrics.

This is achieved by monitoring Malcolm's pausing techniques during narration, for example. Exploitation of punctuation circumscribing phrases, clauses, sentences, or other syntactic divisions also provides clues reflecting the kinds of patterns or rhythms that frame his flow of speech. Modulations of pitch, rate, loudness, and other paralinguistic attributes reflected his attention to rhythms. These are the communicative patterns germane to Malcolm X that evidence his lyrical approach to strengthening responders toward his ideas and weakening them away from those of others.

Most of Malcolm X's lyricism becomes evident in the context of narration. For instance, his description of pan-Africanist unity at Bandung was supremely lyrical. By distinguishing among punctuated clauses to determine typographical structure and omitting non-narrative elements, the poetic nature of the text becomes manifest. Sections from the lengthy passage about the Bandung Conference could have been transcribed as follows:

At Bandung all the nations came together,
the dark nations from Africa and Asia.
Some of them were Buddhists,
some of them were Muslims,
some of then were Christians,

some were Confucianists,
some were atheists.

Using this typography for this passage from *Message to the Grass Roots* renders Malcolm X's lyricism undeniable. Another lyrical narrative contains Malcolm X's frequent revisionist ideas about house Negroes and field Negroes. His lyrical stylistics suggest the following typography:

There were two kinds of slaves,
the house Negro and the field Negro.
The house Negroes—
they lived near the master;
If the master said, "We got a good house here."
Whenever the master said "we," he said "we."
If the master got sick,
the house Negro would say,
"What's the matter, boss, we sick?"
We sick! . . .
Just as the slavemaster of that day
used Tom, the house Negro,
to keep the field Negroes in check,
the same old slavemaster today
has Negroes who are nothing but modern Uncle Toms,
twentieth-century Uncle Toms,
to keep you and me in check,
to keep us under control,
keep us passive and peaceful and nonviolent.
That's Tom making you nonviolent.

It would appear that whenever Malcolm X assumed a narrative mode, he also relied upon lyricism to move respondents toward his perspectives and understandings in *Message to the Grass Roots*. A final sampling reveals an extranarrative lyrical approach to achieving magara. As in the first two examples, this passage about the "Black revolution" is assigned typography suited to Malcolm X's paralinguistic modulations alongside syntactical markers:

When you study the historic nature of revolutions,
the motive of a revolution,
the objective of a revolution,
the result of a revolution,
and the methods used in a revolution,
you may change words.
You may devise another program,
you may change your goal and you may change your mind. . . .
You don't know what a revolution is.

You bleed for White people,
But when it comes to seeing your own churches being bombed
And little Black girls murdered,
You haven't got any blood.
You bleed when the White man says bleed;
You bite when the White man says bite;
And you bark when the White man says bark.
If violence is wrong in America,
Violence is wrong abroad.

Malcolm X tended toward a lyrical approach to structuring his call in order to prompt desired responses from his listeners.

CONCLUSION

In the previous section, I called attention to three forms in which culturally determined discursive styles in the rhetoric of Malcolm X were manipulated to achieve desired shared understandings. It is important to call attention as well to the recorded vocal responses of Malcolm X's Detroit audience. One of the factors contributing to a reliance upon these and other stylistic elements is the consistent manner in which responders filled spaces created by Malcolm X's artistic appreciation of the call-and-response patterns of participatory communication.

Perhaps the most central manifestation of a nurtured presence of nommo, call and response, not only required respondents to help form a message, but afforded Malcolm X the privilege of knowing the degree to which shared or communal understandings were being reached. More than feedback or "noise," as it is characterized under Eurocentric models of communication, response became a guide, directing Malcolm X toward more effective manipulations.

Nommodic dynamics, you will recall, are immaterial substances that do the work of achieving magara. From this perspective, they fuel the work of language. The degree to which we are able to demonstrate that Malcolm X manipulated manifestations of these dynamics correlates with our ability to suggest, in a context of ntu, that he achieved magara—the strengthening of responders' attitudes and ideas toward his own and the weakening of their attitudes and ideas away from those of most civil rights leaders—especially Dr. Martin Luther King Jr.

A significant addition made by this type of critical exercise is the validation of an Africological claim that human communication may be understood within spiritual contexts. All of the observable, audible, and otherwise empirical behaviors of communicators are really scripts for the unseen dynamics that constitute human understanding. Ultimately, there can be no objectivist explanation for the ways in which people come to know, agree, and forge social coordination.

Africological theories treat human behaviors as manifestations of spirit/forces motivating behind and between the words, images, illusions, and other signs. Within the context of ntu, universal life rhythm(s), nommo is the force that achieves the sharing of meanings we experience when we reach agreement and cognitive coordination. Meanings do not reside in our experiences alone. They are part of an engendering or conjuring process not isolated from human skill and stylistic artistry, as we have seen in the rhetoric of Malcolm X.

African American communication has fostered our appreciation for the spiritual dynamics of human communication. These dynamics and their manifestations are *traceable in all human communication*. Anyone with artistry and cultural sensitivity has access to manipulating the manifestations in order to afford nommo facility to produce a kind of magara.

Rhetorical theory and criticism, as we have known it in the West, has long avoided attending to the immaterial essence as a constitutive element of rhetorical studies. Africological theory and criticism opens the door to new ways of explaining and appreciating communication and human understanding. Magara, far outside fundamental Aristotelian preoccupations, is detectable as listeners respond to and guide a communicator's call. "Discovering available means" takes on an entirely new yet related meaning when including nommo alongside the weary triumvirate ethos, logos, and pathos.

We have long labored with only portions of what is available in the achievement of shared meanings, communal understandings, and social coordination. Perhaps by considering spiritual dynamics, our focus will advance more humane, less exclusivist rhetorical and communication studies.

REFERENCES

Asante, M. K. (1987). *The Afrocentric Idea.* Philadelphia: Temple University Press

Asante, M. K. (1990). *Kemet, Afrocentricity, and Knowledge.* Trenton, NJ: Africa World Press.

Asante, M. K. (1993). An Afrocentric Communication Theory. In M. K. Asante (Ed.), *Malcolm X as Cultural Hero and Other Afrocentric Essays* (pp. 171–85). Trenton, NJ: Africa World Press.

Clarke, J. H. (Ed.) (1990). *Malcolm X: The Man and His Times.* Trenton, NJ: Africa World Press.

Dodd, C. H. (1987). *Dynamics of Intercultural Communication,* second edition. Dubuque, IA: Wm. C. Brown Publishers.

Ehrenhaus, P. (1981a). A Conceptual Model of Rhetorical Community. Paper presented at the annual meeting of the Central States Speech Association, Chicago, IL, April.

Ehrenhaus, P. (1981b). The Critical Study of Rhetorical Community: Applications for a Conceptual Model. Paper presented at the annual meeting of the Speech Communication Association, Anaheim, CA, November.

Gonzalez, A., M. Houston, and V. Chen (1994). *Our Voices: Essays in Culture, Ethnicity and Communication: An Intercultural Anthology.* Los Angeles: Roxbury Publishing Co.

Griaule, M. (1948). *Dieu d'eau.* Paris: Fayard.

Jahn, J. (1990). *Muntu: African Culture and the Western World.* New York: Grove Weidenfeld. Originally published 1961.

Klopf, D. W. (1991). *Intercultural Encounters: The Fundamentals of Intercultural Communication,* second edition. Englewood, CA: Morton Publishing Co.

Lustig, M. W., and J. Koester (1993). *Intercultural Competence: Interpersonal Communication Across Cultures.* New York: HarperCollins College Publishers.

Nobles, W. W. (1986). Ancient Egyptian Thought and the Development of African (Black) Psychology. In M. Karenga and J. Carruthers (Eds.), *Kemet and the African Worldview: Research, Rescue and Restoration* (pp. 100–18). Los Angeles: University of Sankore Press.

Paznik, J. (1975). *Artistic Elements in Black English: Implications for Urban Education.* Paper presented at the annual meeting of the National Conference on Urban Education, Kansas City, MO, November.

Samovar, L. A., and R. E. Porter (1994). *Intercultural Communication: A Reader,* seventh edition. Belmont, CA: Wadsworth Publishing Co.

X, M(alcolm) (1992). *February 1965: The Final Speeches.* Ed. S. Clark. New York: Pathfinder.

X, M(alcolm) (1965). *Malcolm X Speaks: Selected Speeches and Statements.* Ed. G. Brietman. New York: Grove Weidenfeld.

Zeigler, D. (Ed.) (1995). *Molefi Kete Asante and Afrocentricity: In Praise and in Criticism.* Nashville, TN: James C. Winston Publishing Co.

CHAPTER 10

Every Man Fights for His Freedom: The Rhetoric of African American Resistance in the Mid-Nineteenth Century

ELLA FORBES

Mass media have presented us with images that represent specific eras of African American history. Often those representations reflect not the African American reality but the wishful thinking of the larger White society (Dates and Barlow 1993, 3). For example, we can readily identify the modern civil rights movement when we see depictions of peaceful protesters being sprayed with fire hoses or attacked by dogs controlled by burly White policemen. During the antebellum period, it is the sketch of an African American male kneeling, hands clasped, chains broken but visible, pleading, "Am I not a man and a brother?" begging Whites to see his humanity and his manhood.

In both instances, the portrayals represent iconic symbols that many Whites are most comfortable with, images that they can, in fact, relate to because they created them. What Whites are discomfited by is the picture of the athletes, gloved fists raised, who protested at the 1968 Mexico City Olympic Games or the militant Africans such as the 1851 Christiana, Pennsylvania, resisters who espoused, and acted upon, Black self-defense when they killed a slaveowner who was attempting to reenslave Africans. Such representations, illustrations of Black agency and self-empowerment, force Whites to confront the reason for Black activism and militancy: White racism. Calls for Black manhood and self-defense bring into question the very tenets upon which the nation is supposedly founded—life, liberty, and the pursuit of happiness for all its citizens—because it is those very things that have been denied, historically, to Africans in America.

However, contrary to the depictions of passive, docile Africans promoted by White mass media, the most prevalent stance for the African American community has been one of resistance. Therefore, militant images more accurately reflect the reality of African American agency and the quest for Black manhood, which have always been a part of the African American experience within the spectrum of African American social and political thought. This can easily be seen upon examining Black rhetoric that has consistently challenged White notions of African American passivity and docility. Mid-1800s periodicals devoted to African issues, such as the *Anti-Slavery Bugle, Douglass' Monthly, Frederick Douglass' Paper, Liberator,* and *Voice of the Fugitive,* are primary source documents for period resistance rhetoric.

This essay will focus on the rhetoric of resistance of African American males during the mid-nineteenth century because calls for resistance, redemptive violence, and Black manhood were the hallmark of this period's social and political thought. "Manhood" is meant in the sense of courage, self-determination, civil and human rights, and communal self-esteem, not necessarily gender. African American women also issued calls for resistance during this period, but those calls usually emphasized Black manhood by linking the manhood of Black males with the liberation of the entire African community.

Implicit in the rhetoric of the mid-1800s was a sense of disconnection and separation from the nation's social and political structure and an acknowledgment of a common interest—that of defying and relieving the burden of oppression. Africans came to understand that, to this end, violent resistance was sometimes necessary. The rhetoric was delivered in speeches, letters, and newspapers, in private and public forums, and in actions. This essay employs the term *African* as opposed to *African American* in many cases to illustrate the isolation from American citizenship that Black writers and speakers challenged.

However, unlike the lawlessness so often exhibited by White Americans toward Blacks, as in the case of the many White riots and physical attacks on Black communities and individuals during this period, Africans championed a redemptive violence, a violence both retributive and retaliatory because it was to be committed in self-defense and for the purpose of liberation. The use of a rhetoric of redemptive violence, manhood, and self-defense was designed to urge Africans to contend against oppression, but more importantly, it sought to establish the African's natural right to resist, and while it emphasized the "elevation" of the African community, it categorically rejected the idea that Blacks were innately inferior to Whites. The willingness of Africans to resort to force to gain basic rights, or at least to suggest it rhetorically, points to the alienation Blacks felt in a nation that showed its hostility so openly toward them. Operating from an axiological position that sanctioned their use of violence to effect their liberty, Africans put this rhetoric into action, believing that every *man* fights for his freedom.

African writers and speakers repeatedly paraphrased an apt line from the nineteenth-century poet Lord Byron's "Childe Harold's Pilgrimage": "Hereditary bondsmen! Know ye not who would be free themselves must strike the first blow? By their right arms the conquest must be wrought?" (Byron 1936, 76). William Parker, Henry Bibb, and Henry Highland Garnet are examples of African men who incorporated Byron's charge in their rhetoric, changing the words, intonation and meaning to fit the African worldview, experience, and need. Using such a statement from a European poet who wrote in support of Europeans' use of force legitimized redemptive violence for Africans and placed the responsibility on Africans for their own self-liberation. Converting standard discourses into vernacular ones is a part of the Black rhetorical tradition. Therefore, armed resistance, consistent with the principles of democracy touted by White America but denied to Black America, became a part of African axiology.

One of the ways in which Africans responded to political and social disenfranchisement was by forming organizations to work for and protect their own interests. A major self-help effort was the Negro convention movement, which began in 1817 as a response to the American Colonization Society's effort to rid the nation of free Blacks. The conventions provided a forum for Africans to protest and coalesce as they recognized and fought against their precarious position in a nation that sanctioned the enslavement of Africans. It was at these gatherings that Africans articulated a cosmology of defiance, calling for the violent overthrow of the slave system, rebellion against oppression, self-reliance, and, sometimes, voluntary emigration from the United States.

Fugitives used their own experiences of self-liberation to vindicate the use of redemptive violence. At one National Negro Convention, Samuel Ringgold Ward told the humorous story of Andrew Jackson, a religious fugitive, who eschewed passive resistance as five slave catchers tried to recapture him. Ward recounts: "Andrew told me, that when they demanded his surrender and return, he pointedly refused, and placed himself in an attitude of defence and defiance. He says, 'they came upon me, and I used a hickory stick I had in my hands. Striking them as hard and as often as I could, with each blow I prayed, 'Lord, save! Lord, save!' Now,' said he, 'had I simply cried, 'Lord, save!' without using my hickory, they would have taken me. Now I know that faith and works go together.' He conquered; flogging the five, as he said, by God's blessing upon the energetic use of his hickory" (p. 176). Reverend Jackson shared a version of the same story and defended his use of violence to secure his freedom in his own narrative by connecting his plight with the American Revolution. He challenged, "if it was right for the revolutionary patriots to fight for liberty, it was right for me, and it is right for any other slave to do the same. And were I now a slave, I would risk my life for freedom. 'Give me liberty or give me death,' would be my deliberate conclusion" (Jackson 1847, 14).

Frederick Douglass also advanced the manhood rights of African men repeatedly by using himself as an example. In answer to an editorial in the *Buffalo Courier* that contended, "Frederick Douglass gets into difficulty wherever he goes," Douglass challenged that he did so because "presuming to be a man, he recognizes himself as entitled to the rights and privileges of a man . . . 'difficulty' is forced upon him by the manhood of himself, and the meanness of the community" *(Frederick Douglass' Paper,* August 20, 1852).

Henry Highland Garnet had been influenced by David Walker's 1829 *Appeal* and in 1848 published *An Address to the Slaves of the United States of America.* Rephrasing Lord Byron, he exhorted enslaved Africans:

> If hereditary bondsmen would be free, they must strike the first blow. . . . To such degradation [as enslavement] it is sinful in the extreme for you to make voluntary submission. . . . It is your solemn and imperative duty to use every means, both moral, intellectual, and physical, that promise success. . . . You had better all die—die immediately, than live slaves, and entail your wretchedness upon your posterity . . . Let your motto be resistance! resistance! resistance! (Garnet 1968, 92)

Garnet first read his address at the National Negro Convention of 1843, where he hoped to have it accepted as a part of the convention's platform. It was rejected by one vote because the faction favoring White abolitionist William Lloyd Garrison's moral suasion view objected to the violence advocated for self-defense. Interestingly, Garnet's opposition was led by Frederick Douglass and Charles L. Remond. Douglass was later to break with Garrison and espouse the use of violence. Remond also renounced nonresistance and supported insurrections by enslaved Africans (Ripley 1991, 50).

Garnet was roundly attacked by the Garrisonians and saw the attack as an attempt to keep Africans submissive to Whites in the anti-slavery movement. This was borne out when Maria W. Chapman, a White abolitionist, wrote: "We say emphatically to the man of color, trust not the counsels that lead you to the shedding of blood. That man knows nothing of nature, human or Divine,—of character—good or evil, who imagines that a civil and servile war would ultimately promote freedom" (*Liberator,* September 22, 1843).

He responded with his usual candor and assumption of equality:

> I was born in slavery, and have escaped, to tell you, and others, what the monster has done, and is still doing. It, therefore, astonished me to think that you should desire to sink me again to the condition of a *slave,* by forcing me to think just as you do. My crime is that I have dared to think, and act, contrary to your opinion. . . . While you must think as you do, we must differ. If it has come to this, that I must think as you do, because you are an abolitionist or be exterminated by your thunder, that I do not hesitate to say that your abolitionism is abject slavery. . . . [You] may rely upon my word, when I tell you I mean "to stand." . . . You say I "have received bad counsel." You are not the only person who has told your humble servant that his humble productions have been produced by the *"counsel"* of some anglo-saxon. . . . I can think on the subject of human rights without "counsel," either from the men of the West, or the women of the East. . . . In the mean time, be assured that there is one Black American who dares speak boldly on the subject of universal liberty. (*Liberator,* December 3, 1843)

A June 2, 1854, article entitled, "Is It Right and Wise to Kill a Kidnapper?" is representative of Douglass' change in position from moral suasion to redemptive violence and reflects as militant an attitude as that of Henry Highland Garnet, his former ideological foe Douglass asserts:

> It may be said . . . for the fugitive slave or his friends that submission . . . is far wiser than resistance. To this it is sufficient answer to show that submission is valuable only so long as it has some chance of being recognized as a virtue. . . . That submission on the part of the slave, has ceased to be a virtue, is very evident. . . . Such submission . . . only creates contempt for them in the public mind, and becomes an argument in the mouths of the community, that Negroes are, by nature, only fit for slavery; that slavery is their normal condition. . . . This reproach must be wiped out, and nothing short of resistance on the part of colored men, can wipe it out. (*Frederick Douglass's Paper*, 1854)

He was firmly out of the Garrison camp when he declared in August 1857:

> "Your humble speaker has been branded as an ingrate, because he has ventured to stand up on his own right, and to plead our common cause as a colored man, rather than as a Garrisonian. I hold it to be no part of gratitude to allow our White friends to do all the work, while we merely hold their coats." (Foner, 1950, 437)

Just a few months after the 1857 Dred Scott Decision, which affirmed the White belief that Africans were not and could not be citizens of the United States, Douglass is speaking to Africans about Black manhood; he is not pleading with Whites to relinquish their bigotry.

He went on to explain why the creation of a worldview that sanctioned redemptive violence was a necessary part of Black axiology—only in that way could the survival of the African community be assured and its manhood redeemed. Douglass avowed,

> The whole history of the progress of human liberty shows that all concessions yet made to her august claims, have been born of earnest struggle. . . . This struggle may be a moral one, or it may be a physical one, and it may be both moral and physical, but it must be a struggle. Power concedes nothing without a demand. It never did and it never will. Find out what any people will quietly submit to and you have found out the exact measure of injustice and wrong which will be imposed upon them, and these will continue till they are resisted with either words or blows, or with both. The limits of tyrants are prescribed by the endurance of those whom they oppress. . . . If we ever get free from the oppressions and wrongs heaped upon us, we must pay for their removal. We must do this by labor, by suffering, by sacrifice, and if needs be, by our lives and the lives of others (Cited in Foner 1950, 437)

Charles Langston of Ohio, brother to John Mercer Langston and ancestor of the poet Langston Hughes, exemplified the Black commitment to redemptive violence and Black manhood. He was a regular attendee at the National Negro Conventions, where he espoused Black resistance. He took part in the 1858 Oberlin-Wellington rescue of John Price, for which he was fined $100 and sentenced to twenty days in jail. In 1859, after John Brown's raid, he maintained that the "renowned fathers of our celebrated revolution taught the world that 'resistance to tyrants is obedience to God,'[1] [that] all men are created equal, and have the inalienable right to life and liberty. These men proclaimed *death*, but *not slavery*, or rather, 'give me liberty or give me death.'" Further, citizens had the right to abolish the government "and to institute a new government" when it failed to live up to its duty of providing "liberty, justice, and happiness." Therefore, John Brown's raid was "in perfect harmony with and resulted from the teaching of the Bible and of the revolutionary fathers" (quoted in Cheek and Cheek 1989, 145).

The young John Mercer Langston, relatively new on the scene, adopted as stringently the militant and self-reliant stance of his brother. He asserted that he had "reviewed with severity the action of the American people in regard to the colored race, and advocated the right and duty of resistance by force of arms, when it was feasible" (*Anti-Slavery Bugle,* December 4, 1858). In that vein, he, too, supported John Brown's efforts, financially and morally, and helped to recruit men for the raid.

Racial hostility, violence, and disfranchisement were the most important issues for Africans during the mid-1800s. A part of the Missouri Compromise, the 1850 Fugitive Slave Law, in its quest to secure the national union, combined all these problems into one bill, reinforcing the belief that the goals of this nation were often inimical to the best interests of Africans. It was the most defining point in African American history up until this point because it highlighted Black isolation and alienation. The new law increased Black rhetorical calls for resistance, redemptive violence, and Black manhood. Martin Delany employed the law to promote emigration as a means of achieving Black manhood. He entitled chapter 16 of his book *The Condition, Elevation, Emigration, and Destiny of the Colored People of the United States* "National Disfranchisement of Colored People," to drive home the point that the law further stripped Africans of citizenship.

> By the provisions of this bill, the colored people of the United States . . . are made liable at any time, in any place, and under all circumstances, to be arrested—and upon the claim of any White person, without the privilege, even of making a defence, sent into endless bondage. Let no visionary nonsense about *habeas corpus,* or a *fair trial,* deceive us; there are no such rights granted in this bill. . . . [There] is no earthly chance—no hope under heaven for the colored

> person who is brought before . . . officers of the law . . . [our] rights and liberty entirely at their disposal.

Addressing the mayor of Pittsburgh, Pennsylvania, Delany used a rhetoric that linked self-defense and Black manhood:

> Whatever ideas of liberty I may have, have been received from reading the lives of your revolutionary fathers. I have therein learned that a man has a right to defend his castle with his life, even unto the taking of life. Sir, my house is my castle; in that castle are none but my wife and my children, as free as the angels of heaven, and whose liberty is as sacred as the pillars of God. If any man approaches that house in search of a slave,—I care not who he may be, whether constable or sheriff, magistrate or even judge of the Supreme Court—nay, let it be he who sanctioned this act to become a law, surrounded by his cabinet as his body-guard, with the Declaration of Independence waving above his head as his banner, and the constitution of his country upon his breast as his shield,—if he crosses the threshold of my door, and I do not lay him a lifeless corpse at my feet, I hope the grave may refuse my body a resting-place, and righteous Heaven my spirit a home. O, no! He cannot enter that house and we both live. (Quoted in Rollin 1883, 76)

He was a man. Delany's use of "Americans," "your revolutionary fathers," and "his country" illustrates his belief that Africans were not truly citizens of the United States.

He argued at the August 1854 National Emigration of Colored People Convention in Cleveland, Ohio, in defense of redemptive violence:

> Should we encounter an enemy with artillery, a prayer will not stay the cannon shot, neither will the kind words nor smiles of philanthropy shield his spear from piercing us through the heart. We must meet mankind, then, as they meet us—prepared for the worst, though we may hope for the best. Our submission does not gain for us an increase of friends nor respectability, as the White race will only respect those who oppose their usurpation, and acknowledge as equals those who will nor submit to their oppression. (Cited in Rollin 1969, 336–37)

Other militant African leaders used the bill to bolster their position that defiance, not pacifism, was the best course. The Fugitive Slave Law caused Frederick Douglass, no longer a Garrisonian, to exhort in 1852:

> Every slave-hunter who meets a bloody death in this infernal business, is an argument in favor of the manhood of our race. Resistance is, therefore, wise as well as just. The only way to make the Fugitive Slave Law a dead letter is to make a half a dozen or more dead kidnappers. . . . The man who rushes . . . to strike down the rights of another does, by that act, divest himself of the right to live: If he be shot down, his punishment is just. . . . [A] colored man . . . is,

therefore, justified in the eye of God, in maintaining his right with his arm. (*Frederick Douglass' Paper,* August 20, 1852)

The Fugitive Slave Law also forced some less militant Africans who had espoused Garrison's doctrine to reassess and change their position. Robert Purvis, a staunch Quaker pacifist, contended in an October 1850 speech at the Pennsylvania Anti-Slavery Society in West Chester that "should any wretch enter my dwelling, any pale-faced spectre among ye, to execute this law on me or mine, I'll seek his life, I'll shed his blood" (*Anti-Slavery Bugle,* November 3, 1850).

Rev. Jermain Loguen commented facetiously, "I want you to set me down as a *Liberator* [Garrison's newspaper] man, I am with you in my heart. I may not be in *hands* and *head*—for my hands will fight a slaveholder—which I suppose the *Liberator* and some of its good friends would not do. But I do not say but they are doing more good in their way than I am in mine. I am a fugitive slave, and you know, that we have strange notions about many things" (*Liberator,* May 5, 1854). His words underscore how some Africans felt about being given advice from well-meaning Whites who had not experienced enslavement.

Rev. Josiah Henson, contrary to but often associated with the negative image of being an Uncle Tom, rebuked Garrison at a meeting at Boston's Belknap Street Church to protest the Fugitive Slave Law on September 30, 1850. Garrison had cautioned the primarily Black assembly that "the fugitives in this city and elsewhere would be more indebted to the moral power of public sentiment than by any display of physical resistance." Rev. Henson rose to contend, "[I]n a crisis for *Liberty or Death,* this speaker [Henson] would not be quietly led like a lamb to the slaughter." In fact, according to Henson, anyone who "condemned resistance on the part of colored people" denounced "the examples of WASHINGTON and JEFFERSON and all Martyrs of Liberty" (*Liberator,* October 11, 1850).

Many Africans voiced their commitment to rebellion at this gathering. Joshua Smith, a caterer, remarked that he hoped no one at the "meeting would preach *peace,* for as Patrick Henry said, '*there is no peace.*' . . . *If liberty is not worth fighting for, it is not worth having.*" He went on to advise every fugitive to "show himself a man" and "arm himself with a revolver—if he could not buy one otherwise, to sell his coat for that purpose." In his own case, he resolved that he "would not be taken ALIVE, but upon the slave-catcher's head be the consequences. When he could not live here in Boston, a FREEMAN . . . '*he had lived long enough.*'" The article comments humorously, "Mr. Smith, in conclusion, made a demonstration of one mode of defence, which those who best know him say would be exemplified to the *hilt*" (ibid.).

Robert Johnson carried this imagery further with his passionate admonition, "[W]e will not go into the depots or elsewhere after the slave-hunter, but when he rushes upon our buckler [shield]—*kill him.*" Charles Lenox Remond declared that he "would not yield to any institution or individual that would abridge his liberties or his efforts for the fugitive, and [I] was happy in believing that the colored citizens of Boston would do their whole duty and defend themselves" (ibid.).

At another meeting called to denounce the Fugitive Slave Law and to advocate resistance, African men in Portland, Maine, met at the Colored Congregational Church on October 8, 1850, and again on October 10, and proclaimed, "Resolved, That, recognizing no authority higher than the law of God . . . we solemnly pledge ourselves to each other, that we will at all times, when it is in our power, feed the hungry, clothe the naked, and give shelter and assistance to the fugitive from American slavery, and will resist unto death any and every effort to take from this city, for the purpose of enslaving him, any person to whom we are united by the ties of common brotherhood." They formed a committee of vigilance and safety "to give notice of the approach of danger; to see that every person is provided with the means of defence, and that places of security are selected; and to give direction to whatever measures may be necessary for our protection." One attendee proclaimed that the "colored people are determined to resist, to a man—and woman, too—any attempt to take a fellow-being back to bondage. Should the slaveholder come hither for that purpose, he will find the colored people are prepared to give him a warm reception. Not a man is to be taken from Portland. Our motto is—'Liberty or Death!'" *(Liberator,* November 1, 1850).

In fact, directives were given to the African community by most Black leaders, passive resisters or not, to use any means necessary to oppose the bill. *The Impartial Citizen* fervently proclaimed,

> Now, this bill strips us of all manner of protection, by the writ of *habeas corpus,* by trial jury, or by any other process known to the laws of civilized nations, that are thrown as safeguards around personal liberty. But while it does this, it throws us back upon the natural and inalienable right of self-defence—self-protection. It solemnly refers to each of us,individually, the question, whether we will submit to being enslaved by the hyenas which this law creates and encourages, or whether we will protect ourselves, even if, in so doing, we have to peril our lives, and *more than peril the useless and devilish carcasses of Negro-catchers.* It gives us the alternative of dying freemen, or living slaves. Let the men who would execute this bill beware. . . . Let them know that to enlist in that warfare is present, certain, inevitable death and damnation. Let us teach them, that none should engage in this business, but those who are ready to be offered up on the polluted altar of accursed slavery. So say the Black men of Brooklyn and Williamsburg [New York] . . . so say the brave 'Negroes of Philadelphia,'. . . and so let all the Black men of America say, and we shall teach Southern slavocrats, and Northern doughfaces, that to perpetuate the Union,

> they must beware how they expose *us* to slavery, and themselves to death and destruction, present and future, temporal and eternal! (*Liberator,* October 11, 1850)

There was opposition to the Fugitive Slave Law, not only in rhetoric but in action. The Henry Long affair in New York, the Shadrach case in Boston, the attempted release of Thomas Sims in Boston, the Christiana resistance in Pennsylvania, and the Jerry rescue in Syracuse, New York, are instances of rebellion against the Fugitive Slave Law. One of the first instances that reinforced African belief in the need for redemptive violence in the face of the Fugitive Slave Law was the Henry Long affair. Long was arrested in New York in January 1851. Abolitionists attempted to use legal means to free him but were not successful. He was returned to Virginia, whence he had escaped. The failure of the abolitionists to secure his release and the spectacle of Long being led shackled through the streets of New York surrounded by two hundred armed policemen made his case a cause célèbre and an argument in favor of physical resistance.

Boston's turn came the very next month. A man nicknamed Shadrach, whose legal name was Frederick Wilkins, had escaped enslavement in May 1850 from Norfolk, Virginia.[2] He settled in Boston and was recaptured there, after the presentation of a fugitive slave warrant, in February 1851. Africans burst into the courtroom, forcibly removed Shadrach from the court's custody, and spirited him away to Montreal, Canada. Eight men, four of them African—Lewis Hayden, Robert H. Morris, James Scott, and John A. Coburn—were indicted, but none was convicted for this action (Campbell 1970, 148–50).

President Millard Fillmore issued orders that federal charges be brought against the rescuers. From Canada, where he had recently fled, Henry Bibb chastised the president:

> The people against whom this proclamation is issued are denominated as "lawless persons." These are the usual cant terms employed by all tyrants, and men of sense attach no importance to them. Laws, from time immemorial, have so seldom been founded in justice, that it is not singular that honest men should invariably be found opposing them. . . . In the proclamation the persons of color are alluded to as chiefly composing the "lawless" mob. We admit the lawlessness of our people—they are outlaws—the only way in which the law recognizes them is in punishment; they are beyond the pale of its protection, consequently they cannot be censured for opposing its execution. (*Voice of the Fugitive,* February 26, 1851)

Ironically, Governor Johnston of Pennsylvania issued a similar proclamation in response to the later Christiana resistance, but as the leader of Christiana's action, William Parker, claimed, echoing Henry Bibb, "[T]he laws for personal protection are not made for us, and we are not bound to obey them. . . . [Whites] have a country and may obey the laws. But we have no country" (Smedley 1883, 115). As such, Africans could not commit treason against a country of which they were no part. Nevertheless, the prosecutors in Castner Hanway's trial in the wake of Christiana cited Shadrach's case in the presentation of their charge of treason against him. Of course, Hanway, a White man, could be charged with sedition because he did not uphold the law of his country.

As a result of Shadrach's escape, security was very tight in April 1851 when Thomas Sims was remanded to his Georgia slaveowner, and the Africans in Boston were unable to rescue him. Sims had been in the city only a little more than a month when he was captured as the result of having a telegram he had sent back to Savannah intercepted. He was attempting to arrange to have his wife, who was free, and his children transported to Boston. During his capture, he wounded one of the posse by stabbing him in the leg, a fact that was used against him in his case before a Boston magistrate.

Three hundred armed federal troops surrounded Sims to prevent abolitionists from rescuing him as he was taken, in the dead of night, to a ship bound for Savannah. The cost of returning Sims was to amount to nearly $20,000, but his return was viewed as a significant victory by those Americans determined to uphold the Fugitive Slave Law. The headline of the April 13, 1851, *National Intelligencer* trumpeted: "Supremacy of the Law Sustained." Turncoat Daniel Webster wrote to President Fillmore that the next step should be to get rid of crazy abolitionists and free-soilers (Levy 1950, 72).

After receiving thirty-nine lashes in Savannah in a public spectacle designed to make an example of him, Sims was sold to a slaveholder in Vicksburg, Mississippi. He again escaped in 1863, during the Civil War, and made his way back to Boston. In 1877, he was employed as a messenger in the Department of Justice in the District of Columbia. Ironically, he received the job through the efforts of Charles Devens, the Boston marshal who had arrested him in 1851 (Robbins 1970, 117–20).

One of the most famous acts of revolt occurred in Christiana, Pennsylvania, as William Parker and his self-defense organization translated rhetoric into action by killing a slaveowner as he attempted to reenslave four fugitives on September 11, 1851. During the conflict, Parker continually exhorted his men to resist: "Don't believe that any living man can take you. . . . Don't give up to any slaveholder." After the revolt, Parker reiterated his commitment; he had "determined not to be taken alive" (Parker 1866, 288). Making no apologies and with no equivocation, Parker used a language of violence to depict the untenable situation he and his fellow fugitives were in. Refusing to nuance his words to conform to established social mores, which demanded Black passivity, he spoke of blowing, beating, and knocking out brains, as well as of pistols and other ammunition. His descriptions are graphic:

> I doubled my fists to knock him down
>
> Bricks, stones, and sticks fell in showers. We fought across the road and back again, and I thought our brains would be knocked out.
>
> I caught him by the throat. . . . Then the rest beat him. . . . If we had not been interrupted, death would have been his fate.
>
> We were then near enough to have killed them, concealed as we were by the darkness.
>
> I told him we would not surrender on any conditions.
>
> I intend to fight. . . . I intend to try your strength.
>
> I told him, if he attempted it, I should be compelled to blow out his brains.
>
> Before he could bring the weapon to bear, I seized a pair of heavy tongs, and struck him a violent blow across the face and neck, which knocked him down. He lay for few minutes senseless. (Parker 1866: 159–60, 162–63, 165, 285–87)

It is evident, though, that the insurgents were not unique in their determination to oppose the imposition of the Fugitive Slave Law. Given the reaction of Africans to the law as illustrated in the rash of speeches and writings advocating defiance of the statute and specific acts of revolt, it is likely that they drew strength from the rhetoric. The Christiana resistance also influenced the same rhetoric. In fact, it became a part of Black militant rhetoric because it was emblematic of Black defiance, collective agency, and African manhood. William and Ellen Craft, themselves escapees from enslavement, after noting that the Thomas Sims rescue had been unsuccessful, acclaimed the actions at Christiana in a November 29, 1851, letter from England: "We were very sorry that the slaveholders were successful enough to get a slave from Boston, but were much pleased with the difficulty they had in doing so. We think a few more such cases as the Christiana affair will put a damper upon slave-catchers" (Woodson 1926, 263).

Immediately after the standoff, Frederick Douglass was praising their manly stand. In Douglass' judgment, the men at Christiana were "so firmly attached to liberty and so bitterly averse to slavery, as to be willing to peril even life itself to gain the one and to avoid the other." He went on to say, "The Christiana conflict was . . . needed to check [the aggressions of slave-catchers] and to bring the hunters of men to the sober second thought." But Black manhood was the most important result of Christiana: "If it be right for any man to resist those who would enslave them, it was right for the men of color at Christiana to resist. . . . Life and liberty are the most sacred of all of man's rights. . . . The man who rushes out of the orbit of his own rights to strike down the rights of another, does, by that act, divest himself of the right to live; if he be shot down, the punishment is just" (*Frederick Douglass' Paper,* September 25, 1851).

In August 1857, Douglass was continuing to praise them as heroes, placing them in the context of other acts of African rebellion, and there were many:

> [E]very mother who, like Margaret Garner, plunges a knife into the bosom of her infant to save it from the hell of our Christian Slavery, should be held and honored as a benefactress.[3] Every fugitive from slavery who like the noble William Thomas at Wilkesbarre, prefers to perish in a river made red by his own blood, to submission to the hell hounds who were hunting and shooting him, should be esteemed as a glorious martyr, worthy to be held in grateful memory by our people. The fugitive Horace, at Mechanicsburgh, Ohio, the other day, who taught the slave catchers from Kentucky that it was safer to arrest White men than to arrest him, did a most excellent service to our cause. Parker and his noble band of fifteen at Christiana, who defended themselves from the kidnappers with prayers and pistols, are entitled to the honor of making the first successful resistance to the Fugitive Slave Bill. But for that resistance, and the rescue of Jerry, and Shadrack, the man-hunters would have hunted our hills and valleys here with the same freedom with which they now hunt their own dismal swamps. . . . Joseph Cinque on the deck of the Amistad, did that which should make his name dear to us. . . . Madison Washington who struck down his oppressor on the deck of the Creole, is more worthy to be remembered than the colored man who shot Pitcairn at Bunker Hill. (Quoted in Foner 1950, 437–38)

Douglass was still using Christiana as a glorious example of defiance in December 1860, the eve of the Civil War: "We need not only to appeal to the moral sense of . . . slaveholders; we have need, and a right, to appeal to their fears." He went on to say how the outcome of the attempted capture of John Thomas in Wilkes-Barre, Pennsylvania, might have been different "[h]ad a few balls there whistled, as at Christiana, about the heads of the slave-catchers." Thomas, a fugitive, was recaptured in September 1853 but escaped into the local river, where he was shot and left for dead. Douglass made the point in his speech that although "the moral suasion people of that vicinity gathered also on the banks," their passive position did nothing to aid Thomas (*Douglass' Monthly,* January 1861).

The Christiana resisters undoubtedly took heart in the knowledge that the prevailing Black attitude mandated opposition to the Fugitive Slave Law. They knew that they would be supported by the African community and they were. Blacks across the country raised money for the moral and financial support of the Christiana resisters and were vocal in their unequivocal backing of the rebels. "At Philadelphia in the space of four months a Special Vigilance Committee for Christiana Sufferers raised $663.41, of which $250 came from Negro contributors in San Francisco. In two successive weeks the Negroes of New York City held meetings with such speakers as Charles B. Ray, J. McCune Smith, William P. Powell, William J. Wilson, J. W. C. Pennington, and White man Lewis W. Paine, who had spent six years in a Georgia prison for giving assistance to a runaway" (Quarles 1969, 211–13). Africans in Columbus, Ohio, lauded the "victorious heroes at the battle of Christiana" for their "manly" stand (*Frederick Douglass' Paper,* November 13, 1851). At a meeting in Chicago the prosperous tailor John Jones "was appointed chairman of a committee to receive donations, the Ladies of Chicago Mutual Protection Society subscribing $10 on the spot" (*Frederick Douglass' Paper,* January 8, 1852).

William McHenry, known as Jerry, had escaped from Missouri and was living in Syracuse, New York, when he was arrested in October 1851, a month after Christiana. He was rescued by Black and White abolitionists from the courtroom but was retaken by marshals. The abolitionists rescued him once again and managed to transport him to safety in Kingston, Canada. Peter Hollinbeck and William Gray, a fugitive, were instrumental in McHenry's final escape (Loguen 1968, 417).

Twenty-six people, twelve of them Africans, were indicted, arrested, or brought to trial for their part in his escape (ibid., 154–56). The government once again attempted but failed to charge them with treason. Bail was set at $2,000 each, a staggering amount for the time. Rev. Jermain Loguen (a fugitive himself), Samuel Ringgold Ward (also a fugitive), Prince Jackson, William Thompson, Harrison Allen, John Lisle, and three other Africans were indicted but managed to escape to Canada. Three Whites were brought to trial but were acquitted, while Enoch Reed, a Black defendant, was convicted. He died, however, before a verdict was handed down on his appeal of his sentence. Jerry lived in Canada until his death in 1853.

Viable Black voices are often silenced by a society intent upon maintaining the racial status quo. White rhetoric, via mass media, implicitly venerates Black passivity because the focus is on a White comfort level. This is done by demonizing Black spokespeople and by excluding their presence in mainstream mass media. It has happened repeatedly to African Americans who speak out against racial injustice: Frederick Douglass, William Parker, W. E. B. Du Bois, Marcus Garvey, the Black Panthers, Malcolm X, and others. Even Martin Luther King Jr. was initially demonized, especially through the efforts of J. Edgar Hoover, the Federal Bureau of Investigation director. His belated elevation to near sainthood by White America serves the ends of those who wish to determine the nature of Black leadership and the "proper" African American response to oppression, one of passivity.

Demonization can be seen in the labels attached to Black leaders—*activist, radical, militant*—as if these are negative attributes. Such labels, however, indicate that the persons so labeled labor in behalf of full citizenship rights for African Americans. They are actively involved in the struggle for freedom, they take radical methods to achieve liberation, they assume a militant or "manly" stance against oppression, and they demand the rights guaranteed under the U.S. Constitution.

Mid-nineteenth-century Black rhetoric gives voice to the militant mindset of the African American community and debunks the Eurocentric notion of an agentless, passive, docile African. The presentation of African American history, especially to children, should reflect the empowering contribution such rhetoric made and can continue to make in the struggle to end oppression.

NOTES

The Anti-Slavery Bugle (Salem, New Lisbon, Ohio) was published by the Quaker abolitionist Benjamin Smith Jones from 1845 to 1861.

Frederick Douglass' Paper (Rochester, New York), formerly the *North Star,* was published by the famous abolitionist Frederick Douglass from 1850 to 1859, when it became *Douglass' Monthly,* which was published until 1863.

Liberator (Boston, Massachusetts) was published by the White abolitionist William Lloyd Garrison from 1831 to 1865. Africans supported the paper financially and morally, supplying articles, editorials, and letters.

1. Thomas Jefferson's crest read, "Rebellion to tyrants is obedience to God."
2. Some sources say his name was Frederick Minkins, Shadrach Minkins, or Frederick Jenkins.
3. Margaret Garner had escaped from Kentucky with her husband, her four children, and her husband's parents in February 1856. During the attempt to recapture them in Cincinnati, Margaret killed her three-year-old daughter, Mary, and tried to kill another to prevent their being taken back into enslavement. After they were retaken, they were sold to a slaveholder in New Orleans, where Margaret died in 1858.

REFERENCES

Byron, G. G. N. (1936). *Childe Harold's Pilgrimage and Other Romantic Poems.* New York: Odyssey Press.

Campbell, S. W. (1970). *The Slave Catchers: Enforcement of the Fugitive Slave Law, 1850–1860.* Chapel Hill: University of North Carolina Press.

Cheek, W., and A. L. Cheek (1989). *John Mercer Langston and the Fight for Black Freedom 1829–65.* Urbana: University of Illinois Press.

Dates, J. L., and W. Barlow (Eds.) (1993). *Split Image: African Americans in Mass Media.* Washington, D.C.: Howard University Press.

Foner, P. S. (1950). *The Life and Writings of Frederick Douglass,* vol. 2. New York: International Publishers.

Garnet, H. H. (1968). *An Address to the Slaves of the United States of America.* New York: Arno Press. Originally published 1843.

Jackson, A. (1847). *Narrative and Writings.* Syracuse, NY: Daily and Weekly Star Office.

Levy, L. (1950). "Sims' Case: The Fugitive Slave Law in Boston in 1851." *Journal of Negro History* 35: 39–74.

Loguen, J. W. (1968). *The Rev. J. W. Loguen, as a Slave and as a Freeman.* Westport, CT: Negro Universities Press. Originally published 1859.

Parker, W. (February, 1866). Freedman's Story. Part I. *Atlantic Monthly*, 17, 152–166.

Parker, William. (March, 1866). "Freedman's Story." Part II *Atlantic Monthly* 17: 276–295.

Quarles, B. (1969). *Black Abolitionists.* New York: Oxford University Press.

Ripley, C. P. (1991). *Black Abolitionist Papers.* Chapel Hill: University of North Carolina Press.

Robbins, J. J. (1970). *Report of the Trial for Castner Hanway for Treason.* Originally published 1852. Westport, CT: Negro University Press.

Rollin, F. A. (1969). *Life and Public Services of Martin R. Delaney*. Originally published 1883. New York: Arno Press.
Smedley, R. C. (1883). *History of the Underground Railroad in Chester and the neighboring counties in Pennsylvania*. Lancaster, PA: The Journal.
Ullman, V. (1969). *Look to the North Star: The Life of William King*. Boston: Beacon Press.
Ward, S. R. (1968). *Autobiography of a Fugitive Negro.* (originally published in 1855). New York: Arno Press.
Woodson, C. G. (1926). *The Mis-Education of the Negro.* Washington, D.C.: The Associated Publisher.

CHAPTER 11

"The Duty of the Civilized Is to Civilize the Uncivilized": Tropes of Black Nationalism in the Messages of Five Percent Rappers

FELICIA M. MIYAKAWA

> *I see rap as being a gardening tool due to the fact that we are planting seeds. We are trying to plant seeds in the minds of Black youth. We are trying to tell the Black youth that they are more than what they are being presented as. We're teaching Black youth that their history goes beyond slavery. Their history goes beyond Africa. Black people are the mothers and fathers of the highest forms of civilization ever built on this planet. (Wise Intelligent of Poor Righteous Teachers, quoted in Eure and Spady 1991, 68)*

The tradition and discourse of Black nationalism in America extends back to the mid-eighteenth century and the height of the slave trade. As social conditions have changed, so too have the goals of Black nationalism. Emancipation and increasing racism, for example, encouraged a back-to-Africa approach in the late nineteenth and early twentieth centuries, and worsening economic conditions in the 1960s helped to spawn a revival of Black self-sufficiency. Although each revival of Black nationalism focuses on different trends and is based in different social conditions, several major themes remain endemic to Black nationalism. Black nationalists are typically concerned with their role in leading and teaching the masses, often support pan-Africanism, and hope to further race pride and solidarity. Each new form of nationalism revises and updates these tropes.

One of the most recent incarnations of Black nationalism is found in rap music. Indeed, as the dominant cultural and musical voice of a generation, hip-hop music of the 1980s and 1990s—particularly hip-hop music based on Islamic doctrines—offers fertile ground for an investigation of the modern legacy of Black nationalism. The late 1980s saw the birth of "conscious" rap; "conscious" MCs and crews took Black nationalism, pan-Africanism, Islamic doctrine, education, political empowerment, and other social causes as their themes. With powerful groups such as Public Enemy fronting this genre, "conscious" rap voiced the woes of social inequality and racism. Many of the most successful "conscious" solo acts and groups of the late 1980s and into the 1990s, such as Public Enemy, Brand Nubian, Poor Righteous Teachers, X-Clan, the Jungle Brothers, Queen Latifah, KRS-One, and the Wu-Tang Clan, had at least nominal ties to Islamic doctrine. In fact, a number of MCs and crews active in the 1980s and 1990s (e.g., Wise Intelligent and Culture Freedom of Poor Righteous Teachers, Rakim, Lakim Shabazz, Brand Nubian, and the Wu-Tang Clan) are members of the Five Percent Nation, a breakaway sect from the Nation of Islam formed in 1964 and still thriving today.

Five Percent rappers use their medium to spread their spiritual message to an international audience. Their lyrics are educational and doctrinal texts and therefore serve as primary sources for the study of Five Percent rhetoric. Based on a mixture of Islamic doctrines (via the Nation of Islam), Masonic mysticism, Kemetic imagery, and social consciousness, Five Percent rhetoric also often espouses revolutionary and separatist Black nationalist leanings.[1] The purpose of this essay is to investigate how the messages of Five Percent rappers make use of, extend, and manipulate three primary tropes of Black nationalist discourse: the role of leadership and teaching, pan-Africanism, and race pride and solidarity. My investigation of each trope includes a brief survey of primary and secondary historical texts in order to contextualize each tropes historical legacy. Although these tropes certainly do not represent the fullness of Black Nationalist discourse, they do illustrate a high level of awareness of this discourse within the Five Percent Nation and, by extension, within the hip-hop community at large.

LEADING AND TEACHING THE MASSES

In *The Golden Age of Black Nationalism, 1850–1925,* Wilson Jeremiah Moses points out that one essential quality of Black nationalism is "the feeling on the part of Black individuals that they are responsible for the welfare of other Black individuals, or of Black people as a collective entity, simply because of a shared racial heritage and destiny" (1978, 19–20). Booker T. Washington is perhaps the most striking embodiment of this sense of responsibility, and took it upon himself to teach his people a modern way of life. Although often asked to take part in politics, Washington felt his purpose lay in the instruction of his people. As he wrote in *Up from Slavery*, "[I]t appeared to me to be reasonably certain that I could succeed in political life, but I had a feeling that it would be a rather selfish kind of success—individual success at the cost of failing to do my duty in assisting in laying a foundation for the masses" (1995, 54). Exactly what Washington chose to teach his students is significant:

> We wanted to teach the students how to bathe; how to care for their teeth and clothing. We wanted to teach them what to eat, and how to eat it properly, and

> how to care for their rooms. Aside from this, we wanted to give them such a practical knowledge of some one industry, together with the spirit of industry, thrift, and economy, that they would be sure of knowing how to make a living after they had left us. We wanted to teach them to study actual things instead of mere books alone. (1995, 74)

In short, Washington wanted to civilize his students, to welcome them into the modern world and provide them with the means to be commercially successful. His goal was to lift his people up by empowering them with skills that would eventually lead to financial and social gain.

In contrast to Washington's emphasis on material gain, W. E. B. Du Bois saw art as the ennobling possibility of the race (Du Bois 1982). Du Bois also shared a vision of education, but instead of holding himself personally responsible for the uplift of his race, he envisioned a "talented tenth," a small group of leaders who would jointly ennoble the race. Du Bois probably took his idea of the talented tenth from Alexander Crummell, an Episcopalian bishop and Black nationalist. In 1897, Crummell asked:

> Who are to be the agents to lift up this people of ours to the grand plane of civilization? Who are to bring them to the height of noble thought, grand civility, a chaste and elevating culture, refinement, and the impulses of irrepressible progress? It is to be done by the scholars and thinkers, who have secured the vision which penetrates the center of nature, and sweeps the circles of historic enlightenment; and have got insight into the life of things, and learned the art by which men touch the springs of action. (Quoted in Bracey, Meier, and Rudwick 1970, 141)

Crummell later suggested exactly who these teachers and leaders should be: "Just here arises the need of the trained and scholarly men of race to employ their knowledge and culture and teaching and to guide both the opinions and habits of the crude masses" (Bracey, Meier, and Rudwick 1970, 142). Here Crummell succinctly differentiates between the teacher and the students; those who teach are "scholarly," whereas those who are to learn are "crude" and hence uncivilized. Whereas Washington would teach his people practical skills for commercial success, Crummell and Du Bois would instead lift the souls of their people to civilization through art and culture. Although their methodologies differed, all three men shared the hope of leading their people to modernity and took their roles as leaders in this effort quite seriously.

Like Washington, Crummell, and Du Bois, the Five Percent Nation wants to civilize their people into a uniquely conscious African American way of life, but not through teaching them basic skills such as caring for their teeth. Instead, the Five Percent Nation takes as its mission the *spiritual* civilization of the masses. Early spiritual training of Five Percenters is essentially based on the lessons of the Nation of Islam.[2] Each lesson is organized in question-and-answer, catechism-like format, and the student must memorize both the question and the answer. Near the end of their training, initiaties move to the two-part "Lost-Found Moslem Lessons," with part one consisting of fourteen questions, and part two of forty questions; together they concentrate on geography, history of the races, and the coming Armageddon. The Five Percent Nation draws both its name and its identity from Lost-Found Lesson no. 2, questions 14 through 16:

> 14. Who are the 85 percent? The uncivilized people; poison animal eaters; slaves from mental death and power; people who do not know who the Living God is, or their origin in this world and who worship that direction but are hard to lead in the right direction.
> 15. Who are the 10 percent? The rich slave-makers of the poor, who teach the poor lies to believe: that the Almighty, True and Living God is a spook and cannot be seen by the physical eye; otherwise known as the bloodsuckers of the poor.
> 16. Who are the 5 percent? They are the poor righteous teachers who do not believe in the teachings of the 10 percent and are all-wise and know who the living God is and teach that the Living God is the Son of Man, the Supreme Being, or the Black Man of Asia, and teach Freedom, Justice and Equality to all the human family of the planet Earth; otherwise known as civilized people, also as Muslims and Muslim Sons. (Nuruddin 1994, 115–16)

The Nation has tried several avenues for educating the "85 percent," each with varying degrees of success. *The WORD,* a bimonthly newspaper limited primarily to the boroughs of New York City and dedicated to Five Percent doctrine, debuted in 1987 but enjoyed only a short publication run. Since the death of Clarence 13X there has been no titular leader of the Nation, no single personality to inspire strict adherence to doctrine. Thus, spiritual education often relies on more personal methods, such as the idea of "each one, teach one." With the help of new technology, the Nation has expanded this concept to "each one, teach thousands" through means such as the World Wide Web.[3] Hip-hop lyrics are another public avenue through which Five Percenters can hope to teach and lead the masses.

Some rappers use the Lost-Found lessons as a basis for lyrical narratives in their desire to spread Five Percent doctrine. The Wu-Tang Clan, for example, open their double-CD compilation *Wu-Tang Forever* (1997) with "Wu-revolution," the end of which reiterates Lost-Found Lesson no. 2, questions 14–16, almost word for word, illustrating the significance of these lessons in Five Percent Rhetoric and identity.[4] The members of Brand Nubian use a similar technique in their "Meaning of the 5%" (*In God We Trust,* 1992), a recording of a Louis Farrakhan speech set to a groove.[5] The details of the speech work out the very essence of Five Percent identity in another neat paraphrase of Lost-Found Lesson no. 2:

> [T]he Honorable Elijah Muhammad said to us that there is 5% who are the poor, righteous teachers, who don't believe the teaching of lies of the 10%. But this 5% are all-wise and know who the true and living God is, and they teach that the true and living God is the Son of Man, the Supreme Being, the Black Man of Asia. They're also known as civilized people, Muslims and Muslim sons. Here is a small percentage of people who know God, and when they know God they have a duty. And that duty is to teach what you know to those who do not know.

Lakim Shabazz also draws from these Lost-Found Lessons in "The Lost Tribe of Shabazz" (*The Lost Tribe of Shabazz,* 1990) but brings personal exegesis to his treatment: Here the 85 percent are "totally ignorant" and make their way through life with a "nigger mentality"; the 10 percent "love greed"; and the 5 percent are "ready to die for the cause" as spelled out by Elijah Muhammad.

Many Five Percent rappers also self-consciously refer to their roles as teachers within their lyrics. Brand Nubian, for example, introduce the purpose of "Allah and Justice" at the beginning of the song: Their goal is to teach righteousness. Poor Righteous Teachers and KRS-One encourage their brethren to return to pro-Black teachings and consciousness at several points in their joint product "Conscious Style" (*The New World Order,* 1996). In the midst of his exhortation, Wise Intelligent, the group's most vocal member, also emphasizes his self-appointed role as teacher: "my task is educate y'all." In another track from the same album, "Gods, Earths and 85ers," Poor Righteous Teachers again capitalize on their self-proclaimed roles as teachers and quote Elijah Muhammad in the process: "the duty of the civilized is to civilize the uncivilized." Wise Intelligent manipulates Elijah Muhammad's words—"the duty of the civilized man is to teach civilization to the uncivilized" (Muhammad 1965, 44)—into a more active role: instead of teaching civilization and its tools, his role instead is to actually civilize, implying that his subjects are unruly and need to be tamed. Wise Intelligent also acknowledges his duty to "make the world recognize that God is Wise," resorting to a clever metaphor. As he raps "God is Wise," he both credits the Almighty with wisdom and refers to his own divinity.[6] For Brand Nubian, their task is not simply to bring knowledge of self to the 85 percent, but also to awaken the masses to the tricks of the White devil. In the midst of a Five Percent doctrinal overview in "Wake Up" (*One for All,* 1990), Grand Puba of Brand Nubian warns the 85 percent, "The devil's a conniver."

Through rap lyrics members of the Five Percent Nation cultivate a messianic mission of bringing the truth of society and humanity to those who are in darkness; their duty is to awaken the 85 percent and lead them to self-knowledge. The average rap fan probably is not aware of the doctrinal rhetoric embedded in Five Percenter lyrics, but it is not the average rap fan that the Nation hopes to reach.[7] As Lakim Shabazz points out in an interview with Charlie Ahearn, those not familiar with Five Percent or Nation of Islam doctrine will not recognize the catch words: "They'll be, like, 'That beat sounds fresh.' They don't really take heed of the lyrics. But some people will hear '1st In Existence' [from his first album *Pure Righteousness*] and it's going to slap them in the face no matter what they be doing" (quoted in Ahearn 1989, 13). Wise Intelligent also admits that his fans only understand his message to a limited degree. Nevertheless, he emphasizes that Poor Righteous Teachers "take it as their duty or obligation to teach and resurrect the poor" (quoted in Eure and Spady 1991, 60). Although Washington and Du Bois were concerned about the cultural and educational needs of their people in the decades after emancipation, the teachings of the Five Percent Nation take responsibility for the spiritual enlightenment of their people. Instead of material prosperity, spiritual enlightenment and knowledge of self are the ultimate badges of civilization in this doctrine.

PAN-AFRICANISM

Pan-Africanism, one of the major themes of Black nationalism, is the belief that the fates and futures of all Black people are somehow tied. Many Black nationalists have sought to establish both cultural and historical ties to Africa and the Diaspora in order to form a sense of identity. In his exhaustive study of pan-Africanism, Imanuel Geiss identifies several themes of pan-Africanism, two of which are especially prominent in the discourse tradition that leads to Five Percenter rap: believing with what Geiss calls "quasi-religious fervor" that the modern world will fall and African civilization will rise, and making reference to the history of Egypt in order to prove that Africans and those of African descent are capable of producing world-class civilizations (Geiss 1974, 96).

Since the mid-eighteenth century, Psalm 68:31 has been the basis for a particular variety of nationalisitic rhetoric, known as Ethiopianism, that arose in the eighteenth century: "Princes shall come out of Egypt; Ethiopia shall soon stretch out her hands unto God."[8] According to Moses, Ethiopianism places the condition of slavery within a broader historical context in an effort to justify why such a violent condition has been visited on the peoples of Africa (1978, 160). Moses identifies various ways in which Black nationalists have interpreted the verse: as a prophecy that Africa would be saved from heathenism, as a prediction of an African economic and industrial renaissance, and as a promise that someday the Black man would rule the world (1978, 157). Moses further explains that the rise of the Black man and, by extension, the East necessitates a concurrent fall of the White man and of Western civilization. Emphasizing the linked fates and futures of all Black men, as well as the fall of the West, Ethiopianism is often at the heart of pan-Africanist rhetoric.

Nineteenth-century nationalist David Walker used this particular psalm to argue that the Black man will someday rule the world; he went to great lengths to establish a historical precedent for this upheaval. Walker worked within the construction of the "jeremiad," a prophetic prediction that the West will soon fall, making way for the resurrection of Africa and the restitution of the Black man's rightful place in the world order.[9] In his *Appeal to the Slaves of the United States of America,* Walker first points out that God is not deaf to the sufferings of his people: "[Slaveholding nations] forget that God rules in the armies of heaven and among the inhabitants of the earth, having his ears continually open to the cries, tears and groans of his oppressed people; and being a just and holy Being will at one day appear fully on behalf of the oppressed, and arrest the progress of the avaricious oppressors" (Walker and Garnet 1994, 13). Walker here refers to slaves as God's oppressed people, a reference to the popular connection drawn between slaves and the Jewish nation. But it is not enough that God will deliver His people; He must also justly punish those who have wrongly treated His chosen ones. Walker's belief in this next premise turns into a warning for America: "I tell you Americans! that unless you speedily alter your course, *you* and your *Country are gone ! ! ! ! ! !* For God Almighty will tear up the very face of the earth ! ! ! ! . . . . Oh Americans! Americans! ! I warn you in the name of the Lord, (whether you will hear, or forbear,) to repent and reform, or you are ruined!!!!!!"[10] (1994, 51–52). He further points out that much of the then-current misery experienced by various European countries is a result of their involvement in the slave trade: They are being punished by God (1994, 15) Walker continues: "God will not suffer us, always to be oppressed. Our sufferings will come to an *end,* in spite of all the Americans this side of *eternity*. . . . 'Every dog must have its day,' the American's is coming to an end" (1994, 25–26). Walker believed the sufferings of slavery would come to an end because he saw slavery within a broader historical time line; his view of history was cyclical and thus predicted the rise of the East. Thus Walker's jeremiad seems to include three steps: that God will recognize the sufferings of Africans and will deliver them; that God will punish the West for the injuries done to the African people; and, finally, that Africa will take its place as a leader of civilization.

Over a hundred years after the publication of Walker's exhortations, the Honorable Elijah Muhammad also predicted the fall of America: "America is falling. Her doom has come, and none said the prophets shall help her in the day of her downfall" (1965, 272). Muhammad's justification is that America will suffer not because of its role in the slave trade (long since abolished and replaced with segregation), but because of God's judgment for more general treachery. He compared American culture to that of ancient Babylon: "[Babylon] was a drunkard; wine and strong drink were in her daily practice. She was filled with adultery and murder; she persecuted and killed the people of God. She killed the saints and prophets of Allah (God). Hate and filthiness, gambling, sports of every evil as you practice in America were practiced in Babylon. Only America is modern and much worse. Ancient Babylon was destroyed by her neighboring nations" (1965, 273). Elijah Muhammad believed with Walker that the fall of the West would exclude Blacks. Muhammad warned, however, that to be saved, his people must embrace Allah and the Nation of Islam: "I warn every one of you, my people, fly to Allah with me! As I warned you, the judgment of this world has arrived! Get out of the church and get into the Mosques and join onto your own kind, the Nation of Islam!" (1965, 283). It is not enough for Muhammad that the West will be punished; his people, too, stand the chance of sharing such punishment because they have been integrated into America and a depraved Western society. The integration sought in the years after emancipation now threatens the future glories of Black people. Their salvation, according to Muhammad, is self-segregation.

The idea that members of the diaspora will someday rule the earth has trickled down into the Five Percent Nation through the teachings of Elijah Muhammad. In "Allies" (*The New World Order,* 1996), a joint effort by Poor Righteous Teachers and the now-defunct group the Fugees, Pras (of the Fugees) taps into the trope of the fall of Western civilization through the same Babylonian metaphor used by Elijah Muhammad. Referring to the "bloodsuckers" of the record industry as "Pharisees," Pras assures us: "All I know is one day that Babylon will be falling." Likewise, Brand Nubian vows in "I'm Black and I'm Proud" (*Foundation,* 1998) that although their people were slaves, justice will prevail since they were "predicted to inherit the earth in the last days."

Psalm 68:31 has especially interested nationalists who emphasize the historical role of Egypt in African and African American culture. Ronald Jackson suggests in the present volume that "rediscovering" an Egyptian heritage provided much of the impetus for modern Black nationalism, yet examination of the role of Egypt in the African American past is not new to the twentieth century. David Walker, for example, carefully established ties between ancient Egypt and modern Blacks, suggesting that the loss of Egyptian civilization is a fall from grace and now the time for redemption is at hand. Once Africa is redeemed, it will take its rightful place as a leader of civilization. As Moses points out, this brand of pan-Africanism allows nationalists to remember that "this present scientific technological civilization, dominated by western Europe for a scant four hundred years, will go under certainly—like all the empires of the past" (Moses 1978, 161).

References to Egyptian culture and civilization are also important in Five Percenter lyrics. Poor Righteous Teachers and KRS-One, for example, jointly proclaim the connections between the scientific leanings of the Five Percent Nation and ancient Egyptian culture in "Conscious Style" (*The New World Order,* 1996). Wise Intelligent refers to Gods and Earths as "Egyptians" and "metaphysicists" who "give birth to understanding." Here Egypt is used as a metaphor for knowledge and culture. Gods and Earths who have "knowledge of self" and "civilize the uncivilized" have access to ancient culture and wisdom. In other lyrics, Egyptian icons are invoked for their symbolic meaning. Brand Nubian uses the Egyptian ideogram for life, the ankh, in their "Dance to My Ministry" (*One for All,* 1990): "an ankh is the key and the key is knowledge, unlocks my lab's door." The ankh, an ancient hieroglyph, here unlocks mysteries of knowledge otherwise hidden from the 85 percent. Lord Jamar's (of Brand Nubian) laboratory is more of a classroom, where knowledge of the Black man's ancient self is taught.

In the late nineteenth century pan-Africanism took a decidedly different turn. Whereas Ethiopianism stresses past and future glories, another brand of Black nationalism often seeks physical repatriation, or the construction of a nation-state, preferably located in Africa (Moses, 1995, 1). This type of pan-Africanism reached its twentieth-century fruition with the work of Marcus Garvey, who developed the Black Star shipping line to physically transport those who wished to go "back" to Africa. As is well documented, Garvey's attempts failed for a variety of reasons. Significantly, however, many of his followers turned to Noble Drew Ali, founder of the Moorish Science Temple, after Garvey was imprisoned.[11] Noble Drew Ali was highly influenced by Garvey and drew heavily from Garvey's teachings (as well as from the Bible and the Koran) for the writing of *The Holy Koran of the Moorish Science Temple of America* (Rashad 1995, 168). But Ali introduced a significant change into the back-to-Africa trend; According to Rashad, it was Noble Drew Ali who was most responsible for the change in desire for physical repatriation to *spiritual* repatriation (1995, 162). Ali considered himself heir to Garvey's doctrine but wanted full rights in American society for his fellow "Asiatic Blackmen" rather than a new society in Africa (Rashad 1995, 172).

The lineage of Noble Drew Ali's ideas is significant. One of his young followers in the early days of the Moorish Science Temple was W. D. Fard, who took over as leader of the Temple after Ali's mysterious death. W. D. Fard's teachings later became the essential teachings of the Nation of Islam as led by Elijah Muhammad, Fard's prophet. Clarence 13X then brought Ali's mystical ideas with him to the Five Percent Nation.[12] Desire for spiritual repatriation is seen in "Black Star Line" (*In God We Trust,* 1992) by Brand Nubian, which not only praises Marcus Garvey, but also shows the difference in ideology between Garvey and Ali (and his followers):

It's the Black Star Line that's leavin' at nine
Here's a paid ticket so you can free your mind . . .
See we got a mental ship somethin' like Noah's Ark
Spark your brain cell now let's set sail.

Brand Nubian explicitly states that this is not an actual ship, but a mental ship. The listener is given a free ticket to escape the concrete jungle of the ghetto in order to show the youth a better way to live. These lyrics are used as a history lesson; they teach the young about the importance of Marcus Garvey and his ideas. Furthermore, Brand Nubian honors Garvey's Jamaican roots by setting these lyrics to a reggae groove and by featuring Red Foxx, a reggae artist. It is Foxx, with his distinctive Jamaican accent, who tells us about Marcus Garvey's history and mission. In this case, the music goes above and beyond the text to link Five Percent rhetoric with Pan-Africanism and the diaspora.

BLACK PRIDE AND RACIAL SOLIDARITY

One of the results of pan-Africanism is race pride; as African Americans learn more about their past and more of the exemplary lives of members of the Diaspora, they take pride in their heritage and in the very color of their skin. Often in tandem with race pride is racial solidarity, the belief that the race will not prosper unless all work together physically, spiritually, and economically.

Arguments for race pride in Black nationalist literature are varied and typically respond to contemporary commentary on Blacks. In the midst of a criticism of Thomas Jefferson, for example, David Walker refuted the contemporary popular idea that, given the chance, Blacks would choose to be White. His justification was that he and his fellow African Americans believed that God made them Black for a purpose and he was grateful to be what God had made him: "As though we are not thankful to our God for having made us as it pleased himself, as they (the Whites) are for having made them White. They think because they hold us in their infernal chains of slavery that we wish to be White, or of their color—but they are dreadfully deceived—we wish to be just as it pleased our Creator to have made us" (Walker and Garnet 1994, 22). Walker was proud to be Black because he was made that way. He valued his Blackness and saw in his people an essentialist moral superiority not found in other races:

> I know that the Blacks, take them half enlightened and ignorant, are more humane and merciful than the most enlightened and refined Europeans that can be found in all the earth. Let no one say that I assert this because I am prejudiced on the side of my color, and against the Whites or Europeans. For what I write, I do it candidly, for my God and the good of both parties: Natural observations have taught me these things; there is a solemn awe in the hearts of Blacks. (1994, 35)

In 1898 Bishop Henry M. Turner proclaimed the beauty of Blackness from a different theological perspective: he claimed that God was a Negro. He pointed out that all people imagine God to look like themselves because the Bible claims God made man in His own image; Blacks should certainly be allowed this same liberty. Without this surety of God's dark skin color, Turner saw no point in worshiping Him: "We had rather be an atheist and believe in no God, or a pantheist and believe that all nature is God, than to believe in the personality of a God, and not to believe that He is a Negro. Blackness is much older than Whiteness, for Black was here before White" (quoted in Bracey, Meier, and Rudwick, 1970, 155). His arguments also suggest an origin myth; it is not only because man is made in God's image that he believed God to be Black, but also because he held that Blackness was the original status of the universe, that light came from darkness as described in chapter 1 of Genesis. His arguments would later be echoed in the teachings of Elijah Muhammad and the Five Percent Nation.

Du Bois recognized that it is not simply a matter of accepting one's Blackness because the Creator has made one Black, since we are trained from birth to recognize pure Whiteness as beautiful; dark skin is thus unpure and unbeautiful in its very opposition to Whiteness. For Du Bois, this was a difference in aesthetics and not a matter of theology. His tack was to retrain his people to see Black as beautiful. In a 1920 editorial in *The Crisis,* Du Bois spelled out just how the African American is trained to recognize beauty only in Whiteness, and he exhorted his people: "Off with these thought-chains and inchoate soul-shrinkings, and let us train ourselves to see beauty in Black" (quoted in Bracey, Meier, and Rudwick 1970, 278).

But Du Bois also used quasi-historical arguments for Black pride. He, like David Walker, investigated the relationship between ancient Egyptian culture and African American culture, but instead of asserting, as Walker did, that African American culture is of value because it *comes from* Egyptian culture, Du Bois tried to prove that the supremacy of ancient Egyptian culture was *due to* the influence of "Negro" blood. In an article entitled "The Negro in Literature and Art," Du Bois claims: "[T]he Negro blood which flowed in the veins of many of the mightiest of the Pharaohs accounts for much of Egyptian art, and indeed, Egyptian civilization owes much in its origins to the development of the large strain of Negro blood which manifested itself in every grade of Egyptian society" (Du Bois 1996, 2). Manipulating the accepted history of Egypt gives Black Americans yet another source of race pride.

With the teachings of Elijah Muhammad and the Five Percent Nation, however, we return to a theological (and quasi-scientific) basis for race pride. The Nation's justification for racial pride comes from their strong belief that Black people were the original people on the planet and the mothers and fathers of civilization, beliefs they share with the Nation of Islam. Elijah

Muhammad claimed that Blacks are the "descendants of the Asian Black nation and of the tribe of Shabazz" (1965, 31) and went on to explain the significance of the tribe of Shabazz and how the tribe came to inhabit the earth.

> You might ask, who is this tribe of Shabazz? Originally, they were the tribe that came with the earth (or this part) 60 trillion years ago when a great explosion on our planet divided it into two parts. One we call earth and the other moon.This was done by one of our scientists, God; who wanted the people to speak one language, one dialect for all, but was unable to bring this about. He decided to kill us by destroying our planet, but still He failed. . . . We, the tribe of Shabazz, says Allah (God), were the first to discover the best part of our planet to live on. The rich Nile Valley of Egypt and the present seat of the Holy City, Mecca, Arabia. (1965, 31)

Rapper Lakim Shabazz bases his entire persona on this origin theory. He has taken the name of the tribe Shabazz as his last name to symbolize his connection with the original tribe, and he titled his second CD *The Lost Tribe of Shabazz* (1990). Brand Nubian refers to both the Tribe of Shabazz and the original-man belief in "Dance to My Ministry" (*One for All,* 1990), reminding their listeners that the tribe was first on earth and is also "definite to be the last." In "Wu-revolution" (*Wu-Tang Forever,* 1997), the Wu-Tang Clan celebrate their origins and further identify the original man as the Asiatic Black man with lyrics that repeat the first Student Enrollment Lesson nearly word for word: "The original man is the Asiatic Black man, the Maker, the Owner, the Cream of the planet Earth, Father of Civilization, God of the Universe."[13]

The Five Percent Nation also draws its race pride from social developments concurrent with the birth of the Nation in the 1960s. Echoing James Brown's cry, members of the Five Percent Nation once again shout "I'm Black and I'm Proud" in the 1990s. In their song "I'm Black and I'm proud" (*Foundation,* 1998), an anthem of allusion both to the 1960s and to the teachings of the Five Percent Nation, Brand Nubian clearly identifies the source of their pride as the origin myth preached by Elijah Muhammad. Paraphrasing the same Student Enrollment lesson, Brand Nubian queries their audience: "Now did you know it was you who was first to walk the earth?" and makes it clear that they are proud to be Black "because the Black man's first." Reference to Black pride of the 1960s is strengthened by sampling James Brown's song of the same name; indeed, the chorus is taken directly from James Brown's hit: "Say it loud . . . I'm Black and I'm proud!" Brand Nubian exhorts their audience to shout out, but their respondents are sampled from James Brown's recording, creating a concrete tie between generations of Black Pride.

Once racial pride has been established, Black Nationalist leaders often exhort their people to solidarity; through solidarity the race will be uplifted and will attain self-sufficiency. As Molefi Asante has argued, Black unity (as well as anti-White aggression) forms a crucial part of both Black Power and

Black Nationalist rhetorics. In a sermon from as early as 1875 Alexander Crummell encouraged his people to counter racism through dependency on each other.

> While one remnant of disadvantage abides in this land, stand by one another! While proscription in any quarter exists, maintain intact all your phalanxes! While antagonism confronts your foremost men, hold on to all the instincts of your race for the support of your leaders, and the elevation of your people! While the implication of inferiority, justly or un-justly, is cast upon you, combine for all the elements of culture, wealth, and power! While any sensitiveness or repulsion discovers itself at your approach or presence, hold on to your own self-respect, keep up, *and be satisfied with,* your own distinctive circles! (Quoted in Bracey, Meier, and Rudwick 1970, 134)

Crummell emphasized that African Americans must be content with self-sufficiency, that they must be willing to support their own people even at the risk of personal economic loss. Du Bois made a similar observation two decades later: "The mass of the Negroes must learn to patronize business enterprises conducted by their own race, even at some slight disadvantage. We *must* cooperate or we are lost" (quoted in Bracey, Meier, and Rudwick 1970, 263). However much African Americans may lose economically, they stand to gain solidarity, a prize beyond jewels.

A century later Brand Nubian also broaches the subject of Black unity in "Wake Up" (*One for All,* 1990) and conclude that unity is a solution to all racial and social ills. Even the title of the album from which this song is drawn, *One for All,* shows their interest in unification. In "Black Star Line" (*In God We Trust,* 1992) they are even more explicit about what this unity means: "doin' for self, keepin' the wealth." They cite Marcus Garvey as the author of this brand of economic solidarity but by extension also echo Du Bois' exhortation to patronize African American businesses. By keeping money and capital within Black communities, Five Percenters—like their nationalist ancestors—hope to gain broader economic power. More importantly, by "doin for self" and "keepin the wealth," Five Percenters encourage and promote racial solidarity, aligning themselves with long traditions of Black nationalism.

Even though the commercialism of hip-hop music may seem to hide lofty motives, Black nationalist tropes have found a new voice through Five Percent rappers. Through the medium of hip-hop music, Five Percenters clearly show us their commitment to teaching knowledge of self to those who are lost, and take pride in the color of their skin and in their heritage. "Knowledge of self" in this doctrine demands an awareness of history and civilization, a willingness to effectively teach "truth" and lead the masses, and an interest in racial solidarity, three tropes deeply embedded in Black nationalist rhetoric. In other words, Black nationalism is part and parcel of Five Percent doctrine.

For the Five Percent Nation, nationalist rhetoric is necessarily couched in religious rhetoric; their revisions of these three tropes redefine nationalism according to their ontotheological world view. Yet in its fullness Five Percent doctrine is more than religious rhetoric; indeed, Wise Intelligent (among many others) explicitly denies that the Five Percent faith is a religion:

> People consider us a religion. This does not have anything to do with religion. This has nothing to do with something which was started up in the past. This has no said birth record. That Blackness that was there at the beginning that created all things in the universe was that of Islam. That's what we're dealing with. When you're saying Islam you're saying I-Self-Lord-Am-Master, or an Independent Source of Life and Matter. For that's showing and proving the ability to create. And from this Blackness came all things in the universe. Here we are that Blackness in manifestation. Being made manifest. (Quoted in Eure and Spady 1991, 65–66)

Wise Intelligent seems to suggest that what he teaches is not a religion, but a worldview, an Africological worldview that places the Black man at the center of civilization, not only in the past, but also in the future (Woodyard this volume). If we understand the references and catch words of the Five Percent rhetorical community, Five Percent rappers methodically instruct us in their vision of Black Nationalism as they teach us the doctrines of their faith.[14]

NOTES

1. See Jackson's essay in the present volume, where he identifies three types of Black nationalism: revolutionary, integrationist, and separatist.
2. In the Nation of Islam, initiates begin with the Student Enrollment Lesson, and then move to Actual Facts, "English Lesson C no. 1, and finally, the Lost-Found Moslem Lessons. Five Percenters use many of the same lessons in a different order, with additional lessons of their own devising. They begin with two lessons not included in the Nation of Islam's indoctrination: the Science of Supreme Mathematics and the Supreme Alphabet. Initiates then move on to the same Student Enrollment Lesson used in the Nation of Islam, followed by English Lesson no. C1 and the Lost-Found Lessons. The Lost-Found Lessons are followed by two final lessons: Actual Facts (borrowed from the Nation of Islam) and Solar Facts (new to the Five Percent Nation). Actual Facts, the Student Enrollment Lessons, the Lost-Found Lessons, and English Lesson no. C1 are all available at www.thenationofislam.org/supremewisdom.html.
3. See, for example, http://www.ibiblio.org/nge/. This site also contains a link to a new Five Percent Web journal entitled *The All Eye Seeing* (http://www.ibiblio.org/nge/thealleyeseeing) as well as subscription information for *The Five Percenter,* a newspaper devoted to Five Percent doctrine.
4. "Wu-revolution" also paraphrases lessons from Lost-Found Lesson no. 1, the Student Enrollment Lesson, and English Lesson no. C1.
5. The sample used here to underlie the speech comes from "T Stands for Trouble" by Marvin Gaye (from the *Trouble Man* soundtrack). I am grateful to Mtume Ya Salaam for identifying this sample.
6. In Five Percent doctrine, each Black man is a God.
7. The effectiveness of rap as a teaching tool for the Nation remains unclear. Various Web sites featuring lyrics posted by ardent fans consistently indicate misinterpretation, and hence misunderstanding of the lyrics. On one Web site, for example, the line "or their origins in the world" from Wu-Tang Clan's "Wu Revolution" reads "and all the orchards in the world." Yet those in the know, including the hip-hop media, give credit to the Nation when credit is due. In a recent article ("On

Ciphers, Centuries and Millenniums") from the January 2000 issue of *The Source,* for example, Bakari Kitwana points out that the hip-hop catchword *cipher* has its roots in the Five Percent Nation.

8. According to Geiss, the psalm verse was first used for Black Nationalistic purposes by Henry Highland Garnet (Walker and Garnet 1974, 105). See chapters 7 and 8 of Geiss 1974 for an extended discussion of both pan-Africanism and Ethiopianism.
9. For an alternative discussion of the jeremiad, see Gilyard's essay in the present volume.
10. All punctuation and emphases are Walker's. Unless otherwise noted, all further punctuation and emphases in this essay are original.
11. For a full narrative of Ali's beginnings, see Wilson 1989.
12. Rashad points out that Noble Drew Ali's brand of Islam is patterned after Sufism, the mystical sect of Islam, rather than on traditional Islam (1995, 171). In many ways the Five Percent Nation seems to draw more heavily on the teachings of Noble Drew Ali than on those of Elijah Muhammad, particularly because the Five Percent Nation relies so heavily on numerology and mystical science. Additionally, Ali drew heavily from Masonry and Masonic symbols, which also appear in Five Percent Nation literature.
13. The term *Asiatic* premiered with the teachings of Noble Drew Ali, who believed that American Blacks were descendants of Moors or ancient Moroccans (Rashad 1995, 162); www.thenationofislam.org/supremewisdom.html).
14. See Woodyard's essay in the present volume for a discussion of rhetorical communities.

REFERENCES

Ahearn, C. (1989). Lakim Gets Busy Dropping Science. *The City Sun* (April 26): 13, 19.

Bracey, J. M., Jr., A. Meier, and E. Rudwick (Eds.) (1970). *Black Nationalism in America*. Indianapolis: Bobbs-Merrill.

Brand Nubian. (1990). *One for All* [CD]. New York: Time Warner.

Brand Nubian. (1992). *In God we Trust* [CD]. New York: Time Warner.

Brand Nubian. (1998). *Foundation* [CD]. New York, Arista.

Du Bois, W. E. B. (1982). *The Souls of Black Folk*. New York: Penguin.

Du Bois, W. E. B. (1996). The Negro in Literature and Art. In C. D. Wintz (Ed.), *The Emergence of the Harlem Renaissance* (pp. 2–7). New York: Garland Publishing.

Eure, J. D., and J. G. Spady (Eds.) (1991). *Nation Conscious Rap*. New York: PC International Press.

Geiss, I. (1974). *The Pan-African Movement: A History of Pan-Africanism in America, Europe and Africa.* Trans. A. Keep. New York: Holmes and Meier.

Moses, W. J. (1978). *The Golden Age of Black Nationalism, 1850–1925*. Hamden, CT: Archon Books.

Moses, W. J. (Ed.) (1995). *Classical Black Nationalism: From the American Revolution to Marcus Garvey.* New York: New York University Press.

Muhammad, E. [Elijah Poole]. (1965). *Message to the Blackman in America*. Chicago: Muhammad Mosque of Islam No. 2.

Nuruddin, Y. (1994). The Five Percenters: A Teenage Nation of Gods and Earths. In Y. Y. Haddad and J. I. Smith (Eds.), *Muslim Communities in North America* (pp. 109–32). Albany: State University of New York Press.

Poor Righteous Teachers. (1996). *The New World Order* [CD]. New York: Profile.

Rashad, A. (1995). *Islam, Black Nationalism and Slavery: A Detailed History*. Beltsville, MD: Writers Inc. International.

Shabazz, L. (1990). *The Lost Tribe of Shabazz* [CD]. New York: Tuff City Records.

Walker, D., and H. H. Garnet (1994). *Walker's Appeal and Garnet's Address to the Slaves of the United States of America*. Nashville, TN: James C. Winston Publishing Co.

Washington, B. T. (1995). *Up from Slavery.* Ed. and introduction W. L. Andrews. Oxford: Oxford University Press.

Wilson, P. L. (1989). Shoot-out at the Circle Seven Koran: Noble Drew Ali and the Moorish Science Temple. *Gnosis* 12: 44–49.

Wu-Tang Clan. (1997). *Wu-Tang Forever* [2 enhanced CDs]. New York: RCA.

CHAPTER 12

Death Narratives from the Killing Fields: Narrative Criticism and the Case of Tupac Shakur

CARLOS D. MORRISON

Gangsta rappers create a variety of imagery in their music. The imagery discussed ranges from life in the hood to full-time "thugging." Yet the harsh reality of life is thugging for far too many gangsta rappers and young African American males in the urban war zones of America. Death is a reality for both African American males and gangsta rappers, but it is often not feared, whether on "wax" (CDs or vinyl records) or in the streets. The question then becomes: How do gangsta rappers talk about death? What kind of stories do they create about death that allows them to deal with it and not fear it? What is their motive for producing a discourse about death? This essay will identify and analyze stories about death in gangsta rap. It begins with a selected review of the literature on rap music from a historical and cultural studies perspective. There will also be a brief review of music in the field of rhetoric. The essay then proceeds with an analysis of gangsta rap lyrics of Tupac Shakur based on the narrative and pentadic approach to rhetorical criticism. The essay ends with suggestions for further research.

RAP MUSIC AND HIP-HOP CULTURE: SELECTED REVIEW OF THE HISTORY

One of the earliest histories on the development of rap music from African culture to the urban streets of New York City is Toop's *The Rap Attack* (1984). Toop discusses rap music's connection to the African oral tradition in general and to the West African griots specifically. Toop further discusses the influence of other Black musical genres on rap such as jazz, bop, R&B, and soul in the 1970s and 1980s.

Fernando's social history of hip-hop culture "explores the complexities of hip hop's words, sounds, images, and attitudes" (1994, xiii). In addition to discussing the political and social history of hip-hop culture, Fernando also brings attention to the business aspect of rap music from the artist's perspective. He provides insight into the meanings of lyrics by allowing the artists to speak for themselves.

Eure and Spady continue to tell the story of hip-hop through oral history. The editors allow "old school" rappers such as Doug E. Fresh, KRS-One, Poor Righteous Teachers, X-Clan, and Sister Souljah to tell how rap developed as a musical and cultural force in Black culture. Furthermore, Eure and Spady discuss the philosophical dimensions of rap when they suggest that rap can be viewed as "rhythmic praxis discourse" (1991, 414). The work by these historians laid the foundation for analysis of rap music by cultural critics by providing a sociopolitical and economic context whereby the cultural production of rap music could be analyzed.

RAP MUSIC AND HIP-HOP CULTURE: SELECTED LITERATURE IN CULTURAL STUDIES

African American cultural critics lead the way in contemporary understanding and critiques of hip-hop culture and music. Scholars such as Tricia Rose, Michael Eric Dyson, bell hooks, Todd Boyd, Houston Baker, and Cornel West have intellectualized the discussion of rap music and hip-hop culture within and outside of the walls of the academy. I believe that it is safe to say that most scholars would agree with Rose's definition of rap music as "a Black cultural expression that prioritizes Black voices from the margins of urban America. Rap music is a form of rhymed storytelling accompanied by highly rhythmic, electronically based music" (1994, 2). However, hip-hop can be defined as the culture that young African Americans co-construct via music, language, dress, graffiti, and so on to create spaces of resistance to oppression, racism, and poverty while living their lives on the margins of society.

Dyson (1991) was one of the first scholars to provide a critical analysis and assessment of rap music and hip-hop culture. Dyson shows that a relationship exists between rap music, Black nationalism, and other forms of African American cultural expression such as storytelling, gospel, and rhythm-and-blues music. Dyson also suggests that rappers are modern-day griots and that Black youth "embrace rap as a symbol of protest; [rap music] is an expression of *negritude*" (p. 5).

Baker, an African American literary scholar, also argued for the study of rap music in the area of Black studies. In his book, *Black Studies, Rap, and the Academy* (1993), Baker suggests that the field of Black studies should provide a context where rap music can be debated, critiqued, and analyzed. Baker also argues for the cultural importance of rap music.

Some scholars, in their analysis of rap music and hip hop culture, have advanced the critique of sexist and misogynistic language in the music (Rose 1994; hooks 1994). Rose and hooks have defined rap, particularly gangsta rap, as Black male cultural space that historically has been resistant to the inclusion of African American women rappers. The Black-male-dominated cultural space in hip hop is often a context where the Black female body is sexualized and subjugated.

In addition to the sexual politics involving rap music, scholars have also focused on the social, cultural, religious, and economic influences on the music (Spencer 1992; Dyson 1993; Kunjufu 1993; Ross and Rose 1994; Boyd 1997; Datcher and Alexander 1997). Critiques concerning rap music were also taken up by nonacademics such as magazine and newspaper writers, community activists, and the rappers themselves (George, Banes, and Romanowski 1985; Costello and Wallace 1990; Nelson and Gonzales 1991; Shabazz 1992; Sexton 1995; Ice T 1994; Chuck D 1997; White 1997; George 1998; Alexander 2000). Thus, historians, cultural studies scholars, nonacademic writers, and journalists have provided a critical and interpretive framework in which to view hip-hop culture in general and rap music specifically. Communication scholars have also provided a critical framework for the analysis of the rhetorical dimensions of music.

MUSIC AND RHETORIC: SELECTED LITERATURE

Researchers within the field of communication have studied the rhetorical dimensions of music lyrics. Scholars have analyzed the rhetoric of music in protest songs and films and have songs about America and the South (Irvin and Kirkpatrick 1972; Thomas 1974; Booth 1975; Smith 1980; Roth 1981; Gonzalez and Makay 1983; Atwater 1995; Morrison 2000). Rhetorical studies emphasizing rap music have focused on analyzing the rhetoric of KRS-One (Aldridge and Carlin 1993), the communicative practices in rap music (Smitherman 1997), Gangsta rap as a cultural commodity (Watts 1997), and rhetorical tropes of Black nationalism in the messages of Five Percent Rappers (Miyakawa in this volume). Moreover, Dangerfield (in this volume) analyzes the rhetoric of hip-hop soul artist Lauryn Hill by using cultural criticism in order to reveal Hill's values, myths, and fantasy themes.

While much headway has been made in the publication of scholarly articles on the rhetorical dimensions of music, academic journals in communication still have not given the rhetorical analysis of rap music serious consideration. However, the rhetorical study conducted by Smitherman was published in the *Journal of Black Studies;* the journal has historically been receptive to reviewing and publishing manuscripts concerning African American rhetoric and communication and Black popular culture.

At times cultural critics and popular cultural scholars are far ahead of communication scholars in recognizing the academic importance of rap music. Thus, a narrative and pentadic criticism of gangsta rap lyrics is a call to communication and other humanities and social science scholars (and editors) to consider the intellectual significance of rap music and hip-hop culture.

NARRATIVE AND DRAMATIC CRITICISM: THE METHODS

As griots, rappers are modern-day storytellers. Through the telling of stories about life in the hood, death, police brutality, or getting paid, rap artists in their own way continue the African oral tradition of storytelling. Through the telling of these stories, rappers attempt to educate, inform, persuade and empower their listening audience while at the same time affirming and validating their sense of selfhood. In an attempt to identify and analyze the way hip-hop artists discuss and engage in talk about death in their stories, this study will rely on the narrative approach to rhetorical criticism. Walter Fisher has made major contributions to the study of narration in the field of communication studies. Fisher defines narration as the "symbolic actions-words and/or deeds-that have sequence and meaning for those who live, create, or interpret them" (1989, 58). Foss defines narrative as "a way of ordering and presenting a view of the world through a description of a situation involving characters, actions, and settings that change over time" (1989, 229). The narrative form is found in a variety of media such as comic strips, songs, and dance (p. 229). Furthermore, Foss suggests that there is a three-stage process to the way in which narratives help us to interpret social reality:

> First, narratives help us identify the central action of an experience; they help decide what a particular experience "is about.". . . Second, narratives establish connections between the central action and the various elements in our experiences or the story. . . . Third, we judge the narratives about reality that are presented to or created by us for such qualities as completeness and consistency and find them either adequate or lacking. (1989, 229–30)

Narrative criticism focuses on two major areas of the narrative: the story and the telling of the story. Foss claims that "the story is the substance or content of the narrative, with its characters, settings, and plot lines; the [telling of the story] is the means by which the content is communicated or the form of the narrative" (1989, 230). Furthermore, Foss outlines "three major steps . . . involved in narrative criticism: (1) analysis of the content and the narrative; (2) analysis of the form of the narrative; and (3) evaluation of the narrative" (p. 230). This essay will focus only on the semantic *content* of Shakur's narrative because the study places an emphasis on the narrative or storytelling aspects of the lyrics. While music is also an important aspect of the rhetorical power of Shakur's lyrics, the words assist in the telling of the story and need to be examined in an effort to develop an understanding of rap apart from the music. Often in the African American cultural context, a greater premium is placed on how words are communicated than on what is communicated. The classic example is the statement made by some Black parishioners after the service in a traditional Black church: "I don't know what the reverend said, but he sure sounds good." It is important to examine the aspect of the discourse that has become neglected (the words of the sermon) as a result of privileging style over substance. This issue has been magnified in rap music, where it has become difficult to understand the words used by the rappers because of the verbal barrier created by the rapper's style.

ANALYSIS OF THE SUBSTANCE OF THE NARRATIVE

In the first stage of the analysis, the rhetorical critic is concerned with analyzing the content or substance of the narrative. Hence, the critic investigates such attributes as setting, characters, events, themes, narrator, and audience. "The setting is the place in which the characters think and act" (Foss 1989, 231). The critic is interested in determining if the *setting* is consistent with the way the characters act or feel, or whether the setting contradicts the mood, action, or feelings of the characters. After an analysis of the setting, the critic identifies the *characters* in the narrative, both main and secondary. "Characters are the people, figures, or creatures who think and communicate in the narrative" (p. 231). After determining the characters, the critic is then interested in the *events* that take place in the story.

Here, the critic is charged with the responsibility of identifying the events or plot lines of the narrative. The critic identifies major and minor events. Foss explains:

> Major events are called *kernels;* these are the events that suggest critical points in the narrative and that force movement into particular directions. They cannot be left out of the narrative without destroying its coherence and meaning. Minor plot events are *satellites;* they are the development or working out of the choices made at the kernels. Their function is to fill out, elaborate, and complete the kernels. Satellites do not have to appear in the immediate proximity of the kernels to which they are linked; they may appear anywhere in the narrative. Satellites are not crucial to the narrative and can be deleted without disturbing the basic storyline of the narrative. (p. 231)

After the critic has determined the major and minor events, he/she turns his/her attention to the *themes.* "A theme is a general idea illustrated by the narrative; it is what a narrative means or is about" (Foss 1989, 232). After determining the theme(s), the critic can focus on the *narrator.*

Here, the critic is concerned with the identification of the narrator in the story. The critic must also determine if a narrator mediates the narrative or not. Foss claims that "in a narrative, mediated by a narrator, the audience is told about events and characters, and the presence of the narrator is more or less audible" (p. 232). After analyzing the narrator, the critic next examines the audience.

At this point, the critic determines whom the narrative is addressed to. "A narrative may be addressed to one person, a group of people or to the narrator him or herself. The audience, just as in the case with the narrator, may be a participant in the events recounted. . . . Nevertheless, a narrative, like all rhetoric, is addressed to someone and is designed to appeal to that person" (p. 232). Having discussed the procedures for analyzing the substance of the narrative, this essay now turns to a brief discussion of the evaluation process.

In the evaluation stage, the critic assesses the substance of the narrative. The critic may focus on determining what was valued in the narrative. "After identifying this value, the critic may ask what the effects are of adhering to this value and whether it is a desirable one" (Foss 1989, 236).

Pentadic criticism is grounded in Kenneth Burke's work on dramatism (Burke, 1969a; 1969b). Burke, a philosopher and literary critic, defines dramatism as the "study of human motivation through terms derived from the study of drama" (Foss 1996, 455). Through dramatism, the critic can determine the semantic dimension of the use of language.

There are two basic assumptions that undergird the dramatistic method. The first assumption is that "language use constitutes action, not motion" (Foss 1996, 455). According to Foss (1996) Burke argues that motion is non-symbolic activity that "corresponds to the biological or animal aspect of the human being, which is concerned with bodily processes such as growth, digestion, respiration, and the requirements for the maintenance of these processes such as food, shelter, and rest" (p. 455). However, action "corresponds to the symbolic or neurological aspect of the human being, which Burke defines as the ability of an organism to acquire language or a symbol system" (pp. 455–56). Thus, humans are motivated to action via language and symbols. When humans strive to achieve in sports, education, or in the sciences, they are motivated by symbols. "To be motivated to act in these areas requires a symbol system that creates the possibility for such desires in the first place" (p. 456).

The second assumption that undergirds dramatism "is that humans develop and present messages in much the same way that a play is presented" (p. 456). Foss further states:

> We use rhetoric to constitute and present a particular view of our situation, just as the presentation of a playcreates a certain world or situation inhabited by characters who engage in actions in a setting. Through rhetoric, we size up situations and name their structure and outstanding ingredients. How we describe a situation indicates how we are perceiving it, the choices we see available to us, and the action we are likely to take in that situation. Our language, then, provides a clue to our motive or why we do what we do. (p. 456)

The critic must describe or "size up" the rhetor's situation in order to identity the rhetor's motive by using five dramatistic elements associated with a play. The five elements outlined by Kenneth Burke are: scene, act, agent, agency, and purpose. Thus, for the critic

> these five terms constitute what Burke called the *pentad,* and they are used as principles or a "grammar" for describing any symbolic act fully: "you must have some word that names the *act* (names what took place, in thought or deed), and another that names the *scene* (the background of the act, the situation in which it occurred); also you must indicate what person or kind of person *(agent)* performed the act, what means or instruments he used *(agency)* and the *purpose.*" (Burke, quoted in Foss 1996, 457)

In conducting a pentadic analysis, the critic follows a two-step process: (1) the critic must apply the five dramatistic elements to the rhetorical artifact from the perspective of the rhetor, and (2) the critic must identify the dominant term in the pentad (Foss 1996). In the analysis under study, the critic will apply the five elements to Tupac Shakur's lyrics; the labeling of the terms will be done from Shakur's worldview. Furthermore, the labeling of the terms and the naming of the dominant term will take place within the context of the narrative approach. Finally, the critic will identify the dominant term in Shakur's rhetoric in an effort to determine Shakur's motive.

In the evaluation stage of the pentadic analysis, the critic will attempt to name Shakur's motive for producing his rhetoric; the critic will also seek to determine Shakur's attitude that undergird the death narratives. "*Attitude,* in this case, designates the manner in which particular means [agency] are emloyed" (Foss 1996, 457). Burke often viewed attitude as the sixth element in the pentad. The results of the critic's evaluation will also take in consideration the findings associated with the narrative approach.

DATA FOR STUDY

Ten songs by rapper Tupac Shakur were chosen for this study. Most of the songs chosen were from Shakur's album *Me Against the World* because this album had the most references to death. The ten songs chosen were "Death Around the Corner," "Lord Knowz," "How Long Will They Mourn Me," "If I Die 2nite," "So Many Tears," "Life Goes On, "High 'Til I Die," Bury Me a G," "I Wonder if Heaven Got a Ghetto," and "No More Pain." Rap lyrics by Tupac Shakur were chosen for four reasons: (1) there are references to death in the title of many of his songs; (2) Shakur had a preoccupation with death; (3) Shakur's lyrics about death were grounded in nihilism; (4) Tupac was murdered in a drive-by shooting at the height of his short career.

TUPAC SHAKUR: THE NARRATOR

Tupac Shakur was born in 1971 in Brooklyn, New York. Shakur's mother, Afeni Shakur, was a Black Panther party member at the time. Later in his life, he moved to Baltimore, Maryland, and attended the Baltimore School for Performing Arts. While unable to finish his training, Shakur left a lasting impression on his teachers. Later, he moved to Oakland, California, with his family. It was in California where Tupac Shakur's entertainment career took off. Shakur joined a group called Digital Underground as a dancer. While the group achieved critical acclaim, Shakur wanted to do more than just dance. After all, he was a lyrical poet who only needed a big break; Shakur's came upon the release of his debut album, *2pacalypse Now.* In addition to rapping, Shakur had a starring role in the movie *Juice* in 1992. In the movie, he played the role of Bishop, a young G (gangsta) who was the embodiment of nihilism in the Black community and in the hood. Young G's or G Niggas have an instinct to kill because their behavior is grounded in nihilism. Cornel West, in his book *Race Matters,* defines nihilism as the "lived experience [in the killing fields of Black America] of coping with a life of horrifying meaninglessness, hopelessness, and (most important) lovelessness. The frightening result is a numbing detachment from others and a self-destructive disposition toward the world" (1993, 14). In discussing nihilism and gangsta rap, Nelson George suggests the following:

> There is an elemental nihilism in the most controversial crack-era [1980s and 1990s] hip hop that wasn't concocted by the rappers but reflects the mentality and fears of young Americans of every color and class living an exhausting, edgy existence, in and out of big cities. Like crack dealing, it may die down, but the social conditions that inspired the trafficking and the underlying artistic impulse that ignited nihilistic rap have not disappeared and will not because, deep in the American soul, it speaks to us and we like the sound of its voice. (1998, 49)

G Niggas do not care about their own lives or the lives of others (except true homies). Their behavior and actions are a product of the killing fields (a place where death is an everyday occurrence). Shakur took time away from acting to release his second album, *Strictly for my Niggaz,* which featured hits such as "Keep Ya Head Up" and "I Get Around."

THE MIND OF THE NARRATOR: TUPAC SHAKUR

The music of Tupac Shakur was filled with contradictions (Williams 1997). On one hand, his lyrics emphasized Black empowerment and pride in one's culture. He even praised the Black single mother in a song entitled "Keep Your Head Up." However, on the other hand, his lyrics often referred to Black women as "bitches" and "hos." In the song "Bury Me a G" (1994b), Shakur says, "I ain't got time for bitches, Gotta keep my mind on my mothafucken riches." In addition to the misogynistic lyrics displayed in his music, Shakur also appeared to have a fascination with death. In a song entitled "High 'til I Die" (1996), Shakur states that I'm "high 'til I die-loced [ready to shoot] 'til they smoke [kill] me—the shit don't stop—'til my casket drop [closes]." Some critics of Shakur have suggested that the contradictions reflected in his music are related to the same contradictions Black youths face in their daily lives particularly Black males. In an article entitled, "Death Wish: Tupac Shakur: Life After Death, Living on Death Row and Killing the East Coast," Strange suggests the following:

> Many different people see Tupac as many different things: hustler, actor, thug, realist, lover, hater, opportunist. But in reality he is all of these. And while this observation may appear to make him unique, it actually simplifies him into the universal symbol of young Black manhood that he is; American society's most vibrant and visible symbol of contradiction, one that comes out looking terrible and beautiful all at once. (1996, 84)

AFENI AND MUTULU SHAKUR: TUPAC SHAKUR'S REVOLUTIONARY CONSCIOUSNESS

In addition to being viewed as a hustler, thug, actor, and opportunist, Shakur was also the embodiment of a revolutionary ethos that he inherited from his mother, Afeni Shakur, and stepfather, Mutulu Shakur. Born Alice Faye Williams in North Carolina, Afeni Shakur, like most youths of the 1960s, grew up watching with frustration the civil rights movement on television in New York. "A member of the notorious Disciples gang as a teenager, Afeni points to two primary factors that channeled her frustrations in a political direction: the historic Ocean Hill–Brownsville, Brooklyn, parent-student strike . . . in 1968 and the formation of the Black Panther Party in New York City" (Powell 1997, 22).

Shakur joined the Panther Party in September 1968. Shortly thereafter, while carrying the rapper-to-be in her womb, she was jailed in April 1969 along with twenty other members of the party (the Panther 21) and " charged with numerous felonies, including conspiracy to bomb several public areas in New York City" (Powell 1997, 22). Shakur was out on bail, in almost no time; then became involved with "Legs," a street hustler and gangster, and Billy, a member of the Panther Party, while still legally married to Lumumba Shakur, one of the lead defendants in the Panther 21 case. Lumumba Shakur later divorced Afeni after he found out she was pregnant.

While "Legs" is credited with shaping Tupac Shakur's antisocial behavior and with being his father (Powell 1997), Mutulu Shakur, Lumumba Shakur's adopted brother, became Tupac Shakur's stepfather and spiritual advisor. Mutulu, who was also a member of the Black liberation struggle, "maintains he was having an impact on the young man, guiding him from street instincts and post-adolescent confusion into a more coherent use of his energies" (Shakur Family 2001, 2). Moreover, Mutulu

> praised the tender songs that Tupac would write, the ones with positive messages about family life and responsibility, like "Brenda's Got a Baby." Together, the step father-and-son team drew up a "Code of Thug Life," which was a list of

> rules discouraging random violence among gangsta rappers. All of this was done away from the glare of media attention. (Shakur Family 2001, 2)

Tupac Shakur's life was influenced by more then just media attention. His life was also shaped by conflicting ideas. While his mother and stepfather shaped his revolutionary thinking, "Legs," who is also credited with getting Tupac's mother hooked on crack (Powell 1997), shaped the rapper's "ride or die" mentality.

Thus, Shakur was a very complex individual whose life was filled with contradictions. One of many contradictions faced by Tupac Shakur during his lifetime was his preoccupation with death. For example, in the song "I Wonder if Heaven Got a Ghetto" (1997a), Shakur states, "I'd rather be dead than a po' nigga—let the Lord judge the criminals—If I die, I wonder if heaven got a ghetto." While he loved life, death was a subject that permeated a variety of his lyrics. In order to understand Shakur's views on death, one must first understand the setting or scene for his narratives about death.

ANALYSIS

THE BLACK COMMUNITY AS THE KILLING FIELDS–THE SETTING OF THE DEATH NARRATIVE(S)

The setting or scene depicted in the stories of gangsta rappers such as Tupac Shakur is a world where young African American men in particular are at war with each other in their communities. These young G's or gangsta warriors are at times warring over territory, drugs, or even gang colors. Sanyika Shakur, also known as Monster Kody Scott, suggests in his book *Monster: The Autobiography of an L.A. Gang Member* that the major objective of the Bloods and the Crips during gang warfare is the elimination of the "enemy." Shakur, who was a member of the L.A. Crips, gives a vivid description of gang warfare in the Black community of Los Angeles:

> Escalation was the order of the day. Entire streets were turned into armed camps to be used as liberated territory, where safe "meeting and mounting up" could be carried out with out not so much as a worry about enemy gunfire. ("Meeting" means a gang gathering to choose a riding party or group of shooters to invade enemy territory. "Mounting up" means starting out on the mission). . . . Our war, like most gang war, was not fought for territory or any specific goal other than the destruction of individuals, of human beings. The idea was to drop enough bodies, cause enough terror and suffering so that they'd [Bloods] come to their senses and realize that we were the wrong set [a gang unit] to fuck with. (1993, 55–56)

In addition to gang warfare, the killing fields of Black America are a place where revenge and retaliation are carried out after the death of one's comrade or homie. In the song "How Long Will They Mourn Me" (1994a), Tupac

Shakur states, "I load my clip before my eyes blurry, don't worry. I'll get them suckas back before you're buried."

The idea of facing death or dying is a twenty-four-hour reality for a G Nigga or ridah who is thuggin, or ballin in the killing fields of urban America. In the face of death, the objective of a G Nigga is survival. In the song "Death around the Corner" (1995a) Shakur proclaims, "Gotta stay high while I survive . . . strugglin and strivin, my destiny's to die."

A G Nigga faces survival in the killing fields where African American men must confront social, economic, and environmental problems on a daily bases. Lack of education among some African American men places them at a disadvantage. "Dropout rates are high, failure is common, performance below grade level is pervasive, and alienation is epidemic. . . . Black males are suspended, expelled, pushed out, and take themselves out of school" (Majors and Billson 1992, 13).

In addition to lack of education, African American males still face high rates of criminality. African Americans make up only a small percentage of the United States population but are disproportionately represented as both criminals and victims of violent crime (Dixon and Linz 2000). High rates of poverty and unemployment have also contributed to the criminal behavior of some African American men.

The killing fields of the Black community are a world where young African American men are at war with other Black men. In a 1996 interview with *Vibe* magazine, Tupac Shakur states the following:

> We all soldiers, unfortunately. Everybody's at war with different things. [Some of us are at war] with ourselves. Some are at war with the establishment. Some of us are at war with our own communities. [I am at war with] different things at different times. My own heart sometimes. There's two niggas inside me. One wants to live in peace, and the other won't die unless he's free. (Powell 1996, 80)

Like Shakur, these young men fight and kill over turf, money, gang affiliation, and dead homies. They also kill in the act of retaliation. Moreover, the killing fields are a world where poverty, unemployment, and illiteracy are a reality for real gangstas, G niggas, and homies.

THE CHARACTERS AND THEIR [ACT] IONS IN THE "KILLING FIELDS"

In Tupac Shakur's stories, G Niggas are the agents (those who produce acts) or street soldiers in the killing fields of urban America who blaze weed and drink until they pass out. The objective of these actors is to maintain their ability to ball (make money and court the attention of women) and sell drugs at all cost. Ballin' and selling drugs are secondary acts (action performed by agents) carried out by G Niggas. However, when confronting the enemy, (playa-haters, tricks, traitors, etc.) their objective is to retaliate. Killing as an act of retaliation is a major act committed by G Niggas. In the song "No More Pain" (1996b), Shakur tells his victim-to-be that "retaliation is a must . . . so watch the guns bust." And in the song "If I Die 2nite" (1995c), Shakur says, "Polishin' pistols, prepare for battle, pass the pump . . . revenge is the method, whenever stepping, keep a weapon close."

G Niggas have no fear of death. As a matter of fact, they welcome death because by dying, they escape the killing fields and the nihilistic behavior it produces. In the song "So Many Tears" (1995b), Shakur states "My every move is a calculated step ta bring me closer to embrace an early death." The G Nigga (Shakur 1996c) continues to reflect on life after death by suggesting that a party be given at his funeral and that Shakur be given "paper and pen so I can write about my life of sin [and] a couple of bottles of gin in case I don't get in [heaven]." Shakur is articulating the life of a ridah where true freedom from the killing fields of urban America comes at the cost of death.

The irony of Tupac's reflection on his life is that death is an act of freedom for himself and most young Black men involved in the gangsta lifestyle. While G Niggas seek to escape nihilism and the killing fields by way of death, homies, who are secondary characters in Shakur's stories, are often the victims of nihilistic behavior. Homies are friends or relatives of G Niggas. Homies can also be G Niggas; however, they are generally thought of as innocent bystanders or "civilians," who live and work in the killing fields of America. In the song "Life Goes On" (1996b), Shakur says goodbye to Kato, his homie, who was shot down in "battle." Shakur states, "Rest nigga cause I ain't worried . . . I got your name tatted on my arm so we both ballin till my dying days."

The negative behaviors and actions (acts of retaliation and revenge, ballin' or smoking weed) of G Niggas and/or homies fit the killing fields that produced them. Thus, "the scene [killing fields] [is] a 'fit container' for the act[ions] of 'G Niggas' " (Larson 1998, 127). The key element that connects the setting with the characters is nihilism. While the development of the killing fields is rooted in nihilism, G Niggas also use the nihilism of the killing fields as agency (instrument used to perform the act) through which the act of retaliation, killing, dying, or ballin,' is carried out.

G NIGGAS' PURPOSE FOR THE ACT OF RETALIATION

"*Purpose* is the reason an agent [G Nigga] acts [retaliates] in a given scene [killing fields] using a particular agency [nihilism]" (Larson 1998, 128). The reason that G Niggas act in retaliation against the enemy is because to do so is to fulfill their allegiance to the rules or code of the streets (Anderson 1999, 32–34). One of the rules of the killing fields faced by G Niggas is the following:

> If a person is assaulted, it is essential in the eyes of his "running buddies" as well as his opponent for him to avenge himself. Otherwise he risks being "tried"

(challenged) or "rolled on" (physically assaulted) by any number of others. Indeed, if he is not careful, he can lose the respect of his running buddies, thus perhaps encouraging one of them to try him. This is a critical consideration, for without running buddies or "homies" who can be depended on to watch his back in a "jam," the person is vulnerable to being rolled on by still others. (Anderson 1999, 73)

In the end, G Niggas must retaliate against the enemy. In doing so, they maintain their juice (respect) with their homies and adversaries. Moreover, it is necessary for G Niggas to strengthen their sense of respect and selfhood as they confront and do battle with death.

DUELING WITH THE REAPER: THE MAIN EVENT IN THE DEATH NARRATIVES

The main event or kernel that seems to intertwine through all of Tupuc Shakur's stories is G Nigga's (Shakur's) showdown with the grim reaper. Minor plots, called satellites, focus on his relationships with his homies, such as Kato. G Nigga is preoccupied with death, which comes as a result of being a "street soldier" who borders on paranoia. Throughout Shakur's stories, G Niggas confront death on two levels: on the killing fields, and within himself. Both of these elements also represent major plots in Shakur's narratives. In the song "Lord Knowz" (1995d) G Nigga, who is contemplating suicide, says, "I smoke a blunt to take the pain out and if I wasn't high I would probably try to blow my brains out. . . . Lord knows." In the song "Death Around the Corner" (1995a), G Nigga claims, "I'm out of breath; make me wanna kill my damn self, but I see death around the corner."

Death was a major theme throughout Shakur's narratives. Elegy was both Shakur's and G Nigga's preoccupation. Thus, death is viewed as a savior that will free them from self-destruction, nihilism, and the killing fields.

SCENE-AGENT: THE DOMINANT RATIO IN THE DEATH NARRATIVES

In addition to determining the major themes and events in Shakur's death narratives, it is equally important for the critic to determine the dominant ratio in Shakur's rhetoric. "A ratio is a pairing of two of the elements in the pentad in order to discover the relationship between them and the effect that each has on the other." Moreover, "discovery of the dominant term provides insight into what dimension of the situation the rhetor privileges or sees as most important" (Foss 1996, 460).

Shakur's rhetoric reveals a scene-agent ratio; he privileges the dramatic element of the scene in his discourse. His situation or worldview is one where the objective or environmental conditions of the killing fields (scene) mold and shape its inhabitants, G Niggas (agents). As far as Shakur is concerned, G Niggas are only responding to the lived conditions, such as poverty, crime, and joblessness, infecting their communities. Thus, Shakur's characters (G

Niggas, homies) are a product of their environment and the scene prescribes their actions—killing, revenge, and/or ballin.

Because scene is privileged in the scene-agent ratio, Burke (1969b) suggests that there is a corresponding school of philosophy associated with scene. "For the featuring of scene, the corresponding philosophic terminology is *materialism*" (Burke 1969b, 128). "Burke believes that persons favoring scene as a key element have a *materialist* philosophy of life. They think that the physical, social and psychological environment in which action occurs can be the cause of good or bad outcomes" (Larson 1998, 127). G Nigga (Shakur) provides evidence in the "death narratives" of environmental forces shaping the outcome of situations. In the song "Life Goes On" (1996b), Shakur discusses the idea of "brothas" falling "victim to tha streetz." And in the song "Death Around the Corner" (1995a), G Nigga claims that "I see death around the corner anyday [and I'm] trying to keep it together, no one lives forever anyway." In the song "So Many Tears" (1995b) G Nigga discusses witnessing death on the killing fields when he states, "Lord knows I've tried, been a witness ta homicide, drive-bys taken lives, little kid die." In "If I Die 2nite" (1995c), G Nigga boldly states his feelings about the way he has been affected by his environment: "I run in the streets and puffin' weed with my peeps, I'm duckin' the cops, I hit the weed as I'm clutchin' my Glock."

Clearly Shakur's rhetoric suggests that his actions—that is, "drama" and retaliation—were the result of a nihilistic life he lived in "tha streetz." Shakur's actions were predetermined by environmental factors such as nihilism that undergird the scene (killing fields). This is the effect that environmental factors rooted in the scene had on the agent (G Nigga) in Shakur's discourse. Thus there is little wonder why Shakur had such a preoccupation with death in his narratives. Shakur's duel with death was a predetermined outcome of the scene-agent ratio and of his narrative. In both the scene-agent ratio and in his narrative, death is a reality that must be faced by all G Niggas as a part of living life in the killing fields of urban America. In the worldview of Shakur, all G Niggas must "ride or die"; this anthem was at the heart of his death narratives. Thus, Shakur faced death by embracing it. His options to do otherwise were limited because of the constraints placed on him (agent) by his environment (scene). In essence, both Shakur and G Nigga could neither avoid nor circumvent their confrontation with death.

Throughout the various lyrics, Shakur is the narrator. Moreover, the narratives are mediated by Shakur via the character G Nigga. Shakur makes other references to himself in the lyrics, such as "I," "my," and "2pac." For Shakur, storytelling becomes a way of extending one's sense of selfhood. It is through this extension of self that Shakur is able to identify with his listeners, homies and G Niggas. Shakur seeks to share substance (views about life in the hood) with his audience. Burke suggest that substance is the "common sensations, concepts, images, ideas, [and] attitudes" (1969a, 21) that people share with one another. By sharing substance with his listeners, Shakur not only extends his sense of self, but more importantly suggests to his homies that he in fact experiences the world of gangsta life as some of them do in their daily lives.

G NIGGAS, STREET SOLDIERS, AND LOVERS OF TUPAC: THE AUDIENCE

In essence, Tupac Shakur's lyrics were addressed to individuals like himself. The message that he was conveying was meant for G Niggas, "big ballers," and the many fans of his music. Shakur's message of balling and death was a message of affirmation and validation for all of the street soldiers. Thus, as far as Shakur was concerned, art and reality were the same, in much the same way as G Nigga and Shakur were identified as one. In communicating the message that he did, Shakur was "keeping it real" even in the face of death while maintaining street credibility.

In addition to his intended audience, White suburban youths also identified with Shakur's message. Moreover, these youths identified with Shakur and his messages as a symbol of rebellion. Shakur and his antiestablishment rhetoric gave White youths an opportunity to vicariously experience Black urban life through the music.

EVALUATION OF THE NARRATIVE

A critical assessment of Tupac Shakur's narrative must begin with an assessment of nihilism in the African American community. As it stands, far too many African Americans who live in the urban centers of this nation face poverty, unemployment, crime, and illiteracy. These are the social ills that create a context whereby hopelessness, worthlessness, and self-loathing can flourish. Developing a love ethic is the only way to defeat nihilism. West states that "nihilism is not overcome by arguments or analyses; it is tamed by love and care. Any disease of the soul must be conquered by a turning of one's soul" (1993, 19). West goes on to say "this turning is done through one's own affirmation of one's worth—an affirmation fueled by the concern of others" (p. 19).

Shakur's narrative represents the absence of a love ethic. His narrative is symbolic of a deep dark void in the killing fields of the Black community, where death and destruction are the order of the day. Death is viewed in Shakur's narrative as a viable and only option for a street soldier to accept. Moreover, he accepts it willingly and with no remorse or regret. It is his final destiny as a soldier. Shakur's narrative also suggests that death by suicide is an acceptable practice during times of war.

Shakur's narrative also communicates the message that death is the street soldier's only savior. Death will save the baller from further destruction in the killing fields. It is only in death that the street soldier finds ultimate peace.

Finally, mental death later followed by physical death begins and ends in the killing fields of urban America. Shakur's narratives suggest that the killing fields first drive the street soldier insane with paranoia. He wonders if his mind is playing tricks on him as he looks over his shoulder for the enemy. Moreover, the street soldier loses touch with reality—friends become enemies and enemies become friends. Shakur's narratives suggest to us that life's contradictions rule the urban environment. Thus, the only way to escape the contradictions of the "killing fields" and become free is through death.

Shakur's narratives, in all fairness, are rhetorically persuasive and demonstrate both narrative coherence and narrative fidelity. Narrative coherence is the ability of the narrative to sound like a story. Shakur meets this criterion by presenting very real characters (G Nigga, homies) that interact and behave in a very consistent and predictable way in the killing fields. Shakur's narratives show a parallel between the urban environment and the individual that is coherent and continuous.

Shakur's narratives also demonstrate narrative fidelity. Narrative fidelity is concerned with the believability of the narrative. The thousands of fans (both White and Black, homies, and G Niggas), and the substantial number of tribute Web sites are evidence that his message is reaching its intended audiences. Shakur's narratives reflected a subjected reality through which many youths identify.

"NAMING" SHAKUR'S MOTIVE

Tupac Shakur's nihilistic attitude motivated him to view death in the manner in which he did. His extreme sense of hopelessness and meaninglessness toward life was often summed up with his middle finger. He was a street soldier who was merely responding to the environmental factors that shaped him and the world in which he balled. Shakur knew that despite his fame and success as a rapper, he was still a ridah who had death breathing at his heels. Thus, "tha streetz" left him only one option: ride or die. Because of Shakur's nihilistic motives, he embraced death openly in his music and unfortunately in his life.

Moreover, the attitude that undergirded Shakur's motive was survival. Despite being a victim of life in the streets, Shakur had a strong desire to survive in the "killing fields" of urban America. During his lifetime, he survived an East Coast–West Cost confrontation, prison life, and being shot. Shakur was eventually shot and killed in a hail of gunfire after leaving the Tyson/Seldon heavyweight bout in Las Vegas in 1996. At that point, death became his savior and set him free from his nihilistic self.

As critics, we must continue to be concerned with not only the message but more importantly how that message registers in the minds and hearts of listeners. We must continue to place a critical lens on the words or lyrics of the message, particularly as it pertains to rap music. As activist scholars, we must also work to change the killing fields of urban America into a space where love, forgiveness, and self-respect can flourish. If we are to validate or reinforce narratives of self-love, this must be done.

There are several reasons why Eurocentric methods are used to study Tupac Shakur's rhetoric: (1) both narrative and dramatistic criticism provided the critic with systemic procedures for the object under study; (2) both narrative and dramatistic criticism place a premium on the symbolic nature of rhetoric; and (3) both narrative and dramatistic criticism allowed the critic to determine Shakur's underlining attitude and motive for his "death narratives."

However, a major drawback of both the narrative and dramatistic methods of rhetorical criticism is the linear procedures the critic is to follow in conducting his/her analysis. The linear nature of the methods tends to constrain the nonlinear or "Afro-circular" (Asante 1987) nature of African American discourse. African American orality is holistic and communal in its orientation (Asante 1987). Thus, the unique communicative nuances (e.g., nommo, style, rhythm) of African American discourse that give the rhetoric its vibrancy and expressiveness could be marginalized as a result of linear Eurocentic methods of analysis.

Future research would assess the form of Shakur's narratives in an effort to see if the form had a bearing on the death theme. An Afrocentric analysis of the form of the narrative would focus on nommo, style, and the importance of rhythm in African American discourse. Does the form alter the emphasis on death or does it reinforce it? Jackson's (1995) development of an Afrocentric method of analysis and Kunjufu's (1993) use of Maat may also be helpful in evaluating hip-hop narrative from ethical and moral standpoint.

REFERENCES

Aldridge, H., and B. D. Carlin (1993). The Rap on Violence: A Rhetorical Analysis of Rapper KRS-One. *Communication Studies* 44: 102–16.

Alexander, F. (with H. S. Cuda) (2000). *Got Your Back: Protecting Tupac in the World of Gangsta Rap.* New York: St. Martin's Griffin.

Anderson, E. (1999). *Code of the Street: Decency, Violence, and the Moral Life of the Inner City.* New York: W. W. Norton and Company.

Asante, M. K. (1987). *The Afrocentric Idea.* Philadelphia: Temple University Press.

Atwater, D. F. (1995). Political and Social Messages in the Music of Stevie Wonder. In L. Niles (Ed.), *African American Rhetoric: A Reader* (pp. 139–47). Dubuque, IA: Kendall/Hunt Publishing Company.

Baker, H. A. (1993). *Black Studies, Rap and the Academy.* Chicago: University of Chicago Press.

Booth, M. W. (1975). The Art of Words in Songs. *Quarterly Journal of Speech,* 103, 2: 73–109.

Costello, M., and D. F. Wallace (1990). *Signifying Rappers: Rap and Race in the Urban Present.* New York: Ecco Press.

Chuck D (with Y. Jah) (1997). *Fight the Power: Rap, Race, and Reality.* New York: Delacorte Press.

Datcher, M., K. Alexander (Eds.) (1997). *Tough Love: The Life and Death of Tupac Shakur.* Alexandria, VA: Alexandria Publishing Group, Inc.

Dixon, T., and D. Linz. (2000). Overrepresentation and Underrepresentation of African Americans and Latinos as Lawbreakers on Television News. *Journal of Communication* 50(2): 131–54.

Dyson, M. E. (1991). Performance, Protest and Prophecy in the Culture of Hip-hop. In J. M. Spencer (Ed.), *The Emergency of Black and the Emergence of rap: A Special Issue of black Sacred Music: A Journal of Theomusicology* (pp. 12–24). Durham, NC: Duke University Press.
Dyson, M. E. (1993). *Reflecting Black: African-American Cultural Criticism.* Minneapolis: University of Minnesota Press.
Eure, J. D., J. G. Spady (1991). *Nation Conscious Rap.* New York: PC International Press.
Fernando, S. H., Jr. (1994). *The New Beats: Exploring the Music, Culture, and Attitudes of Hip-hop.* New York: Anchor Books Doubleday.
Fisher, W. R. (1989). *Human Communication as Narration: Towards a Philosophy of Reason, Value, and Action.* Columbia: University of South Carolina Press.
Foss, S. K. (1989). *Rhetorical Criticism: Exploration and Practice.* Prospect Heights, IL: Waveland Press, Inc.
Foss, S. K. (1996). *Rhetorical Criticism: Exploration and Practice.* Revised ed. Prospect Heights, IL: Waveland Press, Inc.
George, N. (1998). *Hip Hop America.* New York: Viking Press.
George, N., S. Banes, and P. Romanowski (1985). *Fresh: Hip Hop Don't Stop.* New York: Random House.
Gonzalez, A., J. J. Makay (1983). Rhetorical Ascription and the Gospel According to Dylan. *Quarterly Journal of Speech* 69, 1: 1–14.
hooks, b. (1994). *Outlaw Culture: Resisting Representations.* New York: Routledge.
Ice T (as told to H. Siegmund) (1994). *The Ice Opinion.* New York: St. Martin's Press.
Irvin, J. R., and W. G. Kirkpatrick (1972). The Musical Form in Rhetorical Exchange: Theoretical Considerations. *Quarterly Journal of Speech* 58: 272–84.
Jackson, R. (1995). Toward an Afrocentric Methodology for the Critical Assessment of Rhetoric. In L. A. Niles (Ed.), *African American Rhetoric: A Reader* (pp. 148–57). Dubuque, IA: Kendall/Hunt Publishing Company.
Kunjufu, J. (1993). *Hip-hop vs. Maat: A Psycho/social Analysis of Values.* Chicago: African American Images.
Larson, C. U. (1998). *Persuasion: Reception and Responsibility.* Belmont, CA: Wadsworth Publishing Company.
Majors, R., and J. M. Billson (1992). *Cool Pose: The Dilemmas of Black Manhood in America.* New York: Lexington Books.
Morrison, C. D. (2000). The Blackman Is God or at Least a God Term is the Rhetoric of Louis Farrakhan: A Cluster Analysis. (White Man's Heaven is Black Man's Hell). *Encore* 40: 60–78.
Nelson, H., M. A. Gonzales (1991). *Bring the Noise: A Guide to Rap Music and Hip-hop Culture.* New York: Harmony Books.
Powell, K. (1997). This Thug's Life. In A. Light (Ed.), *Tupac Shakur* (pp. 21–31). New York: Crown Publishers, Inc.
Rose, T. (1994). *Black Noise: Rap Music and Black Culture in Contemporary America.* Hanover, NH: Wesleyan University Press.
Ross, A., T. Rose (Eds.) (1994). *Microphone Fiends: Youth Music and Youth Culture.* New York: Routledge.
Roth, L. (1981). Folk Song Lyrics as Communication in John Ford's Films. *Southern Speech Communication Journal* 46, 4: 390–95.
Sexton, A. (Ed.) (1995). *Rap on Rap: Straight-up Talk on Hip-hop Culture.* New York: Dell Publishing.
Shabazz, J. L. D. (1992). *The United States vs. Hip-hop: The Historical and Political Significance of Rap Music.* Hampton, VA: United Brothers Publishing Co.
Shakur, S. (1993). *Monster: The Autobiography of an L.A. Gang Member.* New York: Penguin Books.
Shakur, T. (1994a). How Long Will They Mourn Me. *Thug Life: Volume I* (Interscope Records).
Shakur, T. (1994b). Bury me a G. *Thug Life: Volume I* (Interscope Records).
Shakur, T. (1995a). Death around the Corner. *Me against the World* (Interscope Records).
Shakur, T. (1995b). So Many Tears. *Me against the World* (Interscope Records).
Shakur, T. (1995c). If I Die 2nite. *Me against the World* (Interscope Records).
Shakur, T. (1995d). Lord Knowz. *Me against the World* (Interscope Records).
Shakur, T. (1996a). High 'Til I Die. *Sunset Park* Soundtrack (WEA/Elektra Entertainment).
Shakur, T. (1996b). Life Goes On. *All Eyez on Me* (Death Row and Interscope Records).
Shakur, T. (1996c). No More Pain. *All Eyez on Me* (Death Row and Interscope Records).

Shakur, T. (1997a). I Wonder if Heaven Got a Ghetto. *Thug Life: Volume I* (Interscope Records).
Shakur, T. (1997b). How Long Will They Mourn Me. *Thug Life: Volume I* (Interscope Records).
Shakur Family. (2001). Available: http:angelfire.lycos.com/ga2/family569/.
Smith, S. A. (1980). Sounds of the South: The Rhetorical Saga of Country Music Lyrics. *Southern Speech Communication Journal* 45, 2: 164–72.
Smitherman, G. (1997). "The Chain Remain the Same": Communicative Practices in the Hip Hop Nation. *Journal of Black Studies* 28, 1: 3–25.
Spencer, J. M. (Ed.) (1992). *Sacred Music of the Secular City: From Blues to Rap: A Special Issue of Black Sacred Music: A Journal of Theomusicology*. Durham, NC: Duke University Press.
Strange, A. (1996). Death Wish: Tupac Shakur: Life After Death, Living on Death Row and Killing the East Coast. *The Source* (March): 84–89, 111.
Toop, D. (1984). *The Rap Attack: African Jive to New York Hip-hop*. Boston: South End Press.
Watts, E. (1997). An Exploration of Spectacular Consumption: Gangsta Rap as Cultural Commodity. *Communication Studies* 48: 42–58.
West, C. (1993). *Race Matters*. Boston: Beacon Press.
White, A. (1997). *Rebel for the Hell of It: The Life of Tupac Shakur*. New York: Thunder Mouth's Press.
Williams, F. (1997). Part-time Thuggin': Redefining a Generation by Discarding the Thug Swagger. In M. Datcher and K. Alexander (Eds.), *Tough Love: The Life and Death of Tupac Shakur* (pp. 105–108). Alexander, VA: Alexander Publishing Group, Inc.

Section 5

TRENDS AND INNOVATIONS IN ANALYZING CONTEMPORARY AFRICAN AMERICAN RHETORIC

CHAPTER 13

Lauryn Hill as Lyricist and Womanist

CELNISHA L. DANGERFIELD

Music holds an important place in the history and survival of African Americans. Its rhetorical presence and power can be seen in days past just as it can be seen today. During the days of slavery, the enslaved Africans used music for several purposes. Researchers such as Southern (1977) discuss the role of music in the lives of slaves. Noted orator and abolitionist Frederick Douglass also discussed the role of slave songs in his autobiography (see Douglass 1982). Southern points out that from Douglass' accounts, most slave songs were sung when the slaves were unhappy or upset (1977, 177). In addition, these songs were sung in the fields to announce that a slave—or slaves—would soon attempt to run away. Signifying phrases such as "steal away" and "I'll fly away" were often references to slave breaks that would probably occur later that night (Garner and Calloway-Thomas in this volume; Woodyard in this volume). Directions for travel, news of an ensuing slave uprising, and other hints were often encoded into these songs, and the slave master was usually none the wiser of their actual meaning (Cummings and Moore-Latta in this volume).

Furthermore, the slaves sang songs to get them through the day. As they worked diligently under the hot sun and the watchful eye of their overseer, the slaves chanted lyrics of inspiration. These songs helped pass the workday and gave the impression that the slaves were content. These songs were often completed in the form of call and response, a pattern that is reminiscent of African musical rituals (Jackson 1995). This style of song continues to exist in black churches all over the nation. In fact, it was the call-and-response pattern and the inspirational songs sung in the fields that gave birth to the early "Negro" spirituals, a music form that was the predecessor of what is now called the blues (Roberts 1972).

When one considers the various music forms that have emerged out of Black experiences, the need to understand the complex history behind these music forms becomes apparent. Black music, as a potent rhetorical force, is filled with complex meanings. One need only analyze the rhythms and tones used within Black music forms to see this manifestation. More important, though, are the lyrics to these songs. For black musicians and their audiences, song lyrics are much more than catchy expressions of rhyming words; they are a representation of the sentiments, thoughts, and emotions of a group of people (see Southern 1997). The words to songs, those penned by black artists in particular, tell stories of pain, struggle, and triumph. Nowhere is this more apparent than in the lyrics of today's hip-hop music.

Hip-hop music is one of the newer music forms, only having been in existence for slightly over twenty years (Stewart 1998; Farley 1999). More than just mere poetry set to jazzy beats, this music form, in part, represents the experiences, dreams, and struggles of impoverished, inner-city youth.[1] Henderson (1996) contends that hip-hop fuses poetry and jazz to create a music form that boldly and effectively announces its strong nationalist stance. Rose explains, "Hip hop replicates and reimagines the experiences of urban life and symbolically appropriates urban space through sampling, attitude, dance, style, and sound effects" (1994, 22). Surely, hip-hop music is to today's youth what rock and roll was for the youngsters of the 1950s. However, just as the Vietnam Veterans Memorial defied the norms of architectural design in its day, so too does hip-hop music defy the American-imposed mandate that music merely entertain. Potter (1995) adds support to this notion of hip-hop and rap as postmodern representations.

Hip-hop music is an innovative form of African American rhetoric for many reasons. To begin, it builds upon traditional African American music forms, but it does so much more. It adds to the equation sampled beats and lyrics, media know-how, and public relations savvy. By using sampled beats and (re)making old hits, hip-hop artists (re)use and (re)create music in a conscious effort to recognize those musical artists that have played a major role in developing the hip-hop artist's appreciation for music and his/her own culture. Potter contends, "The *knowledge* which rappers draw on is not only their own day-to-day experience, but also the entire recorded tradition of African American music . . . which it re-reads and [s]ignifies upon through a complex blend of strategies, including samplin', cuttin' (pastiche), and freestylin' (improvisation)" (1995, 22). All of these things meld to create an industry that is worth billions and that has an international audience.

Second, just as slave chants and field hollers were defiant in their day, so too are other black music forms (ya Salaam, 1995); hip-hop is no exception. As a voice for those who have traditionally been voiceless, hip-hop and rap challenge the oppressive forces that seek to keep impoverished blacks muted. Morrison (this volume) notes that hip-hop music shares with the world the range of images experienced daily by artists. Sometimes these images are harsh, but they tell the stories that went untold for so long. Bartlett contends that hip-hop artists have the "second sight" that DuBois spoke of, "that process by which the 'minority' knows the majority not only better than the obverse, but often better than the 'majority' knows itself" (1994, 639). This may help explain why this art form appeals across racial, national, and socioeconomic boundaries. Hip-hop producers are postmodernists in the truest sense, resisting and defying the traditional demands placed on them by society. Smitherman (1997) goes beyond merely labeling these artists and producers as postmodernists and asserts that they are also African griots, or respected community-sanctioned storytellers.

Various hip-hop artists lend support to the belief that this music form is the voice of a silenced group of people. Music artists such as Common, Mos Def, Jill Scott, and the Roots are just a few of the artists who use hip-hop to tell their story, send a message, and create a smidgen of hope for others who have experienced similar circumstances. Moreover, via hip-hop music and rap, these artists have created an art form enjoyed across cultures. Indeed, hip-hop has traveled far beyond the inner-city youths who were the primary audience for hip-hop during its formative years. Today, this style of music is enjoyed by an array of people: middle- and upper-class elites, Whites, and even some in international markets.

While the artists mentioned earlier are important to the hip-hop arena, there is yet another artist who provides one of the most striking examples of a lyricist using hip-hop for a purpose greater than mere entertainment. One need only analyze the work of Lauryn Hill to see the power and the purpose of the spoken word when combined with the musical style that is hip-hop. In her solo debut, Lauryn Hill received critical acclaim for her chart-topping album, *The Miseducation of Lauryn Hill.* As a testament to her accomplishments in the music world, Hill received ten nominations for the 1999 Grammy Awards, and in doing so became the first female artist to accomplish such a feat. As an even greater marker of her talent, it is important to note that the majority of the songs on her album were written and produced by Hill herself.

Lauryn Hill is one of the newest female voices of hip-hop, but for many she is much more. She has stepped into the shoes of predecessors such as Roxanne Shanté, Salt-N-Pepa, and Queen Latifah, and has managed to represent black women and hip-hop with grace. She has been put at the forefront of hip-hop's continued rise and has in effect become a spokesperson for artists, fans, Blacks, and women alike. Moreover, on February 8, 1999, Hill appeared on the cover of *Time* magazine, signaling her importance to the world of hip-hop. This accomplishment announced to the world the realization that hip-hop is a lasting music form and that Hill is a worthy representative. For this reason and many more, Hill's work proves meritorious of further investigation.

This chapter analyzes the song lyrics from Lauryn Hill's solo debut album, *The Miseducation of Lauryn Hill.* A strategy for cultural criticism as described by Roderick Hart (1997) is used to analyze several songs from the album, specifically looking at the use of values, myths, and fantasy themes throughout.

METHOD OF ANALYSIS

The cultural aspects that shape hip-hop music can mystify those who attempt to analyze it. As Rose points out, "The dynamic tensions and contradictions shaping hip hop culture can confound efforts at interpretation by even the most skilled critics and observers" (1994, 21). However, analysis of hip-hop is possible when conducted in a manner that takes into consideration the role of Black culture and experiences in shaping this particular genre on music. By analyzing hip-hop using a method such as cultural criticism, the task becomes easier than one might imagine. When the influence of culture is considered, the interpretations and conclusions, drawn appropriately, link individual experience, social connectedness, and cultural particularity. Culture is such an important part of hip-hop music that disregarding its effects taints textual interpretations and in effect signals shallow observations by researchers. Dyson points out that hip-hop "measures the pulse of black youth culture" (1993, 276). Thus, neglecting this element negates a significant component of hip-hop music. Asante echoes this sentiment by asserting that culture is an inherent part of each person's existence, and it is impossible to divorce oneself from one's culture (1990, 146).

Cultural criticism involves the analysis of values, myths, and fantasy themes. As Hart points out, "One's cultural assumptions, treasure stories, ways of valuing and linguistic preferences are so deeply ingrained within us that we become mute without them" (1997, 234). Nowhere is this truer than within the confines of hip-hop music and for Blacks who use this type of music to give voice to their experiences. This idea is as true for African American and Caribbean cultures as it is for American culture in general. However, Toop (1984, 1991), Rose (1994), and Smitherman (1997) all point out that hip-hop music is filled with elements taken from African traditions.

There are fourteen songs on the album *The Miseducation of Lauryn Hill.* While only five of the songs are analyzed here, it is important to note that certain themes are more apparent in some of the songs than they are in others. For example, the song "Forgive Them Father" expresses values and utilizes both myths and fantasy themes to ensure a greater personal/cultural resonation with the song. One of the mandates for fantasy theme analysis is that several texts be analyzed across a number of rhetorical situations (Hart 1989; Jackson 2000). By analyzing each song on the album as an individual entity, one moves closer to the mandate set forth by this type of analysis. However, while it is important to examine a number of texts, the concepts found within the rhetorical artifact are of primary importance. For this reason, the *concepts* are analyzed as consistent themes throughout the album instead of by analyzing *each song* separately, even though each song is considered a unique text. This brings specific attention to the three concepts of import in cultural criticism: values, myths, and fantasy themes.

ANALYSIS

Using the features outlined in Hart's discussion of cultural criticism, the analysis of hip-hop music can be divided into three areas: values, myths, and fantasy themes. Songs from Lauryn Hill's debut album cannot be excluded from this method of critical analysis. To begin, the songs from this album are analyzed for the presence of value statements.

VALUES

Hart posits that values are beliefs about right and wrong that are deep-seated and persistent. He comments further that they impact "a person's basic orientation to life" (1997, 234). The rhetoric of hip-hop is complete with value statements—some are considered positive, but much more often the negative ones are highlighted. Dyson highlights the role of dueling values in hip-hop music:

> From the ready resources of culture, history, tradition, and community, rap artists fashion musical personae who literally voice their hopes, fears, and fantasies: the self as cultural griot, feminist, educator, or itinerant prophet of black nationalism; but also the self as inveterate consumer, misogynist, violent criminal, or sexual athlete. (1993, 276)

Education is one thing that is extremely important to those within the Black community. The importance of education is underscored by the terms used to describe rappers and the messages that they impart through their music. Potter notes that

> both rappers and scholars partake of a discursive universe where skill at appropriating the fragments of a rapidly-changing world with verbal grace and dexterity is constituted as *knowledge,* and given ultimate value. This parallel emphasis is echoed within rap's own discursive terminologies; a particularly skilled rapper is known as a "teacha" or a "professa," who "drops knowledge" on the mic and gives her/his opponents "schoolin." (1995, 21)

The Miseducation of Lauryn Hill accents the importance of education and the value that has been placed on it. Even the title of the album is indicative of the value placed upon education within the Black community, and the added belief that many Blacks have been miseducated within a traditionally white education system.

The title of the album is a direct reference to the famed text by Carter G. Woodson, *The Miseducation of the Negro*. In this seminal text, Woodson notes how Blacks who have received higher levels of education have been taught, or forced to conform to, Eurocentric ideas. These same Blacks are then asked to take these inconsistent notions back into the Black community and contribute in whatever way possible. In a similar vein, Hill's discussion of dueling values within the Black community speaks to the realization that the miseducation that Woodson spoke of is indeed a reality. Just as Woodson called on Blacks to realize that the ideas pushed on them were not healthy, Hill warns that preoccupation with material things may contribute to continued racial stagnation.

Hill's music tends to emphasize the more positive aspects of Black culture (i.e., self-love, Black love, spiritual relationships with God), but she does bring attention to some of the less positive points. Dyson (1993) appropriately discusses rap artists' ability to meld two areas of importance to the black community, preaching and music; Hill effectively does this throughout the album. For instance, in the song "Doo Wop (That Thing)," she urges both men and women to ponder their present status and consider new ways of behaving and thinking. Toward the beginning of the song, Hill states:

If you did it then, then you probably f——k again
Talking out your neck sayin' you're a Christian

These lines end a verse in which Hill chastises a young woman for having sex with a man after he admitted that his main concern was getting money, not her personal well-being. Hill warns the woman about giving herself to someone who places more importance on money than her body, and particularly for doing so early in the relationship.

Lauryn Hill goes on to say,

Don't be a hardrock when you're really a gem
Babygirl, respect is just a minimum

Hill uses these lyrics to remind the female in this narrative that while she has settled for mediocrity, she deserves more than what she is getting from her male suitor. In this manner, Hill points out the young lady's misguided values, then offers words of support and wisdom that may very well build the young lady's self-esteem and enhance her self-worth.

Hill also talks about values in the song "Forgive Them Father." The song begins with a guest artist, Shelly Thunder, speaking in a Caribbean accent. Hill then enters with a warning that says:

Beware the false motives of others
Be careful of those who pretend to be brothers

The lecture then proceeds with Shelly Thunder adding on to Hill's warning.

Why [is it that for] you to increase, I must decrease?
If I treat you kindly does it mean that I'm weak

This part of the song is a discussion of the warped values that some individuals possess. However, neither Hill nor Thunder advocates hate toward people who have done them wrong. Instead, Hill reverts back to Christian-based values and says, "Forgive them father for they know not what they do."

Hill also discusses values in the song "Lost Ones." She begins the song by talking about the problems that may lie ahead for those who value money more than anything.

It's funny how money change a situation
Miscommunication leads to complication

She then continues her attack on the unfavorable moral acts of those who succumb to the lure of money.

Gained the whole world for the price of your soul
Tryin' to grab hold of what you can't control

With a spiritual undertone, Hill warns that money may lead to evil instead of happiness. She adds that there are other things that should be valued over money—including one's own soul and wisdom.

MYTHS

While the use and reinforcement of values in Lauryn Hill's music and in the music of other hip-hop artists is important, there are other aspects that are central to cultural criticism. This includes the use or presence of myths in rhetorical artifacts. According to Hart, myths are "[m]aster stories describing exceptional people doing exceptional things and serving as moral guides to proper action" (1997, 234). Myths, or at least references to myths, are apparent within hip-hop. However, it is important to note that because of the limited time available within each song, extended tales often are not utilized.

Many of the myths that are used by Lauryn Hill on this album tend to have biblical references. The rhetorical power of stories from the Bible gives the songs on the album even more rhetorical power. One song in particular, "Forgive Them Father," is filled with references to well-known characters in the Bible. The title of the song itself is a reference to the words spoken by Jesus on the cross during his crucifixion. In this famed Bible verse, Jesus asks forgiveness for those who did not believe that he was the son of God and those who betrayed him (Luke 23:34). Lauryn Hill makes reference to these biblical characters and other historical feud as she chants:

Like Cain and Abel, Caesar and Brutus, Jesus and Judas[2]
Backstabbers do this

Another biblical story is referred to in the song, "Final Hour." Thoughts of Moses, Aaron, the children of Israel, and the Promised Land are conjured by the lyrics of this song:

Documented in the Bible
Like Moses and Aaron

This particular mythical reference is important because of the role that this story plays in the cultural beliefs of several groups. The story of Moses and the Israelites, as it relates to African Americans, will be discussed in more detail later in this chapter.

FANTASY THEMES

Fantasy theme analysis is a method of rhetorical criticism that was created by Ernest G. Bormann from the work of Robert Bales on small-group communication (see Bormann 1972; Foss 1989). Fantasy themes refer to "abbreviated myths providing concrete manifestations of current values and hinting at some idealized vision of the future" (Hart 1997, 234). A derivative of symbolic convergence theory, this method of rhetorical criticism "attempts to account for the creation, raising, and maintenance of group consciousness through communication" (Jackson 2000).

Fantasy themes are of key importance within hip-hop and rap because they carry the force of myths while taking up less space and demanding less time within a particular song. These themes help foster group identification and cohesiveness by sharing common visions of the past or the future (Tierney and Jackson 2001). While fantasy themes are often unique to particular cultures, there are those that coincide with the beliefs and experiences of a number of cultural groups. This is especially true within the work of Lauryn Hill. There are two major fantasy themes apparent in Hill's work, that of Blacks as God's chosen people and the importance of motherhood.

Hart (1997) argues that one of the major fantasy themes that exist in this country is the idea of America as the "new Israel." This theme revolves around the idea that the United States is such a force because it has been chosen by God to be a leader and a guiding presence throughout the world. However, while this fantasy theme is valid for all U.S. inhabitants, it is of particular importance to African Americans.

The theme of Blacks as God's chosen people clearly surfaces in the work of Lauryn Hill. While the story of the Israelites is brought to mind by the mere mention of Moses and Aaron, the preceding lines in the song "Forgive Them Father," add more context to Hill's statement. Prior to the mention of both Moses and Aaron, she links the experiences of Blacks to those of the Israelites. Her reference to the laws that "prevented our survival" may refer to those laws and rulings such as those that made slavery legal, those that deemed blacks three-fifths of a person, and those that prohibited blacks from voting (the grandfather clause, reading tests, etc.). However, the harshness of slavery endured by Blacks is enough to establish a relationship between the experiences of Blacks and the Israelites. So similar are the experiences that one of the most well-known abolitionists—Harriet Tubman—was given the nickname "Moses" because of her efforts to free the slaves, just as the Moses of biblical fame had done.

Still, another fantasy theme that is represented on Lauryn Hill's album is that of motherhood being a gift from God and a joyful experience. While this may be true within certain religious circles and within American culture, the same may not be true within other cultures. Thus, this ensures that these beliefs about motherhood meet the mandate that fantasy themes be culture-specific.

Hill dedicates an entire song to her son, Zion. In the song, she discusses the joys of motherhood, along with the realization that it would not be an easy journey. She sings:

Unsure of what the balance held
I touched my belly overwhelmed

The rest of this verse contains elements that are strikingly similar to the tale of the Virgin Mary's visit by an angel in the Bible.

The use of motherhood as a fantasy theme is of particular importance within the Black community. A report issued by Daniel Moynihan in 1965 had a major impact on the shift of attention to Black females and their leadership of households. Since that time, the proliferation of female-headed households and unwed mothers has been the subject of many debates. This reality helps explain why motherhood may be met with mixed reactions in the Black community. Using her voice to shed light on the experience of impending motherhood, Hill confesses the struggles that she encountered after discovering that she was pregnant. In the song "To Zion," she notes her decision to choose motherhood as well as a career. She sings:

Look at your career they said
"Lauryn, baby, use your head"
But instead I chose to use my heart

In these lines, Hill acknowledges her family's push to choose a career—and almost certain financial stability—over being a single mother. Yet while Hill was clearly being steered away from having her son as an unwed mother, she chose motherhood and was able to continue her career, proving that it is possible to have both. To understand this song, one must consider the historical legacy of motherhood in the Black community, as well as Hill's personal explanation for continuing her pregnancy. The pairing of these realities ultimately presents the notion that while motherhood may be a huge undertaking, it is taken seriously within the Black community.

Dyson reminds us that in the past the cultural criticism of Black culture has tended to be "vicious and unjust, reflecting the self-validating sciolism of cultural imperials whose prejudice clouded their reason" (1993, xiv). However, this analysis shows that when racist blindfolds are removed, black culture has many of the same components as other U.S. cultures. After close analysis of *The Miseducation of Lauryn Hill,* it becomes readily apparent that the three aspects of cultural criticism outlined by Hart are evident within Hill's work. Yet the dueling tensions of being both Black and American are ever-present within the songs on this album, just as they are within the everyday experiences of blacks in this country. The unique thing about hip-hop is that it allows for a creative expression of what being young and black in America really means, and cultural criticism proves a suitable method for understanding this cultural domain.

DISCUSSION

In 1903, noted African American scholar W. E. B. Du Bois wrote about the dual identities that many blacks in the United States possess. In *The Souls of Black Folks,* he made the following assertion:

> It is a peculiar sensation, this double-consciousness, this sense of always looking at one's self through the eyes of others, of measuring one's soul by the tape of a world that looks on in amused contempt and pity. One ever feels his twoness,— an American, a Negro; two souls, two thoughts, two unreconciled strivings; two warring ideals in one dark body, whose dogged strength alone keeps it from being torn asunder. (1965, 215)

In line with this sentiment offered almost a century ago by Du Bois, Potter adds "that African Americans, even as they have sought to build from within a full sense of self-authenticity, have had to exist in a nation where the fundamental symbolic structures continually place them in the position of 'Other'" (1995, 3). Hill alludes to this in the final song on *The Miseducation of Lauryn Hill.* She states:

> But deep in my heart the answer it was in me
> And I made up my mind to find my own destiny

In this verse, Hill talks about the inherent struggle that comes with warring against what others say she is as contrasted with her own "true" nature. Thus, the double consciousness that Du Bois spoke of is clearly alive even today, at least as described by Hill.

The rhetoric of Lauryn Hill, and the rhetoric of many other hip-hop artists, is filled with the duality of being American and being Black. This becomes readily apparent when the values, myths, and fantasy themes in songs are analyzed. Not only are points of importance to the Black community noted, but so are things that are of importance to Americans overall. Examples of these competing (and sometimes complementary) ideals are found throughout the song lyrics on the album *The Miseducation of Lauryn Hill.* The lyrics on this album cover areas ranging from love and spiritual relationships to money, career, and sexual relationships.

Hart is careful to point out, "While the values in any culture wax and wane over the years, they are not altered radically except during periods of massive social upheaval . . . values represent basic life orientations" (1997, 237). Many music forms were developed amidst social upheaval, and hip-hop is no exception. This may provide a deeper clue as to why some of the values within the African American community may have shifted over time and why many remain in line with traditional African values. Further, this may explain why there is such a wide array of values referred to in Hill's music.

CONCLUSION

The power of hip-hop lies in its rhetorical strength. This art form, like other black music forms of the past, transcends its position as just another genre of music and has become a mouthpiece for an entire generation. Culture cannot be separated from rhetorical acts, and this idea is supported by Hill's work. *The Miseducation of Lauryn Hill* is a powerful rhetorical artifact that recollects and reinforces the importance of culture, especially within the Black community.

Furthermore, as a rhetorical artifact, the album is a compilation of innovations. Hip-hop and rap are unique spaces in which Blacks freely defy the confines within which they have traditionally been placed. Hip-hop music itself is a postmodern representative of music. It defies the norms of the American status quo and simultaneously both destroys boundaries and re-creates them as more permeable. Yet, even within this defiance of what has traditionally been acceptable, Lauryn Hill resists falling into the "pit of conformity." By writing and producing her own music, Hill steps outside of the boundary that some scholars have tried to create for hip-hop. She counteracts the idea that hip-hop is substantive only because of its use of others' music. By voicing the concerns of an entire group without relying on sampled beats, Hill refuses to neatly fit into a precompartmentalized space. Ya Salaam (1995) asserts that this notion of innovativeness is not only advised within Black music forms, but is even expected. Thus, within the hip-hop genre, Hill is both a representative and a trailblazer.

As a spokesperson for—and a prominent voice within—the hip-hop generation, Lauryn Hill joins the ranks of other greats who have represented music forms that at one time were up-and-coming genres. Hill stands beside Aretha Franklin, James Brown, Little Richard, Miles Davis, B. B. King, and many others who are now synonymous with blues, jazz, soul, and rhythm and blues. Just like its predecessors, which were dismissed as passing fads, hip-hop has withstood the test of time and is now being recognized as a legitimate art form. No matter what else is said, the fact that hip-hop represents Black culture and gives voice to those who have traditionally been silenced cannot be ignored. Hip-hop is a music form that grew out the marginalization of inner-city blacks, and this is a careful reminder that even from its genesis, culture was—and still is—an important part of its rhetorical force.

THE FUTURE OF AFRICAN AMERICAN DISCOURSE

If the work of Lauryn Hill and other hip-hop artists is any indication, the future of African American discourse is bright indeed. These artists have merely picked up where Martin Luther King Jr, Malcolm X, and Marcus Garvey left off. Smitherman (1997) echoes this sentiment and goes as far as to label rap music as "contemporary resistance rhetoric" (1997, 21). While the faces and the method employed by hip-hoppers may have changed, the message certainly has not. It is one of Black uplift, strength, and survival; it is merely cloaked in the garb of rap and hip-hop music (along with money, cars, and women). In many ways, hip-hop is the modern slave song, expressing one's dismay at the oppression experienced daily, offering a smidgen of hope to others, and sharing with others the plan for stealing away from the subjugation that comes as a result of living in Black skin.

While the rhetorical power of our forefathers cannot be forgotten or cast aside, a new day has come and Generation X-ers and Y-ers look to other rhetorical formats for entertainment, direction, and even empathy. As the voice of a new generation, this rhetorical strategy is not only highly effective, but borders on sheer genius. For not only has it reached its primary audience of inner-city black youth, it has expanded beyond those shallow depths and touched people across racial, cultural, and socioeconomic lines. For this reason and many more, the genre of hip-hop is an innovative form of black rhetoric that has exposed the world to the powerful force that is African American rhetoric.

NOTES

1. Although all rappers are not poverty-stricken urban youth, there is a clearly observable trend toward culture, status, and class commentary within rap and hip-hop music.
2. The reference to Cain and Abel and Caesar and Brutus are references to other master stories that have maintained their rhetorical power over the centuries.

REFERENCES

Asante, M.K. (1990). *Kemet, Afrocentricity, and Knowledge*. Trenton, NJ: Africa World.

Bartlett, A. (1994). Airshafts, Loudspeakers, and the Hip-hop Sample: Contexts and African American musical aesthetics. *African American Review* 28, 4: 639–52.

Bormann, E. G. (1972). Fantasy and Rhetorical Vision: The Rhetorical Criticism of Social Reality. *The Quarterly Journal of Speech* 58: 396–407.
Douglass, F. (1982). *Narrative of the Life of Frederick Douglass, an American Slave*. New York: Penguin.
Du Bois, W. E. B. (1965). The Souls of Black Folk. In *Three Negro Classics*. New York: Avon.
Dyson, M. E. (1993). *Reflecting Black: African-American Cultural Criticism*. Minneapolis: University of Minnesota Press.
Farley, C. J. (1999). Hip-hop nation. *Time,* February 8, 54–64.
Foss, S. K. (1989). *Rhetorical Criticism: Exploration and Practice*. Prospect Heights, IL: Waveland.
Hart, R. (1989). *Modern Rhetorical Criticism*. Glenview, IL: Scott Foresman/Little, Brown.
Hart, R. P. (1997). *Modern Rhetorical Criticism* (second edition). Needham Heights, MA: Allyn and Bacon.
Henderson, E. A. (1996). Black Nationalism and Rap Music. *Journal of Black Studies* 26, 3: 308–39.
Jackson, B. G. (2000). A Fantasy Theme Analysis of Peter Senge's Learning Organization. *The Journal of Applied Behavioral Science* 36, 2: 193–209.
Jackson, J. M. (1995). The Changing Nature of Gospel Music: A Southern Case Study. *African American Review* 29, 2: 185–200.
Moyniham, D. P. (1965). *The Negro Family: The Case for National Action*. Washington: U.S. Department of Labor, Department of Policy Planning and Research.
Potter, R. A. (1995). *Spectacular Vernacular: Hip-hop and the Politics of Postmodernism*. Albany: State University of New York Press.
Roberts, J. S. (1972). *Black music of two worlds*. New York: Praeger.
Rose, T. (1994). *Black Noise: Rap Music and Black Culture in Contemporary America*. Hanover, NH: University Press of New England.
Smitherman, G. (1997). The Chain Remain the Same: Communicative Practices in the Hip-hop Nation. *Journal of Black Studies* 28, 1:3–25.
Southern, E. (1997). *The Music of Black Americans*. New York: W. W. Norton and Company.
Stewart, E. L. (1998). *African American Music: An Introduction*. New York: Schirmer.
Tierney, S., and Jackson, R.L. (2002). Interrogating the Fantasy of Whiteness: Implication for Intercultural Alliance Building in the US. In M. J. Collier (Ed.), *Intercultural Alliances*. Thousand Oaks, CA: Sage.
Toop, D. (1984). *The Rap Attack: African Jive to New York Hip-hop*. Boston: South End Press.
Toop, D. (1991). *The Rap Attack 2: African Rap to Global Hip-hop*. New York: Serpent's Tail.
ya Salaam, K. (1995). It Didn't Jes Grew: The Social and Aesthetic Significance of African American Music. *African American Review* 29, 2: 351–75.

CHAPTER 14

The Kink Factor: A Womanist Discourse Analysis of African American Mother/Daughter Perspectives on Negotiating Black Hair/Body Politics

REGINA E. SPELLERS

The body is a sign-emitting text (Bordo 1993; Trethewey 1999). Shilling writes, "Individuals engaged in encounters constantly display information as a consequence of their embodiment even if they are not speaking" (1993, 85). In Erving Goffman's writings (1958, 1963, 1968, 1983) the body is associated with the exercise of human agency. In his work the corporeal has a dual location (Shilling 1993). As a resource that both requires and enables people to manage their movements and appearances, bodies are the property of individuals, yet are defined as significant and meaningful by society. The idea that the body can be viewed as a readable text (Stern and Henderson 1993) is particularly important when seeking to understand the choices individuals make as they construct their aesthetic images. As Shilling notes, "The social meanings which are attached to particular bodily forms and performances tend to become internalized and exert a powerful influence on an individual's sense of self and feelings of inner worth" (1993, 83). Individuals often find themselves negotiating between and making meaning of various discourses of the body. For women of African descent negotiating between and making meaning of different discourses of the body is a critical aspect of their everyday lived experiences.[1]

Black women's ideas about beauty and femininity are largely shaped through a discursive understanding of hierarchies based on hair texture and skin tone (Collins 2000; Banks 2000, Spellers 2000). While the categorization of hair textures (Brownmiller 1984) and skin tone differences may seem trivial from a Eurocentric standpoint, they are central to understanding the Black female experiences of hair/body politics. In Black communities, for example, the terms "good hair" and "bad hair," "light-skinned" and "dark-skinned" are the language (Smitherman 1977; Russell, Wilson, and Hall 1992) that gives shape to both the experience of being discriminated against because of one's features and the act of internalizing negative, external definitions (Rooks 1996). Hair and skin tone become sites of African American women's struggle to define their identity and their relationships to Black men (Kelly 1997; Russell, Wilson, and Hall 1992), to each other (Rooks 1996), and to the dominant culture (hooks 1992). Together, race, gender, and class make a difference in understanding the unique ideological significance of hair in the lives of women of African descent (Banks 2000; Spellers 2000).[2] However, few communication studies have examined how Black women define beauty and construct their aesthetic images with a specific focus on hair. Given how much change is taking place in our culture, especially with respect to ethnic and gender diversity (Dykes 1999; Johnston and Packard 1987; Judy and D'Amico 1997), it is essential for scholars to research and give expression to marginal aspects of Black female cultural experience.

The purposes of this project are to examine the discursive formations that emerge as African American women define beauty and to describe the complex "preverbal" (Jackson 2000) dynamics that emerge for them as they engage in the process of constructing their corporeal representations, specifically their hair. The central questions here are "How do African American women disrupt and challenge dominant notions of the Black female body?" and "What are the implications, if any, associated with these acts of resistance?" In order to address these questions, a womanist framework is employed. This chapter proceeds with an overview of the framework that guided this investigation. Next, a review of representative literature in the area of Black hair/body politics is conducted. Also provided are a description of the methodology and a discussion of the three essential discursive themes that emerged in this investigation. This essay concludes with a discussion of the implications for future research.

WOMANIST FRAMEWORK

Womanism is an example of a self-defined Black women's standpoint that draws from a definition put forth by Alice Walker in her book entitled *In Search of Our Mother's Gardens*. To act "womanish" is to act in bold, audacious, in-charge, serious, and self-defining ways (Walker 1983). It is a term Black mothers use to describe and (usually) admonish "grown-up behavior" in female children—"You're acting womanish." Its usage offers a vocabulary for describing Black feminists or feminists of color who assert their right to identify, name, and reflect on the parameters and character of their experiences from their own perspective (Cummings 1995). Frameworks, such as womanism, that center the perspectives of women of color have the potential to expose new themes (Houston 2000).

Examining the multilayered texture of Black women's lives in relationship to images of Black corporeal inadequacy is an expansion of the womanist principle that the personal is political (Combahee River Collective 1982; Smith 1998). Berger and Luckman (1967) argue that we create social constructs, and in turn, they create us. Stern and Henderson write:

> As long as we live in a racist society, the concept of race will continue to be important; we may envision a world in which this concept has disappeared, but until then, we need to confront its meaning in the lives of those people whose bodies are constructed along racial lines. (1993, 324)

Here, I use the term "body politic" to refer to ways in which discursive formations of race, gender, class, and nation invent symbolic representations of literal bodies. In this way, I merge the human body with the political. In doing so, this study not only recognizes Black women's unique angle of vision via their discourse (Collins 2000), but also helps us to better understand how they construct their corporeal representations in the midst of negative, externally defined images of Black womanhood.

BLACK HAIR/BODY POLITICS

Much of the literature on Black body politics seeks to understand hair in relation to various racial and social ideologies. Scholarship focusing on Blacks and hair emphasize the importance of hair in relationship to Africa (Yarbrough 1984), construction of racial identity (Cross 1991), enslavement (Uya 1993, 94; Diop, 1974), skin color (Russell, Wilson, and Hall 1982), self-esteem (Boone 1996; Queenan 1988), ritual (Boyd 1993; hooks 1996), aesthetics (Spellers 1998), appropriate grooming practices (Tyler 1990), images of beauty (hooks 1992), and intersections of race and gender (Caldwell 1991; Kelly 1997). We have learned much from this literature, such as how hair came to mean so much in African American communities and how these understandings are transmitted and communicated in particular contexts (Caldwell 1997; Cenen and Smith 1983; Jewell 1993; Rooks 1996). However, a review of the research relating to Black body politics reveals two major limitations.

First, few empirical investigations include actual interviews with African American women on the subject of what role hair plays in their lives (Banks 2000). Thus, within this discourse, it becomes difficult to fathom the meaning of the body politic for individual African American women. In this way, articulations of African American female identities are muted. While common experiences may link Black women's lives, they will be interpreted differently by Black women of different classes, ages, regions, sexual preferences, and historical contexts (Collins 1991a; Houston 1992). Projects that investigate Black body politics by actually interviewing African American women may elicit more telling articulations of the complex functions that hair performs in their lives and perceptions.

Second, the notion of critical self-interrogation is a predominant theme within the body of literature regarding Black hair/body politics. Authors stress the value of considering seriously how we, as people of African descent, have participated in the creation, acceptance, and maintenance of negative, externally defined discourses and images of Blackness (Collins 2000; hooks 1992; Russell, Wilson, and Hall 1992). Deconstructing and reconstructing externally defined discourses and images of Black womanhood is a useful and worthwhile pursuit and often reveals a culture's oppressive aesthetic values. Through this approach we also see the anguish that emerges in women's lives as a result of trying to live up to externally defined standards. However, this approach can also be viewed as limiting our understanding of Black hair politics because it simplifies the decolonization process and tends to obscure the complex tensions associated with the role hair plays in the lives and perceptions of African American women. What is required, then, is a theoretical framework that moves beyond explaining the importance of the decolonization process as it relates to Black hair/body politics; rather, the approach used here attempts to actually describe the complex dynamics involved in this process.

METHOD

For this preliminary study, in-depth one-hour interviews were conducted with ten African American female participants. They ranged in age from eight to fifty-nine, in socioeconomic status from poor-but-"didn't-know-we-were-poor" to upper middle class, in education from high school diploma to master's and law degrees, and in family structures from single-parent households to "traditional" nuclear family structures, and yet they all share the mutuality of having to negotiate hair/body politics. All of the women are heterosexual and are identified in this study by a pseudonym. Eight of the participants represent mother/daughter pairs: Kim/Tyisha, Jessica/Denise, Elaine/Carla, Bessie/Vanessa. The remaining two participants, Ruth and Fran, represent an othermother/daughter relationship.[3] All of the participants were interviewed individually.

The interviews followed a semistructured (Kvale 1996) format that allowed room for dialogue (Reinharz 1992), helped to develop a sense of connectedness between the researcher and participants (Collins 2000), and aided in minimizing the unequal power in the researcher-researched relationship (Acker, Barry, and Esseveld 1991). For example, the interviews were strongly interviewee-guided (Reinharz 1992). The first phase of the interview functioned as an icebreaker in which the women were urged to think of the interview as "just a conversation with a few specific questions." There were a few fixed, preset questions posed to each of the participants, such as those that centered on obtaining demographic information. Other questions were more open-ended and were designed to investigate how the participants identify themselves ethnically, how they define beauty, how they have constructed their aesthetic images at various stages in their lives, and how others react to their aesthetic images. In general, interviewees' responses determined when each area was covered, the time spent on each, and the introduction of new or additional issues.

All of the interviews were audiotaped, transcribed, and analyzed for thematic content utilizing the meaning condensation method as described by Kvale (1996). Five steps were involved in the analysis process. First, in order to get a sense of their content, all of the interview transcripts were read through by the researcher. Second, all of the interview transcripts were divided into two columns. Here, the right column featured the participant's responses, which were divided into natural meaning units (Kvale 1996) as determined by the researcher. In the third step, the theme(s) that emerged from the natural meaning unit, as interpreted by the researcher, is stated as simply as possible in the left column of the transcript. The next step consisted of interrogating and analyzing the meaning units and their themes in terms of the specific purpose of the study. In the fifth step, meaning units from all of the interviews were grouped together under corresponding themes and discussed.

In addition to employing the meaning condensation method of analysis, the data and interpretation of them were also tested with one participant. The member check gives participants the opportunity to react to the investigator's reconstructions and representations (Lincoln and Guba 1985). Here, one participant read an early draft of this report and gave an assessment of the overall adequacy of interpretations. Incorporating this technique was a conscious decision that helped to establish the meaningfulness of the findings and interpretations. The following section discusses the metaphor that will be utilized throughout the remainder of this chapter.

THE KINK FACTOR METAPHOR: A DISCUSSION

According to Lakoff and Johnson, "The essence of metaphor is understanding and experiencing one kind of thing in terms of another" (1980, 5). Metaphors play a crucial role in the creation and understanding of human communicative activities. Here, the metaphor of the kink factor attempts to illustrate the complexity of Black hair/body politics as experienced by women of African descent.[4] Within Black culture, *kinky* is usually a negatively connoted word used to describe or express an aesthetic evaluation of hair texture that is tightly coiled or nappy (Smitherman 1997). By evoking the image of tightly coiled hair, the term *kink factor* demarcates the cultural space/dimension between two realities—a Eurocentric worldview and an Afrocentric worldview—as characterized by tension.

In negotiating the body politic, African American women have to learn how to employ certain strategies in order to survive in a culture that devalues their womanhood. Black children have to be prepared to dediate two opposing worldviews (Nobles 1975; Staples and Johnson 1993)—the Eurocentric worldview, which emphasizes control over nature, competition, and individualism, and an Afrocentric worldview, which values cooperation, interdependence, and collective responsibility (Asante 1995; Bekerie 1994). Self-definition and self-valuation are two key strategies employed by African American women as a way to resist dehumanizing systems of domination (Collins 1991a). While these two strategies are closely related, they are distinguishable.

According to Collins (2000), self-definition involves questioning who has the authority to define as well as the act of interrogating or critically examining the very politics underlying the process of definition. She also posits that, in contrast to self-definition, self-valuation involves addressing the actual content of Black women's self-definition. Although the former speaks to the power dynamics associated with the act of defining self and community and the latter addresses the actual content of these self-definitions, both strategies share the common feature of empowering Black women.

Without the skills of self-definition and self-valuation, African American women may become victims of internalized racism. Thus, these tools allow African American women to endure the recurrent psychological assaults to their self-esteem that stem from externally defined controlling images of Black womanhood (Collins 2000). The ability to define and value qualities and attributes of Black womanhood from a Black female-centered framework is essential for Black female survival.

While engaging in self-definition and self-valuation allows African American women to build inner strength and demonstrate their objection and resistance to externally defined controlling images, utilizing these tools presents a unique challenge for them. For example, on one hand, having the ability to be assertive is required if one is to survive in and transcend the harsh environments that circumscribe many Black women's lives. On the other hand, Black women are stereotyped for embracing this quality (Bell 1990).

Gilkes (1983) and White (1985) suggests that many of the attributes extant in Black female stereotypes are actually distorted renderings of those aspects of Black female behavior seen as most threatening to the status quo. Strong, assertive, and aggressive Black women are labeled matriarchs, Mammies, and Sapphires because these attributes challenge White patriarchal definitions of femininity. The historic practice of labeling certain aspects of African American womanhood as "unfeminine" (Collins 2000) has socialized Black women to understand that acts of self-definition and self-valuation are punishable. Black daughters must learn how to survive in interlocking structures of race, class, and gender oppression while simultaneously rejecting and transcending those very same structures (Collins 1991b). Thus, a key part of Black girls' socialization into womanhood involves being able to cope with contradictions and consequences. Utilizing the skills of self-definition and self-valuation presents a certain risk for African American women, yet these skills are key to their ability to survive in, reject, and transcend these interlocking structures of race, class, and gender oppression. This unique dilemma shapes how Black women negotiate the body politic.

The kink factor is a contested zone. Here, elements of contradiction and potential consequences exist that may create certain tensions in the everyday lives of women of African descent. The kink factor metaphor allows us to exploring the notions of self-definition, self-valuation, and survival, and the relationship among them. By evoking the kink factor metaphor we confront static notions of Black female beauty, allowing us to conceive African American women's hair politics as diverse and emergent from historical experiences characterized by the tensions between surviving in and resisting cultural hegemony. It also works to inform our understanding of how African American women negotiate their image, their beauty, and their womanhood.

THEMATIC ANALYSIS

These mothers and daughters of various ages and from diverse social class backgrounds, family structures, and geographic regions have all experienced aspects of the kink factor—the tensions associated with wanting to be self-defined yet also wanting to avoid the consequences associated with self-definition. Three key themes emerged from participants' interviews: kinky hair is a Black thing; kinky hair is nappy by nature; and kinky hair is a state of mine/mind. The themes were derived by examining the discursive formations that were articulated by the respondents. Within my discussion of each theme, I have included an analysis of certain interview segments or discursive fragments that are exemplary of the particular theme under evaluation. While each theme is distinct, there are some overlapping concepts.

KINKY HAIR IS A BLACK THING

The first theme suggests that due to their marginal perspective, African Americans identify with and experience hair/body politics in very unique ways. Specifically, participants were very clear about the fact that culture and gender (Bordo 1993; Banks 2000) make a difference in understanding how dominant definitions of beauty and femininity shape women's identities. For example, as noted in the following interview segment with Carla, a thirty-something successful attorney, Black women have come to understand that a controversial relationship exists between culture, gender, and hair/body politics.

R: And so, hair, it's not an easy thing. For us, for Black women, do you think? Do you think that White women have the same issues?

C: Oh, I think that they have issues. White women aren't satisfied with their hair, they want their hair blonder, or they want their hair darker . . . there is a fraction of Asians who try and perm their hair or cut it.

R: So how is it, or is it different for African American women?

C: Oh, I think that all of us have hair issues. It's just that we have our own because we have the kink issue.

Here, Carla's statements reflect the idea that while dominant definitions of beauty have implications for all women, the intersection of race and gender creates particular issues for Black women. Further, her discourse implies ownership of the cultural significance hair plays within Black communities.

The first theme, kinky hair is a Black thing, also takes into account how the dynamics of race, gender, and class intersect in multiple and interlocking ways (Davis 1981; Houston 1992) to impact how Black women view their relationship with their bodies, specifically their hair. Kim, a married mother of two and (at the time of the study) a full-time graduate student, also seems to recognize the distinct ways these constructs shape the significance hair plays in many Black communities:

K: Now, Black men say they want a woman with some meat on their bones, a brick house. They don't want a woman that they cannot feel when they hold them. So I think Black women are pretty secure with the weight issue. But the hair thing . . . and the color thing . . . well . . .

Kim's comments suggest that Black women construct their corporeal representations with the relationship between skin tone and hair texture foremost in mind.

When discussing notions of corporeal politics it is important to note that certain physical attributes of the Black body are more salient than others (Dickerson 1987; Russell, Wilson, and Hall 1992; Rooks 1996). As Mercer writes, "Within racism's bipolar codification of human worth, Black people's hair has been historically devalued as the most visible stigmata of Blackness, second only to skin" (1994, 101). Hair and skin tone become sites of African American women's struggle to define their identity and their relationships to Black men, to each other (Rooks 1996), and to the dominant culture. In order to more fully understand how Black women negotiate hair/body politics, one must also consider the complex relationship between hair texture, skin tone, and body size for women of color when discussing beauty standards. The fact that dominant standards of beauty affect different groups in different ways gives support for studying the issues and experiences of various groups from their particular worldviews.

Metaphorically, kinky hair is a Black thing because, as the participants' comments reveal, African American women are acutely aware of the fact that their corporeal representations are often subjects of and subjected to a Eurocentric gaze. The following interview segments reveal how racial, class, and gender stereotyping based on one's aesthetic image shape interpersonal relationships in the workplace. Carla feels that it is not her role to "play happy

Negro" (her words), educating Whites about the nuances Blacks experience in America or about aspects of African American history. Below she describes an incident at work where a White female co-worker attempted to compliment her:

> C: One night we were all sitting around and basically we were all just talking and she was like, "Oh, but Carla's not like the average Black person, I mean she's really pretty." And the room was silent.

Historically and in the everyday lives of African Americans, at a glance, our hair and skin tone communicate to some degree, whether valid or not, if we will neatly fit into systems of oppression or if we pose a threat to the status quo. For Black females, to act womanish is to step out of the boundary of acceptable nonverbal and verbal communication (hooks 1989). Likewise, kinky hair is often described as unmanageable (Smitherman 1977), has been characterized as having a mind of its own (Rooks 1996), and is often viewed as a site of struggle for some African American women (Banks 2000; Spellers 1998).

For her co-worker, Carla's law degree, petite frame, light skin, hair that is closer to straight than nappy, and middle-class polish all represent "beauty" and "safety." The sometimes mindless or mindless-seeming responses to the Black female body highlight the oppressive relationship between race, gender, and class. Like being caught in an unexpected rain shower without an umbrella, fully aware that one's processed hair may revert back to its original texture, oftentimes African Americans encounter instances of racism, sexism, and classism that take us off guard and shock us back into reality. We have a nap attack. We have encountered the kink factor.

Oftentimes Black women experience Eurocentric readings of their corporeal texts that are less obvious but nevertheless shocking. Discourses that promote the notion of "socially adaptable" bodies (Bordo 1993) or bodies that are trained, shaped, obedient, and responsive, influence how professional women construct their workplace aesthetic images (Trethewey 1999) and shape their self-esteem. Here, Kim talks about receiving subliminal messages from White corporate America indicating that she did not fit the dominant mode of womanhood:

> K: I was a flight attendant for about three years before returning to school. In that industry, the icon of beauty is even more apparent because you're surrounded by all these statuesque White females . . . you have to wear your uniform a certain way, and the uniforms are for White females of a certain physique. So you might be a size eight in the clothes that you wear, but in theirs you're a size twelve because they don't want anything showing. All of that affected how I felt about myself, and so I began searching.

As Kim's comments suggest, corporate policies dictating appearance and dress code may result in material consequences for professional Black females.

Strict rules about makeup and hair, including the prohibition of certain ethnic hairstyles, can make organizational life difficult for African American women (Russell, Wilson, and Hall 1982). Skin tone, hair texture, and body size preferences may hurt the chances for Black women to succeed in the business world and therefore may impact their earning potential.

Discourses that emphasize a preference for certain appearances, sizes, and shapes of the body often contextualizes social interactions (Shilling 1993). For example, according to Russell, Wilson, and Hall, White supervisors are generally unaware of the color complex, "a psychological fixation about color and features that leads Blacks to discriminate against each other" (1992, 2), yet routinely participate in it by primarily hiring and promoting Blacks with light skin. Intraracial color discrimination in the workplace is also a common occurrence (see Atlanta Trial 1990) and stems from the larger societal problem of institutionalized racism. The experience of the kink factor and color complex combined has material consequences for women of color. As a generator of meaning, the Black female body is tangled in a web of communication that includes society's views and prejudices, self-identity and social identity.

The idea that kink hair is a Black thing is a controversial one and speaks to how these African American women negotiate beauty in the realm of Whiteness. On one hand, attempts to meet dominant beauty standards may require women of African descent to remake themselves in ways that negate their personal value. On the other hand, sisters understand that there are economic and emotional consequences if they do not, as indicated by their aesthetic image, appear to "fit into systems of oppression." Thus, the tensions inherent in the processes of self-definition and self-valuation are heightened.

KINKY HAIR IS NAPPY BY NATURE

The process of decolonization suggests that individuals must take an active role in reconstructing themselves within particular cultural contexts. Hooks argues that "all Whites (as well as everyone else within White supremacist culture) have learned to over-value 'Whiteness' even as they simultaneously learn to devalue Blackness" (1992, 12). Learning to love Blackness in the midst of oppressive conceptualizations of the Black female body can be a painful process. According to hooks, the complex process of decolonization is a critical, difficult, and painful process for all colonized people, in particular for Black folks in America. She writes, "We cannot value ourselves rightly without first breaking through the walls of denial which hide the depth of Black self-hatred, inner anguish, and unreconciled pain" (hooks 1992, 20). Here, decolonization is viewed as not just a way of noticing oppressive standards but also as deconstructing the social origins and cultural markings of the corporeal.

Like decolonization, straightening kinky hair is a process. Kinky hair is hair that is tightly coiled. It is nappy by nature. It resists being tamed. One must work diligently to unkink it. The various techniques utilized to straighten kinky hair, such as the hot comb (which usually involves the process of pulling a heated iron comb through small sections of hair at a time, followed by a curling procedure (that also uses heated irons) and the perm (which is a chemical straightening method), may be painful (Smitherman 1977). As in the process of straightening kinky hair, being able to manage pain and/or cope with the threat of pain is inherent in the process of decolonization. Overall, resisting the temptation to internalize negative images of self may require a process of self-conscious struggle. Thus, one of the tensions among self-definition, self-valuation, and survival involves confronting how we have accepted and maintained externally defined images of Black womanhood. This tension emerged in our discussion of Black hair and body image.

The idea that kinky hair is nappy by nature is an outgrowth of how Black female beauty has been historically defined in the United States. The fact that media images can be a powerful influence on how we see ourselves can be seen in the following interview segments with Elaine and Kim:

> E: Let's talk about doing hair. When Carla was young there was a lot of emphasis on straight hair. Our models were the models that you saw in advertising, and you saw on the screen, and you saw in the media . . . so we desired straight hair.
>
> K: When I was growing up I didn't think about the fact that there were no beautiful Black women on television and the magazines. You didn't see us in a lot of the magazines you read. It [racism] was subliminal but it was there. And so, in a roundabout way, for lack of a better word, my self-confidence was not what it could have been because of the standards of beauty and icons of beauty that I was exposed to. So I grew up thinking the lighter-skinned you were and the straighter your hair, the more beautiful you were.

For African American women, the tensions inherent in the experience of the kink factor involve combating externally defined negative images of beauty.

Internalized racism, a manner of looking and seeing the world in ways that uphold White supremacist values and aesthetics, thereby negating one's own (hooks 1992), often manifests itself in the language African Americans use when discussing the politics of Black hair and skin tone. For example, Jessica provides her definition of "good hair" and "bad hair" as the terms are used and understood in African American culture:

> J: Girls who have nappy hair have bad texture. I mean and if they took care of it, it probably wouldn't be nappy . . . but a good grade of hair is like the hair that's longer, it's straighter, and you don't have to use all the added stuff like perming and relaxing to straighten it. It's sort of like that naturally.

Fran describes her skin tone and how the color complex got played out among her childhood friends:

> F: I'm deep rich chocolate. And I always noticed that when we would hang out with friends they would choose the lighter-skinned girls in everything we did.

Denise also experienced an aspect of the color complex within her own family as a result of being the "brightest or lightest" in skin tone among her four sisters:

> D: So I mean, right now, I might think, "Oh, no, it didn't bother me at all," but if I think back to that particular time and as I struggled with my own issues of color and even being teased, not really so much by my sisters, but maybe picking up on some slight resentment from them . . .

Fran describes a painful experience of being rejected by a Black male friend because he did not like her short natural hairstyle:

> F: He looked at me with my short hair that I had just shampooed and said, "Your hair is shorter than mine. You're bald-headed and you look terrible." And I just felt like my heart was just ripped out. He told me I was ugly, you know? But I didn't know if he told me that because he was upset with me because we had been arguing and this was an opportunity to lash out or because he really felt like that. Anyway, I got a perm real quick.

Engaging in self-defining ways, such as wearing a natural hairstyle, not only involves the possibility of being rejected by Black male acquaintances but also includes the possibility of being rejected by family members as well. While Kim says she is fortunate to have had a man in her life for twenty years who has never complained about her hairstyle choices over the years, she has received less support from other family members. As her following comments indicate, family members expressed disapproval and criticism when Kim decided to "lock" (create dreadlocks in) her daughter's hair:

> K: It came back to me within the same week that everybody in the family had been talking about why I was dreading Tyisha's hair. . . . People would comment that my daughter was too pretty to wear dreadlocks. They would still see her face as pretty but her hair was [considered] ugly.

In the end, Kim decided to untwist her daughter's hair before it "locked" in order to spare her daughter from the pain associated with self-definition and now vacillates between braiding or using the pressing comb to style her daughter's hair.

The ongoing process of decolonization often involves interrogating how one has participated in the maintenance of dominant knowledge claims about beauty. It is a process that often involves thinking about what women themselves define as attractive, what aesthetic representations their partners, family members, friends, and colleagues find appealing, and what messages they encounter from the media in regard to fashion and beauty. For African American women, styling and wearing one's hair from a self-defined standpoint require strength in order to resist and reject external criticism.

While acts of self-definition and self-valuation disrupt and challenge dominant notions of Black womanhood, they are strategies that both involve struggle. For African American women to engage in self-definition and self-valuation, we must confront controlling images and negative representations of our bodies as well as examine how we ourselves may have embraced some of these notions. Examining images of African American womanhood reveals how women of color view their ethnic, gender, and class identities as sources of sorrow, agony, or a burden. However, it also highlights the joyful and prideful aspects of constructing their aesthetic images from self-defined standpoints.

KINKY HAIR IS A STATE OF MINE/MIND

African American females learn how to act womanish from their mothers, othermothers, and sister-friends. Likewise, Black females learn how to negotiate their bodies from watching how other Black females construct their aesthetic images (hooks 1996). Central to understanding how we co-create race, gender, and class as social constructs is the idea that through self-awareness and self-conscious struggle we can control the degree to which social constructs influence how we act, think, and construct our aesthetic images. As performance studies scholars Stern and Henderson suggest:

> In many ways, the body has become a kind of text, or even a set of texts, that we remake not only as we grow up physically and go through puberty and other physical stages but also as we reflect on and engage in psychological and sociopolitical dimensions of experience. (1993, 317)

Many of the women could recall the exact time period when they experimented with different hairstyles or the exact age they were when they gained permission to style their own hair as opposed to having someone else style it for them. Earning the right to style one's own hair can be viewed as a rite of passage for Black females (Rooks 1996). Similarly, Black females must earn the right to act womanish (hooks 1989). Womanism is intertwined with the notion of legacy, and the role of hair in the Black community is intertwined with our unique cultural hair/heritage.

Kinky hair holds the possibility of creativity. It can be twisted, locked, braided, weaved, curled, dyed, fried, and laid to the side. For example, in this study African American mothers and daughters reflect on the various hairstyles that they wore throughout their lifetimes. The choices in hairstyles for these women range from perms (a chemical process to straighten the natural curl pattern of hair) to braided hairstyles, natural unprocessed hair, and dreadlocks (the process of twisting the hair until it locks). These various hairstyles speak to the creativity and agency of self-definition and self-valuation engaged in by African American women.

For the participants, one's chosen hairstyle can be a direct reflection of one's identification with Black culture and communities, but not always. Their comments further suggest that loving Blackness is also a state of mind. Here, the participants stress the importance of looking inside and honoring self regardless of one's external, aesthetic attributes. Additionally, for these mother-daughter pairs, certain hairstyle choices grew out of a sense of the fashion at the time or convenience. For African American women, the power to choose and create their own personal aesthetic image is reflected not only in their hairstyle choices, but also in the specific and creative ways they define beauty.

Ruth, for example, is a fifty-something health care worker who currently wears her hair in a short chemically relaxed style. She takes pride in the fact that she does not dye her hair to mask the fact that it is now completely gray. Here, she dismisses her choice to wear an Afro in the '70s as a fashion statement:

> R: Years ago, when my children were small, everybody had started wearing the Afro, and I wore one. But I wore it out of fashion, I didn't wear it from the heart or "this is us," and power to the people, you know. I wore it because it was a fashion and so happened I thought I looked good with it. *[laughing]*

The fact that Ruth felt that she 'looked good" with this style indicates that hair politics can be linked to issues of self-esteem.

Vanessa often wears a braided hairstyle and views this particular hairstyle choice as a manner of convenience:

> V: I consider it just another style. It's totally convenience. I wonder sometimes how other people perceive me. If they see me as a militant woman because I have these braids in my hair, or if they see it as an alternative. But I view it simply as another alternative. I like them because they are so low-maintenance, but in terms of identity, it's not really an impact.

Although Vanessa states that her decision to wear a braided hairstyle is not linked to aspects of her identity, her concern for how others might view her because of her hairstyle demonstrates that Black hair has certain political connotations. The knowledge that Black hair is political may influence how African American women construct their aesthetic images.

Other hairstyle choices are guided by a sense of coming into an Afrocentric consciousness. According to the models of racial identity development (Cross and Fhagen-Smith 1996), the development of a Black person's racial identity often moves through a process where individuals display overt manifestations of their newfound Black identity such as wearing of ethnic clothing or hairstyles. Coming into a realization of a Black identity is one of the reasons why Kim, who currently wears dreadlocks, decided to cut her hair into a short natural style after the birth of her daughter eight years ago:

> K: I needed to connect to something and so Africa was the natural choice for me. The root. Return to the source. I began to just get that kind of consciousness and a confidence, and so six months after I had my daughter I cut my hair off, down to the scalp, down to the nap. Cut it down to wherever it wasn't straight. It was to make a statement, a political statement, socially and culturally aware statement that I was turning into somebody else. But also I wanted my daughter to know that the same Black female that had brought her into the world, the person that she would look at as probably one of the most beautiful women on the planet, had short hair and natural hair. And so I cut it off. I started growing a flattop and got more compliments than when I had the long straight hair.

Other elements of African American identity also influenced how participants engaged in self-definition. For example, the church plays an important role in Black communities (Peterson 1992). Not only does it shape Black women's social interactions, but one's spirituality can influence hairstyle choices. Some Black women, as indicated in Jessica's comments, consider hair to represent a connection to their spirituality (see Walker 1988):

> J: A woman's hair is her glory . . . I think it's in Corinthians. My neighbor lady was telling me about it—it's in the Bible. You know, that's why I stopped cutting my hair. I came into the Scriptures and I realized what it said about a woman's hair is her glory and I said, "What am I doing cutting my glory? Let me stop cutting off my glory here."

As indicated in the previous interview segments, hair is an important way for African American women to engage in self-definition and self-valuation. As a vehicle to express one's sense of fashion, spiritual awareness or ethnic identity, hair functions to highlight the power dynamics underlying the process of these two strategies. Enacting the power to (re)create the body or (re)define one's identity threatens the validity of externally defined notions of Black womanhood (Collins 2000).

The third theme, kinky hair is a state of mine/mind, also centers on the notions of redefining self and re-creating the body as a way to heal the scars of self-hate. Self-definition influences how these mothers and daughters define beauty. They define beauty in terms of the natural body, intellect, and inner qualities. Vanessa focuses on the natural body:

> V: I think being part of beauty is to be natural. If it looks like you're wearing a lot of makeup, my perception is that you're trying to hide something, or maybe trying to create an image that is different from who you are as a person, or what the [natural] physical traits are.

Eight year-old Tyisha, whose name is a combination of the name of a female relative and a traditional African name, stresses the importance of intellect in her definition of beauty:

> T: I don't think beauty's important because all that matters is how smart you are and if you have a brain.

Elaine, a retired schoolteacher, age fifty-nine, who is married and a mother of two, includes personality and demeanor as a criteria for beauty:

> E: My, I guess I would say my impression of beauty includes some of the physical attributes that you assign to beauty, but also it's that inner quality. That comes across immediately. A lot of times you see people who will have the physical appearance but the way they come across may turn you off. I would not consider that person a beautiful person.

Overall, African American mother-daughter talk about hair/body politics suggests that redefining notions of beauty is a crucial step in deconstructing dominant interpretations of the Black female body.

The realization that one will never measure up to internal or externally defined standards is often the catalyst for engaging in self-definition and self-valuation. Resisting the temptation to internalize negative images of self requires self-conscious struggle. While African American women realize that constructing their aesthetic images in self-defined ways can be both a painful and challenging experience, in the end they find that engaging in the ongoing process of self-definition is worth it. Fran's comment echoes this idea:

> F: This is actually about your heart, your spirit, and your soul. If we spend time trying to please others instead of doing what is in the very depth of our souls, then we could never live up to our true potential because we're gonna always wonder can we tailor our look to serve and help, to make someone else feel comfortable, versus going with our spirit. I think that's what my locks are about.

As Denise's comment below suggests, Black women must reach inside themselves to get beyond the shadow of Eurocentric beauty standards:

> D: I was thinking, even our men tend to judge us how well we conform to the Eurocentric standards. And that is a really hard blow. It would be one thing if the rest of the world is out there living in these standards, and then we live within our community and we're like, "Well, we don't fit those standards and we're perfectly fine with that." It's hard to think that way when we're going to be judged by our men, we're going to be judged by employers . . . so for women, African American women especially, I think it really has to come from inside, to just say that is not my standard . . . that is not

> my children's standard. I can talk to another African American woman and say, "Look, don't think about that because you know, we're different, we're built different."

Overall, African American mothers play an important role in teaching their daughters how to traverse the contradictory path between conformity and resistance (Collins 1991b). Survival skills passed down from generation to generation provide the foundation for African American women to negotiate their aesthetic image in a culture that often negates it. By exercising the power to self-define, African American women begin the process of transcending those images that limit the view they have of themselves. In short, these interviews reveal that self-definition and self-valuation, albeit difficult and problematic at times, nonetheless can be powerful and self-sustaining acts.

CONCLUSION

> We have an obligation as Black women to project ourselves into the revolution to destroy these institutions which not only oppress Blacks but women as well, for if those institutions continue to flourish, they will be used against us in the continuing battle of mind over body. (Lindsey 1970, 89)

As a metaphor, the term "kink factor" describes the tension experienced by individuals of African descent when negotiating the body politic, yet it also leaves room for joy and celebration. For African American women, negotiating the body politic involves weighing the potential material consequences associated with self-definition and self-valuation against the odds of survival. In essence, the participants' experiences of Black hair/body politics reveal that self-definition requires courage. However, as hooks (1989) has warned, when writing about African American women's experiences of multiple interlocking oppressions one must be careful not to characterize them as helpless victims. We, as Black women, do have agency in the performance of our corporeal texts. Learning to love Blackness is an ongoing process, and it is critical to the survival of Black womanhood.

This investigation makes several contributions to the legacy of work that seeks to understand the ways in which African American women struggle to define themselves and make meaning of their bodies within a culture that devalues their self-definitions. First, utilizing a framework rooted in their discourse, attitudes, and beliefs helps us to understand the personal, psychological, and sociopolitical consequences of engaging in self-definition and self-valuation as experienced by women of African descent. Second, by viewing the corporeal text as a primary discursive symbol rather than focusing only on speaking and writing as the principal modes of rhetorical communication that shape and reproduce certain power structures (Mumby 1994), we get a better sense of the complex dynamics associated with Black female hair/body politics. Thus, the metaphor of the kink factor is extremely useful because it gives culturally particular symbolic meaning to tensions experienced by African American women when constructing their aesthetic images.

There are several directions for future research. For example, African American men and children are also faced with having to construct their aesthetic images in face of negative, externally defined images of Blackness. Investigations centering these groups might shed light on their particular experiences of the kink factor. Cross-cultural investigations designed to explore the global impact of the kink factor, such as those concerned with the differences and similarities between African American women, African, Cuban, Haitian, and Puerto Rican women is also a possible direction for future research. Furthermore, with the increase in concern for how cultural diversity will impact organizations (Allen 1995), it might be fruitful to investigate the kink factor as it occurs in the context of organizational settings.

The minor limitations of this study present opportunities for how this present work can be extended. While some of the participants in this present study came from working-class backgrounds, all of the participants are currently middle-class. They are also all heterosexual. Centering future investigations in the voices of poor and/or lesbian women might reveal different nuances.

As these interviews suggest, rejecting controlling and oppressive images of and discourse about Black womanhood often involves self-examination, which can be a liberating act of resistance. Evaluating controlling and oppressive images of Black womanhood can lead to individual and collective efforts toward exposing and altering racist, sexist, and classist institutions and behaviors. By centering our stories in our voices (e.g., González, Houston, and Chen 2000), even when our stories are about how we see ourselves aesthetically, we become empowered. By taking agency in how we define our identity, construct discourse meanings, and live our lives, we return to a personal and cultural imperative to love ourselves. We create an opportunity for our stories to be heard and to be meaningful in a context that has traditionally negated their significance. As such, we open a space for healing.

NOTES

1. I use both *African American* and *Black* to refer to one's racioethnic identity. However, I do make a distinction between these two terms. As a racioethnic identifier, *Black* is used to refer to people of African descent or people of the African Diaspora, while *African American* is used when referring to people of African descent who are natives of the United States. All participants utilized a pseudonym. In the interview segments, both the researcher and the participant are identified by their first initial.
2. Here the term *race* is defined as "a social construct saved on phenotyical variations among groups" (Jackson and Garner 1998).

3. Women who treat biologically unrelated children as if the were members of their own family (Collins 1991b; James 1993).
4. Utilizing this metaphor is not intended to trivialize the role of hair in the lives of African American women, nor is its use here meant to imply that all women of African descent have a particular hair texture.

REFERENCES

Acker, J., K. Barry, and J. Esseveld (1991). Objectivity and Truth: Problems in Doing Feminist Research. In M. M. Fonow and J. A. Cook (Eds.), *Beyond Methodology: Feminist Scholarship as Lived Research* (pp. 133–53). Bloomington: Indiana University Press.

Allen, B. (1995). "Diversity" and Organizational Communication. *Journal of Applied Research* 23: 143–55.

Asante, M. (1995). *Malcolm X as a Cultural Hero.* Trenton, NJ: Africa World Press.

Atlanta Trial Focusing on Color-Bias Charge (1990). *The New York Times,* February 1, A20.

Banks, I. (2000). *Hair Matters: Beauty, Power, and Black Women's Consciousness.* New York: New York University Press.

Bell, E. L. (1990). The Bicultural Life Experience of Career-Oriented Black Women. *Journal of Organizational Behavior* 11: 459–70.

Bekerie, A. (1994). The Four Corners of a Circle: Afrocentricity as a Model of Synthesis. *Journal of Black Studies* 25: 131–49.

Berger, P. L., and C. Luckman (1967). *The Socialization of Reality.* Garden City, NY: Anchor Books.

Boone, S. A. (1996). Perceived Physical Attractiveness, Self-Esteem and Racial Identity in African American Women: A Qualitative Study. Ph.D. Dissertation, Southern Illinois University at Carbondale, 1996. *Dissertation Abstracts International, 57–10B,* 6645.

Bordo, S. (1993). *Unbearable Weight: Feminism, Western Culture, and the Body.* Berkeley: University of California Press.

Boyd, V. (1993). The Ritual. *African American Review* 27, 1: 43–45.

Brownmiller, S. (1984). *Femininity.* New York: Simon and Schuster.

Caldwell, P. M. (1997). A Hair Piece: Perspectives on the Intersections of Race and Gender. In A. K. Wing (Ed.), *Critical Race Feminism* (pp. 297–305). New York: New York University Press.

Cenen and B. Smith (1983). The Blood—Yes, the Blood: A Conversation. In B. Smith (Ed.), *Home Girls: A Black Feminist Anthology* (pp. 31–51). New York: Kitchen Table/Women of Color Press.

Collins, P. H. (1991a). Learning from the Outsider Within: The Sociological Significance of Black Feminist Thought. *Social Problems* 33: 35–59.

Collins, P. H. (1991b). The Meaning of Motherhood in Black Culture and Black Mother Daughter Relationships. In P. B. Scott and B. G. Sheftall (Eds.), *Double Stitch* (pp. 42–60). New York: HarperCollins.

Collins, P. H. (2000). *Black Feminist Thought: Knowledge, Consciousness and the Politics of Empowerment,* second edition. New York: Routledge.

Combahee River Collective (1982). A Black Feminist Statement. In G. T. Hull, P. B. Scott, and B. Smith (Eds.), *All the Women Are White, All the Blacks Are Men, but Some of Us Are Brave* (pp. 13–22). New York: The Feminist Press at the City University of New York.

Cross, W. E., and P. Fhagen-Smith (1996). Nigrescence and Ego Identity Development. In P. B. Pederson, J. G. Draguns, W. J. Lonner, and G. E. Trinble (Eds.), *Counseling Across Cultures* (pp. 108–23). Thousand Oaks, CA: Sage.

Cross, W. E. (1991). *Shades of Black: Diversity in African American Identity.* Philadelphia: Temple University Press.

Cummings, L. (1995). A Womanist Response to the Afrocentric Idea. In C. J. Sanders (Ed.), *Living in the Intersection: Womanism and Afrocentrisim in Theology* (pp. 57–66). Minneapolis: Fortress Press.

Davis, A. (1981). *Women, Race and Class.* New York: Random House.

Dickerson, D. (1987). Not So Black and White. *Allure* (September): 138–49.

Diop, C. A. (1974). *The African Origins of Civilization: Myth or Reality.* Chicago: Lawrence Hill Books.

Dykes, P. Y. (1999). She Works Hard for the Money: The Experiences of African American Women in the Workplace. In T. McDonald and T. Ford-Ahmed (Eds.), *Nature of a Sistuh: Black Women's Lived Experiences in Contemporary Culture* (pp. 91–111). Durham, NC: Carolina Academic Press.

Gilkes, C. T. (1983). From Slavery to Social Welfare: Racism and the Control of Black Women. In A. Smerdlow, H. Lessinger, and J. Lessinger (Eds.), *Class, Race, and Sex: The Dynamics of Control* (pp. 288–300). Boston: G. K. Hall.

Goffman, E. (1958). *Presentation of Self in Everyday Life.* New York: Anchor Books.

Goffman, E. (1963). *Behavior in Public Places: Notes on the Management of Spoiled Identity.* Harmondsworth: Penguin.

Goffman. E. (1968). *Stigma: Notes of the Management of Spoiled Identity.* Harmondsworth: Penguin.

Goffman, E. (1983). The Interaction Order. *American Sociological Review* 48: 1–17.

González A., M. Houston, and V. Chen (2000). *Our Voices: Essays in Culture, Ethnicity, and Communication,* third edition. Los Angeles, CA: Roxbury Publishing Company.

hooks, b. (1989). *Talking Back: Thinking Feminist, Thinking Black.* Boston: South End Press.

hooks, b. (1992). *Black Looks: Race and Representation.* Boston: South End Press.

hooks, b. (1996). *Bone Black.* New York: Henry Holt and Company, Inc.

Houston, M. (1992). The Politics of Difference: Race, Class, and Women's Communication. In L. F. Rakow (Ed.), *Women Making Meaning* (pp. 45–59). New York: Routledge.

Houston, M. (2000). Multiple Perspectives: African American Women Conceive Their Talk. *Women and Languages* 23: 11–17.

Houston, M. and Davis, O. (2000). *Centering Ourselves.* Cresskill, NJ: Hampton Press.

Jackson, R. L. (2000). So Real Illusions Are Black Intellectualism. *Communication Theory* 10(1), 48–63.

James, S. M. (1993). Mothering: A Possible Black Feminist Link to Social Transformation. In S. M. James and A. P. A. Busia (Eds.), *Theorizing Black Feminisms: The Visionary Pragmatism of Black Women* (pp. 44–54). New York: Routledge.

Jewell, K. S. (1993). *From Mammy to Miss America and Beyond: Cultural Images and the Shaping of U.S. Social Policy.* London: Routledge.

Johnston, W. B., and A. E. Packard (1987). *Workforce 2000: Work, Workers for the 21st Century.* Indianapolis: Hudson Institute.

Judy, R. W., D'Amico, C. (1997). *Workforce 2020: Work and Workers in the 21st Century.* Indianapolis: Hudson Institute

Kelley, R. D. G. (1997). Nap Time: Historicizing the Afro. Fashion Theory. *The Journal of Dress, Body, and Culture* 1(4), 339–351.

Kvale, S. (1996). *Interviews.* Thousand Oaks, CA: Sage.

Lakoff, G., and M. Johnson (1980). *Metaphors We Live By.* Chicago: University of Chicago Press.

Lindsey, K. (1970). The Black Woman as Woman. In T. Cade (Ed.), *The Black Woman: An Anthology.* New York: New American Library.

Lincoln, Y. S., and E. G. Guba (1985). *Naturalistic Inquiry.* Newbury Park, CA: Sage.

Mercer, K. (1994). *Welcome to the Jungle: New Positions in Black Cultural Studies.* New York: Routledge.

Mumby, D. K. (1994). *Communication and Power in Organizations: Discourse, Ideology, and Domination* Cresskill, New Jersey: Ablex Publishing.

Nobles, W. W. (1974). Africanity in Black Families. *The Black Scholar,* 6, 10–17.

Peterson, E. A. (1992). *African American Women: A Study of Will and Success.* Jefferson, NC: Mcfarland and Company.

Queenan, P. L. (1988). A Psychoeducational Approach to the Issue of African American Female Attractiveness: A Workshop Design. Ph.D. dissertation, University of Massachusetts, 1988. *Dissertation Abstracts Internationa,* 49–(09a). University Microfilms no. AAI8822678.

Reinharz, S. (1992). *Feminist Methods in Social Research.* New York: Oxford University Press.

Rooks, N. M. (1996). *Hair Raising.* New Brunswick: Rutgers University Press.

Russell, K., M. Wilson, and R. H. Hall (1992). *The Color Complex: The Politics of Skin Color Among African Americans.* New York: Harcourt Brace Jovanovich.

Shilling, C. (1993). *The Body and Social Theory.* London: Sage.

Smith, F. (1998). *American Body Politics: Race, Gender, and Black Literary Renaissance.* Athens: University of Georgia Press.

Smitherman, G. (1977). *Talkin and Testifyin: The Language of Black America.* Detroit: Wayne State University Press.

Spellers, R. E. (1998). Happy to Be Nappy: Embracing an Afrocentric Aesthetic for Beauty. In J. Martin, T. Nakayama, and L. A. Flores (Eds.), *Readings in Cultural Contexts* (pp. 70–85). Mountain View, CA: Mayfield.
Spellers, R. E. (2000). Cornrows in Corporate America: Black Female Hair/Body Politics and Socialization Experiences in Dominant Culture Workplace Organizations. Ph.D. dissertation, Arizona State University.
Staples, R., and L. B. Johnson (1993). *Black Family at the Crossroads.* San Francisco: Jossey-Bates.
Stern, C. S., and B. Henderson (1993). *Performance: Texts and Contexts.* White Plains, NY: Longman Publishing Group.
Trethewey, A. (1999). Disciplined Bodies: Women's Embodied Identities at Work. *Organization Studies* 10, 3: 423–50.
Tyler, B. M. (1990). Black Hairstyles: Cultural and Socio-political Implications. *The Western Journal of Black Studies* 14, 4: 235–50.
Uya, O. E. (1993). The Middle Passage and Personality Change Among Diaspora Africans. In J. E. Harris (Ed.), *Global Dimensions of the African Diaspora* (pp. 83–97). Washington, DC: Howard University Press.
Walker, A. (1983). *In Search of Our Mothers' Gardens.* Orlando, FL: Harcourt Brace Jovanovich.
Walker, A. (1988). *Living by the Word.* Orlando, FL: Harcourt Brace Jovanovich.
White, D. G. (1985). *Ar'n't I A Woman? Female Slaves in the Plantation South.* New York: W. W. Norton.
Yarbrough, C. (1984). Female Style and Beauty in Ancient Africa: A Photo Essay. In I.V. Sertina (Eds.), *The Journal of African Civilizations*, 6(1): 89–97.

CHAPTER 15

An Afrocentric Rhetorical Analysis of Johnnie Cochran's Closing Argument in the O.J. Simpson Trial

FELICIA R. WALKER

INTRODUCTION

On October 3, 1995, the nation watched as the jury foreman read the verdict: "We find the defendant, Orenthal James Simpson, not guilty." O.J. Simpson was acquitted for the murders of his ex-wife, Nicole Brown Simpson, and her friend, Ronald Goldman, in what has been termed the "trial of the century": the State of California versus O.J. Simpson.

Various issues drew widespread attention to the case, such as celebrity status, racism, interracial relationships, media coverage, police corruption and domestic abuse. Simpson's defense team, which included celebrated attorneys Johnnie Cochran, F. Lee Bailey, Robert Shapiro, Alan Dershowitz, and Barry Scheck, was no exception. The tactics, strategic maneuvers, and style of Cochran, the lead defense attorney, increased the dramatics of the trial. His perceived confidence, flamboyancy, and comfort in the courtroom became an apparent unwelcome force for the opposing attorneys, their witnesses, and the judge. Throughout the trial and in his closing argument, Cochran's style was strong and confident. He exhibited flair and passion throughout the trial, but especially during the closing arguments, the final rhetorical act of the trial. With rhythmic phrases, powerful words, and strategic gestures, he advocated for Simpson. Creating his own spiritual atmosphere, Cochran reasoned for the outcome he desired, often in the style of a southern Black preacher. Cochran seemed to bring words to life, using his rhetorical skills to hammer points with conviction and defeat the opposing counsel. Among other things, Cochran persuaded members of the jury as well as members of the viewing audience with his smooth but passionate plea for Simpson's acquittal.

Scholars have studied the styles of African Americans and have cited different characteristics that are observed as common in Black speakers. Cochran's closing argument in the O.J. Simpson double murder trial, as a rhetorical act, provides an opportunity to investigate Cochran's exhibition of traits that are characteristic of African American public discourse.

PURPOSE

This study illustrates the usefulness of an Afrocentric method in the analysis of a rhetorical text produced by a highly acclaimed African American attorney. Additionally, this study demonstrates the appropriateness of a culture-centered approach to rhetorical analysis. Specifically, it investigates the extent to which Cochran drew upon certain characteristics common to African American communication styles during his closing argument in the Simpson murder trial. Other scholars have conducted studies on communication in the courtroom (O'Barr 1982; Smith and Malandro 1985; Childress 1995), effective closing arguments (Spence 1995; Childress 1995; Haydock and Sonsteng 1991), and Black attorneys (Leonard 1977; Segal 1983; Washington 1994). However, absent from the research literature are culture-centered detailed studies on communication styles of African American attorneys during closing arguments.

This study contributes to the body of research grounded in rhetorical analysis and encourages the progression of culture-centered studies. Cultural backgrounds affect behaviors, actions, interpretations, and reactions in communication situations (Greaves 1992). Central to this study is African American culture. Black culture is a reality (Chimezie 1984), and Afrocentric distinctions such as in folklore, music, socialization, family structure, food, values, communication, and more are significant to the need for Afrocentric analyses. While general features of Black culture may be offered, not every feature is expected to appear in a given instance of discourse. Thus, a culture-centered investigation into this rhetorical act that bears heavily on language and communication is most appropriate. Cochran's African American cultural background is relevant in examining his closing argument. Although other cultures that influence language and behavior exist (such as the legal environment), this study investigates only Cochran's communication characteristics from an Afrocentric perspective. In addition, this study contributes to the communication body of knowledge and encourages further qualitative studies in the fields of rhetoric and law.

AN AFROCENTRIC APPROACH

Different cultures have different value systems, language patterns, ideologies, and experiences. Thus, specific cultural approaches to communication often provide exploration into phenomena that may be more insightful than less specific ones. Afrocentricity often acts as one such approach. Afrocentricity is a theoretical perspective based in the cultural image and human interests of people of African descent (Karenga 1988). Much of the research in the area of

Afrocentricity by scholars such as Asante (1987), Akbar (1979), Boykin (1983), and Schiele (1990) is rooted in the assumption that "any meaningful and authentic study of peoples of African descent must begin and proceed with Africa as the center, not periphery" (Abarry 1990, 123). These and other scholars have addressed the concept of Afrocentricity, which grew out of a movement to study phenomena from the perspective of the agency of people of African descent. "Afrocentricity becomes indispensable to our understanding of Black Studies; otherwise, we have a series of intellectual adventures in Eurocentric perspectives about Africans and African Americans" (Asante 1988, 58). An Afrocentric perspective facilitates an understanding of social patterns and institutional patterns that have characterized the actions of African people (Winter 1994). "Different regions of the world that have evolved distinct cultures are entitled to develop paradigms based on the perspectives of the region's qualitatively significant human cultures, histories and experiences" (Keto 1989).

Important in using Afrocentric methodologies is considering the realms that connect the African American to African communication patterns (Jackson 1995; Oyebade, 1990). An Afrocentric approach in conducting a rhetorical analysis should be sensitive to concerns of providing a holistic view. That is, the cosmology of African descendents, including history and culture, needs to be taken into account within any investigation of African American ?? (Cummings and Daniel 1980). "Rhetorical discourse is inherently bound by the culture or subculture in which it is fashioned" (Phillips 1983, 181). An Afrocentric perspective "holds that the whole history and culture of Black people constitute the proper internal frame of reference for giving explanations and critical assessments of Black communication" (Atwater 1995, 142). From the literature, it is clear that a culturally sensitive methodology is supported. Conducting an Afrocentric analysis of Johnnie Cochran's closing argument in the Simpson murder case is an appropriate method for discovering the culturally specific information sought.

AFRICAN AMERICAN COMMUNICATION PATTERNS

This rhetorical analysis of Cochran's argument uncovers the traditional and nontraditional usage of African American communication stylistic devices in an attempt to persuade the fact finder (the jury). The stylistic features of African American communication explored here derive from an investigation of Black language patterns. The features highlighted are as follows: rhythm, stylin', narrative style, call and response, rappin', and signifyin'.

RHYTHM

Fluctuations in pitch, tone, rate, and tempo make up the rhythm. Rhythm also includes rhyming, repetition of sounds, and fluency (Wilson, 1996).

With rhythm, speech often develops a musical quality. The voice is employed like a musical instrument, with improvisations and riffs. Specific use of stress and pitch contribute to rhythm as well. Words pronounced a particular way may indicate special meaning such as sarcasm or disbelief. "[R]hyme remains a basic ingredient of poetry. Its widespread cultural use and approval in nonpoetic contexts is unique to Black speakers" (Smitherman 1977, 145). Rhythm is a tool of persuasion and can be effectively used in closing arguments in a trial. Attorneys may use alliteration or repetition, for instance, to emphasize points to a fact finder.

STYLIN'

Stylin' involves the "way in which verbal and nonverbal cues are demonstrated to achieve a desired effect" (Jackson 1995, 151). It includes usage of rich, descriptive, allegorical phrases. "Stylin' out" refers to performing certain acts and saying certain things with flourish and finesse (Welsh-Asante, 1985). This stylistic feature, which can be visual or aural, is used in conjunction with a speaker's goals to involve the audience in the message. Visual stylin' can be "effected by gestural or symbolic mannerisms" as well as the "arrangement of physical surroundings" (Asante 1987, 39). This may be represented, for example, by the intentional stroking of clothing or purposeful use of accessories. In audio stylin', "words are frequently intoned to give them a soulful quality" (Asante 1987, 39). In persuasive oratory, "the sound of words can often assume as much importance as presentation of arguments" (Asante 1987, 84). African American attorneys may use stylin' to maintain the attention of juries and appeal to their desire to listen. With this, they can attempt to establish more natural and credible relationships with juries.

Stylin' attempts to make words reality and to engage in expressive communication. In this regard, stylin' is directly related to the concept of nommo. Nommo is described as "the generating and sustaining power of the spoken word" (Smith 1972, 295). Nommo involves the generative power of the word to bring things, ideas, and concepts into existence. It is common to African American communication and represents the spirituality of communication, not just the communicative act itself. Stylin' interacts with nommo as a socializing force that encompasses and unifies aspects of language. The gestures, speaking style, verbal and nonverbal cues and finesse of stylin' combine with the spirit and moving power known as nommo to create the life in the communication that establishes the rhetor's desired outcome.

NARRATIVE STYLE

Another major contribution to characteristics of African American communication is that of narration or storytelling. Storytelling relates to the African past, when a griot or the revered elder was responsible for maintaining tribal history. Narrative style is related to lyrical code, which concerns itself with "inventiveness and creativity expressed through language" (Jackson 1995, 151). Because it is a cultural creation and engages a particular group of values for the enhancement of discourse, narrative style is important. Storytelling acts as a measure to ensure that information is passed down through the generations.

> Black narrative style . . . owns a syntax which is informed by the scene or atmosphere. Style does not suggest any fixed limits on how a narrative or song must be delivered. It is sui generis to the performer. The speaker exploits the context he is in to achieve the greatest amount of immediacy and variation [on old themes]. (Harrison 1972, 46–47)

Smitherman notes that the "story element is so strong in Black communication dynamics that it pervades general everyday conversation" (1977, 161). The narrative style may assist lawyers in sharing with the fact finder their version of events. "The relating of events (real or hypothetical) becomes a Black rhetorical strategy to explain a point, to persuade holders of opposing view to one's own point of view, and in general to 'win friends and influence people'" (Smitherman 1977 147–48). In litigation, storytelling is frequently used in opening statements and closing arguments.

CALL AND RESPONSE

Call and response is often found in African American communication, particularly in the Black church (Hecht, Jackson, and Ribeau, 2003). It involves participation from both the audience and the speaker. Call and response is "the ritualistic response from the audience, a feature of story-telling mode common to both contemporary and traditional Black communities" (Harrison 1972, 47). Smitherman (1977) notes that call and response organizes Black American culture generally, and enables traditional Black people to realize a harmonious and balanced state of being that is fundamental to the African worldview. African Americans engage in call and response in various communication situations, though normally in the religious ceremonial setting. "Usually the response is the repetition of the exact word or phrase, or it may be an affirmatory statement such as 'Oh yes,' 'Praise God,' 'Thank you Jesus,' or 'Have Mercy' " (Niles 1995, 84). Call and response relates to nommo and the spirituality of communication among African Americans. As Harrison notes, call and response is a "necessary component of Black speech; it brings spiritual solidity and power to the images created in language" (1972, 54). Call and response, a custom from African heritage, "provides the audience an opportunity to participate and to feedback favorably to the message" (Niles 1995, 84). The courtroom, however, is one setting in which call and response is not deemed appropriate. Typically, a jury does not speak during the course of a trial. Thus, the response portion of call and response would not be expected during a closing argument. However, that expectation, or lack thereof, does not necessarily apply to the call portion. In a closing argument, the attorney may indeed make a call by asking rhetorical questions, posing hypotheticals, using striking statements, and the like. African American attorneys may speak to juries whereby they make a call for a response other than one that is verbal or immediate. Attorneys can arguably make a call in their closing arguments, looking for nonverbal responses (such as the nod of a head) or seeking a delayed response through the verdict.

RAPPIN'

Rappin' (used synonymously to mean ordinary conversation) is an engaging lyrical presentation enwrapped in natural conversation, it involves a distinctive personal flair (Kochman 1972). It is closely linked to African American culture:

> Afro-America's emphasis on orality and belief in the power of the rap [which] has produced a style and idiom totally unlike that of Whites, while paradoxically employing White English words. We're talking, then, about a tradition in the Black experience in which verbal performance becomes both a way of establishing "yo rep" as well as a teaching and socializing force. This performance is exhibited in the narration of myths, folk stories . . . in Black sermons; in the telling of jokes; in proverbs and folk sayings. (Smitherman 1977, 79)

Rappers possess skills in reading their audience and their situation (Smitherman 1994). The "speaker must be up on the subject of his rap, and his oral contribution must be presented in a dazzling, entertaining manner" (Smitherman 1977, 80). Rhetorical strategies sought through rappin' are achieved in several ways. Smaller units of rappin' include exaggerated language, mimicry, proverbial statements, punning, improvisation, image making, braggadocio, and indirection (Smitherman 1977). Black raps are "stylized, dramatic and spectacular" (Smitherman 1977, 80).

SIGNIFYIN'

Signifyin' is a tactic employed in verbal dueling. It is language behavior that attempts to imply, goad, beg, boast and stir up excitement (Kochman 1972). "Signification refers to the verbal art of insult in which a speaker humorously puts down, talks about, needles . . . the listener" (Smitherman 1977, 118). "It is a culturally approved method of talking about somebody" (p. 119), in a manner not meant to be taken seriously. However, signifyin' also functions to make a specific point (usually implied). Signifyin' takes several forms, from witty one-liners to cohesive discourse. It embodies characteristics such as indirection, circumlocution, humor, irony, rhythm, and punning (Smitherman

1977). Other names for signifyin' include crackin', jonin', snappin', cappin', and soundin'.

Though there are other aspects of African American communication (e.g. realism, assertiveness, and conversational tone) these aforementioned traits form the parameters of the analysis of Cochran's closing argument that I will offer. These traits of African American communication are often found in areas such as the Black church, politics, literature, entertainment, and law.

Many of these traits are relevant to courtroom oratory. For example, mainstream society does not embrace African American vernacular English in many settings, but other factors, such as perceived authority, may create an exception. In a court of law, African American attorneys with authority, credibility, confidence, and flair may be able to successfully persuade a fact finder, even when using a nondominant communication system. In conjunction, African American attorneys often code-switch to "acceptable" language to enhance their chances of success.

DISTINCTIVE AFRICAN AMERICAN RHETORICAL FEATURES IN THE CLOSING ARGUMENT

This analysis examines Cochran's closing argument and identifies when and how these characteristics were integral aspects of his rhetorical act. As an African American male, Cochran exhibits stylistic choices that are common in African American communication patterns. He approached his closing argument aware of the gravity of the case, aware of the media's presence, and, perhaps most importantly, aware of the members of the jury—his immediate audience. By the end of the trial, the makeup of the jury had changed several times. During the course of the court proceedings, the jury included Black females and males, Hispanic females and a Hispanic male, White females, and a male of American Indian and White heritage. As a result of several dismissals and replacements, the twelve jurors that actually voted included eight Black females (ages twenty-five to seventy-two), two White females (ages twenty-three and sixty-one), one Hispanic male (age thirty-three), and one Black male (age forty-four) (Rogers 1995). The majority of Cochran's immediate audience consisted of Black females, who could probably, in some ways, identify with Cochran's linguistic style and communication tools.

Cochran's closing argument begins with tactics recommended by several trial experts. He greets the jury in a personable manner, then almost immediately thanks them for their service. He sets up a theme, not for his argument, but for the jury. He guides them through the remainder of their "journey towards justice" (Cochran 1995, 10). Cochran uses this theme to continuously instill in the jurors' minds their major role in the murder trial. Throughout the summation, as Cochran performs the typical closing argument tasks, such as summarizing testimony and arguing the evidence to support his side's position, he incorporates his own rhetorical strategy and style. This analysis via transcript and videotaped coverage investigates Cochran's style from an Afrocentric perspective, focusing on specific features of African American communication.

To the courtroom, Cochran brought his unique rhetorical style, evidenced by aspects of African oral expression and African American culture. This analysis reveals the presence of the listed traits that are characteristic of African American communication: rhythm, stylin', narrative style, call and response, rappin', and signifyin'. The aforementioned characteristics are examined independently.

RHYTHM

Occurrences of rhyming, set tempo, or certain fluctuations in pitch, tone, or rate are indicators of Cochran's use of rhythm. In addition, repetition of phrases or sentences as well as any sounds that have a musical undertone or a timed pattern indicates rhythm (Niles, 1984). Rhythm often combines lyrical balance and cadence with semantic meaning (Smitherman 1977). Cochran's most memorable display of rhythm rang in the minds of viewer across the nation: "If it doesn't fit, you must acquit" (Cochran 1995, 22). This phrase illustrates the use of rhyme, set tempo, and repetition as Cochran repeatedly offers this phrase throughout his summation. He first uses this phrase early in the closing argument, when he rebuts the success of the prosecution's time line. Cochran asks the jury to remember the words like the "defining moment in this trial, the day Mr. Darden asked Mr. Simpson to try on those gloves and the gloves didn't fit" (Cochran 1995, 15). Throughout the closing argument, Cochran uses this phrase to coincide with the themes he advances. He repeats the phrase to accentuate the presence of reasonable doubt. He underscores his belief that the prosecution has failed to meet their burden. Restating "[i]f it doesn't fit, you must acquit" works to persuade the jury in the defense's favor. In the Anglo-African tradition, Cochran imbues the standard legal criteria with Afro American rhythmic particularity to make it memorable and to achieve his persuasive goals.

Cochran consistently repeats one phrase as he works to denounce the prosecution's theory: "It just doesn't make sense." By repeating this statement, Cochran is emphasizing to the jury the failure of the prosecution to meet its burden. He uses this aspect of rhythm in an attempt to place reasonable doubt in the jury's minds. Additionally, while going through the state's theory, Cochran continues to use repetition. In arguing the lack of blood found at Simpson's estate, Cochran repeatedly poses hypothetical questions about the blood:

> If he went in that house with bloody shoes, with bloody clothes, with his bloody hands as they say, where's the blood on the doorknob, where's the blood on the light switch, where's the blood on the banister, where's the blood on the

> carpet? That's like almost white carpet going up those stairs. Where is all that blood trail they've been banting about in this mountain of evidence? (Cochran 1995, 28–29)

With the repetition of "Where's the blood?" Cochran establishes a rhythmic pattern while attempting to leave that question lingering in the minds of jurors in order to establish reasonable doubt.

At one instance while summarizing Simpson's actions after he heard of Nicole Simpson's death, Cochran speaks with a noticeable rhythm. Nearly each sentence in the following excerpt begins with a pronoun followed by a verb. Each is a simple declarative sentence that Cochran delivers succinctly:

> He finds out. He gets the first thing smoking. He comes back here. He goes right to his residence. He talks to the police. He goes downtown with the police. He goes in a room with the police. He has his finger photographed. He gives blood. His lawyers are off someplace else. That's what this man did on June thirteenth. They weren't there then. That's what he did, consistent with innocence. (Cochran 1995, 64)

Cochran uses consistent phraseology as he argues the consistency of Simpson's actions. In portions of the summation, Cochran increases the tempo. When criticizing the prosecution's use of Mark Fuhrman as a witness, he speaks rapidly:

> And so when they try to prepare him, talk to him and get him ready and make him seem like a choir boy and make him come in here and raise his right hand as though he's going to tell you the truth and give you a true story here, they knew he was a liar and a racist. (Cochran 1995, 84)

Immediately after this statement, an emotionally charged Cochran manages to slow the tempo and powerfully deliver these next words: "There's something about good versus evil. There's something about truth. The truth crushed to earth will rise again. You can always count on that" (Cochran 1995, 84).

Continuing the case against Fuhrman, Cochran's repetition of identifying phrases places Fuhrman's involvement in context:

> Let's remember this man. This is the man who was off this case shortly after two o'clock in the morning right after he got on it. This is the man who didn't want to be off this case. This is the man, when they're ringing the doorbell at Ashford, who goes for a walk. And he describes how he's strolling. (Cochran, p. 86)

While recapping points from the first day of closing arguments, Cochran reemphasized a memorable part of the trial and stressed its role in the reasonable doubt: "Then the gloves. The gloves didn't fit. The gloves didn't fit. The gloves didn't fit" (Cochran 1995, 110). Repetition of certain phrases alerts the jurors to flaws and unexplained events in the prosecution's case. Shortly after, Cochran repeats the memorable rhyme: "It just doesn't fit. If it doesn't fit, you must acquit" (Cochran 1995, 110).

STYLIN'

Crafty usage of words and body language denotes stylin'. The determination of this characteristic involves observing verbal and nonverbal combinations of Cochran's communication during the closing argument. Intentional movements that accompany emphasized words illustrate stylin'. Language that appears to sound purposefully allegorical and descriptive also fall under the stylin' technique.

One clear example of Cochran's manipulation of his language and mannerisms occurs moments prior to the first break in his closing argument. Cochran ridicules the prosecution's theory of how Simpson was planning to disguise himself. As he spoke of a knit cap, Cochran physically demonstrated the disguise to highlight his point. Cochran incorporates aspects of stylin' and rhythm as he states:

> He was going to put on a knit cap and some dark clothes, and he was going to get in his white Bronco, this recognizable person, and go over and kill his wife. That's what they want you to believe. That's how silly their argument is. And I said to myself, maybe I can demonstrate this graphically. Let me put this knit cap on (indicating). You have seen me for a year. If I put this knit cap on, who am I? I'm still Johnnie Cochran with a knit cap. And if you looked at O.J. Simpson over there—and he has a rather large head—O.J. Simpson in a knit cap from two blocks away is still O.J. Simpson. It's no disguise. It's no disguise. It makes no sense. It doesn't fit. If it doesn't fit, you must acquit. (Cochran 1995, 22–23)

In conjunction with his speaking, Cochran actually places the cap on his head. He then slightly bounces with a tilt of the head as he reiterates his point to the jury. Throughout the closing argument, Cochran's visual stylin' appears in the form of this bounce and head tilt. For instance, when Cochran tells the jury that Detective Mark Fuhrman is a "lying, perjuring genocidal racist" (Cochran 1995, 70), he stands still, pointing his index finger with each word. Immediately afterward, he nods and bounces slightly as if agreeing with himself. These movements accentuated his argument, placing a confident and often flashy punctuation on his words.

A combination of stylistic devices rings forth at the portion in the closing argument where Cochran discusses the socks, or as he states, "Those socks!" At this point, there is observable change in rhythmic pattern and stylin.' As Cochran introduces the discussion of "those socks," he uses a suspicious facial expression, moves slowly, points with his index finger, and repeats words and phrases for emphasis: "Then we come to those socks. Those socks. They just don't fit. They just don't fit. They just don't fit" (Cochran 1995, 62). Cochran's visual stylin' continued with this type of testimony review. Often as Cochran drew attention to prosecution witnesses, he used the same suspicious facial expression and pointed with his index finger. This type of manipulation of mannerisms and body language influences the effect of the message (Jackson 1995), which in this instance was that the witnesses and their testimony could not be trusted.

Verbally, Cochran emphasized this same distrust by using an acrid tone of voice. For example, Cochran's tone is much harsher when he speaks the names of prosecution witnesses Detectives Vannatter and Fuhrman. He speaks their names quickly and dismissively. When Cochran refers to Detective Fuhrman as an "unspeakable disgrace" (Cochran 1995, 75), one can see how his visual stylin', consisting of pointing fingers and the shaking head, works with his aggressive tone of voice to complement his intended message.

NARRATIVE STYLE

The use of storytelling or its format is identified as narrative style. Sentences that relate events in an ordered sequence, hypothetical situations, and information that involve characters, scenes, and settings are all labeled as narrative style. The use of a narrative style is common in African American communication (Orbe 1995). Storytelling is prevalent in Black neighborhoods and Black churches. "Rarely will Black preachers expound their message in the linear fashion of a lecture" (Smitherman 1977, 150). Instead, they make stories come to life with energy and dramatization. "The reporting of events is never simply objectively reported, but dramatically acted our and narrated. The Black English speaker thus simultaneously conveys the facts and his or her personal sociopsychological perspective on the facts" (p. 161).

Cochran makes no exception during the closing argument. It is not surprising to uncover a narrative element in a trial summation because of the necessity of explaining one party's side of the story. Cochran often delivers excerpts of his closing by telling or retelling a sequence of events. When Cochran explains the attempts by several witnesses to find blood on Simpson's Ford Bronco, he speaks in narrative style. He chronologically explains the actions of witnesses, allowing jurors an opportunity to visualize each step. The narrative style aids in clearer understanding. One can observe through Cochran's reflection of the witness testimony of William Blauzini:

> He gets in the car on the driver's side where he stays almost five minutes, looking down, looking for blood, looking in the front. Remember, he takes his fingerprints or hands and puts them in the mirrors. . . . He looks all over for blood. Then he gets out. . . . He walks around, looks inside the driver's side, looks back, looks all down on the console looking for blood. (Cochran 1995, 74)

Perhaps a more lucid example of Black storytelling style occurs when Cochran reviews part of Mark Fuhrman's testimony. While reliving Fuhrman's investigative actions, Cochran adds flair to the words. He also gestures for visual effect and inserts his own perspectives:

> He's the guy who climbs over the fence. He's the guy who goes in and talks to Kato Kaelin. . . . He's the guy who's shining a light in Kato Kaelin's eyes. . . . Now, he's worried about bodies or suspects or whatever. He doesn't even take out his gun. He goes around the side of the house, and lo and behold, he claims he finds this glove and he says the glove is still moist and sticky. (Cochran 1995, 77)

Cochran uses more energy and makes the events more memorable than the original witness. Avoiding an exact reiteration of the witness' account, Cochran frequently digresses from the testimony to incorporate his own angle on the facts. This type of storytelling is reflective of the narratives in Black communities. Rather than just merely reviewing the facts, Cochran uses sequence, dramatization, gestures, and other devices to convey the theme (Smitherman 1977). Cochran's method of storytelling allows the jury to visualize the events that took place, either from the witness' perspective or from his own perspective. Through his word arrangement and nonverbal accompaniment, he attempts to persuade the jury by making the facts more identifiable and comprehensible.

CALL AND RESPONSE

Call and response involves interaction between the speaker and the audience during the message that often acts as a motivator for the speaker. "Call response is evident in repetition of a theme, stressed and unstressed syllables, short sentences, pauses, passionate intensity of expression, questions, and vocal audience response" (Phillips 1983, 137). As stated earlier, call and response is a feature expected to be absent due to the nature of the courtroom. Typically, in a closing argument, while the attorney addresses the jury in an attempt to persuade them, the jury does not speak. They may listen, they may take notes, but they do not verbally participate in the message. Logically, it would seem that call and response would not be found in Cochran's closing argument. However, the possibility of nonverbal call and response is recognized. Perhaps Cochran made statements or asked questions that elicited a nod of the head or a frown. However, because of the expectation of absence of call and response, the focus is placed on the front end, the call. Even though the traditional concept of call and response requires direct and immediate participation, in a closing argument the lawyer may make a call while the response is either given nonverbally or delayed until deliberations or verdict rendering when it is appropriate for the lead juror to speak. Responses may even occur subconsciously.

"Occasionally, expression seems expertly planned to evoke responses, much as a speaker might prepare persuasive arguments with an eye towards a special kind of reaction" (Asante 1987, 84). Indications of a call in Cochran's closing argument include phrases that are repeated for emphasis (as if putting his own "Amen" on it) and charges and challenges to the jury, as well as rhetorical questions that are deliberately repeated or followed by a pause, giving the jurors an opportunity to answer them mentally.

Several times within the closing argument, Cochran poses hypothetical questions to the jury that denotes a call. Even though the questions are posed hypothetically, the point of Cochran's stylistic choice is for the jury to answer the questions in their minds or in other nonverbal formats. He wants them to respond affirmatively to his question or to the point the question makes. In these instances, Cochran makes a call. The first evidence of this characteristic presents itself at the beginning of the closing argument. Cochran questions the jury: "Have you ever in your life been falsely accused of something? Have you ever been falsely accused? Ever had to sit there and take it and watch the proceedings and wait and wait and wait, all the while knowing that you didn't do it?" (Cochran 1995, 11). Here, Cochran calls for the jury to respond affirmatively in attempts to establish a common ground between them and the defendant. "[C]all response unifies speakers and listeners into a cohesive whole" (Phillips 1983, 142). Cochran wants the jury to identify with Simpson's position and calls for them to do just that.

Repetition of a theme, short sentences, intensity of expression, and questions are characteristics that evidence call-and-response situations (Phillips 1983). Combining a call with repetition, Cochran repeats rhetorical questions when discussing Fuhrman's testimony about using the word *nigger.* Cochran makes a call for the jury to support his allegations that Fuhrman lied on the witness stand: "Did he lie? Did he lie? Did he lie under oath? Did this key prosecution witness lie under oath? And I'm going to end this part and resume with him tomorrow morning. Did he lie?" (Cochran 1995, 78).

In Cochran's concluding remarks, he allots time to appeal to the jury on a humanistic level. The defense has argued all of the evidence, and Cochran now calls the jury to validate all that they have argued. Cochran imparts to the jury once again their power in the case. He incites them to use that power to impart justice:

> It is now up to you. We are going to pass this baton to you soon. You will do the right thing. You have made a commitment for justice. You will do the right thing. . . . By your decision you control his very life in your hands. Treat it carefully. Treat it fairly. Be fair. . . . Don't be a part of this continuing cover-up. Do the right thing remembering that if it doesn't fit, you must acquit, that if these messengers have lied to you, you can't trust their message, that this has been a search for truth. (Cochran 1995, 114)

In that passage, Cochran uses short sentences, refers to a theme of truth, speaks with passionate expression, and incorporates pauses. All of these elements represent a call Cochran is making to the jury. Similar to the styles found in the Black church in a call-and-response situation, Cochran delivers his last remarks in a preachy manner. He speaks of God and references a poem by James Russell Lowell:

> If truth is out there on a scaffold and wrong is in here on the throne, when that scaffold sways the future and beyond the dim unknown standeth the same God for all people keeping watch above his own. He watches all of us and he will watch you in your decision. Thank you for your attention. God bless you. (Cochran 1995, 114–15)

The chosen expression and deliberate stressing and unstressing of syllables at the end of the closing argument clearly indicate Cochran's intention of seeking the jurors' support and affirmation.

RAPPIN'

Rappin' exhibits a highly personalized way of talking that may include several units of expression. While rappin' also is not generally included in the format of a closing argument, the units of rappin' previously listed guided the examination. For example, observances of exaggerated language in the form of rarely used expressions are noted. Imitating the style of another indicates mimicry. Use of proverbs to sound wise or powerful indicates a unit of rappin'. "Proverbs are used to teach, to punish, to praise, [and] in litigation" (Richards 1992, 42), as is seen in the body of Cochran's argument. Playing on the sounds of words denotes punning. Improvisation for originality's sake counts as spontaneity. Boastful expressions of fearlessness and omnipotence count as braggadocio. Points made as innuendo indicate indirection.

While Cochran did not rap in the form of a musical composition, his closing argument did include elements of rappin' as described in African American communication theories. For instance, Cochran emphasized many of his beliefs through innuendo.

Occasionally, Cochran seized the opportunity to put down the prosecution team. Cochran appeared to insult the capability and competence of state attorneys Marcia Clark and Christopher Darden. Cochran managed this through indirection. Without making explicit reference to anyone, he needled Clark and Darden. Cochran implies the irrationality of the prosecution team through innuendo in this passage: "Somebody had to have some good sense in this courtroom. We had to bring this matter to a close. We did what we set out to do, to demonstrate to you reasonable doubt" (Cochran 1995, p. 41). Rather than blatantly saying that the prosecutors have no sense, Cochran uses terms like *somebody* to indirectly make this point.

Reminiscent of the Black rappin' style, Cochran's words to the jury in the beginning of his summation resemble the proverbial statement style: "You know, Sister Rose said a long time ago, 'He who violates his oath profanes the divinity of faith himself'" (Cochran 1995, 9). Cochran speaks here of his and the prosecution's faith in the jury's honesty on the voir dire questionnaire. Later, he uses a proverbial statement to put holes in the state's case while reviewing the lies of Mark Fuhrman: "If you can't trust the messenger, you can't trust the message" (Cochran 1995, 80). Cochran also cites the Bible: "I happen to really like the book of Proverbs and in Proverbs it says that a false witness shall not be unpunished and he that speaketh lies shall not escape" (p. 114). Cochran references the Bible to further denounce the testimony of Mark Fuhrman: "In that same book it tells us that a faithful witness will not lie but a false witness will utter lies. Finally in Proverbs it says that he that speaketh the truth showeth the forthrightfulness but a false witness shows deceit" (p. 114). Cochran uses these proverbial statements to make his points powerfully. This type of proverbial usage is rooted in the Black church. Black rhetorical tradition dictates that the natural leader "must be able to talk, to speak—to preach" (Asante 1987, 47).

SIGNIFYIN'

Finally, Cochran's closing argument is examined for the presence of signifyin'. Signifyin' is an artistic method for humorously putting another down. In this instance, signifyin' may include remarks where Cochran may humorously put down others involved in the murder case. Rather than the tearing down of the opponent's case or a particular procedure, references to an actual person or put-downs of a person in a witty way count as signifyin'.

Signifyin' usually involves personal attacks between people in jest. Not typically an aspect of a closing argument, one would not expect to discover such tactics in Johnnie Cochran's summation. Certainly there was no back-and-forth verbal dueling during the course of closing arguments. However, Cochran did make several comments that could arguably qualify as indirect signifyin'. In other words, Cochran speaks negatively about the prosecution team, specifically Marcia Clark and Christopher Darden. While his comments may or may not be in jest, they are spoken creatively and at times sarcastically. Nevertheless, Cochran's negative imaging of the prosecution team is delivered in a signifyin' style. For example, in his opening remarks, Cochran makes this comment about Marcia Clark, the lead attorney for the prosecution team: "And I think it was Miss Clark who said saying it is so doesn't make it so. I think that applies very much to their argument" (Cochran 1995, 9). His comments act as an indirect attack on Clark and her ability to make an argument.

Textbook closing arguments do not contain personalization by the attorneys involved. Generally, closing arguments argue the law based on one side's version of the facts. Emphasis is on the law and not the attorneys for either side. In this case, however, Cochran and the prosecutors criticize each other on a personal level during their closing arguments. Cochran makes objectionable statements about Marcia Clark on more than one occasion. These statements qualify as signifyin'. One instance of these insults occurred early in the summation:

> By the way—I have to stop at this point. I'm glad Miss Clark doesn't know this, but, you know, if you've ever been to McDonald's, they don't like you to bring hundred dollar bills in there. You know, you can't get a hundred dollar bill changed there generally. Some of these things about common sense, some people don't know. (Cochran 1995, 24)

The court instructed Cochran that he was indeed beyond the evidence with those statements. Despite the court's warnings, Cochran continues in this mode of verbal put-downs. He uses his language behavior to goad and needle opposing counsel Christopher Darden:

> That is how silly what they are talking about in this case [is] as he tries to play out this drama. But let me show you, rather than talk—a picture is worth a thousand words, so let me show this video. You watch this video for a moment and we will talk about it. This is for Chris Darden. (Cochran 1995, 36)

In that passage, after suggesting that Darden's methods are silly, Cochran specifically calls Darden by name.

In concluding his negation of Simpson having a fuse, Cochran reverses the allegation to apply to Darden. This signifyin' technique impacts negatively on Darden's argument and attacks Darden personally: "And so we get all the way back past May into June and there is no trigger, there is no fuse, there is nothing going on. The only fuse, the only trigger is in Mr. Darden's mind. The evidence isn't there" (Cochran 1995, 82). Following Barry Scheck's summation of the more scientific evidence, Cochran resumes and continues to verbally challenge and direct remarks at the prosecution team. In the following passage, Cochran speaks to Christopher Darden concerning the whereabouts of Simpson:

> That is what he was doing, getting the little knapsack out that has golf balls in it. . . . That is what he was doing, Mr. Darden. That is where he was. It is your speculation he is on the side of his house running into an air conditioner. That didn't happen. That is unreasonable. Nobody here believes it. (Cochran 1995, 102)

With this statement, Cochran seemingly stops talking to the jury and speaks directly to Darden. As he does many times in the closing argument, he addresses the prosecution team to goad them, to needle them, to challenge their argument, and to show that it just does not fit.

CONCLUSIONS AND IMPLICATIONS

Characteristics common to African American communication emerged in Cochran's closing argument. Specifically, uncovered traits include rhythm, stylin', narrative style, call and response, rappin', and signifyin'. Overall, Cochran did exhibit features (or parts thereof) of African American communication in his closing argument. He creatively combined the use of these stylistic devices to deliver a successful argument.

This study advocates the use of a culture-centered methodology. Specifically looking to an Afrocentric methodology to investigate characteristics of African American communication in an argument delivered by an African American to a majority African American jury seemed the most logical and most appropriate consideration for the purposes of the study. It encourages the use of an Afrocentric approach in rhetorical analysis. This qualitative study was structured specifically toward the portion of the closing argument delivered by Johnnie Cochran. The study was also limited to a search for six stylistic features of African American communication. The researcher did not examine the closing argument for every characteristic of African American communication found in the literature. The study was also limited to the context of the rhetorical act. An Afrocentric methodology was used to investigate rhetoric that did not occur in an Afrocentric context. However, the focus was not on the environment, but on the orator.

This study has prompted several recommendations for future research. An expansion of this study may determine whether a correlation exists between African American communication patterns and Cochran's success as an attorney. This study could extend to determine if a correlation exists between African American communication patterns and successful African American attorneys. The study can be expanded to investigate African American attorneys in other rhetorical situations, such as opening statements or arguments before the bench. The subject of the study, Johnnie Cochran, could be interviewed to determine his awareness of the stylistic devices observed in the closing argument. This may specifically provide insight as to the influence of a non-Afrocentric setting on African American communication style. At the very least, this work encourages and urges the use of Afrocentric methodologies when studying phenomena that deal with Africans or African Americans. It promotes the healthy incorporation of utilizing culture-centered perspectives to uncover meaning, particularly in communication situations.

REFERENCES

Abarry, A. (1990). Afrocentricity: Introduction. *Journal of Black Studies* 21: 123–25.

Akbar, N. (1979). African Roots of Black personality. In W. D. Smith, H. Kathleen, M. H. Burlew, and W. M. Whitney (Eds.), *Reflections on Black Psychology* (pp. 79–87). Washington, D.C.: University Press of America.

Asante, M. (1987). *The Afrocentric Idea.* Philadelphia: Temple University Press.

Asante, M. (1988). *Afrocentricity.* Trenton, NJ: Africa World.

Atwater, D. F. (1984). A Dilemma of Black Communication Scholars: The Challenge of Finding New Rhetorical Tools. *Journal of Black Studies* 15, 1: 5–16.
Atwater, D. F. (1995). Political and Social Messages in the Music of Stevie Wonder. In L. Niles (Ed.), *African American Rhetoric: A Reader* (pp. 139–47). Dubuque, IA: Kendall Hunt.
Boykin, W. (1983). *The Academic Performance of Afro-American Children.* In J. Spence (Ed.), *Achievement and Achievement Motives* (pp. 324–71). San Francisco: Freeman.
Childress, C. (1995). *Persuasive delivery in the courtroom.* Rochester: Lawyers Cooperative.
Chimezie, A. (1984). *Black Culture.* Cincinnati, OH: University of Cincinnati.
Cochran, J. (1995). *The People of California Versus Orenthal James Simpson.* Los Angeles: Court TV.
Cummings, M. S., and J. L. Daniel (1980). Scholarly Literature of the Black Idiom. In B. Williams and O. Taylor (Eds.), *Working Papers International Conference on Black Communication* (pp. 97–129). New York: The Rockefeller Foundation.
Greaves, G. (1992). An African-Centered Rhetorical Analysis of Selected Calypsoes of Political Commentary of Trinidad from 1988–1991. Ph.D. dissertation, Howard University.
Harrison, P. (1972). *The Drama of Nommo.* New York: Grove Press.
Haydock, R., and J. Sonsteng (1991). *Trial: Theories, Tactics, Techniques.* St. Paul: West Publishing Co.
Hecht, M. L., R. L. Jackson, and S. A. Ribeau (2003). *African American Communication: Exploring Identity and Culture.* Mahwah, NJ: Lawrence Erlbaum Associates.
Jackson, R. L. (1995). Toward an Afrocentric Methodology for the Critical Assessment of Rhetoric. In L. Niles (Ed.), *African American Rhetoric: A Reader* (pp. 148–57). Dubuque, IA: Kendall Hunt.
Karenga, M. (1988). Black Studies and the Problematic of Paradigm: The Philosophical Dimension. *Journal of Black Studies* 18: 395–414.
Keto, T. (1989). *The African-centered Perspective of History.* Creskill, NJ: KA Publications.
Kochman, T. (1972). *Rappin' and Stylin' Out: Communication in Urban Black America.* Urbana: University of Illinois Press.
Leonard, W. (1977). *Black Lawyers: Training and Results, Then and Now.* Boston: Senna and Smith.
Niles, L. A. (1984). Rhetorical Characteristics of Traditional Black Preaching. *Journal of Black Studies* 51, 1: 41–52.
Niles, L. A. (Ed.) (1995). *African American Rhetoric: A Reader.* Dubuque, IA: Kendall Hunt.
O'Barr, W. (1982). *Linguistic Evidence.* New York: Academic Press, Inc.
Orbe, M. (1995). African American Communication Research: Toward a Deeper Understanding of Interethnic Communication. *Western Journal of Communication* 59: 61–78.
Oyebade, B. (1990). African Studies and the Afrocentric Paradigm. *Journal of Black Studies* 21, 2: 233–38.
Phillips, L. C. (1983). *A Comparative Study of Two Approaches for Analyzing Black Discourse.* Ph.D. dissertation, Howard University.
Richards, D. (1992). *Let the Circle Be Unbroken: The Implications of African Spirituality in the Diaspora.* Lawrenceville, NJ: Red Sea Press.
Rogers, P. (1995). The Jurors Unbound: Anonymous No More, the Simpson Trial Jurors Reveal the Personalities Behind the Numbers. *People* 44: 52–53.
Schiele, J. (1990). Organizational Theory from an Afrocentric Perspective. *Journal of Black Studies* 21: 145–61.
Segal, G. (1983). *Blacks in the Law.* Philadelphia: University of Pennsylvania Press.
Smith, A. (1972). *Language, Communication and Rhetoric in Black America.* New York: Harper and Row.
Smith, L., and L. Malandro (Eds.) (1985). *Courtroom Communication Strategies.* New York: Kluwer Book Publishers.
Smitherman, G. (1977). *Talkin' and testifyin: The Language of Black America.* Boston: Houghton Mifflin. Reprint: Detroit: Wayne State University Press, 1986.
Smitherman, G. (1994). *Black Talk.* Boston: Houghton Mifflin.
Spence, G. (1995). *How to Argue and Win Every Time.* New York: St. Martin's Press.
Washington, L. (1994). *Black Judges on Justice.* New York: The New Press.
Welsh-Asante, K. (1985). Commonalities in African Dance: An Aesthetic Foundation. In M. K. Asante and K. Welsh-Asante (Eds.), *African Culture: The Rhythms of Unity* (pp. 71–82). Westport, CT: Greenwood.
Wilson, P. (1996). The Rhythm of Rhetoric: Jesse Jackson at the 1988 Democratic National Convention. *Southern Communication Journal* 61, 3: 252–63.
Winters, C. (1994). Afrocentrism: A Valid Frame of Reference. *Journal of Black Studies* 25, 2: 170–90.

CHAPTER 16

Afrocentric Rhetoric Transcending Audiences and Contexts: A Case Study of Preacher and Politician Emanuel Cleaver II

SHAUNTAE BROWN-WHITE

In his book, *The Souls of Black Folk,* published in 1903, W. E. B. Du Bois prophesied that the enduring predicament of American life would be "the problem of color" (1989, xxxi). This cancerous problem of color would affect all America, but especially the African American who would have to manage his two identities. Du Bois wrote:

> One ever feels his twoness, an American, a Negro; two souls, two thoughts, two unreconciled strivings, two warring ideals in one dark body, whose dogged strength alone keeps it from being torn asunder. . . . The history of the American Negro is the history of strife, this longing to attain self-conscious manhood, to merge his double self into a better truer self. (1989, 2–3)

Almost a hundred years after Du Bois wrote those words, the problem of color still exists, as does the double consciousness of the African American.

DOUBLE CONSCIOUSNESS AND EMANUEL CLEAVER II

No person is more acutely aware of this dilemma than the African American rhetor. While many historical and contemporary rhetors have been successful at merging this "double consciousness," others have found it challenging. The African American politician, perhaps more so than any other rhetor, faces the challenge of merging this double consciousness while maintaining cultural integrity. All politicians face the never-ending challenge of obtaining and maintaining the support of constituents. But African American politicians face even more of a challenge when their constituency is multicultural and they are representing people whose orientations to the world are dissimilar. Former Kansas City mayor Emanuel Cleaver II provides a model of a rhetor who successfully merges Du Bois' double consciousness, as he maintained an Afrocentric orientation to the world while appealing to a broad racially, politically, and culturally diverse audience. This case study will provide an Afrocentric analysis to explain Cleaver's rhetorical effectiveness.

In March 1991, the political face of Kansas City, Missouri, changed as the city found a leader who could bridge cultural, social and political gaps. Emanuel Cleaver was elected as the fifty-first mayor of Kansas City and, more specifically, the first African American to hold the office. Having worked on the city council since the late 1970s, Mayor Emanuel Cleaver had developed the political savvy needed to lead the city. As a United Methodist pastor of a 1,800-member African American church, as well as being nurtured, socialized, and indoctrinated in the African American church tradition, the Rev. Emanuel Cleaver understood the power of the spoken word and the oratorical skills required of a public person.

By the time he announced his bid for mayor, he had successfully built African American, Jewish, Hispanic, and White coalitions. But building coalitions alone was not enough. There were other aspects to be considered. He was seeking office in a city that was 30 percent African American (far less than any other city that had elected an African American mayor), and only 26.5 percent of those African Americans were of voting age. It was clear: In order for Cleaver to win a citywide election in Kansas City, he had to skillfully manage his double consciousness. It was imperative for him to have crossover appeal without losing the African American vote.

Throughout Cleaver's campaign, he was described as being well liked and respected by Whites, while at the same time maintaining his credibility with African Americans. Cleaver also possessed a skill that clearly separated him from other candidates: He was and is rhetorically gifted. News coverage during his 1991 campaign described him as "charismatic and eloquent," "a mesmerizing public speaker," "known for his stirring oratory," and "a smooth speaker grounded in the rich tradition of the Black church" (Leader Sworn In 1991, 23A; Moore 1991, 12A; Raber 1991, 5A; Robbins 1991, 16A). Those oratorical gifts would take Cleaver far during his eight-year tenure as mayor. Rhetorically skilled and a master storyteller, Emanuel Cleaver skillfully crafted his personae for several different rhetorical contexts: secular, sacred, African American, and other. It has been speculated that he is the most sought after speaker in the mayoral history of Kansas City.[1] He managed all of these personae well, as he transcended racial barriers in mainstream America while maintaining integrity and credibility in the African American community. While Cleaver was able to create identification with various audiences, he was still identifiably rooted in the African American culture. His ties to the culture and the community are pervasive in his discourse. Because of his leadership abilities and rhetorical skills, he won the 1991 election and was reelected in 1995. Term limits prevented him from seeking another term. In 1999, Cleaver left office with a 71 percent approval rating.[2] This preacher-politician successfully merged the two parts of Du Bois' double consciousness. Though he is not the first to rhetorically merge this double identity, Cleaver presents a model for how one can be both African and American and not sacrifice the integrity of either identity.

DOUBLE CONSCIOUSNESS AND AFROCENTRICITY

Molefi Asante's theory of Afrocentricity explains, perhaps, one approach that enables the rhetorical critic to explore how the African American rhetor alleviates the predicament of Du Bois' double consciousness. According to Afrocentric theory, one can maintain credibility in the African American community as well as in American society. Afrocentricity is culturally relevant, but not to the neglect of the entire human family. Afrocentric theory recognizes the need for people of the African Diaspora to locate their center of being.[3] Literally, it means placing African ideals at the center of any analysis that involves African culture and behavior (Asante 1987, 1988, 1990, 1993). Afrocentricity is an orientation that determines how one views the world and how one defines oneself. The African American rhetor who embraces an Afrocentric orientation is ultimately concerned with liberation. All Afrocentric discourse, implicitly or explicitly, addresses the issue of liberation. While addressing liberation, Afrocentric rhetoric also has the burden of transcending ideologies, "whether political or racial, in order to perform the task of continuous reconciliation" (Asante 1987, 167). Thus, by its very definition, Afrocentric rhetoric must transcend barriers. It can be argued that Emanuel Cleaver's rhetoric successfully fulfills the functions of Afrocentric discourse, while simultaneously transcending many rhetorical barriers.

PURPOSE OF THE STUDY

The purpose of this case study is to explore the limits of Afrocentricity within multidimensional sacred-secular contexts. Afrocentricity is a cultural orientation. Thus, if a speaker is Afrocentric in his or her worldview, a critic will find some of the same markings of Afrocentricity in the rhetor's discourse when he or she is speaking to an African American audience as well as to a mixed or predominantly White audience. This study proposes three arguments: (1) Afrocentric rhetoric, which focuses on viewing the world through the conceptual and cultural lenses of an African, has the ability to transcend political, racial, and other rhetorical barriers; (2) an African American rhetor can maintain his or her cultural integrity and appeal to others outside of his or her culture; and (3) Emanuel Cleaver is Afrocentric in his orientation toward the world and remains true to that orientation in his political speeches and sermons, regardless of audience or context.

Since it has been argued that Cleaver is an effective speaker, the primary purpose of this case study is to explain how his rhetoric functions and offer explanations for its effectiveness. Specifically, this study identifies the primary markings of Afrocentric rhetoric that exist in Cleaver's sermons and speeches to both African American and predominantly White audiences. Daniel and Smitherman (1976) argue that there is a religious background to all African American rhetoric. Thus, some of the same principles, themes, and perhaps even style will be found in sacred and secular contexts.

CRITICAL METHOD

The ultimate goal of Afrocentric rhetoric is to eliminate chaos and create harmony and unity. With this in mind, the goal of the Afrocentric critic is to determine the degree the speaker contributed to the elimination of chaos, made peace among incongruent views, and created the opportunity for harmony and balance (Asante 1987). Harmony and balance should be attained without the speaker losing integrity, meaning without divesting the person's cultural orientation.

Asante and Jackson offer several different interrelated themes to examine Afrocentric discourse which will be used in this analysis. Asante presents three primary themes in Afrocentric discourse: (1) human relationships, (2) humans' relationship to the supernatural, and (3) humans' relationships to their own being. All Afrocentric discourse, implicitly or explicitly, addresses the issue of liberation. A critic must assume that a successful presentation of one of these three themes will occur while trying to achieve liberation (Asante 1987, 167). Similarly, Jackson (2000) enlists the themes of liberation, community, and relational ethics in order to discuss the human conditions. The Afrocentric mind is highly communal and values collective over individual advancement. The "I" and the "we" are one in Afrocentric discourse (Asante 1987, 105; Daniel and Smitherman 1976, 31–32). Community is of utmost importance, and Jackson (2000) argues that relational ethics reinforce what is meant by community: "Each community creates and maintains its ethical standards, and the value placed upon the standards are emphasized within relationships with others" (36). Jackson poses several investigative questions to be asked by the critic when doing an Afrocentric analysis. A primary question is: What does the text inform about liberation and/or relational ethics?

Afrocentricity, as a theoretical frame, is used in this study to explain how the rhetoric of Emanuel Cleaver functions. The second inquiry of this study is to assess how Emanuel Cleaver eliminates chaos and restores harmony and unity. The study examines how, through his rhetoric, Cleaver addresses issues of community, relational ethics, and human relationships with the supernatural, others, and oneself, while addressing the issue of liberation.

TEXTS AND TRANSCRIPTS

Twenty-five texts of Emanuel Cleaver's sermons and speeches were collected between June 1996 and May 1998. There are twelve sermons and thirteen political speeches included in this study (see apendices). The texts were acquired by (1) audiotapes provided by the church where Cleaver serves as pastor, (2) videotapes or manuscripts provided by the mayor's office, or (3) the researcher audiorecording a speech or a sermon while it was being delivered. Once the tapes were obtained, the researcher transcribed them with minimal editing. Meaningless sounds such as verbalized pauses or coughing were edited out. Grammatical errors, responses from the audience, and the like were unedited. The transcripts reflect the precise words that Cleaver spoke. The researcher transcribed the majority of the audio and videotapes (fifteen), and a transcription service transcribed the remaining tapes.

ANALYSIS

Emanuel Cleaver, the rhetor, has successfully merged the double consciousness described by W. E. B. Du Bois almost one hundred years ago. Cleaver, both preacher and politician, trafficking in an African American world as well as the world of others, has managed to transcend racial, political, ideological, and sacred-secular barriers by the power of his rhetoric. This section supports the argument that Cleaver is both Afrocentric and remains true to that orientation through his rhetoric. The analysis demonstrates how Cleaver fulfills the functions of Afrocentric rhetoric. All Afrocentric rhetoric, implicitly or explicitly, addresses the issue of liberation, embraces the principle of community, and provides guiding principles for relational ethics.

In this study, twenty-five texts were collected and analyzed. However, one sermon and one political speech, which best demonstrate the three Afrocentric concepts (liberation, principle of community, and relational ethics), are highlighted.

LIBERATION

As established earlier, all Afrocentric rhetoric, implicitly or explicitly, addresses the issue of liberation primarily for people of the African Diaspora, but not to the exclusion of others. The two primary themes that address the issue of liberation in Cleaver's rhetoric are the themes of social justice and the exercise of agency and responsibility.

Cleaver's ministry, which is a ministry that advocates social justice, also informs his political beliefs. The African American preacher and church have always been concerned with social issues that affect the African American community. Cleaver's theology and his political activism are guided by the principle of social justice. In a general sense, Franklin defines social justice ministries as a "tradition that seeks public righteousness through community activism, political advocacy and preaching" (1997, 42). Thus, preaching and activism are interrelated. In his or her analysis of America, a social justice theologian focuses on the root causes of social problems, which include but are not limited to economic inequality. The sermon that most poignantly demonstrates Cleaver's commitment to social justice is "A Left-Handed Army" (Appendix A). This sermon is highlighted as well as the keynote speech Cleaver made at the Turner Construction Management Training Program (Appendix B).

Emanuel Cleaver has enjoyed a long-standing relationship with the Jewish community. In fact, an overwhelming majority of Jewish citizens supported him in both elections as mayor (E. Cleaver, personal communication, December 22, 1999). One of the long-standing relationships he has developed is with the people of Temple B'nai Jehudah, where he and the rabbi have exchanged pulpits once a year for the last fifteen years, in honor of the Martin Luther King Jr. holiday.

In the sermon "A Left-Handed Army," Cleaver demonstrates how Afrocentricity is concerned with liberation for African Americans, but not to the exclusion of others. For Cleaver, the reason social injustice still exists is because too many people whose immediate group is not affected by discrimination and racism have become too comfortable and complacent in witnessing and accepting injustice.

To resolve this tension between complacency, apathy, and bitterness from the experience of one's own injustice, Cleaver uses the metaphor of a "left-handed army." The reference is to a biblical text (Judges 20:16), where the tribe of Benjamin forms an army of wounded soldiers. They were by birth right-handed but lost their right hands in combat. This left-handed army is to be the exemplar for the audience in fighting injustice. With the use of vivid images, Cleaver paints the picture of the army for the audience:

> These men had lost the use of their right arm in battle. In ancient days when men fought in hand-to-hand combat, the first goal was to wound your adversary's right arm. If you could just wound his right arm, you would have successfully defeated him.
>
> And so it came about that in the tribe of Benjamin, in this tribe alone, there were hundreds of fighting men who were lame of the right hand. So, they formed this south pawed army—seven hundred chosen men. These seven hundred men had the perfect excuse for avoiding combat. They had only their left hand, and they were by birth right-handed. They had obviously given their right arm in the defense of their country. They could have requested their military pension and waited on their monthly government check. They had the best excuse in the land.

This is a culture-specific reference for this Jewish audience to whom he is preaching. This Old Testament reference to the tribe of Benjamin helps to create identification with the audience and transcend religious barriers between him and the audience. While Cleaver establishes identification with the audience by using this metaphor as a major theme throughout his sermon, this is the only reference that directly relates to the experiences of the Jewish audience. All of the other references come from Cleaver's experiences as an African American. He makes references to playing dominoes in college with the other African American athletes as well as playing the dozens (yo' mama jokes), the Civil War African American regiment, and his family origin in Ghana (later purchased as slaves in America). All these references demonstrate his connection to the African American community. Here, Cleaver demonstrates his ability to maintain cultural integrity while appealing to those outside the African American community. While remaining grounded in the African American community, it is the metaphor of the left-handed army that bound him, his Jewish audience, and the few African Americans in the audience as well. This left-handed army appeals to the human family.

The images of the soldiers in the left-handed army invite the audience to visualize the army that Cleaver sees. In most of Cleaver's stories, he wants the audience to identify with the characters; thus, the audience is to see themselves as part of the army. Being left-handed represents being wounded. All the excuses the audience uses so as not to fight—apathy, complacency, and an "it's-not-my-group" attitude—are nonissues compared to being physically wounded in a war. The contemporary war is the fight against social injustice, which affects African Americans, the Jewish community, and others. For Cleaver, joining the army is an obligation, not an option. The left-handed soldier overcomes his or her wound and joins the army anyway, which is what God has commanded Cleaver and the audience to do:

> People asked me why would I march with a group of Hispanics in Rosedale Park a few years ago because a woman had been mistreated at the supermarket. Yet, you can tell, I am not Hispanic, but that is still my brother and sister. I will not allow in my silence anything to be perpetrated on the Jewish people in this community while I sit in silence. If something happens, I will be there. Not for you, but for me. Because God has commanded me to join a left-handed army.

In this sermon, Cleaver unites himself and members of the audience in the left-handed army, the army committed to fighting social ills despite wounds of discrimination, bitterness, and complacency. Cleaver argues that liberation is going to be achieved only through action, and social justice cannot be attained until everyone develops a staunch intolerance for injustice committed against anyone in the human family.

While the sermon "A Left-Handed Army" deals with liberation on a philosophical level, Cleaver's speech to the Turner Construction Management trainees addresses liberation on a practical level as he lobbies for the continued support of affirmative action.

The keynote speech given to the management trainees of Turner Construction Company was delivered in February 1998. The audience primarily consisted of Hispanics and women in construction. In the speech, Cleaver emphatically insists that the grim reality of racism and discrimination still exists in America, and it has affected and continues to affect the audience members. Thus, affirmative action is still necessary.

One of the first tasks Cleaver sets out to do is to justify the need for affirmative action and attack the erroneous view that affirmative action is a handout of jobs and contracts to unqualified people. For Cleaver, affirmative action *is* an opportunity. He uses his personal experience of being admitted and attending seminary to support his argument:

> Now, affirmative action doesn't mean that you get to do things that you don't know how to do. I mean, I would, I attribute my master's degree to the affirmative action program. They did not say, "Cleaver, we're going to start you off with five A's and a B." They didn't. I would have taken it, but they didn't. [*Audience laughter*] What they said was, "Look, in the history of our school, we've only had two African Americans." This was in 1972. "We've only had two. We want to change, and so we will pay your tuition to go to school here." Now, all I wanted was to be enrolled. I was stupid enough to believe that I could compete with the people in my class. And three years later when I graduated, I demonstrated that I had been able to compete. Affirmative action doesn't mean putting me in school and giving me A's. It means simply putting me in school.

While Cleaver exposes the ills of America as he justifies the need for affirmative action, he also challenges the audience to exercise agency and take responsibility for their own success or failure. In this speech, Cleaver seeks to empower the audience as he challenges them not to define themselves as victims. While affirmative action is necessary, the audience cannot depend on it. To support his argument and challenge his audience, he calls on the African American cultural ancestor of Madame C. J. Walker. Walker, an entrepreneur, was the first African American and first woman to become a millionaire in the 1920s—without the benefit of affirmative action or a federal grant. Cleaver argues, "[T]his Black woman was worth $2.6 million because she had vision, she had commitment, and she had the guts to go into business." More importantly, he uses Walker as an exemplar of one who exercised agency in defining her success.

Cleaver appeals to harmony and unity with his audience through the shared experiences of discrimination that has affected the African American and Hispanic communities as well as the women who are a part of an industry dominated by men. More than likely, many of the audience members have experienced some form of discrimination. However, it is not just their shared experience of discrimination that connects them; it is also the shared experience of having to overcome the obstacles that lie before them. It is the shared experience of exercising agency and self-definition while achieving personal and social liberation that also unites them.

As demonstrated through the sermon "A Left-Handed Army" and the keynote address at the Turner Construction Management trainee luncheon, one is able to see Cleaver's worldview toward liberation. Liberation is an imperative for all members of the human family, and the audience must develop an intolerance for injustice against any member of the human family, not just their own group. Consistent in much of Cleaver's discourse is the idea that liberation can be achieved only through the work and initiative of the people who are seeking liberation. The Turner Construction keynote address demonstrates this. But also in the sermon "Wait for the Lord," Cleaver challenges the congregation that while they are waiting for the Lord to act or answer prayers, they must work. While Cleaver affirms social programs such as affirmative action to rectify the ills of society, he is also an advocate of hard work, initiative, and preparation. He challenges the audience to personify these important values. Finally, liberation is a collective responsibility. If one person achieves liberation but others are not free, it is in vain. This idea is informed by the Afrocentric idea of the principle of community.

PRINCIPLE OF COMMUNITY

Afrocentric thought advocates the principle of community or the idea that the "I" and "we" cannot be separated. Collective achievement is valued over individual advancement. Cleaver's themes related to the principle of community are closely tied to liberation. Liberation cannot be attained without communal efforts. His primary themes related to community include collective responsibility, collective identity, and the value of family and extended family. In this section, the sermon "Stuck Up People" (Appendix A) and Cleaver's 1996 Democratic National Convention speech (Appendix B) are discussed.

"Stuck Up People" was preached at Metropolitan Missionary Baptist Church on February 23, 1998. Cleaver preaches annually at Metropolitan as part of their Black History Month activities. Metropolitan would be considered a church deeply grounded in the traditions of the African American church culture. In this sermon, Cleaver identifies the spirits and attitudes that are detriments to community: pride, selfishness, and ingratitude. He uses the biblical story of Saul to demonstrate how pride is destructive and how that attitude can manifest itself in the audience. Through the use of imagery, Cleaver is able to create audience identification with Saul:

> It's a bad thing when somebody becomes stuck up. Saul had everything going for him. He came from an influential family. He grew up in one of the better neighborhoods. He was one of the few kids in his school to drive a late-model chariot. He was not only voted the most handsome boy in the class, but according to the Bible, he was the most handsome man in the kingdom.

Saul represents African Americans who have achieved material and financial success. In this sermon, Cleaver asserts that sometimes people are failures not because they didn't succeed, but because they did. Like Saul, who separated himself from God and became arrogant and ungrateful, a threat to the principle of community is when African Americans separate themselves from God:

> At least, during Black History Month, we ought to pause and remember that while we might have a leather attaché case today, that maybe, maybe, maybe, maybe we were a lot closer to the Lord when we carried our stuff in a sack. [*Audience applause*]

While separation from God is the fundamental threat to community, separation from the community is also perilous. The separation of the community manifests itself in the form of jealousy and ingratitude. These attitudes challenge the idea that collective achievement is valued over individual achievement. Cleaver challenges his audience to reconcile the detrimental attitudes with those principles that will build stronger communities and lead to continued collective achievement: gratitude, selflessness, and humility.

Cleaver reconciles these conflicting views by telling the story of Saul and how his pride led to his own destruction, but he also offers reasons the audience ought not be full of themselves and pat themselves on the back too quickly. Cleaver pays homage to cultural ancestors when he does a roll call of those who have come before them.

While Cleaver pays homage to cultural ancestors, it is also a reminder to the audience that many have come before them, achieved great things, and paved the way. It is also on their shoulders that the African American community now stands. In this sermon, Cleaver alerts the audience to the dangers of being preoccupied with their own accomplishments. Ultimately, it is a threat to the community and the principle of collective identity. Cleaver further reconciles this tension by arguing that God provides the opportunity for collective and individual achievement, and his experience is proof of the argument:

> We have right now 427 Black mayors in America. You better give God the glory! Nobody deserves glory but God! See I know, I know, I know, I know, I know, I know, I know in my own [*inaudible*] of measurement, I was not supposed to be the mayor of this city! I know! I know! You know I know! I wasn't supposed to be mayor! I only had 27 percent of the Black vote. I only had $130 in the bank. I know! I know! I was not supposed to be the mayor of this town! It was God who clothed me and put in that [*inaudible*]. I I I I I I I know! It was God!

The implicit audience of the sermon is middle-class Black America, of which he is a part. Cleaver challenges the audience not to let the very thing that the cultural ancestors fought to achieve be the destruction of the contemporary African American community. He implores, "Let us never get to a point where we believe that through our intellect, through our articulation, through our importance, that we've been able to get over!" "Stuck Up People" does not necessarily define community, but Cleaver uses it to address the issue of collective achievement and individual responsibility. Sometimes individual success can be the failure of the group. While there are more economically and socially successful African Americans today than there were thirty or forty years ago, the very thing that the group has fought to attain is what is threatening their collective identity, responsibility and achievement.

While "Stuck Up People" emphasizes collective achievement and identity, Emanuel Cleaver's 1996 speech made at the Democratic National Convention best exemplifies his conceptualization of community and collective responsibility. Cleaver was a part of a forum in which President Bill Clinton gave those who differed from him or the party an opportunity to speak. Cleaver addressed the issue of the Republican-crafted welfare reform bill that had been recently signed by Clinton. Cleaver's critique of the bill is focused less on Clinton and more on the Republicans, as he defends Hillary Clinton and her book *It Takes a Village,* which had been attacked a few weeks earlier at the GOP Convention.

In the speech, Cleaver sets out to reconcile incongruent views between Republicans and Democrats and even within the Democratic Party—primarily White conservatives who espouse that it is the responsibility not of the community (the village) but rather of the parents to raise children. Cleaver and his life story are the supporting evidence that it does take a village to raise a child. He declares at the beginning of the speech that he is "a self-proclaimed poster child for the American dream," and begins to tell his story of origins in a three-room shack with no electricity and plumbing. He reconciles these competing views by clearly emphasizing the value and role of family. The village does not substitute for parental love and guidance or other familial ties, but they work together. Despite being poor, he said, "my three sisters and I grew up knowing we could always count on a lavish outpouring of parental love. We lived in the projects, but thank God, the projects didn't live in us." He goes on to add, "But, my friends, mere family never made a person prosperous, principled or polite. It take a whole village to raise a child and it takes many villages to raise a nation."

Cleaver declares that he is not only the product of loving, grounded parents who took the time to instill in him a sense of pride, but also a product of the village. The village certainly helped to raise him. He pays homage to his elders as he calls on their names to bear witness to his argument:

> I had plenty of help from my village. I had Ervin Garnett, my football coach. I had Mr. Freeman, my Cub Scout leader. I had Mrs. Alma Holland, an English teacher who took a special interest in me and demanded that I learn to speak before a crowd. I remember the woman who threatened to call my daddy when

> Tommy Nelson and I pulled a watermelon from her backyard garden. Rev. Ball played his part, too. Every person in this convention hall was raised by their village.

This roll call serves two functions. It provides evidence for his argument, but it also affirms the elders and the values of the African American community—the village. Additionally, the story is one that rings true for people beyond the African American community.

As stated earlier, the themes of liberation, community, and relational ethics cannot be easily demarcated and distinguished from one another; all three themes are tightly interwoven. This speech is no different. Cleaver is primarily concerned with our human relationships and answers the question of what our responsibility is to others, or rather, whether we have responsibility to someone other than ourselves. Cleaver boldly says yes. Through his story, he reconciles the tension between conservatism (which he asserts shows no compassion for others) and the fact that the welfare system does need to change with the values of the village and community. It is through the village, Cleaver argues, that America will be able to achieve greatness and provide "at least the economic basics for all our citizens to ensure that even the least amongst us can shop as can I and my family."

In other speeches and sermons, Cleaver demonstrates the principle of community by establishing collective identity. He does this remarkably well. No matter who the audience or what the context, Cleaver is able to establish community. Consistent throughout his speeches and sermons is a shared identity. He is always a part of that identity. For instance, in the Turner Construction keynote luncheon, Cleaver makes several references to when "we" were elected, as opposed to when "I" was elected. In his speech at a meeting of Freedom, Inc., an African American political club, to gain support for downtown economic development, Cleaver, though he does not live in that community, quickly situates himself as part of the community. Some of the constituents of Freedom, Inc. come from public housing. Cleaver identifies with that experience, and demonstrates that he is still a part of the community by his tireless efforts to spend money in that community. In his sermons, though he functions as a preacher, preaching to God's people, he still is a part of the flawed human condition. Based on the human condition, he and the audience, the audience and itself, and the audience and others not present are bound together based on this condition.

RELATIONAL ETHICS

Relational ethics reinforce the value of community but also provide a standard of conduct that people ought to use to govern their relationships with others. Relational ethics are tied to the principle of community; therefore, some of the ideas overlap. Cleaver's themes of relational ethics include compassion, humility, gratitude, and respect for the community. The sermon "Standing Afar" (Appendix A) and a radio-broadcast speech addressing an incident between the African American community and the police (Appendix B) are highlighted to demonstrate Cleaver's definition of relational ethics.

"Standing Afar" was delivered September 8, 1996, at St. James United Methodist Church. In the sermon, Cleaver identifies the characteristics and behaviors that violate the relational ethics of the community: being cold, cold-hearted, insensitive, and self-absorbed. He uses the story of Peter and examines his actions after Jesus had been betrayed. In John 18:18, it states, "Now the servants and officers had made a charcoal fire outside because it was cold, and they were standing warming themselves. Peter also was with them standing and warming himself." Thus, Peter becomes the audience's example of the behavior that they should not embrace but which they so often personify. Peter is the audience, but in the sermon, Cleaver reconciles the tension between who the audience is and who they ought to be.

"Standing afar" is Cleaver's phrase that indicates being cold or cold-hearted. He asserts that too many people do not want to get close because it reminds the audience of things they don't want to deal with or address. Cleaver goes on to argue that the audience stands afar when they show no compassion and look at the experiences of other people:

> There is little compassion for those caught in the grips of self-perpetuating "underclassness." The majority of Americans, according to opinion polls, believe the Welfare Reform bill is good and fair, in spite of the fact that it promises to punish the children of the poor. . . . [I]f you stand afar with no intimate knowledge of, or experience with, people on welfare, it's easy to become cold-hearted.

Cleaver admonishes the audience not to stand afar, but rather to get close to one another and show compassion, which is one of the ethical principles that should guide relationships. But, another important principle is gratitude. The audience cannot afford to stand afar because it is a sign of ingratitude toward others who have made a way for the audience:

> However, if you're like me, you will not want to be caught standing afar warming yourself. Why? Because someone paid the price of experiencing the cold winds of sacrifice in order that you and I could reach the point where we stand. Some mother stood in the cold waiting on a bus to go to work to earn money to buy you a dress, to buy you some shoes, that you might go to school [*Audience harmony indicators*]. Some grandmama, some Big Mama, some auntie saved a little money cleaning a house in the rich part of town in order to buy some stuff to send to you [*audience harmony indicators*] . . . And, so because that happened, I feel guilty anytime I'm standing by the fire, anytime I'm just concerned about warming Emanuel Cleaver, I feel guilty because somebody has already

> worked, somebody has already cried, somebody has already prayed to allowed me to make it [*audience harmony indicators*].

For Cleaver, showing compassion is not an option but an obligation, if for no other reason to remember those who have made a way for the audience ahead of them. Compassion and gratitude are two governing principle of relational ethics, but members within the community also must show respect for the community and toward one another. Cleaver addresses this ethic in the following speech highlighted in this section.

In the summer of 1996, the Kansas City police and some members of an African American neighborhood had a confrontation. An African American police officer shot a young African American man who was an alleged drug dealer. According to police reports, the suspect resisted arrest and pulled out a gun and aimed it at the police officer. The crowd in the neighborhood maintained that the suspect did not have a gun and that the police used excessive, unnecessary force. What resulted was a standoff between sixty police officers and a hundred African American members of that community (Eberting and Rice 1996, A1; Sanchez and Collins 1996, B1).

Three days after the incident, Emanuel Cleaver addressed the community on a local African American radio station. The purpose of his address was to calm the anxieties and frustrations of some factions of the community and to support the police's actions. Cleaver faced a unique dilemma: He was a part of the African American community, and he was also a member of the police board of commissioners. He overcomes these barriers and prescribes the ethics that should govern the relations of the community. Of the texts collected in this study, this is probably the only one where he directly confronts and even attacks members of the audience.

As a member of two conflicting groups, one of the first things Cleaver does is situate himself as part of the African American community while at the same time differentiating between the "lawless" and "law-abiding" citizens within that community. Cleaver defines and appeals to unity and harmony among the law-abiding citizens. He defines them as:

> [m]odel citizens . . . men and women who work their jobs eight hours a day, raise their families, maintain their property, worship God and try to do the right thing on a daily basis . . . [they are] active in the Santa Fe or Washington/Wheatly Neighborhood Associations, who meet with the police regularly to support the efforts to rid their neighborhoods of baneful bullies who brandish weapons and sell drugs.

These are the people who were not involved in the incident, who are tired of threats that exist to the principle of community, and to whom he appeals to unite against the people who don't practice good citizenship. Cleaver describes the other member of the community who were involved in the confrontation as "low-life, lawless, licentious lackies who sell drugs to our children, shrink our property value in our neighborhoods, create fear in our souls and break into our homes."

By differentiating between these two groups, Cleaver is defining the ethics of good citizenship that ought to govern the relationships within the community. Ultimately, the primary relational ethic promoted by Cleaver in this speech is respect for the community by engaging in activities that enhance, not devalue the physical, psychological and emotional aspects of the community. Also, by differentiating between the two groups, it made it possible to overcome the situational barrier of the historically tenuous relationship between the police and the African American community. Cleaver was able to defend the actions of the police. He does this successfully in addition to discrediting the recounts of the incident given by the "lawless."

Another issue Cleaver addresses is the role the media played when they describe the incident as a "riot." It is linked to relational ethics in the sense that Cleaver asks the audience not to allow outsiders (the media), who have no genuine interest in the community, to make exploitative comments define what goes on in the community. Cleaver asks the audience, "Why in the world should we buy into someone else's analysis of our community as a group of defective dumbbells who burn and loot our own neighborhoods?" No one can better assess the events that took place than the members of the community, and in addition, the media analysis is laced with racist interpretations.

In this address, Cleaver makes an effective appeal to the restoration of harmony and balance within the community as he defines the relational ethics of the community and calls for law-abiding citizens to unite against the lawless and the media. However, unlike many of Cleaver's other political speeches and sermons, he does not attempt to unite the entire audience. He makes distinctions within the audience and does not attempt to restore the unity in the African American community between the two factions. Interestingly, the speech was well received by the "law-abiding" citizens and the media (Hood 1996, C6).

One can see that Cleaver's rhetoric fulfills the functions of being Afrocentric as he consistently addresses the issues of liberation, the principle of community and relational ethics. With each of these principles, Cleaver urges his audiences to move out of their comfort zone to achieve liberation, fulfill their obligation as a community, and operate within the standards of relational ethics. Cleaver appeals to harmony and unity in all of his audiences, but not at the expense of xenophobia and unrealistic appraisals of the social ills that face America. He appeals to a genuine principle of community and chastises those who affirm shallow community relations.

DISCUSSION

W. E. B. Du Bois argued in 1903, almost one hundred years ago, that African American men and women struggle with a "double consciousness." This double consciousness reflects the fact that African Americans are both African and American, but sometimes these two identities are competing with each other. No one knows this better than the African American rhetor, especially the politician whose constituents and audiences are diverse. Kansas City mayor and United Methodist pastor Emanuel Cleaver is an exemplar for merging this double consciousness. This case study makes three propositions:

1. Afrocentric rhetoric, which focuses on viewing the world through the conceptual and cultural lenses of an African, has the ability to transcend rhetorical barriers.
2. An African American rhetor can maintain his or her cultural identity and appeal to those outside of his or her culture.
3. Emanuel Cleaver is Afrocentric in his orientation to the world and remains true to that orientation in his political speeches and sermons, regardless of audience or context.

Emanuel Cleaver, as seen through his rhetoric, is Afrocentric in his orientation. Cleaver is an effective Afrocentric speaker for three reasons: (1) his authenticity in his self definition and how he situates himself in the African American culture; (2) his communal orientation, which does not exclude those outside of the African American community; and (3) his connection to and understanding of the human condition and the common needs and issues that face all of his audiences.

Emanuel Cleaver has an authentic relationship with the African American community, and that authenticity is constant, regardless of audience. By authenticity, I mean he does not change how he defines himself or his relationship with the African American community based on the audience. Through his rhetoric, the audience can see his connection to African American culture. It is clear that Cleaver situates himself in African American culture through his references to personal experiences and those experiences germane to the African American community. These are experiences with which an African American audience can relate, but Cleaver's cultural references also appeal to non-African Americans. He embraces an African-centered worldview where there is no demarcation between spiritual and secular/material worlds. How Cleaver situates himself in African American culture is natural—he does not intentionally create a self-definition or relationship with a community; it is simply his orientation. While he has an authentic relationship with the Diaspora, he is also able to connect with those not a part of the Diaspora through his communal orientation (which is also a marking of Afrocentric rhetoric) and his ability to connect with people through identification in the human condition.

One of the goals of Afrocentric discourse is reconciliation that transcends racial, political, and ideological barriers. One way that Cleaver overcomes barriers is to create a sense of community with his audience. Emanuel Cleaver in most cases immediately creates a "we-ness" between him and his audience, no matter if he is talking about the challenges that face the African American religious community or economic development that affects Hispanic and women contractors. From a Eurocentric paradigm, this sense of "we-ness" is often characterized as consubstantiality or identification, which presumes preparation of an audience analysis. From the audience analysis, identification is constructed. Burke argues that a natural division among people exists, "Identification is compensatory to division. If men were not apart from one another, there would be no need for the rhetorician to proclaim unity" (1969, 22).

However, in Afrocentricity, this simultaneous connection between the speaker and audience is the result not of a planned audience analysis or logical arrangement of ideas, but rather of an orientation to the world that holds the idea that all people are connected. Thus, a natural connection with the audience already exists. So while Cleaver is situated in the African American culture, he is also a part of a larger community—the human family. Again, this is a natural orientation for Cleaver, which is one of the reasons he is consistent across audiences and contexts.

This case study of Emanuel Cleaver's rhetoric provides a map for the scholar as well as the practitioner to understand how to create culturally transcendent rhetoric. Political speakers often make the mistake of not maintaining a consistent identity across diverse audiences. For instance, he or she constructs a self-definition with one audience that can vary or completely change with another audience. One of the primary reasons for Emanuel Cleaver's effectiveness is his ability to maintain a consistent and authentic self-definition with various audiences. From this, rhetorical critics as well as rhetors can see that it is not necessary to reinvent an identity for each audience. Rather, one can maintain his or her identity and, from an Afrocentric perspective, operate with the worldview that both the speaker and audience are already connected through their membership in the human family.

Cleaver also appeals to the values and needs of the human family. These values and needs of the human family emerge in his rhetoric through his themes. Cleaver's themes are consistent in his sermons and political speeches with African American and mixed audiences. His specific themes fit into the broad-based themes examined in this study. Cleaver's themes of liberation include social justice, pride, work ethic and initiative. The "principle of community" themes include collective identity, collective responsibility, and the value of extended family. Compassion, humility, gratitude, and respect for the community inform Cleaver's views on relational ethics. All of these themes are related to the African Diaspora and are a part of the Judeo-Christian tradition as well. While Emanuel Cleaver is an effective political speaker, I argue that his experience as a preacher also impacts this effectiveness. Like Afrocentricity, the Judeo-Christian tradition is concerned with reconciliation and uniting the human family. Emanuel Cleaver's authentic relationship with the African Diaspora, his communal orientation, and his ability to unite his audiences by showing their connection to the human condition make him an effective Afrocentric rhetor.

APPENDIX A

Sermon Occasions and Audiences

SERMON TITLE	DATE DELIVERED	OCCASION	AUDIENCE
"The Kingdom of God is Within You"	7/28/96	St. James Service (= SJ)	African American (= AA)
"Wait on the Lord	8/18/96	SJ	AA
"Standing Afar"	9/8/96	SJ	AA
"Stay on the Beam"	9/22/96	SJ	AA
"There Is a God Somewhere"	9/29/96	SJ	AA
"The Frustrations of Life"	2/2/97	SJ	AA
"Sham Battles"	2/9/97	SJ	AA
"Nothing to Draw With"	5/4/97	SJ	AA
"The Broad Margins of Life"	1/7/98	United Methodist Meeting on Evangelism	Mixed
"A Left-Handed Army"	1/23/98	Temple B'nai Jehudah King Holiday Pulpit Exchange	Jewish
"Stuck Up People"	2/23/98	Metropolitan Baptist Church Black History Program	AA
"Will a Man Rob God?"	5/24/98	SJ	AA

APPENDIX B

Political Speech Occasions and Audiences

SPEECH EVENT	DATE DELIVERED	OCCASION	AUDIENCE
Radio Address	6/96	Address incident between police and African American community	African American (= AA)
DNC National Convention	8/27/96	Welfare reform	Mixed = (M)
Kansas City Police Academy	12/10/97	Commencement	M
Luncheon with Community Leaders and Press Conference	9/22/96	Discuss allegations of race discrimination and lawsuit against Dillard's	M
United Methodist Evangelism Meeting	1/5/98	Opening remarks	M
Harley Davidson Plant	1/6/98	Celebration of first motorcycle made in Kansas City	M
Freedom, Inc.	1/6/98	Election support for downtown development	AA
Allied Signal	1/9/98	MLK holiday	M
Kansas City's Children Coalition	1/23/98	United Methodist meeting on evangelism	M
Cleveland Chiropractor College		Commencement	M
Seventh State of the City Address	2/19/97	City Hall	M
Turner Construction	2/98	Keynote speaker	Hispanic/ Women
Eighth State of the City Address	2/18/99	City Hall	M

NOTES

1. Though there is no way to really test this speculation, Mayor Cleaver's personal assistant, Sherry Jackson (personal communication, December 8, 1999) verified that on average, the former mayor made five keynote addresses a week, excluding welcoming remarks.
2. S. Jackson (personal communication, March 30, 2000).
3. Afrocentric theory is pan-African. It is concerned with looking at what is common to the people of African heritage wherever they may be found in the world (Asante 1988, 1993). However, to simplify the terms, I will use *African American* with the understanding that Afrocentricity is related to the Diaspora.

REFERENCES

Asante, M. K. (1987). *The Afrocentric Idea.* Philadelphia: Temple University Press.

Asante, M. K.(1988). *Afrocentricity.* Trenton, NJ: Africa World Press, Inc.

Asante, M. K. (1990). *Kemet, Afrocentricity and Knowledge.* Trenton, NJ: Africa World Press, Inc.

Asante, M. K. (1993). *Malcom X as Cultural Hero and Other Afrocentric Essays.* Trenton, NJ: Africa World Press, Inc.

Burke, K. (1969). *A Rhetoric of Motives.* Berkley: University of California Press.

Daniel, J., and G. Smitherman (1976). How I Got Over: Communication Dynamics in the Black Community. *Quarterly Journal of Speech* 62: 26–39.

Du Bois, W. E. B. (1989). *The Souls of Black Folk.* New York: Bantam Books. Originally published 1903.

Eberting, C., and G. Rice (1996). Mayor: KC Can't Overreact to Minicrises; Tensions in the Area Remain High Following the Weekend of Violence. *Kansas City Star,* June 4, B1.

Franklin, R. M. (1997). *Another Day's Journey: Black Churches Confronting the American Crises.* Minneapolis: Fortress Press.

Hood, R. (1996). Holding Thugs Accountable. *Kansas City Star,* June 7, C6.

Jackson, R.L. (2000). Africalogical theory building: Positioning the Discourse. *International and Intercultural Communication Annual* 22: 31–41.

Leader Sworn In as Kansas City Mayor. (1991). *Los Angeles Times,* April 11, A23.

Moore, J., Jr. (1991). Minister Voted 1st Black Mayor of Kansas City. *Los Angeles Times,* March 27, A12.

Raber, T. R. (1991). Black Cleric Favored in Kansas City Mayoral Run-off. *USA Today,* March 23, 2001.

Robbins, W. (1991). Old Outpost of Slavery Joins Era of Black Mayor. *New York Times,* March 27, A20.

Sanchez, M., and T. Collins (1996). Tension Lingers in Aftermath of Shooting, Clash; Saturday's Standoff with the Police Leaves and Uncertain Future. *Kansas City Star,* June 3, B1.

Section 6

VISIONS FOR RESEARCH IN AFRICAN AMERICAN RHETORIC

CHAPTER 17

The Future of African American Rhetoric

MOLEFI KETE ASANTE

The rhetorical history of African Americans extends as far back as the revolts of the enslaved and will stretch into the future until there is complete cultural and intellectual liberation. I have always believed that the presence of Africans in the United States represents a journey for human freedom. It is this quest that has been at the cutting edge of all rhetoric that establishes itself as formidable discourse within the context of American society.

There are several elements to such a rhetorical tradition, and, of course, inherent in this liberation foundation are the prospects for the future. It is my intention in this essay to explain what I believe to be the major themes and rhetorical currents that will engage the African American rhetor of the future. Indeed, the contours of my discussion will embrace many of the ideas already expressed by the numerous authors in this text.

Any meaningful journey must have a destination, and the role of the rhetor must be to interpret and expound on the direction that will lead to the appropriate place. This task, which must be undertaken by the rhetors of the future, will hark back to the precepts of earlier rhetors and rhetoricians. In order to examine more precisely these issues, I will clarify what I understand as the principal categories of rhetoric for future African American rhetors (those who speak or write for the public), examine the principal characteristics of a new rhetoric for the future, explore cultural themes, suggest historical periods as a way of projecting the future, make a brief excursion into postmodernity, and discuss how classical connections are important as emerging issues.

CATEGORIES OF RHETORIC

It is possible to categorize rhetoric as either ordinary or grand. The first category is concerned with the mundane issues of daily existence, such as how we organize ourselves to carry out the most personal and sometimes menial duties of the day. What it takes to convince the insurance company that I deserve a lower rate for my automobile coverage might be considered ordinary (even though it is not necessarily thought to be ordinary by the person needing a lower rate). But most of the discourses in the African American tradition have been within grand rhetoric. What it takes to convince a nation that African Americans should be compensated for the slave labor of their ancestors is of an entirely different order. On this issue or one of similar substance the rhetor interrogates and discovers all means for convincing the public that the great cause of liberation is worthwhile for humanity. The redressing of the historical wrong of enslavement is a significant part of the African American quest. When it will be completed is hard to say, but what is easy to say is that so long as the moral right of people to be free exists within the conscience of humanity, there will be a discourse on it and African Americans will be in the vanguard.

All of our discourse for the past three hundred years has been a commentary on liberation. Whether we speak of Malcolm X (see Woodyard in this volume) or Harriet Tubman, David Walker or the Marcus Garvey, Sojourner Truth (see Pennington in this volume) or Maulana Karenga, the great orators have been devoted to discovering ways to reconcile us to our role in the nation's history. Because of our orators, we have remained the conscience of the nation that enslaved us. If this is an unending drama, it is so because there is no end to our suffering, to our feeling of being divested of rights, privileges, opportunities, and responsibilities because of our previous condition of enslavement.

One can examine our past centuries to gain some appreciation of the future of African American rhetoric. During the seventeenth century, our rhetoric was merely the pleadings of the enslaved who remembered the gods of our own traditions. In the eighteenth century, we petitioned colonial legislatures on the basis of their own documents. By the nineteenth century, we had Maria Stewart, David Walker, Henry Highland Garnett, Frederick Douglass, and Booker T. Washington. When the twentieth century opened, Du Bois was out front, but there were also Marcus Garvey, Ida B. Wells, Martin Luther King Jr., Malcolm X, and Fannie Lou Hamer. While we do not know who the personalities will be that will define the twenty-first century, we do know what issues will be predominant.

CHARACTERISTICS OF RHETORIC

The rhetoric of the twenty-first century will have three characteristics. It will be based on discourses on correctives, reconciliation, and challenges to the last vestiges of the doctrine of White supremacy. Every speaker who takes the platform as an African American rhetor and every writer of essays will have to deal with one or all of the characteristics of the rhetoric of the twenty-first century in order to establish meaningful presences in the nation. The best rhetors will be those who imbue their speeches, essays, and discourses with correctives, reconciliation, and challenges to White supremacy. This is the grand rhetorical tradition.

Let me briefly discuss what I mean by these characteristics. In the discourse on correctives I mean that there will be a healthy discussion about the need for reparations. This will come not as a threat but as a rational attempt to address the issue of justice. Various rhetors, on different platforms over time and in varying circumstances, will debate not the validity of reparations but the manifestation of those reparations in concrete terms. This will be a continuation of the road taken by our earliest men and women of courage. One cannot forget how David Walker in the *Appeal to the Colored Citizens of the World* placed his life at risk by demanding that Africans be treated fairly or that Africans revolt against the institution of enslavement (Walker 1974). The issue of reparations will prove to be intractable as millions of people begin to learn about the extent of slavery's horrors. There will be seminars, symposia, and workshops to explain to the public the nature of enslavement in human history and especially the holocaust of African enslavement in the United States. This will be a future topic for the public platform. Indeed, in the Mission Statement for the Million Man March/Day of Absence, Maulana Karenga wrote:

> Historically, the U.S. government has participated in one of the greatest holocausts of human history, the Holocaust of African enslavement. It sanctioned with law and gun the genocidal process that destroyed millions of human lives, human culture, and the human possibility inherent in African life and culture. It has yet to acknowledge this horrific destruction or to take steps to make amends for it. (1996, 785)

This is a profound charge that is laid at the door of justice, and it will be addressed and readdressed by future African Americans until the issue is redressed. This is the reality of the future discourse.

Reconciliation as a discourse topic will happen so long as there is a serious collective response to the discourse on correctives. Both of these discourses must go on in order for the moral position of the African American rhetor to be guaranteed; otherwise, there will be a one-sided and perhaps one-audience debate. It is necessary for the public speaker to make public his or her commitments to correctives and to reconciliation if he or she seeks to develop communicator credibility. From all evidence, from the time of Merikare until now, good speech, that is, speech that is believable, must have an ethical base. There are no speeches by hate-mongers that have gone down in history as great speeches. There will never be such speeches because the overwhelming judgment of history is a moral one and the speaker who imperils the forward march of human dignity will not live in the minds of the future. It is the champion of righteousness that is the true victor in rhetorical traditions (Karenga in this volume).

Therefore, the doctrine of White supremacy cannot stand the test of time, and the African American speaker who is devoted to the task of challenging privileges based on the false and flimsy grounds of color entitlement will be accorded high status. In shaping the trend toward the future of African American rhetoric, the best scientists and scholars of communication will look to those who best articulate arguments against the greatest weakness of the American nation—privilege based on White skin—as the true keepers of the future.

THE EMERGING THEMES

Indeed, something else, culture, will manifest itself in the way the rhetors organize their messages and discourses. I believe that the best rhetors will demonstrate reliance on the following emerging African American cultural themes: spirituality, musicality/rhythm, emotional vitality, resilience, humanism, communalism, orality and verbal expressiveness, realness, and soul style. What I mean by spirituality is recognition of the spiritual forces in life, like belief in a higher power and some form of universal order. Musicality/rhythm refers to the connectedness of all movements as personified in the musical beat. Emotional vitality is the openness conveyed in the folk culture of ordinary African American people. Resilience is the ability to bounce back from disappointment, oppression, and crisis. Humanism is the expression of concern for human beings, their condition, interests, and achievements. Communalism is a sense of community as expressed in people coming together for special missions. Orality and verbal expressiveness mean the cultivation of style designed to impress and persuade. Realness is the need to face life the way it is, without pretense. Soul style is the rhetor's own distinctive creativity on an activity. These themes will inevitably define the contours of classical African retentions and contemporary innovative African American rhetorical theory and research.

THE PERIODS OF AFRICAN AMERICAN RHETORIC

The rhetors of the morrow will have to study the periods and tropes of the gallant women and men of the twentieth century to know what must be said. I believe that the study of those rhetors will have to be done within the vein of African American theoretical and critical contexts. The issues that create opportunity for our speakers and writers will determine if they will be propelled into the future. It is how one chooses to treat the issues that will determine if a persona could be established out of the common anonymity of the age. This is why new texts must be written and edited and new criticism written to identify the elements of greatness and the patterns of failure in the discourse. It seems clear to me that what would have been called a great speech by a White South African during the rule of the White minority would have been considered a failure by Africans. A Hitlerian speech denouncing Jewish people would have had a different response from German Nazis and Jews, respectively. This is the way life is; it is really about how one chooses substantive subjects and then develops the themes for success. Questions must be asked and answers sought for the relationship of the future speakers and writers to African culture in its reemergence in the United States. Indeed, it may mean that the rhetorical criticism we did in the past, where we failed to explore many dimensions of the cultural context, was only as good as our knowledge in the twentieth century. Now that we understand connections, resiliency, and the patterns of culture more than we did in the past, we can begin the process of rewriting the criteria for excellence in African American rhetoric. Thus, I believe that the future of the rhetoric in our composite African American community will be in the relationship the rhetor has with African culture. This does not mean some naive nationalism or nativism, but rather a strong engagement with composite African cultural values, norms, mores, and beliefs.

THE CLASSICAL CONNECTION

I am convinced that we will never be able to create a proper criticism of our own rhetoric until we reattach ourselves to our classical traditions. I am not talking here about Greek and Latin, but about *mdw ntr,* that is, the language and culture of the ancient Egyptians, usually translated "divine utterance." This is the beginning of our liberation from the mental enslavement that has gripped us since our arrival in the Americas. Africans in the United States cannot afford to forget that we did not change our origins simply by crossing the sea. We left Africa as Africans and arrived on the shores of the Americas as Africans. However, in the heads of many Africans we became something entirely different from what we were when we left. This modification in Africanity is of a different order than what happens to a European or Asian person who arrives here. The European remains essentially encapsulated in the history, culture, folklore, and symbolism of Europe even while he or she is engaging in politics or economics in America. The same is true for the Asian. Only the African American has been corrupted in a historical linkage and ancestral connections. But the rhetor of the future must give attention to the issues of pan-Africanism, that is, the connection of all Africans by virtue of historical processes where we underwent similar experiences vis-à-vis Europe.

The postmodernists believe that the negation of essentialism, indeed an improbability, leads to freedom. There are many Africans who have followed after the principles of this new intellectual religion only to discover that when you penetrate its core it is nothing more than the collective subjectivity of Europe, which remains the greatest essentialist fact in modern history. For the African American rhetorical theorist, there can be no genuine "African" approach to rhetoric without some attention to the cultural issues that confront us as descendant or native Africans. If this is an essentialist rendering, then I am prepared to say that the future of African American rhetoric is an essentialist undertaking so long as the commonality of our experience necessitates the reaffirmation of the uniqueness of our quest for liberation from mental, cultural, intellectual, and economic oppression. It is only in this way that we remain the vanguard of freedom in the North American context.

CONCLUSIONS: A BRIEF EXCURSION ON POSTMODERNITY

While I am not opposed to all principles of postmodernity, and could not be, I am opposed to all attempts to annihilate the African presence in science, history, and culture by defining us out of existence. Like globalization, it is another attempt of the ruling classes to preach democratization while holding on to their own powerful positions. No French person is preaching the anti-Frenchness of the French, and certainly no English are trying to find the negation of Englishness. It remains the African who must submit, not the European essentialists who maintain their cultural power over us to the extent that some Black postmodernists are so confused that even as they rail against essentialism they declare that they want their books to be shelved in the African American section in the bookstore. If there is no such community of interest, then it is unreasonable to argue for it on one's own accord. I have a fundamental belief in the presence and continuation of the African American community in the United States and the African communities in the Americas for the foreseeable future and therefore remain optimistic about the role of African American rhetoric. I agree with the African Brazilian intellectual Abdias do Nascimento, who says,

> Western culture has reached the point of exhaustion. Her validity has extinguished itself and produced the crossroads at which humanity must confront itself. An empire is perplexed. It seems as though those societies which are most deeply westernized are less able to deter this growing process of deterioration. In this way a not only important, but urgent, role is opened to the creative potential of all men and nations. It is when there arises in one place—in another place, something—perhaps an historic mystery: the culture of a specific area, until now marginalized, projects itself toward the area of ecumenical expansion. (1996, 756)

This brings me to another issue that must be confronted by the rhetor of the future, which is the determination of who is and who is not an African American. This comes about because of the growing complexity of identity in the Americas. First of all, the rhetor will have to appreciate the diversity of the African diaspora. There are more Africans in Brazil than in the United States, and since Brazil is an American nation, the African Brazilians could claim to be African Americans. This is so for many Central and South American peoples.

Many Africans in Brazil see this specific North American dominance as a part of North American dominance in general. In other words, as they have come to realize, the use of the term "African American" by the African in North America robs the South American African of any effective use of the term when in fact the larger number of Africans is on the South American continent, not the North American continent. In that sense we have inherited here in North America the same presumption as the Whites in North America who call themselves "Americans," obliterating that reality in terminology for South American Whites as well as for all other North American Whites, such as Mexicans and Canadians, who are also Americans. I do not know how this issue will be resolved, but I know that the African American rhetors of North America will eventually have to speak to it. Indeed, the evolution of our consciousness will demand that we address all unresolved issues of identity. Mark Christian has written in his book *Multicultural Identity,* that "at the dawn of a new millennium, there is still a great need for understanding how inextricably interwoven the human family actually is. All we can state with confidence is this: all roads lead us back to Africa" (2000, 123).

A FINAL WORD ON THE FUTURE OF THE AFROCENTRIC ENTERPRISE IN RHETORIC

Clearly the most effective way for African Americans to regain a sense of sanity in the world is to reject dislocation and to reclaim our place as participants in the human drama. Enslavement, segregation, and political and economic oppression were meant to strip us of our sanity and to marginalize us forever. We have escaped both fates and are now poised to reassert an ethical leadership that derives from our own subject place, that is, seeing ourselves as agents in the world rather than objects or victims. This is the liberating, indeed liberalizing future that I see for African American rhetoric.

REFERENCES

Christian, M. (2000). *Multicultural Identity: An International Perspective.* London: Macmillan.

Karenga, M. (1996). "The Million Man March/Day of Absence Mission Statement," in M. K. Asante and A. Abarry (Eds.), *African Intellectual Heritage.* Philadelphia: Temple University Press.

Nascimento, A. D. (1996). "Cultural Revolution and the Future of the Pan African Culture." In M. K. Asante and A. Abarry (Eds.), *African Intellectual Heritage.* Philadelphia: Temple University Press.

Walker, W. (1974). "Appeal to the Colored Citizens of the World." In H. Aptheker (Ed.), *One Continual Cry.* New York: Citadel Press.

CHAPTER 18

The Discourse of African American Women: A Case for Extended Paradigms

DORTHY L. PENNINGTON

Perspective taking is necessary to begin this chapter, in order to view African American women's discourse in light of a common discourse produced by African American women and men. It is true that African American women carry a "double burden," of being Black and female in a White-male-dominated society. This is described by St. Jean and Feagin as "gendered racism," which involves negative White reactions, individual and institutionalized, to Black female characteristics (St. Jean and Feagin 1998, 15–16). And while St. Jean and Feagin argue that gendered racism separates the experiences of Black women from those of Black men, I believe that the common heritage of African American women and men should be acknowledged. Much of what is true of African American women's discourse is true of African American discourse in general. Because of a shared past that includes slavery and its legacy of racism, African American women and men produced a common discursive tradition. The descriptions of African American women's discourse in this chapter, therefore, are aimed not at portraying it as dichotomous to African American men's discourse, but rather at stating what is true for African American women's discourse.

Understanding African American discourse, in general, requires going beyond the textual analysis of words to comprehending words or other forms of discourse as a part of a larger cultural and rhetorical context comprised of dynamically interrelated parts, including spirituality. The discourse of African American women is historically grounded in religion and spirituality, although there are notable exceptions and variations. This chapter presents the view that spirituality for African American women is an archetypal epistemology, as shown in much of the incarnational discourse that is produced by them. In this chapter, I use the discourse of Sojourner Truth, born Isabella Baumfree, nineteenth-century orator, as an archetype of African American women's discourse to show the need for extended rhetorical paradigms when studying African American women's discourse. For me, Sojourner Truth is a meaningful choice. Having portrayed her in a historical (stage) characterization for a number of years, I am intimately familiar with the experiences and broader context surrounding her discourse. I use as an archetypal example her famous Akron, Ohio, speech, given in 1851, titled by others "Ar'n't I a Woman?" The most widely publicized (and now controversial) written version of this speech was done by Frances Gage, who was at the convention where Truth delivered this address, but who reported her memory of the speech some twelve years after Truth gave it, on May 29, 1851. The Gage version, written in 1863, reads:

> Well, children, where there is so much racket there must be something out of kilter. I think that 'twixt the negroes of the South and the women at the North, all talking about rights, the White men will be in a fix pretty soon. But what's all this here talking about?
>
> That man over there says women need to be helped into carriages, and lifted over ditches, and to have the best place everywhere. Nobody ever helps me into carriages, or over mud-puddles, or gives me any best place! And arn't I a woman: Look at me! Look at my arm! I have ploughed, and planted, and gathered into barns, and no man could head me! And arn't I a woman? I could work as much and eat as much as a man—when I could get it—and bear the lash as well! And arn't I a woman? I have borne thirteen children, and seen them most all sold off to slavery, and when I cried out with my mother's grief, none but Jesus heard me! And arn't I a woman?
>
> Then they talk about this thing in the head; what's this they call it? ["Intellect," whispered someone near.] That's it, honey. What's that got to do with women's rights or negro rights? If my cup won't hold but a pint, and yours holds a quart, wouldn't you be mean not to let me have my little half-measure full?
>
> Then that little man in black there, he says women can't have as much rights as men, because Christ wasn't a woman! Where did your Christ come from? From God and a woman! Man had nothing to do with Him. . . .
>
> If the first woman God ever made was strong enough to turn the world upside down all alone, these women together ought to be able to turn it back, and get it right side up again! And now they are asking to do it, the men better let them. (Quoted in Foner and Branham 1998, 227–28)

However, because Gage's version of Truth's speech is now questionable (Mabee 1993, 67–82), Mabee presents what is now determined to be a more authentic version, as recorded in the *Bugle* newspaper of Salem, Ohio, closer to the time that Truth delivered the speech. In providing contextual commentary for the speech, the *Bugle* reported:

> One of the most unique and interesting speeches of the Convention was made by Sojourner Truth, an emancipated slave. It is impossible to transfer it to paper, or convey any adequate idea of the effect it produced upon the audience. Those only can appreciate it who saw her powerful form, her whole-souled, earnest gesture, and listened to her strong and truthful tones. She came forward to the platform and addressing the President said with great simplicity:
>
> May I say a few words? Receiving an affirmative answer, she proceeded; I want to say a few words about this matter. I am a woman's rights [sic.]. I have as much muscle as any man, and can do as much work as any man. I have plowed and reaped and husked and chopped and mowed, and can any man do more than that? I have heard much about the sexes being equal; I can carry as much as any man, and can eat as much too, if I can get it. I am as strong as any man that is now.
>
> As for intellect, all I can say is, if woman have a pint and man a quart—why can't she have her little pint full? You need not be afraid to give us our rights for fear we will take too much—for we won't take more than our pint'll hold.
>
> The poor men seem to be all in confusion and don't know what to do. Why children, if you have a woman's rights give it to her and you will feel better. You will have your own rights, and they won't be so much trouble.
>
> I can't read, but I can hear. I have heard the Bible and have learned that Eve caused man to sin. Well if woman upset the world, do give her a chance to set it right side up again. The lady has spoken about Jesus, how he never spurned woman from him, and she was right. When Lazarus died, Mary and Martha came to him with faith and love and besought him to raise their brother. And Jesus wept—and Lazarus came forth. And how came Jesus into the world? Through God who created him and woman who bore him. Man, where is your part?
>
> But the women are coming up blessed be God and a few of the men are coming up with them. But man is in a tight place, the poor slave is on him, woman is coming on him, and he is surely between a hawk and a buzzard. (Mabee 1993, 81–82)

I present the view that this speech is an archetype of African American women's discourse and that its analysis requires an extended rhetorical paradigm. I also present the view that no particular paradigm is necessarily privileged for the analysis of African American women's discourse. Rather, the paradigm blueprint that I present later in this chapter is culturally based, recognizing the point at which rhetoric, culture, and intercultural communication intersect (Starosta 2000).

ARCHETYPE

The term *archetype* here refers to a primary or dominant image, impression, or symbol that recurs often enough in a body of literature or orature to be considered as an element of the whole experience. An archetype (image, impression, symbol) results from a shared past and from individual and collective memories of a shared past. A Jungian, psychological view of an archetype is that it reflects motifs that crop up in myths, fairy tales, fantasies, and dreams, among other places, and that an archetype is based on a collective unconscious. Jung stresses the view that an archetype is "irrepresentable," is determined by its form rather than its content, and is transcendent (1963, 392–93). For me, to say that Sojourner Truth's discourse is archetypal of African American women's discourse has three implications. First, her discourse, intricately internalized in her persona as a spiritualist, presents an image, impression, or form for spirituality in African American's discourse. Using this image or form, African American women's discourse provides the content suitable for an individual speaker's situation. At the same time, however, much of African American women's discourse reflects a transcendent spiritual identity among the women. Second, and reflexively, Truth's discourse, in general, is archetypal for African American women's discourse in that it reveals the role of the unconscious, particularly dreams and imagination, in reflecting the motifs emerging from her discourse and that of other African American women, especially that pertaining to their conversion experiences and incarnation (the divine dwelling in flesh). Third, as archetypal, Sojourner Truth's discourse represents both the religious/spiritual and the psychological forms reflected in the paradigm blueprint that I present later in this chapter, reflecting rhetorical theology and rhetorical psychology.

A REVIEW OF PARADIGMS

Existing paradigms for the analysis and criticism of African American discourse are broadly categorized as being either Eurocentric or Afrocentric in method (Jackson 1995). Listed among Eurocentric paradigms are the traditional neo-Aristotelian approach, Bitzer's "rhetorical situation," the dramatistic approach, fantasy theme analysis, and the narrative approach. The Eurocentric approach views reality from a western-centered ideology. The Afrocentric approach, originated by Asante, is founded upon the principles of Afrology, a genuine acceptance of the African past and the endorsement of a contextual analysis; it is the African-centered study of concepts, issues, and behaviors, and has four components: rhetorical condition, rhetorical structure. rhetorical function, and ethical standard (Jackson 1995).

Other rhetoric scholars have contributed to the discussion of the distinct features of Eurocentric, Western systems of rhetoric, such as Scott (1975) and Ehninger (1975) in their colloquy "A Synoptic View of Systems of Western Rhetoric." Scholars who explain the distinct features of Afrocentric discourse include Asante in his primal Afrocentric exposition, *The Afrocentric Idea* (1987), and Jackson in his discussion of Africological theory building (2000).

While the broad categories of Eurocentric/European and Afrocentric/African provide a clear conceptual frame for rhetorical bases, not all scholars value making such binary cultural distinctions. For example, Rogers (1998) questions the accuracy and ideological function of categories such as "European" and "African," arguing that because culture represents a critical praxis, the terms "European" and "African" can and should be viewed as useful critical and theoretical tools but not as fixed, singular, and essential categories. For African American women's discourse, the recognition of a paradigm that reflects praxis is shown to be of value. Scholars such as Logan (1999), who combines Eurocentric and Afrocentric paradigms in her analysis of the persuasive discourse of nineteenth-century African American women (e.g., combining theorists such as Perlman and Olbrets-Tyreca with Afrocentric concepts, such as nommo and African communalism) and Collins (1991), who combines feminist and Afrocentric paradigms, are aware of the multiple, complex identities reflected in African American women's discourse that occurs at points of praxis. Both Logan and Collins realize that African American women practice multiple identities in ways that are not reflected in simple theoretical constructs and frames.

Sojourner Truth's discourse is archetypal of the discourse of African American women who function in both Eurocentric and Afrocentric contexts. And some scholars add an additional category by classifying Truth as a feminist (Painter 1996). This contributes to a complex discursive map of Truth's identity, as shown in her "Ar'n't I am Woman" speech. Truth was born into slavery in the state of New York in 1797 and was later emancipated. Her public speaking career took her to places where she, as an African American woman, was often in the minority. She combined her unique background as a former slave with a publicly articulated interest in religion, abolition, women's rights and equality, and temperance. While accenting her rhetorical condition (the rhetorical situation combined with the racial hierarchy in America), she made reference to most of these issues in her 1851 speech: it was as a slave that she had "plowed and reaped and husked and chopped and mowed," having "as much muscle as any man" (showing her perception of her equality with men); her enactment of the vital contribution that a former slave could make to society was an implicit case for the abolition of slavery; and her valuing religion was shown by her reference to the divine, pointing to the important matters of faith in God, love, beseeching Jesus, God as the life giver, believing that God was on the side of women, sanctioning their cause (mythication, as defined by Smith 1995b); and her reverence for God was shown in an act of worship—"blessed be God."

In establishing a broader context for this speech and its effectiveness, and in keeping with Jung's definition of an archetype being irrepresentable, it is essential to note the newspaper reporter's view that it is impossible to transmit to written form the impact of Truth's speech on the audience and the impact of her tone, her nonverbal gestures, and her powerful physical form. And although the report fails to indicate whether Truth sang on that occasion, Painter informs us that whenever Truth spoke in public, she also sang, so that singing was an integral part of her rhetorical presentation (1996, 3). And in keeping with the praxis of a complex identity for Truth as archetypal, her 1851 speech is also a combination of the two broad thematic categories identified for African American discourse: the religious and the secular (Smith 1995c, 18–25.)

While many paradigms are usefully employed for analyzing African American women's discourse, it is important to answer an essential rhetorical question posed by Ehninger (1975) in the colloquy cited earlier in this chapter. Envisioning the expanded scope of rhetoric "to encompass all of the arts—the nonverbal as well as verbal—by which minds can be changed, the new rapprochement between the methods of rhetoric and the methods of criticism, and the impact which behavioral studies are having upon our understanding of the rhetorical transaction," Ehninger ends with a classic question: "Will it be possible to find a single epistemic base for rhetoric?" (1975, 453). My view is that the answer to this question depends on the size and type of the unit of analysis. For African American women's discourse, I present the view that the archetypal epistemic base is that of spirituality and religion, as shown in Sojourner Truth's discourse, with her "Ar'n't I am Woman" speech being an example.

Truth's life story reveals numerous instances where she expressed having a personal relationship and conversations with God. Mabee explains that over the years, Truth continued the direct communication with God that she had begun while still a slave. "In her middle years, she still said, 'I talks to God and God talks to me.'. . . When she was converted, she claimed that she saw God directly and felt overwhelmed by His presence" (1993, 232–233). Her conversations with God sometimes assumed a dialogic form, such as when God reportedly changed her name from Isabella Baumfree to Sojourner Truth in 1843, as she describes:

> When I left the house of bondage, I left everything behind. I wa'n't goin' to keep nothin' of Egypt on me, an' so I went to the Lord an' asked Him to give me a new name. And the Lord gave me Sojourner, because I was to travel up an' down the land, showin' the people their sins, an' bein' a sign unto them. Afterwards I told the Lord I wanted another name 'cause everybody else had two names; and the Lord gave me Truth, because I was to declare the truth to the people. (Mabee 1993, 45)

At other times, Truth's communication with God assumed the form of a monolog, such as when she used prayer as both a personal and a rhetorical tool. An example of this was when her son, Peter, was returned to her after being illegally sold into slavery in the state of Alabama; she exclaimed, "Oh,

Lord Jesus, look! See my poor child! Oh Lord, render unto them double for all this!" (Mabee 1993, 19).

As in the case of Sojourner Truth, religious and spiritual references are commonly found in the collections of discourse by African American women that I investigated, making Truth's 1851 speech archetypal of African American women's discourse. Of more than fifty speeches analyzed, almost half of them contained religious or spiritual references (see the Notes section of this essay for the collections consulted and a list of speeches).

RELIGIOUS AND SPIRITUAL DISCOURSE IN CULTURAL PERSPECTIVE

Sojourner Truth's discourse as archetypal of African American women's discourse can be explained by viewing discourse as a part of a larger cultural context. According to Bridges, "African American spirituality is the essence of African American culture and religion and the impetus for the struggle for freedom of the African American community in America" (2001, 1). With the view that African American culture in general is essentially spiritual, African American women are noted as being particularly inclined toward the spiritual. Compared to men, African American women audience members are more likely to be involved in the religious speech situation in an audible and visible manner, whereas male listeners are more inclined to be similarly involved in the secular rhetorical situation (Smith 1995a, 28). Bridges explains the essence of African American spirituality and she also distinguishes between spirituality and religion:

> Spiritual identity . . . is the result of an actual encounter with the Divine wherein the human being cannot bypass participation in what Bruce calls a "transpersonal ultimacy" that requires the person to live out cultural values that foster true community. Religion teaches humankind to appreciate God's love, but spirituality challenges human beings to directly experience the transformative power of God's love. Religion is a belief system or reflection on the nature of ultimate reality. Spirituality is the method and manner by which the ultimately real actually touches the depth of being of the human personality, transforms it and causes it to long for true community. (2001, 2)

Observing Bridges' distinctions between religion (a belief system) and spirituality (the method and manner by which the ultimately real touches and transforms the human personality), it is possible that religious and spiritual discourse, while similar in form, could perceptibly have different origins or perceptibly different manners of expression. African American women's religious discourse and their spiritual discourse, which I classify as incarnational, may both acknowledge the influence of a higher power but label that power in different ways. Taylor and Houchins, two different authorities on African

American spirituality, provide clarifying perspectives on the breadth of meaning for spirituality. Taylor explains that in operating in the spiritual realm, or being "in the spirit," African American women live from within and focus inward through prayer, meditation, or any spiritual communion that makes them feel centered and calm (1993, xxi–5). It is unclear from Taylor's description what is precisely the source of the spirit. Spirit, for her, could conceivably be a higher, nonanthropomorphic power, on one hand, or a human internal power, on the other. Conceivably, extending Taylor's perspective, African American women's spirituality may be expressed without the use of God-terms (such as God, Jesus, the divine, the Holy Spirit) and without references to the divine as being the ultimate source. On the other hand, much of African American women's spirituality is expressed in terms of incarnational theology, found in the texts of their discourse, something that is historically common in African American women's spiritual texts, as Houchins (1988) explains: In incarnational theology "the Logos, the Word—not simply the utterance, but the breath/the spirit of Creation—not only is spoken/breathed into the world, but also the world is heard in return through the intercession of the incarnational Christic being." The incarnation, then, is discursive, like prayer (1988, xxvii). I would call Taylor's view the rhetorical psychology of African American women's spirituality, and Houchins's view I would call the rhetorical theology of African American women's spirituality.

Of spirituality, Bridges says further that the conversion process, viewed as God's intervention with the self, in community, is crucial to African American spirituality (2001, 83). Spiritual identity for African American women, I believe, is an archetype that transcends divisions and reflects African American women's quest for true community.

Sojourner Truth's conversion experience illustrates her direct encounter with the divine and her embodiment of spirituality. According to Mabee (1993, 22–23), during Truth's conversion, she saw Jesus for the first time in her life. She later recalled, "I felt Him come between God and me as sensibly as I ever felt an umbrella raised over my head." On another occasion, she gave a vivid description of her encounter: "My voice sounded like a hiccough. I seen him! I saw the hair on his head, and I saw his cheek; and I saw him smile."

Archetypally, Truth's thought life led to her having a vision of Jesus. Her conversion experience, Mabee says, "and her subsequent struggle to respond to God's voice within her—led her . . . toward a conviction that she could be an instrument of God. They led her, regardless of her race, class, gender, or education toward feeling empowered to 'perfect' herself and the world" (Mabee 1993, 23). Truth viewed herself as an agent of the divine, and she held conversations with God. As an embodiment of divine presence, her discourse was incarnational—the Word revealed in human form, divine presence made manifest in the human condition—and her discourse also reflected communication to her from God.

While her 1851 speech clearly referenced the divine, as alluded to by Houchins, it also conveyed the ambivalent incarnational discourse shown by Taylor's view in which the spirit could be perceived as having a human genesis. Truth's speech conveyed a sense of human agency in her making herself nominally equivalent to the ideology of woman's rights—"I am woman's rights"—and her portraying her physical capabilities in ways that showed her perceived equality with men; moreover this speech showed a human strength in her that seemed larger than life, and certainly greater than that perceived for women during that time period. During her years as a slave, she had learned to look within herself (an example of Taylor's view of spirituality as looking within oneself) to derive a model for behavior, for Truth had few existing models. White women were not a model for her, and neither was she a part of a large institutionalized system of plantation slavery, such as that which existed in the southern United States, where other African American women similarly situated as slaves could have demonstrated the expected forms of behavior. Therefore, Truth's discourse serves as an archetype for a broad-based view of African American women's spiritual discourse.

My claim that Truth's discourse is archetypal of African American women's discourse is supported by examples of other African American women's discourse. Maria Stewart and Mary Shadd, among others, delivered spiritual, incarnational discourse. Stewart remarked that God "hath unloosed my tongue, and put his word in my mouth; in order to confound and put all those to shame that have rose up against me" (quoted in Foner and Branham 1998, 136). Her report of her conversion experience resembles the form found in Sojourner Truth's self-report of her own conversion. In her 1883 speech "What If I Am a Woman," Stewart relates:

> Borne down with a heavy load of sin and shame, my conscience filled with remorse; considering the throne of God forever guiltless, and my own eternal condemnation as just, I was at last brought to accept of salvation as a free gift in and through the merits of a crucified Redeemer. . . .
>
> After these convictions, in imagination I found myself sitting at the feet of Jesus, clothed in my right mind. For I had been like a ship tossed to and fro, in a storm at sea. Then was I glad when I realized the dangers I had escaped; and then I consecrated my soul and body, and all the powers of my mind to his service, and from that time, henceforth, yea, even for evermore, amen. (Quoted in Foner and Branham 1998, 1336–7)

Archetypally, Stewart's imagination placed her in Jesus' presence, transformed. This speech contains numerous references to God, and through mythication, it also bases women's empowerment in Jesus.

In both the cases of Truth and Stewart, their experiences with God became their epistemology—their way of knowing and of validating knowledge claims—and gave them faith and confidence to go forth as He directed them.

Mary Shadd's speech "Break Every Yoke and Let the Oppressed Go Free," given in 1858, is another example of discourse that conforms to the archetype illustrated by Truth and Stewart. This speech by Shadd is a sermon, and for this reason, it would be expected to have the archetypal form of religion and spirituality, which it does. On the other hand, it provides a different content for the element of transformation involved, as described in the experiences of Truth and Stewart. Rather than describing the personal transformation that resulted from an encounter with God, Shadd uses the form of religion and spirituality to prescribe a negative, ironic transformation in regard to the Fugitive Slave Act of 1850. She argued that this act forced humans to renounce their natural tendency to aid someone in distress and to instead deliberately abort the liberation of fellow humans. She decries the fact that those who enjoyed their freedom were

> called upon as a man to deny and disobey the most noble impulses of mankind to aid a brother in distress—to refuse to strike from the limbs of those not bound for any crime the fetters by which his Escape is obstructed. The milk of human kindness must be transformed into the bitter water of hatred—you must return to his master he that hath Escaped, no matter how Every principle of manly independence revolts at the same. (Quoted in Foner and Branham 1998, 320–21)

In Shadd's and in other African American women's discourse, the archetype of spirituality and religion as epistemology calls for an extended discourse paradigm.

As a qualifier, it should be noted that not all African American women's discourse is religious or spiritual. There are recorded examples of discourse that clearly belong in the secular category, for example, Lucy Parson's 1866 speech "I Am an Anarchist," and Angela Davis's 1971 speech "I Am a Black Revolutionary Woman." And some African American women's discourse contains both religious and secular images, such as Victoria Earle Matthew's address "The Value of Race Literature," given in 1895, and Lucy Craft Laney's speech "The Burden of the Educated Colored Woman," given in 1899. Indeed, much of African American women's discourse classifiable as religious and spiritual contains secular images and could not be claimed to be exclusively religious or secular. As far as the categories of religious and secular discourse are concerned, it is easier to classify secular discourse because, operationally, it contains no religious or spiritual images.

CONNECTING THE PAST WITH THE PRESENT

Most of the discourse by African American women cited so far in this chapter comes from collections of discourse devoted exclusively to African Americans and which also contain a significant amount of discourse by African American women. Unfortunately, most of these collections are limited to nineteenth-century discourse. They include Foner and Branham's *Lift Every Voice: African American Oratory, 1787–1900;* Logan's *With Pen and Voice: A Critical Anthology of Nineteenth-Century African American Women;* and Newman, Rael, and Lapsansky's *Pamphlets of Protest: An Anthology of Early African American Protest Literature, 1790–1860.* An earlier (1972) volume of African American discourse edited by Foner, *The Voice of Black America,* covers a broader historical period, from 1797 to 1971. However, Foner's newer volume of African American oratory, co-edited with Branham, contains a much more extensive amount of discourse by African American women than the earlier volume.

Currently, an ideal addition to existing collections of discourse devoted exclusively to African Americans would be one equivalent to the 1998 collection edited by Foner and Branham, but which would cover the period from 1900 to the present. There are other collections of African American discourse on women of the twentieth century, with one example being Parham's *Barbara C. Jordan: Selected Speeches* (1999). The speeches in this collection, however, are secular in nature and do not provide an example of the type of discourse that this chapter highlights as needing greater paradigmatic development.

More recently, however, related research that I conducted on African American women's discourse presented in oral interviews and narratives (Pennington 1999), indicates a continuing predominance of the religious and spiritual archetype described in this chapter. Six African American women participated in extended oral interviews concerning their reasons for voluntarily, and often suddenly, leaving the workplace. In terms of demographics, the participants were similar in age, but their geographic locations, educational levels, and religious identification varied. Their locations ranged from the South to the Midwest to the East; their educational levels ranged from those having some college to those holding earned doctorates; and their religious identification ranged from those who were deeply religious to those who were not religious at all. Despite demographic differences, the women's discourse showed a common spiritual, incarnational form that transcended demographic differences. To summarize my findings, spiritual, incarnational dialogue with the Divine or with the Spirit within themselves (some simply said "a voice") influenced their decision to quit their jobs. Arbitrarily listed by number here, participant 1 spoke of the role of prayer in her decision to leave her academic professorial position; participant 2 spoke of consulting God and of His speaking to her directly about the day that she was to quit her corporate job; participant 3 spoke of hearing a voice telling her that she no longer belonged in her position as an office manager of an academic unit, although she did not give divine attribution to the voice; participant 4 related how she prayed prior to quitting her corporate position; participant 5 talked of the strong, fervent prayers that she made in deciding to leave her academic professorial position; and participant 6 described the continuous, vivid dialogue between herself and God through which He directed her to move to an unfamiliar city, leaving her job, by default (Pennington 1999).

These examples of African American women's discourse being linked to spirituality and religion are not unique. It is no coincidence that Sojourner Truth and Maria Stewart shared similar concerns, though they lived two centuries apart from one another. Spirituality is a cultural continuity that traverses generational boundaries (Hecht, Jackson, and Ribeau 2002).

A NEW PARADIGM BLUEPRINT

With the examples of an archetype provided in this chapter, I present and reiterate the view that African American women's discourse is archetypally religious and spiritual. Furthermore, for African American women's discourse, I advance the notion of spirituality as epistemology, that is, spirituality as a way of knowing and of validating knowledge claims.

Communication scholars have an opportunity to participate in developing paradigms that contribute to our ability to formulate theory and criticism tools for African American women's religious and spiritual discourse. I end this chapter by offering a blueprint for such a paradigm (see Figure 1). My blueprint presents some discourse forms not specifically mentioned in this chapter but which are heuristically derived and manifested from the prototypes listed. Examples of some of these forms—including nontraditional ones—which should be included in such a paradigm are prayers (for example, the public prayers of Sojourner Truth and of Maria Stewart, found in Washington's [1994] collection); songs and music, which Sojourner Truth included in her rhetorical presentations; narratives; myths; folktales; visions; and dreams, among other archetypal forms. For example, one of the participants in my study (Pennington 1999) reported on how her dreams contributed to her spiritual epistemology. And what could also be heuristically included in archetypal spiritual forms is an African American rhetorical form called "tuning"; tuning is a performance mode practiced in religious settings, worship, using sound utterances that imply a divine presence that is somehow other than the spoken parts of the sermon, as explained by Baldwin (2001). Extending further the study of the "sounding" effect often mentioned in African American discourse would require an investigation of the linguistic field called ideophones, more formally studied in African-influenced Atlantic creole discourses—again, a heuristic possibility.

This paradigm blueprint (see Figure 1) provides a way to conceptualize African American women's religious and spiritual discourse. It makes allowance for the possibility that for some women, spirituality is different from religion. Some women's spiritual discourse results from a theological base, as

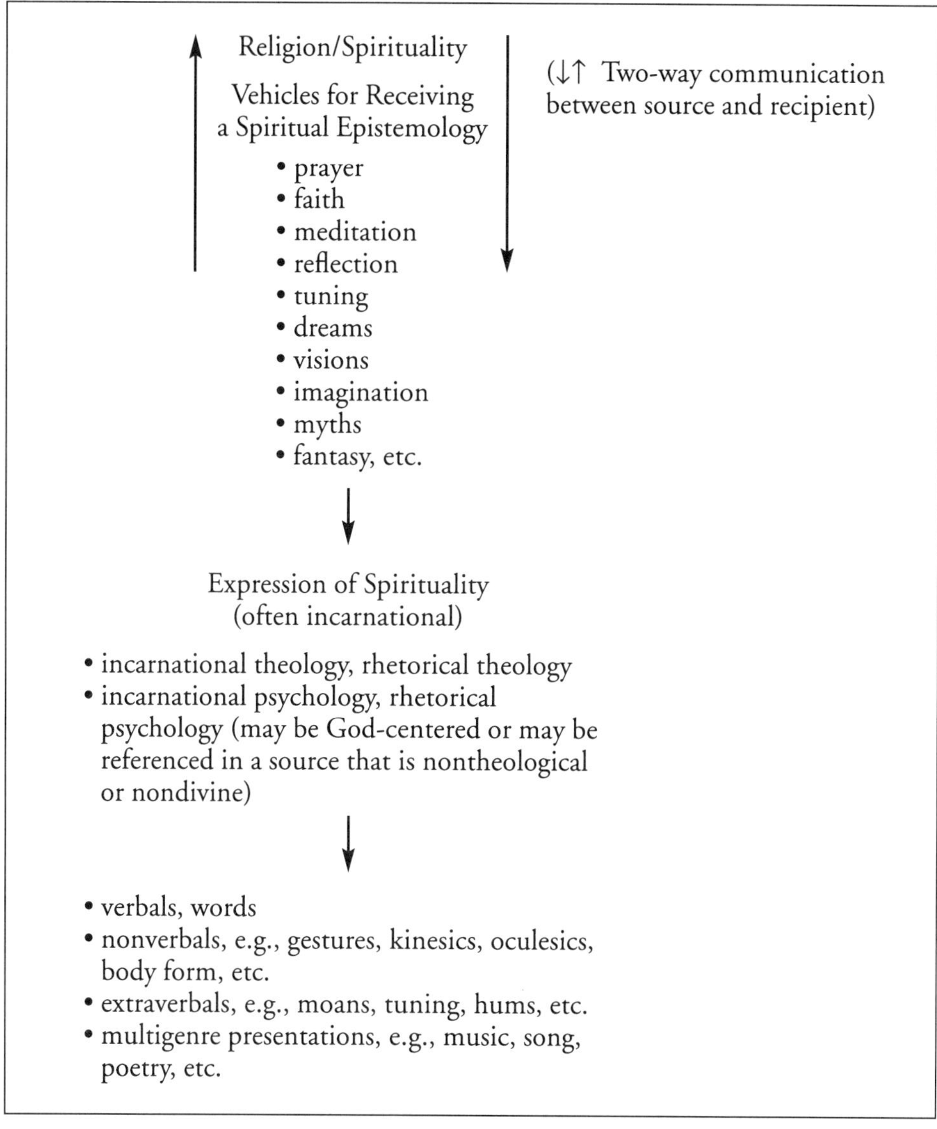

Religion/Spirituality
Vehicles for Receiving a Spiritual Epistemology
• prayer
• faith
• meditation
• reflection
• tuning
• dreams
• visions
• imagination
• myths
• fantasy, etc.
(↓↑ Two-way communication between source and recipient)
Expression of Spirituality (often incarnational)
• incarnational theology, rhetorical theology
• incarnational psychology, rhetorical psychology (may be God-centered or may be referenced in a source that is nontheological or nondivine)
• verbals, words
• nonverbals, e.g., gestures, kinesics, oculesics, body form, etc.
• extraverbals, e.g., moans, tuning, hums, etc.
• multigenre presentations, e.g., music, song, poetry, etc.

Figure 1 A Paradigm Blueprint of African American Women's Religious-Spiritual Discourse

explained by Houchins, while for other women, spiritual discourse derives from the psychology of a spirit within themselves, as explained by Taylor. This paradigm blueprint is an addition to existing ones, all of which have value if they provide insight into African American women's discourse.

African American women's discourses are vast and varied. It is imperative that rhetorical tools for analyzing these discourses are also multitudinous (Houston and Davis 2001). Some of these discourses are distinctively Afrocentric, some are feminist, and others may be considered Eurocentric or some combination of the above. Models for examining the spiritual dimensions of African American women's discourse, such as the one presented here, must continue to be introduced, refined, and utilized to facilitate understanding of a set of rhetorical experiences scantily studied, especially in the fields of communication, English, and African American studies.

NOTES

Examples of discourse containing religious/spiritual references, in the archetypal mode of Sojourner Truth:

Source: P. S. Foner, and R. J. Branham, editors, *Lift Every Voice: African American Oratory, 1787–1900.*

1. Margaret Odell, "Valedictory Address," 1822
2. Sarah M. Douglas, "The Cause of the Slave Became My Own," 1832
3. Maria W. Stewart, "Why Sit Ye Here and Die?" 1832
4. Maria W. Stewart, "What if I Am a Woman?" 1832
5. Clarissa Lawrence, "We Meet the Monster Prejudice Every Where," 1839
6. Lucy Stanton, "A Plea for the Oppressed," 1850
7. Sara G. Stanley, "What, to the Foiling Millions These, is This Boasted Liberty?" 1856
8. Frances Ellen Watkins, "Liberty for Slaves," 1857
9. Sarah J. Woodson, "Address to Youth," 1863
10. Frances Ellen Watkins Harper, "The Great Problem to be Solved," 1875
11. Olivia A. Davidson, "How Shall We Make Our Race Stronger?" 1886
12. Mary V. Cook, "Woman's Place in the Work of the Denomination," 1887
13. Anna Julia Cooper, "Women's Cause Is One and Universal," 1893
14. Victoria Earl Matthews, "The Awakening of the Afro-American Woman," 1897

Source: S. W. Wilson, editor, *With Pen and Voice: A Critical Anthology of Nineteenth-Century African American Women.* This list excludes those titles were are also listed in Foner and Branham.

1. Maria W. Stewart, "An Address Delivered Before the Afric-American Female Intelligence Society of Boston," 1832
2. Frances Ellen Watkins Harper, "Duty to Dependent Races," 1891
3. Frances Ellen Watkins Harper, "Woman's Political Future," 1893
4. Anna Julia Haywood Cooper, "Womanhood a Vital Element in the Regeneration and Progress of a Race," 1886

Source: R. Newman, P. Rael, and P. Lapsansky, editors, *Pamphlets of Protest: An Anthology of Early African American Protest Literature, 1790–1860*

1. Elizabeth Wicks, "Address Delivered Before the African Female Benevolent Society of Troy," 1834
2. Maria W. Stewart, "Productions," 1833

Source: G. Lerner, editor, *Black Women in White America*

1. Sojouner Truth, "I Suppose I Am About the Only Colored Woman That Goes About to Speak for the Rights of Colored Women," 1853
2. Fannie Lou Harner, "It's in Your Hands," 1971

REFERENCES

Asante, M. K. (1987). *The Afrocentric Idea.* Philadelphia: Temple University Press.

Baldwin, J. A. (2001). *Seven Signature Sermons by a Tuning Woman.* Lewiston, NY: The Edwin Mellen Press.

Bridges, F. W. (2001). *Resurrection Song—African American Spirituality.* Maryknoll, NY: Orbis Books.

Collins, P. H. (1991). *Black Feminist Thought: Knowledge, Consciousness, and the Politics of Empowerment.* New York: Routledge.

Ehninger, D. (1975). Colloquy: A Synoptic View of Systems of Western Rhetoric. *Quarterly Journal of Speech* 61: 448–53.

Foner, P. S. (1972). *The Voice of Black America: Major Speaker by Negroes in the United States, 1797–1971.* New York: Simon and Schuster.

Foner, P. S., and R. J. Branham (Eds.) (1998). *Lift Every Voice: African American Oratory.* Tuscaloosa: University of Alabama Press.

Hecht, M. L., R. L. Jackson, and S. A. Ribeau (in press). *African American Communication: Exploring Identity and Culture,* second edition. Mahwah, NJ: Erlbaum.

Houchins, S. E. (1988). *Spiritual Narratives.* New York: Oxford University Press.

Houston, M., and O. Davis (Eds.) (2001). *Centering Ourselves: African-American Feminist and Womanist Studies of Discourse.* Cresskill, NJ: Hampton Press.

Jackson, R. L. (1995). Toward an Afrocentric Methodology for the Critical Assessment of Rhetoric. In L. A. Niles (Ed.), *African American Rhetoric: A Reader.* Dubuque, IA: Kendall-Hunt Publishing Company.

Jackson, R. L. (2000). Africalogical Theory Building: Positioning the Discourse. Rhetoric in Intercultural Contexts. In A. Gonzalez and D. Tanno (Eds.), "Rhetoric in Intercultural Contexts," *International and Intercultural Communication Annual* 22: 31–40.

Jung, C. G. (1963). *Memories, Dreams, Reflections.* New York: Pantheon Books.

Logan, S. W. (1995). *With Pen and Voice: A Critical Anthology of Nineteenth Century American Women.* Carbondale: Southern Illinois University Press.

Logan, S. W. (1999). *We Are Coming: The Persuasive Discourse of Nineteenth-century Black Women.* Carbondale Ill.: Southern Illinois University Press.

Mabee, C. (1993). *Sojourner Truth: Slave, Prophet, Legend.* New York: New York University Press.

Newman, R., P. Lapansky, and P. Rael (2000). *Pamphlets of Protest: An Anthology of Early African American Protest Literature, 1790–1860.* New York: Routledge.

Painter, N. I. (1996). *Sojourner Truth: A Life, a Symbol.* New York: W. W. Norton.

Parham, S. (Ed.) (1999). *Barbara C. Jordan: Selected Speeches.* Washington, DC: Howard University Press.

Pennington, D. L. (1999). *African American Women Quitting the Workplace.* Lewiston, NY: The Edwin Mellen Press.

Rogers, R. A. (1998). A Dialogue of Rhythm: Dance and the Performance of Cultural Conflicts. *Howard Journal of Communications,* 9, 5–27.

Scott, R. L. (1975). Colloquy: A Synoptic View of Systems of Western Rhetoric. *Quarterly Journal of Speech,* 61: 439–47.

Smith, A. L. (1995a). Nature of the Black Audience. In L. A. Niles (Ed.), *African American Rhetoric: A Reader.* Dubuque, IA: Kendall-Hunt Publishing Company.

Smith, A. L. (1995b). Strategies of the Revolutionists. In L. A. Niles (Ed.), *African American Rhetoric: A Reader.* Dubuque, IA: Kendall-Hunt Publishing Company.

Smith, A. L. (1995). Topics of Revolutionary Rhetoric. In L. A. Niles (Ed.), *African American Rhetoric: A Reader.* Dubuque, IA: Kendall-Hunt Publishing Company.

Starosta, W. J. (2000). On the Intersection of Rhetoric and Interculural Communication. In A. Gonzalez and D. Tanno (Eds.), "Rhetoric in Intercultural Contexts," *International and Intercultural Communication Annual,* 22: 149–61.

St. Jean, Y., and J. R. Feagin (1998). *Double Burden: Black Women and Everyday Racism.* Armonk, NY: M. E. Sharpe.

Taylor, S. L. (1993). *In the Spirit.* New York: Amistad.

Washington, J. M. (Ed.) (1994). *Conversations with God: Two Centuries of Prayers by African Americans.* New York: Harper Collins Publishers.

About the Contributors

Adisa A. Alkebulan (Ph.D., Temple University) is Assistant Professor in the Department of Africana Study at San Diego State University. He received his undergraduate degree in pan-African studies at Kent State University, and both his M.A. and Ph.D. at Temple University. His research area is pan-African languages in the Western Hemisphere with an emphasis on the language spoken by Africans in the United States. He has also done research in Africa and Europe on language and colonialism in Africa. He is currently developing on Afrocentric method of clarifying pan-African languages as well as criteria for clarifying thieves and theorists on the subject.

Molefi Kete Asante (Ph.D., University of California, Los Angeles) is Professor, Department of African American Studies, Temple University. He is the author of forty-seven books, including *The Afrocentric Idea, African Intellectual Heritage, The Egyptian Philosophers, African American Atlas,* and *African American History: A Journey of Liberation.*

Deborah F. Atwater (Ph.D., State University of New York at Buffalo) is former head of the Department of African and African American Studies and Associate Professor of Speech Communication at the Pennsylvania State University, where she teaches courses on cross-cultural communication and Black rhetoric. She has published in *Communication Education, Communication Quarterly, Journal of Black Studies, Western Journal of Black Studies,* and *Rhetoric Society Quarterly*. While her research interests include intercultural communication, African American rhetoric with an emphasis on African American women. Recently, she has traveled to South Africa, Russia, Finland, and Italy as part of cross-cultural communication exchanges.

Shauntae Brown-White (Ph.D., University of Kansas) is Assistant Professor at Miami University of Ohio, where she has a joint appointment in Black world studies and communication. She received her B.A. in journalism from Howard University, her M.A. in speech communication from the University of Alabama, and her Ph.D. in communication studies from the University of Kansas. Dr. White's research interests include African American public address, African American music, and African American women and their relationship with their hair. Currently, she is working on project examining how pastors' wives negotiate their identity.

Carolyn Calloway-Thomas (Ph.D., Indiana University) is Associate Professor in the Department of Communication and Culture at Indiana University. She is the co-author of *Intercultural Communication: Roots and Routes,* co-editor of *Dr. Martin Luther King Jr. and the Sermonic Power of Public Discourse,* and author of various articles on African American rhetoric and intercultural communication. Together with Professor Thurmon Garner, she is co-author of the forthcoming book *What if I Am a Woman: The Rhetoric of Sisterhood and Struggle.* She holds editorial positions with three journals and is the book editor of the *Howard Journal of Communications.* Currently a Carnegie Scholar, Professor Calloway-Thomas has also won other prestigious fellowships, including a Ford Fellowship and a Fulbright Scholarship to Nigeria to study what is African about African American communication.

Melbourne S. Cummings (Ph.D., University of California, Los Angeles) is Professor and Chair of the Department of Communication and Culture at Howard University. She teaches courses across the discipline in rhetoric, public address, nonverbal and intercultural communication. Her publications span the areas of African American communications—rhetoric, poetry, song, comedy, and others. She has served on major planning, organizational, and policy boards in regional, national, and international communication associations, and has traveled extensively in Africa, Europe, and Asia as part of intercultural exchanges in communication, international education, and religion.

Celnisha L. Dangerfield (B.A., Clark Atlanta University) received her M.A. in communication theory within the Department of Communication Arts and Sciences at the Pennsylvania State University, where she now holds the position of Lecturer. She is a summa cum laude graduate of Clark Atlanta University and previous undergraduate summer fellow at both Brown University and New York University. Her research interests are related to cultural identity negotiation as evidenced in varying contexts from mass media to interpersonal relationships. Ms. Dangerfield is also developing a paradigm she has coined "race shock."

Ella Forbes (Ph.D., Temple University) is Associate Professor in the Department of African American Studies at Temple University, where she was among the first graduates of the department, the first Ph.D. program in African American studies in the nation. Her areas of interest include African resistance movements (especially during the antebellum period), mass media and the African American community, African women, and public policy and its impact on the African American and global communities. Dr. Forbes is the author of *African American Women During the Civil War* (Garland Publishing, 1998) and *"But We Have No Country": The 1851 Christiana, Pennsylvania Resistance.* She is the co-author of *American Democracy in Africa in the Twenty-First Century?*

Thurmon Garner (Ph.D., Northwestern University) is Associate Professor in the Department of Speech Communication at the University of Georgia. He graduated from the Department of Communication Studies at Northwestern University in Evanston, Illinois, in 1979. His general area of study is in rhetorical communication, with an emphasis in rhetorical criticism and African American discourse. His publications have appeared in such outlets as *The Journal of Black Studies, The Quarterly Journal of Speech,* and the *Journal of Language and Social Psychology.*

Sandra L. Herndon (Ph.D., Southern Illinois University at Carbondale) is Professor and Chair of the Graduate Program in Communications at Ithaca College, where she teaches primarily organizational communication. The author of numerous journal articles, book chapters, and conference papers, she has published three anthologies and served on the editorial board for a variety of scholarly journals. Her research interests range from intercultural and interracial communication, gender and communication, and the impact of technology on organizational communication to qualitative research methods. She has traveled both to South Africa and to the People's Republic of China as part of intercultural exchanges in the field of communication.

Ronald L. Jackson II (Ph. D., Howard University) is Associate Professor of Culture and Communication Theory in the Department of Communication Arts and Sciences at the Pennsylvania State University. He is author of *The Negotiation of Cultural Identity.* Forthcoming are five books entitled: *African American Rhetoric(s): English Studies Perspectives; African American Communication: Exploring Identity and Culture* (with Michael Hecht and Sidney Ribeau); *Negotiating the Black Body: Intersections of Communication, Culture and Identity; Essential Readings in African American Communication Studies* (with Carlos Morrison); and *Pioneers in African American Communication Research* (with Carlos Morrison and Trina Wright). Dr. Jackson's theory work includes the development of two paradigms coined "cultural contracts theory" and "Black masculine identity theory."

Maulana Karenga (Ph.D., University of Southern California, Los Angeles) is Professor and Chair of the Department of Black Studies at California State University, Long Beach. A socioethical philosopher in African culture, he is an authority on ancient Egyptian ethical philosophy and wrote his second dissertation on *Maat, the Moral Ideal in Ancient Egypt: A Study in Classical African Ethics.* Dr. Karenga is the author of numerous scholarly articles and books, including *Introduction to Black Studies; Selections from the Husia: Sacred Wisdom of Ancient Egypt; Kwanzaa: A Celebration of Family, Community and Culture; Odu Ifa: The Ethical Teachings;* and *Kawaida: A Communitarian African Philosophy.* An activist-scholar of national and international recognition, Dr. Karenga has played an important role in Black political and intellectual culture since the '60s and has lectured on the major campuses in the United States and in Africa, the People's Republic of China, Cuba, Trinidad, Britain, and Canada. He is also Chair of the Organization Us and the National Association of Kawaida Organizations and the creator of the pan-African cultural holiday Kwanzaa and the Nguzo Saba (The Seven Principles) and author of *Kawaida* philosophy out of which they were created.

Judi Moore Latta (Ph.D., University of Maryland) is Professor and Chair of the Department of Radio, TV, and Film at Howard University. She is a television producer, an award-winning producer of more than seventy radio documentaries, and the recipient of the George Foster Peabody Award for her work as senior producer of the National Public Radio/Smithsonian Institution series *Wade in the Water: African American Sacred Music Traditions.* She has also received production award recognition from the Corporation for Public Broadcasting, the American Women in Radio and TV, the National Education Association, the National Association of Black Journalists, and the National Federation of Community Broadcasters. Her research interests include cultural narratives and the politics of production.

Mark Lawrence McPhail (Ph.D., University of Massachusetts) is Professor of Interdisciplinary Studies and Communication at Miami University in Oxford, Ohio. He is the author of *The Rhetoric of Racism Zen in the Art of Rhetoric: An Inquiry into Coherence* and *The Rhetoric of Racism (Revisited): Reparations or Separation?* His work has been published in *The Quarterly Journal of Speech, Critical Studies in Mass Communication, Howard Journal of Communications,* and *American Literary Review.* His research interests include rhetorical epistemology, language and race relations, and Eastern philosophy and spirituality.

Felicia M. Miyakawa is a Ph.D. candidate in musicology at Indiana University (Bloomington). Her areas of interest are diverse and include hip-hop music and culture, Black nationalism, popular music, American music, and the music and poetry of fourteenth-century French composer Guillaume de Machaut. She is especially interested in interdisciplinary studies and is currently working on a project that examines musical themes in African American short fiction from the Harlem Renaissance through the Black arts movement. Her dissertation, an in-depth analysis of Five Percenter lyrics and music, is tentatively entitled "God Hop: Music, Message, and Medium in Five Percenter Hip Hop."

Carlos D. Morrison (Ph.D., Howard University) is Assistant Professor of Speech Communication and Theatre Arts at Fort Valley State University. He received his Ph.D. in intercultural communication and rhetoric from Howard University. Dr. Morrison teaches courses in African American rhetoric and communication, persuasion, public address, and communication theory. His research focuses on Black popular culture and rhetoric, social movements, Afrocentricity, and African American rhetoric. His most recent publication examined the rhetorical meaning of Louis Farrakhan's song "White Man's Heaven Is a Black Man's Hell."

Dorthy L. Pennington (Ph. D., University of Kansas) is Associate Professor at the University of Kansas, where she has a dual appointment in the Departments of African and African American Studies and Communication Studies. She has served as a consultant to the U.S. Department of Defense in race relations and equal opportunity management, and to the U.S. Commission on Civil Rights on minority women in the labor force. She has contributed numerous scholarly writings in intercultural communication and rhetoric and is a coauthor of one of the pioneer books on interracial communication (*Crossing Difference . . . Interracial Communication,* 1976). Her most recent book is titled *African American Women Quitting the Workplace,* a field study of reasons why African American professional women are voluntarily leaving the workplace in increasing numbers. Her Ph.D. is from the University of Kansas in communication.

Elaine B. Richardson (Ph.D., Michigan State University) is Assistant Professor of English at Pennsylvania State University. Her research interests include the teaching of rhetoric and composition to African American vernacular English speakers and linguistic and cultural development and diffusion of African American culture. Dr. Richardson is the author of various articles that have been published in *The Journal of English Linguistics, Computers and Composition,* and *The Journal of Pidgins and Creoles* among others. She is also author of *African American Literacies,* recently released by Routledge.

Regina E. Spellers (Ph.D., Arizona State University) is Assistant Professor in the Department of Communication at Western Michigan University. She earned her doctoral degree from the Hugh Downs School of Human Communication at Arizona State University. Her research interests include ethnic identity, Black hair/body politics, and organizational socialization. Spellers also holds an M.B.A. in international marketing.

Orlando L. Taylor (Ph.D., University of Michigan) is past President of the National Communication Association and current Dean of Howard University's Graduate School of Arts and Sciences. Professor Taylor is a member of numerous national boards, including the board of directors for the Council of Graduate Schools, of which he is Chair. Professor Taylor is a pioneer in the fields of Black language studies, intercultural communication, sociolinguistics, educational linguistics, and communication disorders. Recipient of an honorary doctorate of letters degree from Purdue University, Dr. Taylor is a prolific scholar whose most recent books include *Making the Connection: Language and Academic Achievement Among African American Students* (1999) and *Language Acquisition Across North America: Cross-Cultural and Cross-Linguistic Perspectives* (1998).

Felicia R. Walker (Ph.D., Howard University; J.D., Emory University) is Assistant Professor of Culture and Communication in the Howard University School of Communications. She is also Director of the Howard University Martin Luther King Jr. Forensics Mock Trial and Speech Teams, two-time national champions. Her research interests include African American communication and courtroom rhetoric.

Jeffrey Lynn Woodyard (Ph.D., Temple University) teaches communication and Africana studies at Stetson University in DeLand, Florida. Completing a Ph.D. in African American Studies at Temple University while focusing on African American communication affords an Africological orientation to his rhetorical studies. His research appears in several journals including the *Journal of Black Studies, Journal of Pastoral Care,* and *The Griot.* He has written book chapters exploring Afrocentric approaches to rhetorical studies. Woodyard has served as Chair of the National Communication Association, African American Communication and Culture Division, and as Associate Editor of *Communication Education.* A native of York, Pennsylvania, he has been a faculty member at Shippensburg University of Pennsylvania and Georgia State University in Atlanta.

Richard L. Wright (Ph.D., University of Texas) is Professor of Sociolinguistics in the School of Communications at Howard University, where he has been a faculty member for twenty-five years. A former Fulbright scholar to Guatemala, he received his master's and doctoral degrees from the University of Texas. For the past twenty-five years, Dr. Wright has been a national consultant involved with public schools in the areas of early language development and early learning. His teaching and research interests emphasize early language learning, sociopsychological factors in language development and language use, assessing language ability, cultural dynamics in communication, and language issues in the Black community.

Index